Volume 2

Garland Folklore Casebooks

General Editor
Alan Dundes
University of California, Berkeley

Reprinted by permission of the Society of Antiquaries of London

The Much Suffering or Afflicted Eye
(see page 284)

THE EVIL EYE
A Folklore Casebook

edited by
Alan Dundes

GARLAND PUBLISHING, INC. • NEW YORK & LONDON
1981

Library of Congress Cataloging in Publication Data

Main entry under title:

The Evil eye.

(Garland folklore casebooks; v. 2)
1. Evil eye—Addresses, essays, lectures. I. Dundes, Alan. II. Series.
GN475.6.E95 398'.41 80-8513
ISBN 0-8240-9471-9 AACR2

Printed on acid-free, 250-year-life paper
Manufactured in the United States of America

Folklore Casebook Series

The materials of folklore demonstrate remarkable variation. Each of the cultures which share a particular item of folklore, for example, a myth, a folktale, a custom, a folk belief, has its own special version of that item. Sometimes individuals within a given culture will have their own idiosyncratic variations within the larger culturewide tradition. Students of folklore who study the folklore of only their own group may fail to appreciate the range of variation in folklore. By bringing together different studies of the same item of folklore, I hope to provide a means of demonstrating both the ways in which folklore remains constant across cultures and the ways in which folklore is inevitably localized in different cultural contexts.

With respect to the distribution of an item of folklore, there are two all too common erroneous assumptions. The first assumption is that the item of folklore is peculiar to one culture. Those anthropologists, for example, who are unwilling to be comparative, typically assume or assert that a given folktale is unique to "their" people, meaning the people among whom they have carried out their fieldwork. The critical theoretical point is that one cannot tell whether or how a folktale is really unique to one culture without knowing if the same tale is found in other cultures. Once one has examined other versions of the tale, then and only then can one comment intelligently on just how a particular version of that tale reflects the culturally relative characteristics of a given society.

The second erroneous assumption, equally irritating to professional folklorists, is that a given item of folklore is universal. This is the opposite extreme from the first assumption. Rather than presuming that the item is unique to one culture, the universalist (typically a literary or psychologically oriented student) simply posits the existence of the item in all cultures. Yet the facts do not support this position any more than the other. Most items of folklore have limited areas of distribution. For example, there are Indo-European folktales reported from India to Ireland, but most of these tales are *not* found among Australian aborigines, the peoples of Melanesia and Polynesia, South American Indians, etc. Similarly, there are folktales found in North and South American Indian tradition which are not found in Europe. If one takes the trouble to check the sources cited by universalists, he or she will normally find little if any reference to the traditions of the peoples of New Guinea, native South America, sub-Saharan Africa among other areas.

One cannot say a priori what the distribution of a particular item of folklore might be. One needs to consult the scholarship devoted to that item before venturing an informed opinion. Chances are great, however, that the item will not be limited to a single culture nor will it be worldwide. One aim of the Folklore Casebook series then is to show by example something about the range and spread of individual items of folklore.

Questions about the geographical distribution of an item of folklore are not the only ones worth asking. Even more important are questions about meaning and interpretation. Far too often, students of folklore simply collect and report. Pure descriptions of data are surely a precondition for serious study, but they do not offer a substitute for significant analysis. Unfortunately, the majority of writings about a particular item of folklore never attempt anything more than mere description. The discipline of folklore began several centuries ago with the collection of antiquities and presumed "survivals" from earlier periods. It was not until the late nineteenth century and especially the twentieth century that the crucial study of how folklore functions in context may be said to have begun. In most cases, the application of sociological, anthropological, psychological and other theories and methods to folkloristic data has yet to be undertaken. One reason for this is that most theorists in the social sciences are just as unaware of the nature of folklore data as folklorists are unaware of the theories and methods of the social sciences. One intent of the Folklore Casebook series is to bring data and theory together—at least for students of folklore.

Folklore has always fascinated members of many academic disciplines, e.g., scholars in classics, comparative literature, Bible studies, psychiatry, sociology, but despite its interdisciplinary appeal, the study of folklore has rarely been interdisciplinary. One can find lip service to the notion of interdisciplinary study, but scholars and their work for the most part tend to be parochial. Anthropologists cite only the work of fellow anthropologists, psychiatrists only the work of other psychiatrists. Similarly, folklorists too are not always open to considering studies of folklore made by nonfolklorists. Accordingly, students who come upon a specific problem in folklore are commonly restricted by the limited disciplinary bias and knowledge of their instructors.

One difficulty in being truly interdisciplinary involves a mechanical problem in locating the previous scholarship devoted to a problem. Folklore studies appear in an incredible and often bewildering variety of books, monographs, and professional periodicals. One needs sometimes to be a virtual bibliographical sleuth to discover what other scholars have said about the subject one has chosen to research. Yet the credo of the true scholar should be that he should begin *his* work where other scholars have ended theirs. With this in mind, one other aim of the Folklore Casebook series is to bring together under one cover a representative sampling of the scholarship relevant to a single item or problem. Hopefully, it will encourage students of folklore not to be parochial in outlook but rather to be willing if not anxious to explore all possibilities in investigating the folklore research topic they have selected.

The topics covered in the Folklore Casebook series are of sufficient general interest to have received the critical attention of numerous scholars. Topics such as the evil eye, the flood myth, the bullfight, Christmas, the custom of couvade, or the folktale of Oedipus would be examples of topics appropriate for casebook treatment. In most instances, whole books or monographs have been devoted to the topics. However, for the most part, the selections chosen for the Casebook have been taken from periodicals. Assembling representative essays from a variety of sources seemed to be the best means of achieving the various goals of the Casebook series. Students who wish to explore further the topic of one of the Casebooks would be well advised to consult the book-length treatments available. In each Casebook, the editor will provide some bibliographical references for the student who wishes to go beyond the necessarily limited materials contained in the volume.

The selections included in the casebooks will be presented as they originally appeared, wherever possible. To be sure, essays written in foreign languages will be translated for the casebook, but individual words or phrases in foreign languages may be left untranslated. It is important for students of folklore to be aware of the necessity for learning to read foreign languages. Because the different selections were written independently, it is inevitable that some repetition will occur. Students must realize that such repetition in scholarship is not unusual. In folklore in particular, the repetition of data is often desirable. As indicated above, folklorists are often concerned with the question to what extent is an item of folklore in one culture similar to or different from an apparently comparable item in another culture.

The scholarly apparatus including footnote and bibliographical reference style have also been left intact wherever possible. Differences between the humanities and the social sciences exist with respect to reference techniques as any scholar who has had occasion to rewrite or recast an essay to conform to the requirements of another discipline can very well attest. Leaving the footnotes in their original form also serves to demonstrate the partial nature of scholarship. Probably no one scholar ever controls all the relevant data and has read all the books and essays pertaining to his subject. For one thing, few scholars can read all those languages of the world in which germane material has been written. For another, there remains the perennial information retrieval problem which normally precludes even locating all the possible sources. Still granting the unavoidably incomplete nature of most scholarship, the student can still see differences in how well an individual scholar succeeded in finding source materials. Some writers make little or no attempt to consult sources—almost pretending that they are the first to ever contemplate the issue under consideration. Others seem to make a pedantic fetish out of citing esoteric and fugitive sources. In the final analysis, the criteria for the inclusion of an essay in a casebook did not include counting the number of references contained in an author's footnotes. Rather the criteria concerned the clarity of the description of the data and the degree of insight attained in the analysis of the data. It should be understood that not every important essay written about the topic or theme of a casebook could be included. Some essays were simply too long while others may have been superseded by later studies.

Despite limitations, it is hoped that the sampling of scholarship presented in the Folklore Casebook series will assist students of folklore in undertaking research of their own. Whether they are stimulated to continue the study of the particular topic treated in a casebook or whether they use one or more of the essays as a model for the investigation of some other topic, the ultimate goal is the upgrading of the quality of folklore research. As the discipline of folkloristics continues to grow, its success and its achievements will unquestionably depend upon how well future students study the materials of folklore.

Alan Dundes, General Editor
University of California, Berkeley

Contents

The Evil Eye: A Folklore Casebook xiii

The Research Topic: Or, Folklore Without End 3
Arnold van Gennep

Praise and Dispraise in Folklore 9
Eugene S. McCartney

An Incantation in the 'House of Light' Against the Evil Eye 39
Stephen Langdon

Proverbs (23:1–8) and the Evil Eye in "The Wisdom of Sirach" 41

The Evil Eye Among the Hebrews 44
Aaron Brav

The Evil Eye in South Indian Folklore 55
A. Stewart Woodburne

The Evil Eye in Iran 66
Bess Allen Donaldson

The Shilluk's Belief in the Evil Eye 78
Rev. D.S. Oyler

The Evil Eye and Infant Health in Lebanon 86
Jamal Karam Harfouche

The Evil Eye in Some Greek Villages of the Upper Haliakmon Valley in West Macedonia 107
Margaret M. Hardie (Mrs. F.W. Hasluck)

The Evil Eye in Roumania, and Its Antidotes 124
A. Murgoci

The Jettatura and the Evil Eye 130
Giuseppe Pitrè

Scoring Aboon the Breath: Defeating the Evil Eye 143
Thomas Davidson

The Evil Eye Among European-Americans 150
Louis C. Jones

The Evil Eye in Its Folk Medical Aspects: A Survey of North America 169
Wayland D. Hand

Reflections on the Evil Eye 181
Richard G. Coss

The Evil Eye: Forms and Dynamics of a Universal Superstition 192
Helmut Schoeck

The Evil Eye—Envy and Greed Among the Patidar of Central Gujerat 201
D.F. Pocock

The Evil Eye 211
Géza Róheim

Envy and the Evil Eye Among Slovak-Americans: An Essay in the Psychological Ontogeny of Belief and Ritual 223
Howard F. Stein

Wet and Dry, the Evil Eye: An Essay in Indo-European and Semitic Worldview 257
Alan Dundes

The Evil Eye: A Folklore Casebook

The aim of this casebook is to sample the scholarship concerned with the evil eye. The evil eye has attracted the attention of scholars from a variety of academic disciplines. The voluminous bibliography of evil eye studies includes writings by anthropologists, biblical scholars, classicists, folklorists, missionaries, ophthalmologists, psychiatrists, and sociologists, among others. By far the majority of discussions of the evil eye represent anecdotal reportings of the phenomenon in a single cultural context, often without any reference to the occurrence of the same or similar phenomena elsewhere. Yet these anecdotal accounts of the evil eye are not without value, for they provide those scholars interested in theory the critical raw material which can be drawn upon to test one or another theoretical notion.

An attempt has been consciously made to select essays representing the variety of approaches. Accordingly essays have been taken from sources as diverse as *Ophthalmology* for 1908, *Sudan Notes and Records* for 1919, the *International Review of Missions* for 1935, and the *Emory University Quarterly* for 1955. The intent was to immerse a student in the kinds of materials available to any scholar who might wish to undertake a study of the evil eye. Most of the essays in the initial part of the casebook tend to be reportorial in nature. As one reads about the evil eye in India, in Iran, and in other countries, one will surely begin to notice familiar details. And this is precisely the point. Rather than simply taking some purported authority's word for the assertion that the evil eye exists in cultures A and B, the student will have the opportunity to see for himself what the evidence is like from those cultures.

The final essays in the casebook are aimed more at the interpretation of facts. The student may or may not find a given interpretive essay reasonable or persuasive. In some cases, he may have more evidence at his disposal than did the writer of the theoretical essay.

Some readers may be dismayed by the variety of interpretations offered. But learning about the diversity of theoretical arguments is just as important as learning about the diversity of folklore itself. It may be difficult for a novice to realize there may be conflicting or equally plausible ways of analyzing data. Theoretical approaches represented in this casebook include: the comparative, the functional, and the psychoanalytic, among others. But rather than learning about theoretical approaches in the abstract, the student can see how these approaches can be applied to illuminate (or obscure) a common set of facts, namely those relating to the evil eye.

In sum then, the aim of this casebook on the evil eye is not just to provide source material on a single widespread folk belief complex, but also to give some insight into the process or nature of inquiry whereby scholars examine data and seek to understand that data.

THE EVIL EYE

The Research Topic: Or, Folklore Without End

*Arnold van Gennep**

The first task in research is to select an appropriate topic to investigate. This is true whether one plans to engage in fieldwork or wishes to work in the library, relying upon field reports made by others. Having chosen a topic, the researcher, ideally, should begin his work where previous scholars have ended theirs. To do this properly, it is obvious that one needs to discover precisely what is already known about the subject to be studied. This often requires considerable bibliographical (and linguistic) expertise. Many investigators either because of ignorance or laziness or the unavailability of published sources conduct their field or library research as though they were the very first to ever consider the problem. Although there may be something to be said in favor of undertaking research with an open or unbiased mind, most of these parochial efforts typically result in rediscovering something which is already known to many scholars. On the other hand, all knowledge is partial. No one can ever know all the information relevant to a particular problem. Hence an attempt to locate and read every single word ever written on a given subject before *beginning one's own analysis may be endlessly futile. There is also little point in accumulating bibliography for bibliography's sake. The difficulty is that one never knows*

* Reprinted from Arnold van Gennep, *The Semi-Scholars* (London: Routledge & Kegan Paul, 1967), pp. 32–36.

ahead of time which of a large group of writings on a subject will prove to be fruitful and stimulating. So one usually feels obliged to read as widely as possible before formulating one's own hypotheses to be tested in the field or against the data contained in library sources.

The plight of the compulsive researcher is beautifully delineated in a delightful parody written by the great French folklorist Arnold van Gennep (1873–1957) who is perhaps best known for his major theoretical work on rites of passage. (It was van Gennep who coined the phrase and used it in the title of his important book Les rites de passage *in 1909.) As to why van Gennep chose the evil eye to make his point, it is difficult to say. Possibly van Gennep was inspired by the case of Jules Tuchmann, an ex-musician who was largely self-trained in library research. During the last decades of the nineteenth century, Tuchmann evidently spent hour upon hour, day upon day, in the Bibliothèque Nationale in Paris reading anything he could find on the evil eye. His ransacking of classical, historical, and ethnographic reports resulted in what would have been a veritable monograph-length compilation of assorted and sundry jottings on the evil eye. These valuable extrapolations appeared in a series of more than ninety segments in the French folklore journal* Mélusine, *beginning in the second volume in 1884 and ending finally in the eleventh volume in 1912. Tuchmann was not a candidate for a higher degree but his dogged and relentless pursuit of evil eye references may have suggested the portrait of the "young man" so skillfully drawn by van Gennep. For more about Tuchmann, see Henri Gaidoz, "Jules Tuchmann,"* Mélusine, *11 (1912), 148–151. For van Gennep's own superb scholarship, see* The Rites of Passage *(London: Routledge and Kegan Paul, 1960), his incredibly comprehensive multi-volume* Manuel de folklore français contemporain *(1937–1958), or other of the numerous works listed in Kitty van Gennep,* Bibliographie des oeuvres d'Arnold van Gennep *(Paris: A. & J. Picard, 1964). For details of van Gennep's life and career, see Nicole Belmont,* Arnold Van Gennep: The Creator of French Ethnography *(Chicago: University of Chicago Press, 1979).*

I

The Young Man, pale and earnest, at sixteen read *The Future of Science*, at seventeen the complete works of Nietzsche in Henri Albert's translation, and at eighteen resolved to be a great scholar, all this in a continual effort to improve himself. When he had passed his matriculation examination, The Young Man left his province, registered at the Sorbonne, got his degree, and then went to his teacher and said:

"I believe I have it in me to be a great scholar. Would you please give me a research topic?"

"But of course, willingly! A research topic, you say? Very well: prepare a doctoral thesis on the Evil Eye. You know the scientific method: first you compile a complete bibliography, then you go through the literature, and eventually you make an advance in the subject. When you have done that, come back and see me. I shall then instruct you how to prepare your monograph."

II

The Young Man thanked him effusively. He was an orphan, and had an annual income of 2,400 francs. The next day, as soon as the doors opened, he went into the Bibliothèque Nationale, sat down in seat No. III, and started to work.

In those days neither the *Revue des Traditions Populaires* nor *Mélusine* yet existed. The Young Man therefore had to compile his bibliography volume by volume, journal by journal, title by title. After several years of uninterrupted labour, and taking advantage of the periods when the library was closed to classify his notes, The Young Man had extracted from the French literature everything that had to do with the Evil Eye.

The French facts, however, were directly connected with the facts of classical antiquity. A new effort, and all the Latin and Greek authors were reduced to notes.

The interpretation of ancient texts is often difficult. The least of them has been the object of innumerable commentaries, which a conscientious scholar could not ignore. The Young Man therefore made a bibliography of commentators, limiting himself, though, to copying the titles in Hungarian, Finnish, Basque, Albanian, and other hirsute languages, scarcely understanding what exactly they meant.

He then perceived that the Evil Eye occupied a preponderant place in the preoccupations of savages; so all the collections of voyages, all the missionary accounts, and all the ethnographical journals took their places also in his pigeon-holes. All the same, towards his thirty-fifth birthday, The Young Man concluded that his bibliography was "quite complete."

III

He then proceeded to the second part of his programme: going through the literature. He took out his bibliographical notes one by one, and set himself, pen in hand, to read all the French, Greek, Latin, Italian, Spanish, and German authors on whom he had made out references. This took him about twelve years.

Then he realized the necessity to learn the Scandinavian and Slavonic languages, and Finnish and Hungarian. He launched himself at this task with enthusiasm and drove the librarians mad at the Bibliothèque Nationale, the School of Oriental Languages, the Sorbonne, the Museum of Natural History, the Musée Guimet, and the International Ethnographical Institute with his pursuit of untraceable works.

This methodical life had led him to make economies; for he spent money wildly in procuring pamphlets, extracts from journals, and clippings from newspapers which, on the strength of their titles, he thought were of decisive importance.

His researches aroused interest at the School of Oriental Languages, and he was most kindly supplied with references to Armenian and Georgian publications, Chinese encyclopaedias, and Turkish, Persian and Arabic manuscripts. It would have been ridiculous, shameful, and unscholarly to neglect these valuable sources of information.

The Young Man learned Arabic, Persian, Turkish, Chinese, Armenian, and Georgian; then at one go he devoured Japanese, Tibetan, Sanskrit, twenty or so languages of India, Malay, Javanese, Samoan, Maori, and Tasmanian, a dead language; finally, he assimilated the languages of the three Americas, from Eskimo to Fuegian.

By the age of fifty-four, he knew 843 languages and dialects, his bibliographical references numbered 27,000, and as for his notes he did not know exactly how many there were; at any rate, he had 22,312 cartons, each containing on the average from four to five hundred slips of paper. Some years later, he estimated roughly that there were about 12,000,000 notes in his collection.

IV

At this point he decided that the time had come to pass on to the third part of his programme: the investigation of his topic. He was afflicted, however, by a preliminary scruple. He went to unbosom himself to his teacher.

The teacher had long since retired. He lived near Paris in a tiny house with a large garden. In his house he had neither books, nor paper, nor ink. He received his visitor courteously.

"I am The Young Man," said the latter, "to whom you suggested, some years ago, a magnificent research topic."

"Oh, really? A research topic? Do tell me, what topic was that? My memory has deteriorated, and you must excuse me if I do not place you at once."

"There is nothing to be surprised at in that, sir. You told me not to come back and see you until I had reached that stage of scientific research which consists in examining the subject-matter and writing it up. Not without trouble, I am now at that point. I think I may say that I now know more than anyone else in the world about the Evil Eye."

"Ah, the Evil Eye!"

"Yes, the Evil Eye. But before writing my monograph, sir, I should like your advice on two serious questions. First, ought I to give my evidence *in extenso*, accompanying it with a commentary in note form, or ought I rather to write the commentary in a discursive style and content myself with summing up my evidence?

"Second, should I publish such evidence, either in whole or in part, in the original—Algonkin, Pali, Icelandic, Savoyard, and so on—or should I instead translate it into French, or perhaps into Latin on account of the obscene passages?"

"The grave questions that you have put to me, my dear pupil, cannot be answered without mature reflection," said the teacher. "Come back and see me one of these days, and I shall give you my opinion. It is now for me to ask you a question, though. While you have been investigating your topic, have you thought about keeping your bibliography up to date?"

V

The Young Man made a despairing gesture. Without saying a word, he went away, rushed into the main room of the Bibliothèque Nationale, dropped into seat No. III, which by a semisecular tradition was regarded as his quasi-property, and feverishly attempted to make up for lost time.

Death came to him in this very seat, breaking a cervical vertebra. In his will, he left his fortune and his notes to his excellent teacher. The latter accepted the money, but as for the eighteen million notes—no one knows what became of them.

Praise and Dispraise in Folklore

*Eugene S. McCartney**

Because the evil eye was occasionally mentioned in the writings of ancient Greece and Rome, classicists were among those scholars who investigated the subject. Although some classicists like Professor McCartney of the University of Michigan were aware of some of the scholarship devoted to contemporary accounts of the evil eye, many tended to restrict their discussions to citations from classical sources with enough references to modern reportings to demonstrate the continuation or "survival" of the evil eye from classical antiquity.

In this essay, Professor McCartney's stated subject is the danger which may result from an act or statement of praise rather than the evil eye per se. But as the reader will soon see, the articulation of praise very much belongs to the folk belief complex we know as the evil eye. Professor McCartney's abundant knowledge of classical sources and his concentration upon the evils of praise as well as the apotropaic efficacy of dispraise give the reader a useful perspective on the classicist's approach to the study of the evil eye.

We are told by Plutarch (*Mor.* 59A) that a field remains unaffected by commendation, whereas a man who is praised beyond his deserts is puffed up and destroyed.[1] Today, also, praise may turn a person's

* Reprinted from the *Papers of the Michigan Academy of Science, Arts and Letters*, Vol. 28 (1943), 567–593.

head,[2] but in the realm of superstition its consequences are literal rather than figurative, and it is devastating physically as well as spiritually. It is often resorted to by people who have the evil eye. Its harmful potentialities may, in fact, be summed up in the same striking words with which an American scholar described those of this malign power:

> The Evil Eye may be the cause of every ill in mind, body or estate that flesh is heir to; briefly, of misfortunes which in modern times are covered by insurance, attributed to the weather or for which the remedy is sought by recourse to a lawyer, a physician or a gun, according to the temperament of the loser. Above all, the Evil Eye is responsible for those slow, wasting diseases and nervous or mental disorders for which the untutored mind can find no explanation in the circumstances of the person afflicted. Anyone may be blighted by it, babies in the cradle especially.[3]

The blasting effects of praise are not confined to human beings, for it destroys cattle, vegetation, and even objects without life. In the main the dangers have come from three sources: (1) the inadvertence or the ignorance of well-meaning people who let slip complimentary remarks; (2) the envy and malevolence of those who have the evil eye; and (3) the jealousy of the gods,[4] who permit no mortal to be supremely beautiful or happy or prosperous without paying for his blessings by counterbalancing woes and adversities. In modern times even fairies have been resentful of the bestowal of praise, especially in Ireland. Expressions of admiration and the display of love and affection have likewise brought heavy calamities. These and related aspects of praising I desire to illustrate by examples from both ancient and modern Greece and Italy, from several other countries bordering on the Mediterranean Sea, and from a few places remote from the classical lands.

It happens that numerous ancient beliefs about praise and the evil eye that are recorded in colorless statements of fact by Greeks and Romans are strikingly paralleled by modern ones in story settings. In the Mediterranean countries material of this kind illuminates the superstitious past more clearly and accurately than a novelist can re-create the atmosphere of a bygone era. Especially close analogues to classical notions may be found in books dealing with the lore of Gaelic-speaking parts of Scotland. Many examples have been collected by R.C. Maclagan, *Evil Eye in the Western Highlands,*[5] a volume which cannot fail to give the reader a better understanding of classical ideas about the dangers of praising.

A meager generalization about praise occurs in Pliny the Elder (*Nat. Hist.* 7.16). He says that certain families in Africa who were gifted with powers of fascination employed praise as a means of killing cattle, blighting trees, and causing the death of children: ". . . quorum laudatione intereant probata, arescant arbores, emoriantur infantes." A Roman's understanding of Pliny's brief statement may be found in Aulus Gellius (*Noct. Att.* 9.4.7–8): ". . . esse quasdam in terra Africa hominum familias voce atque lingua effascinantium qui si impensius forte laudaverint pulchras arbores, segetes laetiores, infantes amoeniores, egregios equos, pecudes pastu atque cultu opimas, emoriantur repente haec omnia, nulli aliae causae obnoxia."

This circumstantial account of Aulus Gellius is far more interesting than the few matter-of-fact words of Pliny, but it may be somewhat misleading. As we shall see, in general folk practice it is by no means essential that the praise be lavish or casual or unguarded, ("si impensius forte laudaverint"), nor do the persons or things singled out for attention have to be in a particularly flourishing condition. Like the jealous gods, the evil eye may prefer to strike down the exalted and the prosperous,[6] but it may blast any person or any thing attractive enough to call forth a compliment, whether spontaneous and sincere or premeditated and malicious. "And the same bad effect can be produced by the look or glance of the eye of the man who, while uttering words of praise or congratulation, makes a mental reservation whereby he produces the exactly opposite effect of that which his words seem to wish to make."[7]

One may well ask how the evil effects of praise were communicated from one person to another. Some of the ancients thought that feelings of envy aroused on seeing something excellent filled the atmosphere with a pernicious quality and that an envious man transmitted his own envenomed exhalations to the things nearest to him.[8] The eye was the window of the mind or soul,[9] and for this reason, probably, a glance from the envious was supposed to corrupt and contaminate the air.

There are many aspects of the subject of praising, and one story or one quotation may illustrate three or four of them. For this reason my arrangement of material is sometimes arbitrary. Furthermore, pertinent cross references are omitted, since their introduction would encumber the article and make it unduly long.

Praise of Infants

We know that infants, children, and those in the bloom of youth were especially susceptible to the evil eye,[10] for many precautions were taken to guard them against exposure to it. Some Greek mothers went so far as to refuse to show children to their fathers (Plut., *Mor.* 682 A), and an old Roman granny or aunt would lift a baby from the cradle and apply spittle to the forehead in an effort to protect it from danger (Persius, 2.31–34). A Roman nurse tending a baby spat three times in its face if a stranger entered the house or if someone saw the child while it was sleeping (Pliny, *Nat. Hist.* 28.39). The peril was so imminent that the Romans created a special goddess of the cradle, Cunina (Lactant., *Div. Inst.* 1.20.36). Ancient lore would tend to confirm, therefore, Pliny's record of the deadliness of praise bestowed upon infants. At the present time an unguarded compliment or an admiring glance may be equally disastrous. A modern Greek admonition that stresses the welfare of the newborn babe runs as follows: "Do not be too eager to compliment a mother on the birth of an infant, but remain at least half an hour in the house before entering her room, lest rejoicing turn to lamentation."[11]

We find that the Osmanli women of Turkey are best pleased when the new arrival is totally ignored and so is spared the risk of having the evil eye cast upon it. "If, however, feminine curiosity and interest in babies are too strong to allow of the infant's being entirely overlooked, the *hanŭms*, after spitting on it, conceal their admiration under some such disparaging remarks as 'Nasty, ugly little thing!' to show that they bear no malice."[12]

Part of an account of the Turkish ceremony after the birth of a child is worth quoting here:

> . . . Very little notice is taken of the baby, and even then only disparaging remarks are made about it, both by relatives and guests, such as *Murdar* (dirty), *Chirkin* (ugly), *Yaramaz* (naughty). If looked at it is immediately spat upon, and then left to slumber in innocent unconsciousness of the undeserved abuse it has received. Abusive and false epithets are employed by

> Turkish women under all circumstances worthy of inviting praise or admiration, in order to counteract the supposition of ill-feeling or malice underlying the honeyed words of the speaker, which are sure to be turned against her in case of any accident or evil happening to the subject of the conversation.[13]

The danger caused through praising a child in the cradle may be illustrated by a story related by a Moor of Tripoli early in the nineteenth century:

> . . . A person possessed of the evil eye, being once on a journey, chanced to enter a cottage where he saw an old woman, and a child which lay sleeping in a cradle; he requested that some milk might be given him to quench his thirst, but there was unfortunately none in the house; having remained some time to repose himself, he was observed to gaze steadfastly on the infant, and [having] admired its beauty, he soon after departed; on the mother's awaking next morning, she found her child dead! occasioned of course by the evil eye of the preceding day.[14]

A half century ago superstitious mothers in the northeastern part of Scotland took measures to shield their babes from the dangers of praise. "To guard the child from being *forespoken*, it was passed three times through the petticoat or chemise the mother wore at the time of the accouchement. It was not deemed proper to bestow a very great deal of praise on a child; and one doing so would have been interrupted by some such words as 'Gueede sake, haud yir tong, or ye'll forespyke the bairn.' "[15]

The Slavs have a similar superstition, and a Russian nurse has been known to spit in the face of one who praised her ward without uttering the precautionary "God forbid."[16] In Germany, likewise, parents and nurses have had misgivings when their children were praised.[17]

Young children are protected from the effects of the evil eye with as much solicitude as babes. The English traveler Edward Dodwell relates an interesting experience on the island of Corfu in the first decade of the nineteenth century. His account runs as follows:

> . . . I was taking a view near a cottage, into which I was kindly invited, and hospitably entertained with fruit and wine. Two remarkably fine children, the sons of my host, were playing about the cottage; and as I wished to pay a compliment to the

> parents, I was lavish in my praises of their children. But when I had repeated my admiration two or three times, an old woman, whom I suppose to have been the grandmother, became agonized with alarm, and starting up, she dragged the children towards me, and desired me to spit in their faces. This singular request excited so much astonishment, that I concluded the venerable dame to be disordered in her intellects. But her importunities were immediately seconded, and earnestly enforced, by those of the father and mother of the boys. I was fortunately accompanied by a Greek, who explained to me, that in order to destroy the evil effects of my superlative encomiums, the only remedy was, for me to spit in the faces of the children. I could no longer refuse a compliance with their demands, and I accordingly performed the unpleasant office in as moderate a manner as possible. But this did not satisfy the superstitious cottagers; and it was curious to see with what perfect tranquillity the children underwent the nasty operation; to which their beauty had probably frequently exposed them. The mother then took some dust from the ground, and mixing it with some oil, from a lamp which was burning before a picture of the Virgin, put a small patch of it on their foreheads. We then parted perfectly good friends; but they begged me never to praise their children again.[18]

Over fifty years ago the household of a Greek lady in Smyrna showed in the presence of a guest how dangerous it is for a child to be praised even by members of the immediate family.

> . . . Her little grandson, who had just arrived from Europe, was, during luncheon, an object of great interest to his grandmother and aunts, who overwhelmed him with laudations. To every complimentary remark, however, made to, or about him, by either this lady or her daughters, another would exclaim, "No! garlic! garlic!" (Οχι! σκόρδον! σκόρδον!), at the same time pointing at the child, thus threatened with the evil eye, the first and second outstretched fingers. For the evil eye may also be cast unwittingly, . . . and it is impossible in the Levant to speak admiringly or approvingly of any person or thing without being met with the exclamation, "*Kalé!* don't give it the evil eye!" (καλή, μὴ τὸν ματιάζῃς!)[19]

Tourists who are unaware of the existence of this superstitition about praising may inadvertently incur some risk of bodily harm, as we learn from the words of a classical scholar: "I have seen in modern

Greece, within twenty miles of Delphi, a party of American and Canadian women in danger of being stoned because in the little village of Arachoba, inhabited by Albanians, they had artlessly praised the beauty of the local children."[20]

A Greek physician who traveled about the Aegean Sea early in the nineteenth century found the belief widely current among the peoples of the Levant:

> . . . ils tombent d'accord entre eux que lorsqu'on parlera de la bonté ou de la beauté de quelque objet, soit animé, soit inanimé, ils ajouteront, en une langue quelconque, *Dieu le préserve*; c'est ainsi que les Grecs disent en soufflant de la salive sur l'objet qu'ils flattent, *na min ambascathi*, ou *mati na min to piassi*. Les Turcs, qui se soumettent strictement à cette pratique, ne manquent jamais de dire, en pareil cas, le mot *machalach!* (ce que Dieu a fait). Cette influence, selon eux, se faisant sentir particulièrement aux enfants, on a recours pour les garantir à l'ail et à la couleur bleue. Les personnes riches font monter en argent une pierre bleue de quelque nature qu'elle soit, et une racine d'ail, qu'on suspend au bonnet que l'enfant porte habituellement.[21]

Examples of similar beliefs may be adduced from other lands bordering on the Mediterranean Sea.

> The people of Palestine do not like to hear themselves complimented unless at the same time you use the name of God. Otherwise they believe such expressions are bound to bring misfortunes and possibly troubles and death. If you call a boy or a girl pretty its mother's heart is filled with terror, and she straightway throws out her hand, extending the index and little finger in a way supposed to ward off the devil and to prevent the evil consequences of your remark. If you wish to praise the beauty of a child you must begin the sentence with, "May God surround thee." After that you may go on as you please. If you pat the child on the head and fail to use this sentence, the mother upon returning home will take the child into a room and put it in the middle of the floor. She will then take a shovel and gather dust from each of the four corners, and throw it in the fire, crying: "Fie on thee, evil eye."[22]

A passage published in 1743 concerning the evil eye among the Egyptians is informative:

> They have a great notion of the magic art, have books about it, and think there is much virtue in talismans and charms; but particularly are strongly possessed with an opinion of the evil eye. And when a child is commended, except you give it some blessing, if they are not very well assured of your good will, they use charms against the evil eye; and particularly when they think any ill success attends them on account of an evil eye, they throw salt into the fire.[23]

In the second decade of the last century an English traveler found in northern Africa an Arab belief part of which reminds one of the passage quoted above from Aulus Gellius, but, according to it, almost anyone could work injury by resorting to praise:

> The "Evil Eye" is of all other mischiefs most dreaded, and for a stranger to express particular admiration of a child, a horse, or any other valuable, is to bring on it or its possessor certain misfortune; this may, however, be averted by passing over the object a finger wetted with saliva, or by the equally efficacious charm of an open hand, either attached to the clothes as an ornament or tattooed on the skin.[24]

The Walloons entertain similar notions: "Une sorcière peut jeter un sort à un animal ou à un enfant, le rendre malade ou le fair périr, en faisant son éloge, en disant qu'il est beau, qu'il est bien portant, etc."[25]

There is a record of a Scottish woman who was alarmed when a visitor remarked to her: "You have a pretty, dear boy there." Forthwith the mother turned the child's face to her and began to spit in it as hard as she could to prevent any bad effect from the other woman's Evil Eye.[26]

Since the powers that injure with the evil eye are so unsuspecting as to believe everything they hear, children may be protected by addressing to them words that are the opposite of endearments. An excellent example of such deceit occurs in Prosper Mérimée's *Colomba*,[27] which has a Corsican setting:

> . . . "Va, coquine," disait-il, "sois excommuniée, sois maudite, friponne!" Brandaccio, superstitieux comme beaucoup de bandits, craignait de fasciner les enfants en leur addressant des bénédictions ou des éloges, car on sait que les puissances mystérieuses qui président à l'*Annocchiatura* ont la mauvaise habitude d'exécuter le contraire de nos souhaits.

The southern Slavs are likewise afraid to use expressions that show admiration:

> Für „ein schmucker, prächtiger Junge, ein schönes Mädchen, ein gesundes Kind, ein tüchtiges Pferd, ein munteres Füllen" usw., sagt man gewöhnlich: „ein wahnwitziger, lahmer Junge, ein verunstaltetes Mädchen, ein verkehrtes (verwahrlostes) Kind, ein verwittertes Ross, ein schäbiges Füllen" usw.[28]

In accordance with the same principle the Rabbis of Palestine used to advise one to call a pretty son "ugly darky,"[29] and the Chinese have applied to their children the names "dog," "hog," "puppy," "flea," and so forth.[30] A guarded suggestion has been made that "our familiar habit of calling our children 'scamp' and 'rascal,' when we are caressing them, may be founded on a worn-out superstition of the same kind."[31]

Praise of Youths

Attractive boys and girls who were nearing adulthood were still young enough to fall victims to the evil eye. There is an interesting story about a very comely boy eighteen years old. His father, who owned a bath, refused to allow him to bathe in the presence of men because he feared their envy.[32] Since a point is made of mentioning the beauty of the boy one is warranted in concluding that the father was afraid it might elicit a complimentary remark or an admiring glance. In the *Aethiopica* (3.7) Heliodorus tells us that a beautiful girl who had taken part in a procession became sick and retired to her room. Her condition is attributed to her having been seen by some spiteful eye.

In a quotation from a lost Roman play,[33] the *Setina* of Titinius, a lover exclaims: "Paula mea, amabo." At once he sees that his words may injure her, and hence he is quick to make an admonition: "Pol tu ad laudem addito praefiscini." The purpose was, we are told, "ne puella fascinetur."

Praise of Adults

The blighting power of praise was feared by adults also. Those who saw the beautiful hetaera Laïs would make sacrifice, and in the midst of their wonderment would take the additional precaution of praying to the gods and exclaiming, ἀπίτω φθόνος τοῦ κάλλους! ἀπίτω Βασκανία τῆς χάριτος (Aristaen., *Epp.* 1.1).[34] The peril of praise to men of modern Greece is exemplified in a striking story collected by a student of modern Greek folklore:

> . . . I have heard of an ancient dame of Salonica who had the reputation of possessing an evil eye. Many of her achievements were whispered with becoming awe. One day, it was said, as she sat at her window, she saw a young man passing on horseback. He seemed to be so proud of himself and his mount that the old lady . . . could not resist the temptation of humbling him. One dread glance from her eye and one short cry from her lips: "Oh, what a gallant cavalier!" brought both horse and horseman to their knees.[35]

The Gypsies, who are of a passionate nature, have deliberately employed praise as a means of inflicting injury:

> Iskander, isolated, haughty, was sad, angry, and cruel. He asked for neither counsel nor advice, and listened only to the flatterers who chanted his growing megalomania. Ben Sasra understood.
>
> "Their chants of praise are funeral chants. No man could outlive such praise. Our books say: Praise is deadly. There existing no material weapon to destroy Iskander, the Indians are using the most deadly spiritual one: praise."[36]

German Jews of a half century ago believed that dire consequences followed the bestowal of praise: "Il faut éviter de vanter les qualités de ceux qu'on aime; sinon on pourrait leur faire perdre ces qualités ou même occasionner leur mort."[37]

Self-Fascination

In ancient Italy it was risky for a man to say nice things about himself, for he could fascinate himself, as Plautus shows. In the *Rudens* (458–461) a slave who flatters himself because of his skill in drawing water from a well suddenly recalls the peril of such utterances and exclaims *Praefiscine!* In the *Asinaria* (491–493) a slave takes the precaution of saying *Praefiscini* before he mentions his own uprightness and good reputation. An illuminating passage occurs in the *Florida* (16) of Apuleius: "To meet with the favor of the people, to please the senate, to gain the approval of officers and leaders—I would speak without bewitchment (*praefiscine dixerim*)—in some measure has been my lot."

Self-esteem may be dangerous even though not manifested in words. Narcissus felt a consuming passion for the beautiful reflection of himself in a pool and so pined away and died (Ovid, *Met.* 3.402–510), but perhaps this was not fascination. A certain Eutelidas, however, did bewitch himself when he was enravished by his own beauty (Plut., *Mor.* 682B), and it was believed that young children might fascinate themselves by the reflection of their own gaze (*ibid.* 682F). Theocritus (6.34–39) represents Damoetas as spitting thrice upon his breast when he finds beautiful a reflection of himself in the water.

There is a good modern example of self-fascination, for a story is told of a Sicilian with an evil eye so powerful that he bewitched himself on accidentally catching sight of himself in a mirror.[38] According to an English superstition recorded seventy years ago, a bride who wished to take a last admiring look into a mirror after completing her toilette left one hand without a glove.[39] Possibly the lack of perfection in her attire had a protecting effect.

Praise and Ill Health

Even when self-adulation does not cause self-fascination it may bring punishment from another source, as is shown by a Hungarian story: "Well, there is no doubting it, pretty little Helen got overlooked, but only because she came to believe that she was so pretty that everybody kept looking at her, and her only. She developed a perpetual headache."[40]

The most common results of praise, even though not bestowed by one with the evil eye, are sickness and ill health. Remarks about well-being are tantamount to praise of one's health, and they have been feared in many parts of the world.

In one of his letters Pliny the Younger (*Epist.* 5.6.45–46) sets forth the charms of his Tuscan villa. He says that he is unusually strong in both mind and body. Never have the members of his household enjoyed better health. He has not lost a single one of those whom he brought with him. Then, becoming frightened, he exclaims: "Venia sit dicto." It is hard to tell whether Pliny was praising or boasting, but such words concerning health were an entirely adequate cause for alarm. The following striking parallel is taken from an interesting collection of West Indian superstitions dated 1875:

> The feeling is by no means uncommon that to talk much of the health of a family, is a way to bring sickness on them. In the course of pastoral visitation, the clergyman will perhaps say, in a house where there is a large family, that he never has occasion to go to that house for visitation of the sick, so healthy is the household. He will be respectfully, but very decidedly asked not to speak too much about it, as it has been noticed that if this be done, sickness comes upon the family soon after.[41]

A rather similar idea has been recorded from the Orkneys:

> When a healthy child suddenly becomes sickly, and no one can account for the change, the child is said to have been "forespoken." Or when a stout man or woman becomes hypochondriac, or affected with nervous complaints, he or she is "forespoken." Some one has perhaps said "He's a bonny bairn," or "Thou ar' lookin' well the day;" but they have spoken with an *ill tongue*. They have neglected to add, "God save the bairn," or "Safe be thou," &c.[42]

An English writer states that "We need not go out of England to know that many people would rather you said anything to them than 'How well you are looking' "[43] We find Hotspur exclaiming:

> No more, no more; worse than the sun in March,
> This praise doth nourish agues.[44]

In *Far from the Madding Crowd* (Chap. 15) Thomas Hardy makes effective use of the superstition that it is unlucky to praise one's health. On asking a rustic friend how he is Gabriel Oak receives the cautious reply: "Oh, neither sick nor sorry, shepherd; but no younger."[45] This accords with German folk belief: "Spricht Jemand von seiner, oder eines Anderen Gesundheit oder Glück, so sagt er dabel dreimal 'unberufen,' damit nicht Gesundheit in Krankheit, Glück in Unglück sich wende."[46]

In this general connection the second stanza of Poe's "Lenore" is pertinent:

> "Wretches, ye loved her for her wealth and hated her for her
> pride,
> And when she fell in feeble health, ye blessed her—that she died!
> How *shall* the ritual, then, be read? the requiem how be sung
> By you—by yours, the evil eye—by yours, the slanderous tongue
> That did to death the innocence that died, and died so young?"

More or less similar examples may be found much farther afield. Among the superstitious people of Bombay a person who falls ill after having been praised is said to be a victim of the evil eye.[47] The Malays believe that "it is unlucky to remark on the fatness and healthiness of a baby, and a Malay will employ some purely nonsensical word, or convey his meaning in a roundabout way, rather than incur possible misfortune by using the actual word 'fat.' '*Ai bukan-nia poh-poh gental budak ini*' ('Isn't this child nice and round?') is the sort of phrase which is permissible."[48]

The Display of Affection

The manifestation of deep love or affection, especially for a child, is a kind of admiration, and may prove as deadly, but the danger comes chiefly from the jealousy of the gods. An informative passage occurs in the *Epictetus* (3.24.84–85) of Arrian:

> Whenever you grow attached to something, do not act as though it were one of those things that cannot be taken away, but as though it were something like a jar or a crystal goblet, so that when it breaks you will remember what it was like, and not be troubled. So too in life; if you kiss your child, your brother, your friend, *never allow your fancy free rein, nor your exuberant spirits to go as far as they like*, but hold them back, stop them, just like those who stand behind generals when they ride in triumph, and keep reminding them that they are mortal.[49]

The same general idea occurs in Euripides (*Alc.* 1133–1135). as Admetus showed his deep love for his wife, whom he expected never to see again, Heracles becomes somewhat fearful and says: "You have her. May there be no jealousy from any of the gods."

In Ian Maclaren's story of "Domsie" in *Beside the Bonnie Brier Bush* the following reflections are addressed to the mother of a boy who, after winning high honors in school and being much praised by relatives and others, had come home to die:

> Ay, ay, it's a sair blow aifter a that wes in the papers. I wes feared when I hear o' the papers: "Lat weel alane," says I to the Dominie; "ye'ill bring a judgment on the laddie wi' yir blawing." But ye micht as well hae spoken to the hills. Domsie's a thraun body at the best, and he was clean infatuat' wi' George. Ay, ay, it's an awfu' lesson, Marget, no to mak' idols o' our bairns, for that's naethin' else than provokin' the Almichty.
>
> It was at this point that Marget gave way and scandalized Drumtochty, which held that obtrusive prosperity was an irresistible provocation to the higher powers, and that a skilful depreciation of our children was a policy of safety.

Another good example of the danger of loving intensely may be found in Kipling's story "Without Benefit of Clergy,"[50] in which a mother, desirous of guarding against the repetition of a fatal mistake, says:

> "It was because we loved Tota that he died. The jealousy of God was upon us," said Ameera. "I have hung up a large black jar before our window to turn the Evil Eye from us, and we must make no protestations of delight, but go softly underneath the stars, lest God find us out. Is that not good talk, worthless one?"
>
> She had shifted the accent of the word that means "blessed," in proof of the sincerity of her purpose. But the kiss that followed the new christening was a thing that any deity might have envied. They went about henceforth saying: "It is naught—it is naught," and hoping that all the powers heard.

The Germans, also, believe that they may bring disaster upon children by loving them too much. "Auch Kinder werden häufig krank gelobt. Starkes Loben gilt als verdächtig."[51] Uttering the word "unberufen" or "unbeschrien" protects children from the effects of endearments,[52] just as it does from those of excessive praise.

Failure of Egyptian Bedouins to take precautions after a display of affection brings serious results:

> Der Ausdruck „maschallah“ lässt sich ungefähr mit „Gott verhüte Schlimmes“ übersetzen und muss stets hinzugefügt werdern, wenn man ein lebendes Wesen lobt. Sonst lasst sich Unheil oder Tod von dem betreffenden Menschen oder Tier nur dadurch abwenden, dass man sie dem unvorsichtigen Lobredner schenkt.[53]

Praise and Divine Jealousy

As a rule, the gods reserved their hostility for the prosperous, the mighty, and the prideful among men, but praise might enter into the good fortune that they resented and counterbalanced by calamity.[54] I shall give three illustrations of the fear that happiness and success aroused among the ancients.[55]

In speaking to the elders of Argos Clytaemnestra, who has been reunited with Agamemnon, after his absence at Troy gives expression to her great joy and praises her husband rather fulsomely. When she realizes how laudatory she has been she exclaims: φθόνος δ' ἀπέστω (Aesch., *Agam.* 904). Agamemnon seems even more alarmed than she is, and he warns her that for praise to be seemly it must come from the lips of others. He beseeches her not to make his path subject to jealousy by strewing it with carpets (*ibid.*, 916–922). In the *Rhesus* (342–345) of Euripides the chorus entreats Adrasteia, the child of Zeus, to ward off the jealousy caused by their uttering whatever is dear to their hearts.

An overenthusiastic reception of an offical was tantamount to praise of the kind that aroused the envy of the gods. On one occasion when Germanicus Caesar, the grandson of the deified Augustus, was in Alexandria the cordial greetings of the populace greatly frightened him.[56] He deprecated their acclamations of him as a god and threatened to appear before them less frequently unless they restrained themselves. According to Sir Walter Scott, Gustavus Adolphus was equally perturbed by the worship of a throng as he rode through the streets of Nuremberg. The novelist puts these words into the mouth of the great general: "If you idolise me thus like a god, who shall assure you that the vengeance of Heaven will not soon prove me to be a mortal?"[57]

Praise of Cattle

So far as I am aware, Pliny the Elder and Aulus Gellius are the only classical authors who tell us that praise kills animals, but the shepherd in Vergil, *Eclogues* 3.103, may have been thinking of an admiring glance when he said: "Nescio quis teneros oculus mihi fascinat agnos."[58] Later examples of deadly commendation of beasts are easy to find.

Early in the thirteenth century Gervase of Tilbury, in his *Otia Imperialia*,[59] written to amuse a king, advises the reader not to marvel that the words of the wicked can kill animals. He says that in the kingdom of Arles there was a man whose praise was so infective that a horse or any other domestic animal which he noticed in this way either died or was in danger of death. In the sixteenth century a witch of Savoy who was arrested at the door of a stable in which someone was putting a yoke on oxen exclaimed: "Ho! les gaillards boeufs, Dieu les gard!" One of them died soon after.[60] In Oldenburg a witch has been known to kill a pig merely by saying: "Das ist ja ein schönes Schwein."[61]

Similar beliefs have flourished in Scotland, where the most casual, innocent, or commonplace expression of admiration of an animal has been dire enough to cause sickness or death, for example: "a splendid sow," "a grand cow," "Hasn't the cow the big udder?" "You are a bonnie cow," "You [a horse] have got fine limbs."[62]

Just as a man may injure himself by self-admiration, so he may harm his own animals by "thinking too highly of them."[63] A certain Scottish farmer had to be kept in the house "when his own cattle were being taken in from pasture, in case by admiring them he might be the means of doing them an injury."[64] In a work dated 1691 we have a Scottish parson's word for it that a man in his parish killed his own cow by commending its fatness, and even "shot a Hair with his Eyes, having praised its swiftness, (such was the Infection of ane evill Eye)."[65]

The efficacy of belittling remarks as a means of warding off the evils that attend praise is beautifully illustrated by a Scottish story:

> . . . A man ploughing, who thought very well of his horses, said to his master on seeing another he knew approaching, "Here comes —, and he will ruin both the horses if he can, for he has the Evil Eye." His master said, "I'll tell you what you will do, and if

> you do it he can do the horses no harm. When he begins to praise either or both just begin to run them down, and be sure you say as much against them as he shall say for them." He of the Evil Eye came up, and commencing with "What a fine pair of horses you have," went on to enumerate their good points. The servant objected that they looked better than they were, that their looks were the best of them, and for every point in their favour the other mentioned, the lad said something to counterbalance it. The other began to show signs of impatience, and went on his way not very well pleased with the way his opinions of the horses had been disputed. "Well done, you have saved the horses," said the master. "Did I do right?" said the lad. "Yes, indeed, you could not have said more than you have said."[66]

Among the Scottish people, too, we find saliva employed as a protection against praise:

> If a person came and saw a cow or other creature belonging to you, and he began to praise it, *e.g.* if he were to say, *tha ùth mór aig a bhoin*, "the cow has a big udder," or anything similar of a complimentary nature, this act of praising was called *aibh-seachadh*; and as it might lead accidentally to *gonadh*, or evil eye, or wounding of the cattle, as a preventative it was customary to say to the person making the complimentary remarks: *Fliuch do shūil* = "wet your eye." This wetting of the eye was generally performed by moistening the tip of the finger with saliva, and moistening the eye with it thereafter.[67]

According to a work published in 1722, natives of backward districts of Ireland were equally afraid of praise bestowed upon their animals: "If one praise a horse, or any other creature, he must cry, God save him, or spit upon him; and if any mischief befalls the horse within three days, they find out the person who commended him, who is to whisper the Lord's prayer at his right ear."[68] A somewhat earlier writer tells us that "the wild Irish spat upon a horse when they praised it."[69]

An offer to purchase an animal is a compliment—a dangerous one. In English lore, "It is very unlucky to bid a price for an animal, such as a cow, pig, or horse, when it is not for sale, for if this is done the animal is sure to die."[70] Such a fate befell a horse owned by a Scot. "A man taking a valuable horse from the west coast of Kintyre to Tarbert, was after leaving Musadale, offered a considerable sum for it. He said he would not, could not sell the beast, and though the offer was raised to sixty pounds, he still refused and went on his way. Before he reached Tayinloan the horse fell dead on the road."[71] In Palestine a man who is asked whether he will sell a horse must reply "Yes," but he puts a prohibitive price upon it. "At such times he usually requests the would-be purchaser to stop thinking of his horse for fear it may bring misfortune."[72]

Praise of Vegetation

Modern lore provides parallels that enable us to understand quite readily the ancient belief that certain families in Africa could blight trees with their praise. In the Greece of today a blooming garden may stir envy into action,[73] but an experience of an English consul's daughter in Turkey gives us a better idea of the way praise may destroy a tree. Her account is as follows:

> I knew a lady at Broussa [Brusa] whose eye was so dreaded as to induce her friends to fumigate their houses after she had paid them a visit. She happened to call upon my mother one evening when we were sitting under a splendid weeping willow-tree in the garden. She looked up and observed that she had never seen a finer tree of its kind. My old nurse standing by heard her observation, and no sooner had our visitor departed than she suggested that some garlic should at once be hung upon it or it would surely come to grief. We all naturally ridiculed the idea, but as chance would have it, that very night a storm uprooted the willow. After this catastrophe the old woman took to hanging garlic everywhere, and would have ornamented me with it had I not rebelled.[74]

In Scotland, too, it was believed that crops were exposed to the perils of forespeaking (or excessive praise).[75]

Among the Romans untrue remarks were made about the condition of first fruits. They would say: "These are old; we desire other, fresh, fruits."[76] What happens when good fruit receives its due may be illustrated by a modern story with a setting on the Greek island of Sikinos, in the Cyclades: "Old Kortes, the ex-demarch, told me that he had an apple tree covered with lovely fruit; some one with the evil eye went past and said, 'Oh, what lovely apples!' Two hours afterwards they returned that way, and found not a single apple on the tree, and basketfuls lying on the ground."[77]

The Greeks protect trees laden with fruit by a clove of garlic hung from their branches.[78] In parts of India people used to suspend an old shoe from the branches of a tree that bore beautiful blossoms or good fruit.[79]

There is an interesting English saying: "Previous to St. John's day we dare not praise barley."[80] Evidently young vegetation, like young children, was particularly susceptible to the dangers immanent in praise.

Just as belittling remarks served to protect children from the evil eye, just as ribald jests safeguarded the triumphing general,[81] and just as calling persons bad names saved them from harm,[82] so maledictions warded off peril from seeds that were intended to become flourishing crops. In order to insure a good growth of cumin the Greeks cursed and abused the seed while sowing it.[83] The Romans sowed rue to a similar accompaniment (Pallad. 4.9.14). Among the Cyprians ability to curse seems to have been almost a prerequisite to successful farming, for they spoke of "sowing curses."[84] Sometimes the Romans offered prayers that seeds might never come up (Pliny, *Nat. Hist.* 19.120). Raillery and abuse were believed at times to promote fertility,[85] but it seems clear that curses were also supposed to throw the maleficent powers off their guard, for they disdained to pay attention to anything inferior or despised.

Praise of Inanimate Things

In modern Greece inanimate objects, especially attractive ones, such as a new house, are liable to be injured by the evil eye.[86] Admiration called forth by "the rosy colour and the seductive smell" of a pie might bring about its immediate ruin.[87] A note at the end of *The Last Days of Pompeii*, by Bulwer-Lytton, tells how a Neapolitan lady became distracted when she heard a man with the evil eye praising her cap. Calling the contents of a churn of butter beautiful may make the butter scatter on the churn and become froth.[88] In Scotland praise of a plow has caused it to break into two parts.[89]

An old English saying urges one to "praise the day when it is over."[90] The German and Danish version is: "Praise a fine day at night."[91] Whatever may be the superstitious background of these adages they do remind us of Solon's admonition to Croesus not to admire the good fortune of a man while there is still time for it to change (Plut., *Solon* 27.5).

The Egyptians have shown great ingenuity in keeping things from being praised. "You order, for instance, a new boom for your boat, and when you go to see it, your heart sinks to find it with a splice, as though it had already been broken. Such a fine new boom, your dragoman tells you, would be sure to attract the Evil Eye, with direst consequences, and so the fates must be hoodwinked in this way."[92]

Giving a little present to one who admires an object counteracts his praise.[93] Neapolitans have even offered to give to guests possessions for which they have expressed a liking.[94]

Fairies and Praise

In Ireland attractive children who are praised come to grief through the agency of fairies, as we may see from a story told by an old man of the Aran Islands:

> One day a neighbour was passing, and she said when she saw it on the road, "That's a fine child."
>
> Its mother tried to say, "God bless it," but something choked the words in her throat.
>
> A while later they found a wound on its neck, and for three nights the house was filled with noises.
>
> "I never wear a shirt at night," he said, "but I got up out of my bed, and all naked as I was, when I heard the noises in the house, and lighted a light, but there was nothing to it."
>
> Then a dummy came and made signs of hammering nails in a coffin.
>
> The next day the seed potatoes were full of blood, and the child told his mother that he was going to America.
>
> That night it died, and "Believe me," said the old man, "the fairies were in it."[95]

"God's name destroys the power of the fairies," and it appears in protecting words. "*Māmdeud* (God save you), *Slaunter* (your good health), and *Boluary* (God bless the work), should be said respectively when you enter a house, when you drink anything, and when you come to people at work; such expressions show that you have no connection with the fairies and will not bring bad luck."[96]

From a Scottish source we learn that the danger from the fairies was greater when a baby was pretty and its beauty charmed all who saw it.[97]

Excessive Praise

In the quotation from Aulus Gellius emphasis is laid upon the lavish bestowal of praise. This aspect of my subject is well illustrated in the plays of Euripides, who was thoroughly acquainted with Greek popular lore. He makes Orestes say to Pylades (*Orest.* 1161–1162): "I shall cease praising thee, since there is some grief even in this, praising too much." Iolaus knows that excessive praise arouses envy (ἐπίφθουου), for he has often been heavy of heart because of it (*Heracl.* 202–204). An illuminating comment on this subject was addressed to Achilles by Clytaemnestra (*Iph. in Aulis,* 980–981): "The good somehow hate those who praise if they praise to excess."

Tertullian (*De Virg. Vel.* 15) is almost as explicit as Euripides. After making a general statement to the effect that there existed among the *ethnici* something to be feared which they called *fascinum* he explains that it was the unhappy result of unbounded praise or glory ("infeliciorem laudis et gloriae enormioris eventum"). Another interesting record of this idea is to be found in Vergil (*Ecl.* 7.27–28):

> Aut si ultra placitum laudarit, baccare frontem
> Cingite ne vati noceat mala lingua futuro.

Classical ideas about unrestrained praise would be readily understood in parts of Scotland, for a book on Scottish lore says: "Praise beyond measure—praise accompanied with a kind of amazement or envy—was followed by disease or accident."[98] Meeting great praise with praise still more extravagant was a homeopathic remedy practiced by Scotsmen.[99]

Moderation in Praise or Abstention from It As a Matter of Courtesy

The words I have quoted from Euripides, "I shall cease praising thee, since there is some grief even in this, praising too much," show that a considerate Greek refrained from dangerous commendation of a friend. As we have seen, a Roman lover might tell his beloved to say *Praefiscini* to avert the consequences of unguarded praise. Doubtless *Praefiscini dixerim*, in addition to proclaiming the good intentions of the speaker,[100] also served to put the recipient of praise on his guard, so that he might use an antidotal formula for himself.[101] In some of the mountainous parts of Italy people have been known to say "Si mal occhio non ci fosse," by which they meant that the praise would be acceptable if sincere and unattended by envy.[102]

From a work dated 1546, by an Italian physician of Verona,[103] we learn that Italians who wished to praise someone would utter the safeguarding wish, "Verba nostra tibi non noceant."[104] We are informed that "A person who should wander through Italy, and especially through Southern Italy, praising all he saw, would soon come to be considered the most malevolent of men."[105]

Being sparing of commendation is a matter of courtesy in several parts of the world.[106] One writer goes so far as to say that ". . . it was a universally recognised rule of good manners and morals, that every one in praising another should be careful not to do so immoderately, lest he should fascinate even against his will."[107]

Summary of Methods of Averting Evils Arising from Praise

It has become evident that there are many ways of taking out insurance against the harmful effects of being praised. A brief summary of them follows.

A sovereign remedy for praise already bestowed is saliva or spittle,[108] to which the popular imagination ascribes many virtues.[109] Moistening the eye with saliva has been practiced in Scotland. Other effective precautionary measures are skillful depreciation, mock dispraisal, and disparaging or belittling remarks. Raillery and abuse have been employed to forestall the effects of praise. Overpraising an object that has been lauded and setting a higher valuation upon things for which an offer has been made are homeopathic devices.

Certain safeguarding expressions such as φθόνος δ' ἀπέστω and *Praefiscini* were common among the Greeks and Romans, and many parallels to them can be found in the lore of other nations.[110] At times the blessing of a deity is invoked. The mere utterance of the word "garlic" may afford protection and, of course, garlic itself was a prophylactic, as was *baccar* in Roman times. Giving gifts, or even making an offer to do so, is still another means of securing safety from the ill results of praise.

Charms and talismans are often resorted to in an effort to ward off the evil eye, and ornaments may be worn to divert attention from the wearers.[111] Parents may allow children to go unkempt[112] in order to escape the notice of the malign powers or even may dress boys in girls' clothes,[113] but I have no classical illustrations of these two devices. Presumably all methods effective against the evil eye have been and still are effective against praise.

The examples I have given show that both the ears and the eyes of the gods and other envious powers may be deceived. Several of these practices do not reflect credit upon the intelligence of the beings whose hostility is feared.

Conclusion

As we have seen, the ideas under discussion are widespread, and their similarity, even in the way praise operates to injure and destroy, is striking. The Latin countries naturally inherited some of these superstitions from the Romans, but he would be rash who would venture to state that they originated in a common center. The presence of geometric designs on vases made by nations separated by oceans is by no means proof of borrowing; it is, rather, evidence that nations may express themselves in the same way when they reach similar stages in their development. Envy of one's prosperous neighbors is far from being a rarity, and there is always someone who gloats over a failure. The immense continuing popularity of "Casey at the Bat" has been explained as due to its having caught the spirit of the mob, which likes to witness the downfall of the mighty. A prize fight in which a champion is likely to lose his crown always draws a big crowd. The versatility of a youthful film actor is said to have aroused marked dislike among some people because they "are appalled and offended by such assorted virtuosity." In *The Keys of the Kingdom*, by A. J. Cronin, we find these words put into the mouth of a priest who, apparently, was oblivious to the glories of this world: "Perhaps the greatest strain is thrown upon our moral vision by the spectacle of another's success. The dazzle hurts us."

Numerous passages about φθόνος and *invidia* in the classical languages show that Greeks and Romans experienced difficulty in looking with equanimity upon the success of friends and countrymen and their rise to prominence and distinction.[114] Thessalian women stoned Laïs to death because they were envious of her beauty.[115] I am inclined to believe that the ancients were far more addicted to envy than we are.[116] Aeschylus (*Agam.* 832–837) goes so far as to declare that there are only a few men "in whom it is inborn to admire without envy a friend's good fortune. For the venom of malevolence settles upon the heart and doubles the burthen of him afflicted of that plague: he is himself weighed down by his own calamity, and repines at sight of another's prosperity."[117] The Romans often gave expression to similar ideas.[118] Since the gods were endowed by man with many of his own thoughts and characteristics, they, as well as human beings, nursed feelings of jealousy, chiefly of the mighty and the proud. Solon tells Croesus that anything in which the gods are concerned is full of jealousy and trouble.[119]

In the ancient world a man who wished to escape the perils attendant upon eminence and success would have done well to follow the example of Timoleon, a member of one of the noblest families of Corinth. He never allowed a proud or boastful word to pass his lips. When he heard his praises heralded for a great achievement he humbly announced that he was grateful to the gods for making him the human instrument to carry out their wishes.[120]

In closing I quote a remarkable generalization made by Professor W. G. Sumner, in *Folkways*,[121] on the basis of comparatively scanty material: "It follows from the notion of the evil eye that men should never admire, praise, congratulate, or encourage those who are rich, successful, prosperous, and lucky. The right thing to do is to vituperate and scoff at them in their prosperity. That may offset their good luck, check their pride, and humble them a little."

NOTES

The following works will be referred to by the authors' names only: G.F. Abbott, *Macedonian Folklore* (Cambridge, 1903); F.T. Elworthy, *The Evil Eye: An Account of This Ancient and Widespread Superstition* (London, 1895); W. Gregor, *Notes on the Folk-Lore of the North-East of Scotland* (London, 1881); R.C. Maclagan, *Evil Eye in the Western Highlands* (London, 1902); B. Schmidt, "Der böse Blick und ähnlicher Zauber im neugriechischen Volksglauben," *Neue Jahrb. f. klass. Altertum*, 31 (1913): 574–613; S. Seligmann, *Der böse Blick und Verwandtes* (Berlin, 1910); W.W. Story, *Castle St. Angelo and the Evil Eye* (London, 1877).

1. Cf. Luke iv. 26: "Woe unto you when all men shall speak well of you."

2. Cf. Emerson, *Compensation*: "Blame is safer than praise. I hate to be defended in a newspaper. As long as all that is said is said against me, I feel a certain assurance of success. But as soon as honeyed words of praise are spoken for me I feel as one that lies unprotected before his enemies."

3. K.F. Smith, "Pupula Duplex," *Studies in Honor of Basil L. Gildersleeve* (Baltimore, 1902), p. 293. The great work on the evil eye is, of course, that of Seligmann (as cited in the introductory note). It supersedes a remarkable contribution to the subject by Otto Jahn, "Über den Aberglauben des bösen Blicks bei den Alten," *Berichte der königlich sächsischen Gesellschaft der Wissenschaften zu Leipzig*, Phil.-hist. Classe, 7 (1855): 28–110. See also B. Schmidt; F.T. Elworthy; W.B. McDaniel, "The Pupula Duplex and Other Tokens of an 'Evil Eye' in the Light of Ophthalmology," *Class Phil.*, 13 (1918): 335–346. Material of special interest for my subject will be found in the *Handwörterbuch des deutschen Aberglaubens* (Berlin and Leipzig, 1927–), under the articles "Auge," I: 685–690; "berufen, beschreien," I: 1096–1102; and "loben," V: 1311–1316. An article on "unberufen" is announced for a supplement to the *Handwörterbuch*.

4. See, for instance, H.V. Canter, "Ill Will of the Gods in Greek and Latin Poetry," *Class. Phil.* 32 (1937): 131–143; Karl Nawratil, θεῖον ταραχῶδες, *Philologische Wochenschrift*, 60 (1940): 125–126.

5. For bibliographical data see the introductory note.

6. Cf. Abbott, p. 140: "The curse [of the evil eye] is to be dreaded most when its object is in an exceptionally flourishing condition: a very healthy and good-looking child, a spirited horse, a blooming garden, or a new house, are all subject to its influence."

7. Sir E.A. Wallis Budge, *Amulets and Superstitions* (London, 1930), pp. 354–355.

8. Heliodorus, *Aethiop.* 3.7; Plut., *Mor.* 681F.

9. Lactantius says that the thoughts and wishes are often seen in the eyes (*De Opificio Dei*, 8.12) and that they are, so to speak, the windows of the mind (*ibid.* 9.2). Quintilian (*Inst. Orat.* 11.3.75), who studied the matter from the standpoint of the orator, declares that the mind or soul is revealed through the eyes. Pliny (*Nat. Hist.* 11.145) assures us that no part of the body gives a clearer index of the mind, and he

concludes that the mind has its seat in the eyes ("Profecto in oculis animus habitat"). Cicero (*De Orat.* 3.221) states that the eye is the only part of the body that registers all changes of the mind.

10. Alexander of Aphrodisias asks (2.53) why certain people fascinate young children especially. Cf. Plut., *Mor.* 680D. Pliny, *Nat. Hist.* 7.16, notes that *puberes* were particularly susceptible to the evil eye. The gypsies of Spain believe that because of "the tenderness of their constitution" children were more easily blighted than older people. See George Borrow, *The Zincali: An Account of the Gypsies of Spain* (London, 1907), p. 115. Cf. Verg., *Ecl.* 3.103: "Nescio quis teneros oculus mihi fascinat agnos."

11. *Folk-Lore Journal*, 1 (1883): 220. Cf. Abbott, pp. 141–142.

12. Lucy M.J. Garnett, *The Women of Turkey and Their Folk-Lore: The Jewish and Moslem Women* (London, 1891), p. 475.

13. *The People of Turkey: Twenty Years' Residence among Bulgarians, Greeks, Albanians, Turks, and Armenians*, by a Consul's Daughter and Wife [Mrs. John Elijah Blunt], edited by Stanley Lane Poole (London, 1878), p. 5.

14. E. Blaquière, *Letters from the Mediterranean, containing a Civil and Political Account of Sicily, Tripoly, Tunis and Malta* (London, 1813), II: 70–71.

15. Gregor, pp. 7–8.

16. Jacob Grimm, *Deutsche Mythologie*, besorgt von E.H. Meyer (Berlin, 1872), II: 923.

17. John Aubrey, *Remains of Gentilisme and Judaisme, 1686–87*, edited and annotated by James Britten (London, 1881), p. 80. Cf. *Handwörterbuch des deutschen Aberglaubens*, s.vv. "berufen, beschreien," I: 1098.

18. Edward Dodwell, *A Classical and Topographical Tour through Greece during the Years 1801, 1805, and 1806* (London, 1819), II: 35–36.

19. Lucy M.J. Garnett, *The Women of Turkey and Their Folk-Lore: The Christian Women* (London, 1890), p. 146. See also Mrs. Murray-Aynsley, *Symbolism of the East and West* (London, 1900), p. 144.

20. M. Hutton, *The Greek Point of View* (New York, 1925), p. 162. Cf. Abbott, p. 141.

21. M. Zallones, *Voyage à Tine, l'une des îles de l'Archipel de la Grèce* (Paris, 1809), pp. 156–157.

22. Frank G. Carpenter, *The Holy Land and Syria* (Garden City, New York, 1928), pp. 80–81. Cf. Elijūb Abēla, "Gebräuche in Syrien," *Zeitschrift des deutschen Palästina-Vereins*, 7 (1884): 102. See also W.M. Thomson, *The Land and the Book* (New York, 1860), I: 219, and Edgar Thurston, *Omens and Superstitions of Southern India* (London, 1921), p. 116.

23. Richard Pococke, *A Description of the East and Some Other Countries* (London, 1743), p. 181. See also E.W. Lane, *Manners and Customs of the Modern Egyptians* (London, n.d.), p. 259.

24. G.F. Lyon, *A Narrative of Travels in Northern Africa in the years 1818, 19 and 20* (London, 1821), p. 52. I am informed that contemporary Arabs have a prayer which is said to take away the evil arising from praise not only of things present but also of those hoped for or desired.

25. Eugène Monseur, *Le Folklore Wallon* (Brussels [1892]), pp. 90–91.

26. Maclagan, p. 126. Cf. Mrs. Murray-Aynsley, *op. cit.* (see note 19), p. 140.

27. Chapter 17. In his *Notes d'un voyage en Corse* (Paris, 1840), p. 188, Mérimée records the reply of Corsican mothers when their sons are praised: "Nun me l'annochiate."

28. F.S. Krauss, *Volksglaube und religiöser Brauch der Südslaven* (Münster, i. W., 1890), p. 42.

29. Rabbi Emil G. Hirsch, "The Evil Eye," *The Folk-Lorist*, 1 (1892): 73.

30. S. Wells Williams, *The Middle Kingdom* (New York, 1883), I: 797.

31. Story, p. 160. Calling people bad names is a rather common means of protection against the evil eye. See J.G. Frazer, *The Magic Art and the Evolution of Kings* (New York, 1935), I: 280.

32. *Acta Joannis*, ed. Th. von Zahn (Erlangen, 1880), pp. 24–25. See Campbell Bonner, "Demons of the Bath," *Studies Presented to F. LL. Griffith* (London, 1932), pp. 203–208.

33. Charisius, *Inst. Gram.* Liber II, in H. Keil, *Grammatici Latini*, I: 212.

34. Similar examples of the fear of praise may be found under the headings "Excessive Praise" (p. 29) and "Moderation in Praise . . ." (p. 30).

35. Abbott, pp. 145–146.

36. K. Bercovici, *Alexander* (New York, 1928), p. 266.

37. J. Tuchmann, "La Fascination," *Mélusine*, 4 (1888–89): 253. Cf. D.S. Weissenberg, "Kinderfreud und -leid bei den südrussischen Juden," *Globus*, 83 (1903): 316.

38. G. Pitrè, *Usi e costumi, credenze, e pregiudizi del popolo siciliano* (Palermo, 1889), IV: 238. Cf. Seligmann, I: 179.

39. *Chambers's Journal of Popular Literature, Science, and Arts*, 48 (1871): 233.

40. Margit Luby de Benedekfalva, "Treatment of Hungarian Peasant Children," *Folk-Lore*, 62 (1941): 112.

41. Charles J. Branch, "West Indian Superstitions," *The Contemporary Review*, 26 (1875): 770–771.

42. *Notes and Queries*, I, 10 (1854): 221.

43. V.S. Lean, *Collectanea* (Bristol, 1902–04), II: 475.

44. *I Henry IV*, IV.i.111–112.

45. See also J.W. Wickwar, *Witchcraft and the Black Art* (London, n.d.), p. 72.

46. *Zeitschrift für Ethnologie*, 15 (1883): 90. See also Lean, *op. cit.* (see note 43), II: 466; Angelo S. Rappoport, *The Folklore of the Jews* (London, 1937), p. 77.

47. R.E. Enthoven, *The Folklore of Bombay* (Oxford, 1924), p. 229.

48. W.E. Maxwell, "The Folklore of the Malays," *Journal of the Straits Branch of the Royal Asiatic Society*, 7 (1881): 27–28. Other references are: an anonymous article, "The Evil Eye," *The Celtic Magazine*, 12 (1887): 415–416; Borrow, *op. cit.* (see note 10), pp. 118–119; J.C. Lawson, *Modern Greek Folklore and Ancient Greek Religion* (Cambridge, 1910), pp. 9–10; Maclagan, pp. 52, 53, 76, 77, 118, 127; Mrs. Murray-Aynsley, *op. cit.* (see note 19), p. 144; A. Polson, *Our Highland Folklore Heritage* (Dingwall and Inverness, 1926), pp. 114–116; Rappoport, *op. cit.* (see note 46), pp. 72–78; Story, p. 159; J. Tuchmann, "La Fascination," *Mélusine*, 3 (1886–87): 412.

49. W.A. Oldfather's translation in the Loeb Classical Library. The italics are mine.

50. Chap. 3. The story is one of those in *Mine Own People*. Similar incidents are recounted by Pearl S. Buck, *The Good Earth* (New York, 1931), p. 54, and *East Wind, West Wind* (London, 1931), pp. 181–182. See also James Napier, *Folk Lore: or, Superstitious Beliefs in the West of Scotland within This Century* (Paisley, 1879), pp. 34–35.

51. L. Strackerjan, *Aberglaube und Sagen aus dem Herzogtum Oldenburg*[2] (Oldenburg, 1909), I: 374.

52. Seligmann, I: 192–193; *Handwörterbuch des deutschen Aberglaubens*, I: 1097; Schmidt, p. 579.

53. R.T.K., "Unter den Beduinen der ägyptische Wüste," *Globus*, 75 (1899): 193.

54. See, for example, the references given on page 131 of the article by Canter (see note 4).

55. I do not have space to discuss the subject of praise and the gods. It is closely tied up with notions about ὕβρις, a subject treated in many articles.

56. F. Preisigke, *Sammelbuch griechischer Urkunden aus Ägypten* (Strassburg, 1913), Vol. I, No. 3924.

57. *A Legend of Montrose*, Chap. 14.

58. Cf. Servius *ad loc.*: "Et per transitum, pulchrum se pecus habere significat quot meruit fascinari."

59. Page 37 in the edition of Felix Liebrecht (Hannover, 1856).

60. J. Tuchmann, "La Fascination," *Mélusine*, 5 (1890–91): 230. Cf. P. Sébillot, *Le Folklore de France* (Paris, 1904–07), 3: 126. See also the quotation from Monseur on page 16.

61. Strackerjan, *op. cit.* (see note 51), I: 374.

62. Maclagan, pp. 12, 56, 8 (cf. 78), 168, 62, respectively.

63. Maclagan, pp. 71–72.

64. Maclagan, p. 40. In the same work may be found examples of dire results from praising chickens (pp. 79, 88), ducks (p. 66), pigs (pp. 12, 79), cows (pp. 8, 56, 71, 77, 85, 168, 206), horses (pp. 39, 62, 63, 74, 88), cattle and animals in general (pp. 70, 72, 87, 114). Cf. Blunt, *op. cit.* (see note 13), pp. 242–243; Carpenter, *op. cit.* (see note 22), p. 81; Miss A. Goodrich-Freer, "The Powers of Evil in the Outer Hebrides," *Folk-Lore*, 10 (1889): 266–267; A. Goodrich-Freer, *Outer Isles* (Westminster, 1902), pp. 236–237; Gregor, p. 8; Lane, *op. cit.* (see note 23), p. 259; Roswell Park, *The Evil Eye, Thanatology, and Other Essays* (Boston, 1912), p. 11.

65. Robert Kirk, *The Secret Commonwealth of Elves, Fains, and Fairies*. The Text by Robert Kirk . . ., 1691. The Comment by Andrew Lang . . ., 1893 (London, 1893), pp. 54–55.

66. Maclagan, p. 117.

67. G. Henderson, *Survivals in Belief among the Celts* (Glasgow, 1911), pp. 27–28. Cf. Goodrich-Freer, *Outer Isles* (see note 65), p. 237.

68. Quoted by William Camden, *Britannia* (London, 1722), II: 1421.

69. Aubrey, *op. cit.* (see note 17), p. 42.

70. E.M. Wright, *Rustic Speech and Folk-Lore* (London, 1913), p. 219. Cf.

Elworthy, pp. 12–13. I once roomed in an attractive bungalow which caught the fancy of a passer-by. He stopped and asked the owners whether it was for sale. They were unwilling to sell, but the stranger asked them to set a price. They refused to do so, and my landlady, now much wrought up, became almost frantic in her effort to prevent him from making an offer.

71. Maclagan, p. 88.

72. Carpenter, *op. cit.* (see note 22), p. 81.

73. Abbott, p. 140; Schmidt, p. 578.

74. Blunt, *op. cit.* (see note 13), p. 242.

75. Gregor, p. 8.

76. Pliny, *Nat. Hist.* 28.23: "Cur ad primitias pomorum haec vetera esse dicimus, alia nova optamus?"

77. J. Th. Bent, *The Cyclades, or Life among the Insular Greeks* (London, 1885), p. 185.

78. Abbott, p. 141.

79. J. Tuchmann, "La Fascination," *Mélusine*, 8 (1896–97): 257.

80. R. Inwards, *Weather Lore*[3] (London, 1898), p. 35.

81. See, for example, Suet., *Julius*, 49.4 and 51.

82. See note 31.

83. Theophr., *Hist. Plant.* 7.3.3; 9.8.8; Plut., *Mor.* 700F–701A; Pliny, *Nat. Hist.* 19.120.

84. Hesych, s.v. ἀρὰς ἐπισπεῖραι.

85. J.G. Frazer, *Pausanias's Description of Greece* (London, 1898), III: 268.

86. Abbott, p. 140; Schmidt, p. 578.

87. Abbott, p. 146.

88. Maclagan, p. 122.

89. Maclagan, p. 39.

90. Thomas Wright, *Essays on Subjects Connected with the Literature, Popular Superstitions, and History of England in the Middle Ages* (London, 1846), I: 148.

91. R. Christy, *Proverbs, Maxims, and Phrases of All Ages . . .* (New York and London, 1887), II: 430.

92. S.H. Leeder, *Veiled Mysteries of Egypt and the Religion of Islam* (London, 1923), p. 40.

93. Maclagan, p. 122.

94. W.S. Walsh, *Handy-Book of Literary Curiosities* (Philadelphia, 1925), p. 347.

95. John M. Synge, *The Aran Islands* (Dublin, 1911), p. 5.

96. G.H. Kinahan, "Notes on Irish Folk-Lore," *Folk-Lore Record*, 4: 104, 112.

97. Compare a story recorded by Napier, *op. cit.* (see note 50), pp. 40–41.

98. Gregor, p. 35. See also p. 8, and compare Hirsch, *op. cit.* (see note 29), p. 73: "The Jews also took precautions against 'beschreien,'—against praising beyond bounds person or object."

99. Maclagan, p. 118; Adela Goodrich-Freer, *Outer Isles* (see note 65), p. 237; *Folk-Lore*, 10 (1889): 266.

100. Dodwell, *op. cit.* (see note 18), II: 35.

101. Elworthy, p. 33.

102. Dodwell, as cited in note 100.

103. Girolamo Fracastor, *De Sympathia et Antipathia Rerum*. I have taken the quotation from Vincentius Alsarius, *De Invidia et Fascino Veterum*, an interesting work which is reproduced by Graevius, *Thes. Antiq. Roman.*, XII: 889–899.

104. Of course, this is a translation from Italian into Latin, in which the text is written.

105. Walsh, *loc. cit.* (see note 94), p. 347.

106. Blunt, *op. cit.* (see note 13), p. 245; Lane, *op. cit.* (see note 23), p. 256; Elworthy, pp. 17, 32; Story, p. 159.

107. Story, p. 156.

108. Cf. Abbott, pp. 140–141; Schmidt, pp. 591–592.

109. See, for example, J.E. Crombie, "The Saliva Superstition," *The International Folk-Lore Congress of 1891*, pp. 249–258; F.W. Nicolson, "The Saliva Superstition in Classical Literature," *Harvard Studies in Classical Philology* 8 (1897): 23–40; R. Selare, "A Collection of Saliva Superstitions," *Folk-Lore* 50 (1939): 349–366; J. Hastings, *Encyclopaedia of Religion and Ethics*, XI: 100–104.

110. Seligmann, II: 365–367; Schmidt, pp. 581–582; J. Tuchmann, "La Fascination," *Mélusine*, 9 (1898–99): 105–106; Elworthy, p. 17; James Kelly, *A Complete Collection of Scotish Proverbs* (London, 1721), p. 120, No. 57.

111. Abbott, p. 142.

112. Lane, *op. cit.* (see note 23), pp. 57–58.

113. See A.M. Spoer, "Simulated Change of Sex to Baffle the Evil Eye," *Folk-Lore* 37 (1926): 304: cf. *ibid.* 24 (1913): 385; Frazer, *op. cit.* (see note 85), II: 266; *idem, Adonis, Attis, Osiris* (London, 1914), II: 260–261.

114. In the brief *Lives* of Cornelius Nepos we find many records of the actual or supposed influence of envy (*invidia*) upon the careers of great men. See *Alcibiades*, 4, 7; *Chabrias*, 3; *Cimon*, 3; *Datames*, 5; *Dion*, 6, 9; *Epaminondas*, 7; *Eumenes*, 7, 10; *Themistocles*, 8; *Timoleon*, 1 (". . . nonnulli enim laesam ab eo pietatem putabant et invidia laudem virtutis obterebant"); *Timotheus*, 3; *Thrasybulus*, 4.

115. Plut., *Mor.* 768A.

116. They carried the fear of it even to the grave. Cf. *CIL*, IX: 2043: "Hic tumulus parvus nihil habet invidiae nec nimium iactat."

117. Translation of H.W. Smyth in the Loeb Classical Library.

118. Cf. "Est enim hoc commune vitium magnis liberisque civitatibus ut invidia gloriae comes sit et libenter de eis detrahant quos eminere videant altius . . ." (Nepos, *Chabrias*, 3); "Quam sit adsidua eminentis fortunae comes invidia altissimisque adhaereat . . ." (Vell. Paterc. 1.9.6); "Numquam eminentia invidia carent" (*ibid.*, 2.40.4); "Verum nulla tam modesta felicitas est quae malignitatis dentes vitare possit" (Val. Max. 7.7, Ext. 2). Many examples like these have been collected by Atto Vannucci, *Proverbi Latini* (Milan, 1879), p. 99.

119. Herod. 1.32: τὸ θεῖον πᾶν ἐὸν φθονερόν τε καὶ ταραχῶδες.

120. Nepos, *Timoleon*, 4.

121. P. 515. Boston, Ginn & Co., 1913.

An Incantation in the 'House of Light' Against the Evil Eye

*Stephen Langdon**

The evil eye is older than Greek and Roman civilizations. Its very widespread distribution in an area extending from India throughout the middle east and Europe also points to its probable great antiquity. Texts mentioning evil eye that we have from Sumer suggest that it existed in the third or fourth millennium B.C. This would make the evil eye more than five thousand years old. This may not be old in comparison with the age of the earth or even with the age of man, but it is venerable enough in the light of man's written records of his own history.

One difficulty in appreciating the oldest texts extant concerning the evil eye stems from the fragmentary nature of some of these texts. Often there may be considerable scholarly debate over the proper reconstruction and translation of such fragments. The following Sumerian text, however, appears to be fairly representative. Especially noteworthy is the evil eye's depiction as a roving independent entity and its deleterious affect upon both the rains from heaven and the milk from cows. For additional Sumerian texts, see Erich Ebeling, "Beschwörungen gegen den Feind und den bösen Blick aus dem Zweistromlande," Archiv Orientální, *17 (1949), 172–211.*

* Reprinted from Stephen Langdon, *Babylonian Liturgies* (Paris: Librairie Paul Geuthner, 1913), pp. 11–12.

1. The eye *ad-gir*, the eye a man has. . .
2. The eye afflicting man with evil, the *ad-gir*.
3. Unto heaven it approached and the storm sent no rain; unto earth it approached and the fresh verdure sprang not forth.
4. Unto the oxen it approached, and their herdsman was undone.
5. Unto the stalls it approached, and milk . . . was no longer plentiful.
6. Unto the sheepfolds it approached and its production. . .
7. Unto the homes (of men)it approached and vigor of men it restrained.
8. Unto the maiden it approached and seized away her robes.
9. Unto the strong man . . . severed.
10. Marduk beheld it.
11. What I know thou also knowest.
12. Seven vases of meal-water behind the. . .
13. Seven vases of meal-water behind the grinding stones.
14. With oil mix.
15. Upon (his) face apply.
16. As thou sayest the curse,
17. (Thy) neck toward the sick man raise.
18. May the queen who gives life to the dead purge him.
19. ....
20. May Gunura her boat. . .
21. Curse.   Incantation of the house of light.

Proverbs (23:1–8) and the Evil Eye in "The Wisdom of Sirach"*

In view of the antiquity of the evil eye in the Middle East, it should come as no surprise to learn that it is mentioned in the Bible as well as in various apocrypha. The following texts taken from the Book of Proverbs and Ecclesiasticus may serve to exemplify the biblical occurrences. Ecclesiasticus, or the Wisdom of Jeshua, the Son of Sirach, seems to have been written in Hebrew in the second century B.C.

In the biblical context, the evil eye appears to refer to stinginess and envy—in contrast to a good or generous eye. Yet it is likely that this usage is related to the more general evil eye folk belief complex. For discussions of this issue, see C. Ryder Smith, "An Evil Eye (Mark vii. 22)," Expository Times, *53 (1941–1942), 181–182; C.J. Cadoux, "The Evil Eye,"* Expository Times, *53 (1941–1942), 354–355; C. Ryder Smith, "The Evil Eye,"* Expository Times, *54 (1942–1943), 26; Henry J. Cadbury, "The Single Eye,"* Harvard Theological Review, *47 (1954), 69–74.*

from Proverbs

1. When thou sittest to eat with a ruler, consider diligently what *is* before thee:

2. And put a knife to thy throat, if thou *be* a man given to appetite.

*Reprinted from *The Holy Bible* and *The Apocrypha,* trans. by Edgar J. Goodspeed (Chicago: University of Chicago Press, 1938), pp. 249, 282–283, 290, by permission of The University of Chicago Press.

3. Be not desirous of his dainties: for they *are* deceitful meat.

4. Labor not to be rich: cease from thine own wisdom.

5. Wilt thou set thine eyes upon that which is not? for *riches* certainly make themselves wings; they fly away as an eagle toward heaven.

6. Eat thou not the bread of *him that hath* an evil eye, neither desire thou his dainty meats:

7. For as he thinketh in his heart, so *is* he: Eat and drink, saith he to thee; but his heart *is* not with thee.

8. The morsel *which* thou hast eaten shalt thou vomit up, and lose thy sweet words.

from "The Wisdom of Sirach"

Wealth does not become a niggardly man,
And what use is money to an envious man?
The man who withholds from himself amasses
for others,
And others will enjoy his goods.
If a man is evil to himself, to whom will he be
good?
For he will not take any pleasure in his own
money.
There is nobody worse than the man who is
grudging to himself
And that is the penalty of his wickedness.
If he does any good, he does it through
forgetfulness,
And shows his wickedness in the end.
He is a wicked man who has an envious eye,
Turning away his face, and pretending
not to see human souls.
A covetous man's eye is never satisfied with
what he gets,
And wicked injustice dries up the heart.
An evil eye begrudges bread,
And is in want of it at his own table.

. . . .

Do not appear before the Lord empty-handed,
For all these things must be done because they
are commanded.
The offering of an upright man enriches the
altar,
And its fragrance reaches the Most High.
The sacrifice of an upright man is acceptable,
And the memory of it will not be forgotten.
Glorify the Lord with a generous eye,
And do not stint the first fruits of your hands.
In all your giving show a joyful face,
And dedicate your tithes with gladness.
Give to the Most High as he has given to you,
With a generous eye, and as your hand has
found.
For the Lord is one who repays,
And he will repay you seven times over.

. . . .

Do you sit at a great table?
Do not gulp at it,
And do not say, "How much there is on it!"
Remember that an envious eye is wrong.
What has been created that is worse than the
eye?
That is why it sheds tears on every face.
Do not reach out your hand wherever it looks,
And do not crowd your neighbor in the dish;
Be considerate of him of your own accord,
And be thoughtful in everything.
Eat like a human being what is served to you,
Do not champ your food, or you will be
detested.
Be the first to leave off for good manners' sake,
And do not be greedy, or you will give offense.
Even though you are seated in a large com-
pany,
Do not be the first to help yourself.

The Evil Eye Among the Hebrews

*Aaron Brav**

Besides classicists, students of the ancient Near East, and biblical scholars, there is yet another group which has traditionally been much interested in the evil eye. This group consists of medical practitioners specializing in the treatment of the eye. It is no accident that the most ambitious survey of the evil eye ever attempted was by an oculist from Hamburg. S. Seligmann's two volume Der Böse Blick und Verwandtes *published in 1910 or his 1922 revision* Die Zauberkraft des Auges und das Berufen *have remained the standard definitive sources for cross-cultural documentation of the details of the evil eye folk belief complex. Oculists and ophthalmologists, of course, have their own interest in the evil eye inasmuch as they may encounter cases of it in the conduct of their daily practice. A more recent book-length study from this quarter is Edward S. Gifford,* The Evil Eye: Studies in the Folklore of Vision *(New York: Macmillan, 1958). Doctors and men of science might be expected to look down at such "superstitions" as the evil eye and so we can understand the author's relief (which may also be attributed to religious conviction) that the Bible "is free from the stigma of this superstition." We have already seen, however, that the evil eye does occur in the Bible.*

The study of the evil eye in Jewish tradition, relying heavily upon Talmudic materials but also upon folk practices is well established. Representative of the scholarship are: M. Grünbaum, "Beiträge zur vergleichenden Mythologie aus der Hagada," Zeitschrift der

* Reprinted from *Ophthalmology*, 5 (1908), 427–435.

Morgenländischen Gesellschaft, *31 (1877), 183–359 (see esp. pp. 258–266), Rabbi Emil G. Hirsch, "The Evil Eye,"* The Folk-Lorist, *1 (1892), 69–74, Regina Lilienthal, "Eyin ho-re,"* Yidisch filologye, *1 (1924), 245–271, Adolf Löwinger, "Der Bose Blick,"* Menorah, *4 (1926), 551–569, Harry Friedenwald, "The Evil Eye (Ayin Haraah),"* Medical Leaves (1939), 44–48, and Samuel D. Shrut, "Coping with the 'Evil Eye' or Early Rabbinical Attempts at Psychotherapy," American Imago, *17 (1960), 201–213.*

Medical superstition as a result of inadequate knowledge of natural phenomena was a dominating factor in the past, and to a considerable extent holds sway even to-day. This superstition is as old as the human family, and, of course, the Hebrews are not entirely free from it. It finds its origin in the fact that primitive mankind considered all terrestrial phenomena the direct manifestation and steady interference of supernatural powers. It was during this period of evolution that disease was ascribed to the direct interference of the Deity in the affairs of man. Of course this superstition is of theologic origin, and traces of its existence even at the present time are still prominent in the eyes of the observer. The ancient Hebrews, as well as many other nations, also considered disease to be the direct punishment from God for the shortcomings of men. The Talmud teaches that "no man cuts his finger here below unless it had been first determined upon from on High."[1] In fact, the Talmudic dictum is: "All comes from above except heat and cold;"[2] that is, all diseases, excepting those due to heat and cold which are, therefore, preventable, are directly sent unto mankind from God.

Medical superstition appears in several forms, depending upon the origin of the supernatural cause. Primarily it was of a religious origin, later it received a philosophic form and some have assumed a physical character. It is often impossible to trace the origin of certain superstitions: this is especially the case with the evil eye. This superstition is very widely spread and holds sway over multitudes in many countries. The ignorant Hebrews of Russia, Poland, Roumania and Hungary believe in the power of the evil eye. It was a prevalent belief among the ancients that some people possess the power to bewitch and do harm by spiteful looks, that their glance is highly poisonous, producing disease which eventually causes death. Not only was this belief common among the ignorant classes but also among the members of the higher spheres of social life. It is still a common belief of the ignorant masses of various peoples. We shall, however, confine our efforts in this paper to the evil eye among the Hebrews. An attempt to analyze the origin, the nature of this superstition, its growth and development leads us into a sea of uncertainty; all we can say is that it is prehistoric in conception.

In limiting our field of investigation to the Jewish people we must, of course, have recourse to the Biblical writings. It is of interest to note that no mention of it is made in the sacred literature. The Biblical term (rah ayin) means a jealous eye, i. e., an eye that envies, a miser's eye. We do, however, find evidences of this superstition in the Talmudic writings, and to give it an authoritative force the writers of the Talmud have tried to inject it into the Bible by means of interpretation. Thus, for instance, the sentence, "And the Lord will take away from thee all sickness,"[3] is so interpreted as to mean the evil eye.[4] The priestly blessing, "God bless thee and protect thee," is, according to Midrashic interpretation, a protection against the evil eye.[5] Jacob's advice to his children not to enter Egypt by one gate is also taken as a warning against the influence of the evil eye.[6] The Midrashic version is, "Ye are strong, ye are nice, enter not the gates of the city together, do not stand at one place so that the evil eye may not overpower you."[7] The story of Sarah and Hagar, as given in Midrashic literature, is interpreted to convey the idea that Sarah has thrown an evil eye upon Hagar. Ishmael, the son of Hagar, at the age of 27, was so crippled that his mother had to carry him on her shoulder, the evil eye being responsible for his lameness.[8]

Another interesting statement in this connection is that Sarah, having thrown an evil eye upon Hagar, caused her to abort her first child.[9] The evil eye has been considered an etiologic factor in the causation of abortion. The specific order given by Joshua to the spies to hide themselves in the forest was a means of protection against the evil eye.[10] These are some of the interpretations or injections of the evil eye superstition into Biblical literature. Considering the original text, we need not hesitate in emphatically stating that the interpretations are entirely groundless and that the sacred literature is free from the stigma of this superstition.

In Talmudic times the belief in the evil eye must have been very prevalent; this can be seen from the frequent references to it in the

Talmud. In Talmudic language it is known as "En Bisha" or "En Rah;" the latter has remained the popular term, meaning an evil eye. Much importance is also attached to it in Midrashic literature. The evil eye brings great misfortune to this world.[11] It had ruled over Israel and caused it to bow to the golden calf,[12] and as a result they suffered destruction and were compelled to go into exile to Babylonia.[13] The pupils of Akiba were all destroyed by the evil eye.[14] That some of the Talmudists have shared in this belief and its power for evil can be gathered from the following extreme doctrine, that only "1 per cent. of all the dead died from natural causes, while the other 99 per cent. die of the evil eye." This extravagant claim is backed up by a special investigation of Rab, who in a certain burial ground held communication with the dead, and after this peculiar method of experimentation announced the important result, "ninety-nine by the evil eye and one in a natural way."[15] It is interesting here to mention that the same extravagant claim had been made by Maimonides, the great Jewish philosopher and physician, for the excessive indulgence of sexual intercourse: "One per cent. dies of other diseases and 99 from over-indulgence in the sexual passion."[16] How far the Jews believed in the efficacy and power of the evil eye may also be surmised from the fact that they have incorporated in the morning prayer an invocation for the protection against the evil eye.

Susceptibility of the Evil Eye

Just as in other diseases, there are predisposing factors to the evil eye. The attractive and beautiful are, of course, most susceptible, for it gives rise to envy and jealousy. Children are very susceptible to its influence, and especially male children. In fact, it was considered a good omen when the first born child was a girl; she was supposed to have a natural immunity against the evil eye.[17] This superstition has changed, and the people no longer think it is a good omen if the first born baby is a female child.

The causes that produced this change are, of course, potent factors in our social life: (a) The desire to perpetuate the family name. (b) The religious desire to have some one to say the Kaddish prayer after the dead (only boys are entitled to this privilege in orthodox circles). (c) The comparative trouble in raising a boy and a girl. (d) The necessity for providing a dowry for a daughter.

Great men are susceptible to its influences. According to Rabbi, after they were rescued from the fiery furnace, Elieser, Hannaniah, Mishual and Asariah were killed by the many eyes that were directed at them in astonishment.[18] When the people demanded that Judah should come up to the pulpit from his school bench his father, the patriarch Simon Ben Gamlial, said, "I have only one dove among you; do you wish to take him from me by destroying him?" meaning that if Judah is placed in the leader's position the evil eye from the audience will do him harm.[19] The evil eye is apt to be operative in public places: it is said that the evil eye had its power even over the two tablets of the covenant because they were given in public.[20] "Street venders or those who display their goods in public never see the blessing of success." Rashi explains this to be on account of the evil eye.[21] Judging by the amount of display of goods in public by the Jewish venders this superstition has evidently disappeared. Women are also very susceptible to the evil eye; an indication of this fact is to be found in the peculiar circumstance that the word "woman" (Nushim) in numerical value equals the word "En rah."[22]

Some great men have the power of the evil eye. When Rabbi Elieser Ben Hyrcanus was shut out of the place of teaching, every spot upon which he turned his eyes was burned up; even a grain of wheat upon which his glance fell was half burned while the other half remained untouched, and the pillars of the gathering place of the scholars trembled.[23] Simon Ben Johai and Rabbi Jochanan could with their looks transform people into a heap of stones.[24] According to Kabbalistic literature, one should rather walk 100 miles out of the way to avoid meeting a man who possessed an evil eye.[25] An object found should not be placed before the public on account of the evil eye.[26]

Immunity

Natural immunity, according to Talmudic literature; the sons of Joseph have absolute immunity against the evil eye. Says Rabbi Jochanan, "I am of the children of Joseph, over whom the evil eye has no power."[27] The evil eye may, according to some writers, be working unconsciously without any intention to do harm; in fact, according to one author, every one possesses the evil eye, and it would, indeed, be more frequent a cause for evil but for the resisting power of men counteracting the evil influence.[28] This opinion is not shared by all. According to Naphthali Katz, it is essential that one concentrates his mind to the desire of producing an evil eye in order to be effective. It is also necessary when looking or giving an evil eye that one eye be closed. As long as both eyes are open, man is in the image of God and, therefore, can not do evil; but when he closes one eye he then resembles the Sitra Achra, an evil-producing demon, or the Keteb Merirah, and is able to do evil by giving an evil look.[29] It would follow from this that the one-eyed man has a more potent influence in the evil eye superstition, and such was really the general belief, for while the blind in both eyes were the object of pity, the blind in one eye were shunned by the people and considered the offspring of Billeam.

It is customary among the ignorant, and, for that matter, even among the semi-cultured and religious Jews, when speaking of some beautiful child or person, or on success, or anything that is apt to provoke the evil eye, to add the words "Unbeshrien," i. e., "not to be over cried," as a pacification so as not to be understood that the desire is to provoke the evil eye. Another term often employed is "Kein En Horah,"i. e., "No evil eye." This is mostly used by the Russian, Polish and Roumanian lower classes. They consider women in their puerperal state especially predisposed to this danger. The new born baby is apt to be influenced by the evil eye and should, therefore, not be shown to strangers. The bride is exposed to the danger of the evil eye and should, therefore, be veiled during the wedding ceremony. This practice is also common among the Chinese.[30]

How common is the belief in the evil eye among the Jews may be learned from the fact that there are specialists devoted to the cure of this condition. They are known as "Unsprechers."

The evil eye has power not only over persons but also over animals and inanimate things. Bad luck or sudden business reverses are attributed to the evil eye. The following rule, enunciated in the Talmud, corroborates this statement: "Man should not stand in the field of his neighbor when it is in full bloom for fear of the evil eye."[31]

The Evil Eye Theory

It is not my intention to enter into a discussion on the theory of the evil eye as found in general literature: relating to various other nations, I can only refer the readers to Elworthy's book on the evil eye, where several theories are advanced. From the Jewish sources only two theories are to be considered. One is the old ghost theory, the other is a new scientific theory of evaporation. The ghost theory depends upon the belief that numerous evil spirits exist in the eye which at certain occasions, under provocation, may do harm to others, cause disease and even death. The ancient Jews were, of course, believers in ghosts and the bulk of the Jewish, as well as non-Jewish, public still believes in evil spirits.

It is not amiss to remark here that the leaders of many churches still preach the power of Satan and devils as part of their dogmatic religious convictions. These spirits hover everywhere and are also to be found in the eye. Rabbi Hunnah says that one has a thousand to his left and a thousand to his right side.[32] According to Rab, the feeling of oppression around the bride comes from them; they are invisible but may be seen. "Place finely sifted ashes around your bed and in the morning you will see their footprints."[33] It is highly probable that the practice among the Jews to cover the eyes of the dead with pieces of porcelain is to guard against the evil spirits hovering in them. It is very easy to transfer the evil spirits from place to place and finally lodge them in the eye through which the evil eye is produced. It must also be observed that the treatment for the evil eye and for demons is practically the same: incantations, amulets and magic formulas. Of course witchcraft has also been considered an evolution of the ghost theory, and witches and sorcerers were supposed to have control over some spirits. Thus prayers to ward off demonic influences, as well as the evil eye, found their way into Jewish liturgy.[34]

The theory of evaporation is explained in the following way: The eye, like the skin, has pores through which some waste products evaporate. This vapor is highly poisonous in nature and may produce disease and even death. The writer of this theory goes even further and tries to use the principle of refraction to explain his superstitious belief by saying that the evil eye is more effective when these vapors have passed a convex or collecting glass, for after the refraction of these emanations they come to a focus at one point and are, therefore, more potent. Beware, then, of the man who wears convex glasses![35] The conclusion is correct but the premises wrong.

According to this theory, we all have the power to "overlook;" thus a good man may occasionally possess an evil eye against his own will. This is, of course, not the case in the ghost theory, where concentration of mind and a desire to do harm is essential.

Diseases attributable to the evil eye are not of a special character, manifesting a well-defined symptomatology. Any disease at all, and especially those coming on suddenly, are considered by the populace to be caused by it. Puerperal conditions, even sepsis, diseases of the new-born are often spoken of as being "overlooked."

The treatment of the evil eye is rather interesting. In principle the Jews use the same protective measures as other peoples, namely, incantations, amulets and some special formulas; but the methods are different. When one gets suddenly ill the first thing to do is to think of the last person that visited the house, so as to trace the etiologic factor to him; then the diagnosis of having been "overlooked" or an "evil eye" is suspected. The next step in the procedure is to demonstrate the correctness of the diagnosis. They take a glass of water and put into it seven burning coals; if these remain floating then the diagnosis is not correct, at least not with any degree of certainty; but if they sink to the bottom then the correctness of the diagnosis has been established beyond any shadow of a doubt. In this country this experimental process is not practiced. The reason for its decline is in the difference of the nature of coal used for fuel. The hard coals used in this country are not well adapted for this purpose, for they all sink in water.

The diagnosis having been experimentally established, the next thing to do is to take some object belonging to the sick, a cap or a handkerchief, and take it over to the "Unsprecher" specialist, who by some incantation will cure the evil eye by driving it away. There are several incantations in use, but I shall give here only one form, which I found in the book "Kaf Achath" entitled an "Empirical and Experimental Incantation for an Evil Eye." "I conjure ye, ye all spirits of foul eyes, black eyes, white eyes, blue eyes, green eyes, long eyes, short eyes, broad eyes, narrow eyes, straight eyes, distorted eyes, round eyes, sunken eyes, prominent eyes, seeing eyes, speaking eyes, split eyes, flowing eyes, man's eyes, woman's eyes, husband's eyes, wife's eyes, mother's eyes, daughter's eyes, eyes of a woman and her relations, young man's eyes, old man's eyes, virgin's eyes, old woman's eyes, widow's eyes, legally married woman's eyes, divorced woman's eyes, all evil eyes that exist in the world, that saw and spoke with an evil eye upon N. the son of N., I decree and conjure you by the holy celestial eye, a unique eye, a broad eye, an eye that is the most white, an eye that is completely white, an eye that is all right, an open eye, a providential eye, an eye that is all merciful, compassionate, embodying all compassion, an eye that is all, an eye that has no blemishes, an eye that is neither red nor beautiful, an eye before which all evil eyes are hidden and to which all are subordinated, an eye that guards Israel: as it is written, 'The guard of Israel neither sleepeth nor slumbereth;' and it is also written, 'The eye of the Lord is upon those that fear him and hope for his mercy.' By this celestial eye I decree and conjure ye, ye all evil eyes, that ye depart and flee and run and keep aloof from N., son of N., and from his household and you shall have no power to prevail over N., the son of N., and his house neither by day nor by night, neither when he is awake nor in dream, neither in any of his members of his 248 members nor in any of his sinews of his 365 sinews, from to-day and hereafter."[36] This is, of course, no prayer, and while the incantation is offered in the name of God it is not an appeal to God to interfere in behalf of the sick; the underlying principle is in the power of the "Unsprecher" to drive away the evil. A formula as a prophylactic means is given in the Talmud: "Whoever is on the point to enter a city and is afraid of the evil eye should place his right thumb in his left hand and his left thumb in his right hand and say, 'I, N., son of N., am of the seed of Joseph, whom the evil eye may not touch'."[37] A horse can be protected against the evil eye by hanging between his eyes the tail of a fox.[38]

These are some protective measures found in literature and which are not in use at present. To protect a child from the evil eye, "Take the kernel of an almond, make a hole in it, place three little white stones found in the gizzard of a black rooster and add to it a little mercury, close the opening with a little wax and let the child wear it."[39] For a protective amulet, "Take a silver or copper piece of metal and inscribe the Hebrew letter H, and let the child wear it."[40] An amulet is supposed to act either by attracting the evil eye to its important self and away from the victim or it acts as a repellant. The psychic value is not discussed in this paper.

To cure an evil eye take a glass of water, place into it seven burning coals and repeat the following sentence: "And the people cried unto Moses and he prayed to God and the fire was extinguished;" then give the patient to drink from the water.[41] The following is the most popular antidote practiced in this country: Take a handful of salt and pass it around the head of the child that has been "overlooked;" throw a little of it in each corner of the room and the remainder over the threshold. Another popular remedy: the mother kisses the child that has been "overlooked" three times, spitting after each kiss. In Poland if a child has been "overlooked" by the evil eye the mother counteracts this spell by licking the head of the child three times, and spitting several times, repeating the following formula: "Ny hory, Ny hory, Ny buri, Ny kory," which in Polish means "Neither mountain nor forest, nor barley nor oats." Another practice among the Polish element to counteract the influence of the evil eye: spit three times on your finger tips and each time make a quick movement with your hands in the air. It is perhaps to this superstition that we may ascribe the origin of the hand motion so commonly employed by the Jews during conversation, originally having waved their hands to ward off the supposable influence of the evil eye. In praising a good looking person it is well to say, "May the Eternal guard him from evil." When the ghosts wish to do harm they first praise him by saying how beautiful he is.[42]

There are a number of incantations, prayers and formulas to be found in various books; space, however, will not permit me to quote them all. Some of the remedies are very complicated and difficult to prepare. Urine, hair, nails and the feces of the newborn child have been employed in them. It is well, however, to remark in due credit to the chroniclers of these old practices that after having given a complete list of them the conclusion reached is "That they who in case of sickness do not rely on these popular remedies but consult the physician are blessed."[43] In conclusion let me say that while some critics think that the phylacteries and fringes used by the Jews during the prayer was a protection against the evil eye, I can not share in this opinion, for the reason that while women are the most susceptible to the evil eye, yet they are free from wearing them. Again, the reason given especially for wearing of fringes is so clear that we have no right to transplant the moral influence and substitute a superstitious element which, as already stated in the outset of this paper, is not to be found in the Biblical writings.

NOTES

1. Chulin, 97–b.
2. Kethuboth, 30.
3. Deuteronomy, vii, 15.
4. Baba M., 107–b.
5. Num. R., 12.
6. Genesis R. xc, 1.
7. Midrash, Gen. R., 53: Jalkut Genes 14; Num. R., 12–6.
8. Sepher Habrith, part 1.
9. Mid. Gens., R. 53.
10. Sotha, 36–b; Baba B., 118–a.
11. Jalkut Hiob, 908: Lev. R., 17–3.
12. Num. R. 12–4.
13. Jalkut Echa, 997.
14. Jebu 62; Sanhed 93–a.
15. Baba M., 107–b.
16. Maimonidies Yad Hach.
17. Baba B., 141–a.
18. Baba M., 84–b.
19. [Reference omitted by author.]
20. Likkutiim.
21. Sabbath Mkom Shenhogi.
22. Nephesh Chajim.
23. Sabbath, 33–b.
24. Baba M., 84-a; Baba K., 11-a.
25. Zohar Achre Moth.
26. Sabbath.
27. Berachoth 20–a.
28. Sepher Habrith.
29. Orach Mishor 4-a.
30. Cornhill Magazine, 1879.
31. Baba M.
32. Berachoth 6–a.
33. Ibid.
34. Sepher Chasidim.
35. Sepher Habrith.
36. Kaf Achath.
37. Berachoth 55–b.
38. Tosephtha Sabbath.
39. Toldoth Adam.
40. Jalkut Reubenin P. Wajehl.
41. Toldoth Adam.
42. Orach Mishor.
43. Sepher Chasidim.

The Evil Eye in South Indian Folklore

*A. Stewart Woodburne**

By far the vast majority of reports on the evil eye consist of little more than anecdotal listings of cases and cures, innocent of any attempt to analyze or interpret the data gathered so assiduously. Yet these fact-filled accounts are not without interest or value. From reading such accounts, one can discover—through comparison—just what is common to the evil eye complex in different cultures and what is peculiar to particular individual cultural contexts. The following description of the evil eye in south India originally published in a professional missionary publication is not atypical. From it one can see that the serious scholar cannot afford to neglect the often vital information sometimes available only in such missionary or early traveler's reports.

For additional information on the evil eye in southern India, see Edgar Thurston, Omens and Superstitions of Southern India *(London: T. Fisher Unwin, 1912), pp. 109–120. For other representative reports in India, see John DeCunha, "On the Evil Eye among the Bunnias,"* Journal of the Anthropological Society of Bombay, *1 (1886–1889), 128–132, William Crooke,* The Popular Religion and Folk-Lore of Northern India, *Vol. II (Delhi: Munshiram Manoharlal, 1968), pp. 1–84, or William Crooke and R.E.Enthoven,* Religion & Folklore of Northern India *(New Delhi: S. Chand & Co., 1972), pp. 276–307, and Clarence Maloney, "Don't Say 'Pretty Baby' Lest You Zap It with Your Eye—The Evil Eye in South Asia,"*

* Reprinted from the *International Review of Missions*, 24 (1935), 237–247.

in Clarence Maloney, ed., The Evil Eye *(New York: Columbia University Press, 1976), pp. 102–148.*

The belief in the evil eye is very common in India, being recognized even in the sacred books both of Hinduism and Islam. It is a Hindu belief that the eye gives forth the most powerful of all emanations from the body. "Eat not the bread of him that hath an evil eye," is an ancient injunction and one that has been well observed. The possibility of transferring some evil from one person to another by sight is commonly held. It is not always possible for the victim to realize when the evil eye is being cast, for even a look of admiration may be a cloak for it. This is especially the case regarding admiring glances directed at children and domestic animals, particularly young ones. A look of admiration is regarded as resulting in a cow's wasting away and her supply of milk drying up. Sometimes the owner sees a look of admiration and offers the person some milk with the purpose of counteracting the effect.

The evil eye is believed to be rooted in jealousy. Hence the apparently admiring glance of a woman who has no children, or possibly no sons, at the son of another woman will, it is feared, carry the blight of jealousy. A similar emotion may be behind admiration for a cow. The person who is suffering from some physical defect such as blindness, deafness, lameness, or one who is a hunchback or an albino is greatly feared, as it is regarded as certain that such a person will be jealous of those blessed with health and soundness of body, and so will be ready to cast evil glances toward them. The Hindu belief is that the crises of life are particularly precarious from the standpoint of susceptibility to the evil eye. So at times of childbirth, puberty and marriage one must be more than usually careful to take precautions against evil influences. Probably the element of spite is mingled with envy, since deformities themselves are commonly credited to the evil eye, and then there is the added belief that "misery likes company."

The Hindu believes that the evil eye is commonly cast by women, rarely by men, but occasionally even by deities. A few animals also, specifically the jackal and the serpent, are possessors of the evil eye. Many South Indians, especially women, smear lampblack on their eyelids with the twofold purpose of protection from the evil glances of others and prevention against casting such themselves. It is curious that the Malayalis make use of a certain bachelor-demon, Vudikandan, to treat cases affected by the evil eye. The secret method of treatment is never divulged to outsiders. This demon is not invoked in any other rite and he can only be used in the daytime. The planet-god Sani (Saturn) is notorious for the burning gaze of his evil eye.

The Sanskrit word commonly used for the evil eye is *drishti* which literally means sight. In some cases they use a compound word *kripadrishti* to indicate the opposite kind of glance, especially when referring to a god. It means a look of favour or grace. This indicates that the power the eye possesses of sending forth emanations need not necessarily be maleficent. The Muslims use the Urdu word *nazar*. They think that a human being or animal changes for a worse condition of some sort if any one looks on his beauty or wealth with envious or hungry eyes.

Belief that the eye is an instrument for transmitting powerful emanations involves many collateral beliefs. Polluted people are under certain prohibitions about looking at the heavenly bodies. For example, a pregnant women must not look at an eclipse. In certain unfavourable circumstances a father must not look at his new-born child until a propitious time, and then he must first see only its reflection in a pot of oil. The chief mourner after performing a funeral rite must not look back. As a corpse leaves the house one must not look back. In certain rites of casting out demons with mimetic magic, after throwing away the paraphernalia one must not look back. Much care must be taken as to the objects that a woman sees during pregnancy, as it will affect her child. Even idols are susceptible to the evil generated by the looks of an unclean person, and so such persons are prohibited from entering temples. In fact, in some rites of worship the devotee covers his eyes with his right hand, and in a few even the priest is blindfolded.

The power of the evil eye is exercised to the harm not only of people and animals, but also of buildings, gardens and crops. Buildings in course of construction are to a peculiar degree susceptible. To call a building beautiful may spoil it. Masons and carpenters are in great dread of the evil eye's spoiling their work and they will frequently leave some little part of a building incomplete, thinking thereby to avoid the effect of the evil eye. Similarly a weaver will leave a flaw in his cloth and an artist will leave some little defect in his work, the idea prevailing that a completed piece of work is more liable to injury from evil glances than one incomplete. Another method to which many resort is that of placing grotesque and lewd figures in front of houses under construction, on temples and in fields where the crops are growing. These figures naturally attract the attention of everybody, including those who have power of the evil eye, and that means that the building or crop escapes the accursed look. In front of some temples are to be found stones containing the imprint of the foot of a man or deity (*padagatti*) the purpose of which also is to deflect evil glances.

An evil eye gets its evil character from the person's own potentiality. The eye is that part of the person through which his evil influence is transferred. In general, one may say that there are two methods of dealing with the evil. The one is to devise some protective instrument or rite by which persons may be made immune from the influence. The other is to attempt to nullify the evil that suffuses the person who casts the evil eye. In the latter case a plan to which they frequently resort is to obtain something belonging to the evil-eyed individual and burn it. A piece of cloth worn by the individual will do. Nail parings or hair are also good. It is not always possible to get a possession of the person, and so substitute rites are tried such as throwing pepper into the fire while repeating the person's name, repeating his name while burning a horseshoe, and placing fire upon his shadow. Both the name and the shadow are considered parts of the person. It is a commonly accepted axiom of magic that what is done to a part is done to the whole; hence these efforts of overcome the influence of the evil eye.

Among the Koravas a somewhat analogous rite to nullify an evil tongue is to make a mud figure of a man on the ground and then place thorns over the mouth as if to pierce its tongue. Persons who have suffered from it walk around the figure, crying and beating their mouths. The louder the noise the better will be the effect.

Cutting the neck of a fowl half through and then allowing it to flutter about, or inserting a red hot splinter in its anus to madden it with pain are considered effective means of counteracting an evil tongue. If a cock should happen to crow after the neck of the fowl has been cut, it is an especially good omen for the effectiveness of the counter-magic.

Some of the means in current use in South India for counteracting the effects of the evil eye are as follows:

1. In Malabar a *mantra* is addressed to Bhagavati, the translation of which is:

> I prostrate myself to Bhagavati. When Sri Paramesvara and Parvati went hunting, Sri Parvati was under the influence of the evil eye. Sri Paramesvara put away this influence. Do thou unto this case of evil eye likewise. My oath is on my *guru*.

The word *guru* (literally, priestly teacher) in such formulas always refers to the deity. This *mantra* is repeated on each of sixteen grains of rice which are let one by one into oil. The mixture is then stirred while the following untranslatable *mantra* is repeated: "*Om peputi vorrupoti yerrika swaha yen guru vinana*." The oil is handed in silence to the victim, who rubs his head with it in silence and is thereby cured of the evil eye.

2. The Koravas are a caste of thieves. If an excursion of housebreaking has been made, the implement used for the purpose is frequently soldered at the sharp end with *panchalokam* (five metals) to counteract the possible effects of the evil eye.

3. Among the Mandulas, a caste of Telugu medicine men, an anklet made of the hair of the child's mother and tied round the right ankle is considered efficacious in warding off the influence of the evil eye from a child.

4. Among the fisher people of the Tamil country it is customary to pour a few drops of milk with a fig or betel leaf on the foreheads of a couple during the marriage ceremony to counteract any possibility of harm from the evil eye. Marriage is of course one of the critical periods of greatest susceptibility.

5. Among the Porijas of the Oriya country a gourd (*cucurbita maxima*) is suspended over the threshold of a house where a marriage is taking place. When the bride and groom come in front of the house, a tall man cuts the gourd with his axe and it falls to the ground. Thus the possible influence of the evil eye is averted and the couple can enter the house in safety.

6. Another method of countering the effect of the evil eye on marriage occasions is to touch the cheeks of the bridegroom with *mai* or *coryllium*. During the earlier stages of marriage the bride and bridegroom are freed from the influence of the evil eye by waving and throwing in eight different directions balls of variously coloured rice.

7. Huge bamboo and wicker figures are frequently carried in the van of marriage or temple processions to avert the glances of any persons with the evil eye.

8. When red bricks are piled up for use in the construction of a house, it is a common practice to sprinkle *chunam* (lime) water over them to ward off the evil eye.

9. To remove the effects of the evil eye at times people will burn an old broom, chillis and salt together before the person who is affected. At other times cocoanut shells, salt, chillis and some grains are burned before the affected individual. In some instances camphor is burned. In such cases special precautions are taken that small children should not see these things, because they have been magically charmed and are potential sources of danger.

10. The Telugus have a ceremony called *degathudupu* for counteracting the effect of the evil eye. In a small vessel a mixture is made of a number of articles, including a lime cut in two, some water in which saffron and turmeric have been mixed, and rice mixed with turmeric. This vessel is then brandished three times in each direction around the man suffering from the effects of the evil eye. The contents of the vessel are then thrown away on some path. The belief is that whoever first crosses that path will be attacked by the evil eye. The wearing of shoes by the man passing over the place where the *degathudupu* has been thrown out serves as counter-magic in protecting the pedestrian.

11. Another method of counteracting the influence of the evil eye is to cook the lungs of a sheep or goat and place on a leaf with five morsels of boiled rice coloured differently. A few hairs, one or two left eyelashes, one toe-nail from the left foot, three copper coins, a small earthenware vessel, a paper with a crude figure painted in black, one lime cut in two, one egg and a cocoanut smeared with turmeric are placed upon a leaf and waved three times around the person, who spits on it. They are then taken outside the village where the egg and the cocoanut are broken. The one who carries them must return without turning his head about, no matter what may happen. After reaching home, he must wash his hands and feet before entering the house. Meanwhile the lime and turmeric are mixed in water and a little charcoal is added. The patient looks at his face in this water and it is then turned around him and, after he spits in it, it is thrown into the street. Lastly, a piece of camphor is burned on a plate, and is waved

around the man and thrown into the street. The effects of the evil eye being now counteracted, he is finally bathed in hot water and allowed to sleep.

12. To counteract the effects of the evil eye of a witch, a mixture of rice, curds, milk and cooked beans and peas is placed in an earthenware pot. Then some marks are made on the pot with red clay, and the person affected is made to smell the contents of the pot, after which it is placed in a spot where four roads meet.

13. Amulets are frequently worn to attract the first glance of a person and thus avert the possibility of evil. Bright and shining amulets are considered most efficacious. Amulets of a phallic character are frequently used. Some amulets are worn beneath the clothes and this class is considered particular effective for counteracting injuries. Other amulets contain written texts from scriptures, cabalistic figures and *mantras*.

14. Obscene figures are regarded as likely to attract the attention of persons with evil eyes and so divert their gaze. Consequently they are used on temples, new houses and in fields. Straw figures in temples and in front of houses and images frequently represent couples in the act of copulation.

15. A representation of the eye itself is among the devices employed to divert the evil eye.

16. Certain colours are thought to possess protective value—red and blue especially so.

17. In fields the common method of diverting the evil eye is to erect a pole with a pot on it on which spots of lime are daubed. Rags are used sometimes instead of the pot.

18. The waving of *arrati* is practised as a rite to relieve persons believed to be victimized by the evil eye. In that case a vessel containing a circular plate is filled with water containing saffron, lime and some rice. This is waved before the afflicted person and some of the wet rice is thrown on his or her head. The ceremony is usually performed by an elderly woman. After an idol has been taken in procession through the streets, it is subjected to the same ceremony to counteract any evil influence from a gaze to which it was unconsciously subjected.

19. An infant may be protected by tying some of the hair of an elephant to its wrist.

20. The claw of a tiger tied as an amulet about the neck is a good protective for children.

21. A root of the turmeric plant is also used as an amulet to ward off the evil eye.

22. A small gold or copper plate with an image of the god Hanuman, hung about the neck, is said to protect effectively.

23. A cure which is recommended is to make a cloth wick, dip it in oil, hang it on a rod and, waving it around the person afflicted, light it at the lower end. As it burns sparks will drop, and these are said to be the effects of the evil eye dropping away.

24. Still another prescription is to make a small clay image of a deer and a *namum* (ψ), and place it with some grains on a plate. This is waved about the afflicted person and afterwards given to a Brahman.

25. Another prescription is to wave a handful of chillis and salt around an afflicted person and then throw them into the fire.

26. To counteract the evil eye salt is sometimes carried round a person and then thrown into water, while these words are repeated: "Vanish, you evil eye, whosoever you may be."

27. On occasions ten or fifteen brooms are taken, turned round the afflicted person, set alight at one end and then stood in a corner with the burning end downwards. This is a common practice among Tamil Brahmans.

28. Some of the lower castes follow the custom of turning a black hen three times round a person, after which its neck is cut and it is thrown away at a spot where four roads meet.

29. A faqir may have the power of casting the evil eye and a special formula is given to counteract his evil influence. It consists of cooked rice and vegetables which have to be carried to a spot where four roads meet and thrown away there.

30. A cat also has the power of casting the evil eye. The prescription for counteracting its effects is to roast a fish over the head of the afflicted person and then to feed the cat with it.

31. The Madigas or leather workers sacrifice a goat at marriages to the marriage pots. The sacrificer then dips his hands in the blood of the victim and impresses the palms on the walls of the room. This is apparently a protective device against the influence of the evil eye.

32. When a Brahman lad is being initiated by investiture with the sacred thread, at the appropriate time the father introduces to him the *Gayatri mantra* (a sacred verse). This being a time of crisis, both

father and son are covered by a cloth as a protective against the evil eye.

33. Some of the castes and tribes resort to tattooing the body, in some cases as a measure of protection against the evil eye.

34. Some objects take on a character of sanctity because of their association with *puja* (rite of worship). *Darbha* or *kusa* grass and the leaves of the sacred *tulasi* plant (basil) are considered to be of protective value.

35. Some shells are regarded as valuable for counteracting the malign influences of the evil eye. Many shells have small holes in them. One traditions states that these shells are attuned so harmoniously to the wearer that they will split if an evil eye is cast on them. The conch shell is used in summoning worshippers at a temple and in funeral processions, and is especially powerful as a protective against all sorts of evil influences.

36. Mothers will sometimes make the faces of their children grotesque by painting black marks on the cheeks, forehead or chin, so as to enable them to avoid the possible admiring gaze of an evil-eyed individual.

37. The Badagas of the Nilgiri Hills have a protective rite that they perform at the Sakalathi festival on behalf of their children. It consists of making a cake on which butter and rice are placed and into which three wicks soaked in castor-oil are placed and lit. The cake is waved about the heads of the children of the household.

38. Some of the Paraiyans have a waving ceremony to protect a girl from the malign influence of the evil eye at puberty. Ten lumps of flour paste are placed on a sieve and waved before her; afterwards coloured water and burning camphor are also waved before her.

39. In 1906 when a royal wedding was in progress in Travancore, a group of Nayar girls, attractively dressed, went in procession before the royal palanquin to avert the evil eye from the wedding group.

40. The Telugu Malas, who correspond to the Tamil Paraiyans, shortly before a wedding make two marks on the wall on either side of the door into the wedding house. The marks are made by the palms of hands smeared with charcoal and are intended to avert the evil gaze.

41. Muslims make marks similar to those just mentioned, but with hands having outspread fingers that have been smeared with red paint. These marks are made on the exterior of mosques and Muslim buildings to avert the evil eye.

42. The Tanjore *District Gazetteer* says that Tamil Paraiyans sometimes take the impression of a dead man's hand in cowdung and stick it on the wall as a protective device.

42. At all Hindu weddings in South India, when the bride and the bridegroom are seated opposite each other, they show each other some salt, chillis and cakes, and then let them drop. On account of their attractive appearance, and being the central figures in the ceremony, they are the subjects of the gaze of everybody, and particularly susceptible to the bad influence of the evil eye. The act mentioned is intended to avert any calamity from this source. Their feet are also coloured with a mixture of saffron paste and lime to add to their protection.

44. On other occasions some saffron water is poured over the legs of newly married couples while *mantras* are being repeated—also as a protective device.

45. Certain thorny plants and thistles are regarded as possessing virtue and counteracting the influence of evil eyes. These are often hung on the tops of buildings under construction.

46. The gaze of a leper is evil among the Malayalis. To avert any calamity they immediately look up at the sun.

Magic and sorcery frequently take the form of rites and practices designed to counteract the evil effects of malicious influences. The evil eye is one of the malevolent influences that the people of South India seek to control or avoid. There is scarcely any normal process either of human life, animal life or of nature, that is not subject to the injurious glance of the evil eye. All sorts of evils are attributed to this source. In consequence, we have those varied devices and practices to offset the ills emanating from the evil eye.

People who are suspected of casting the evil eye are treated as sorcerers whose powers are to be curtailed. Various means are used to that end. Some people believe that by extracting the sorcerer's tooth his power will be dissipated. One informant told of a Uriya girl whose illness was believed to be the result of sorcery. A certain man was suspected of having cast an evil eye on her. He was caught by her friends and two of his front teeth were knocked out by a hammer. One method in vogue in the Deccan is to make the person suspected of casting the evil eye drink water in which old shoes have been soaked. Other methods include the use of *yantras* (geometrical figures magically contrived), the recitation of *mantras* or of names and words believed to possess potency, the wearing of amulets and charms, and sometimes the celebration of religious rites.

We have in connexion with these beliefs and practices another illustration of the intimate association of the religious and magical. Though the operations of the evil eye are interpreted from the magical point of view, one of the means considered to be most effective for control is the religious. Religious rites themselves are commonly supposed to contribute to the merits of those who celebrate them, and to put him in possession of a power that will enable him to counteract such malevolent influences as that of the evil eye. It is well always to have the gods on one's side in struggles against evil.

The Evil Eye in Iran

Bess Allen Donaldson*

Moving from India to Iran, we find the evil eye equally well entrenched. The familiar dangers of praise and the utility of such conteractants as verbal formulas and prophylactic amulets are very much in evidence. The influence of the Koran is apparent, but it should also be noted that the evil eye is found in the ancient Iranian Zoroastrian literature. For a discussion of the latter, see Leó J. Frachtenberg, "Allusions to Witchcraft and Other Primitive Beliefs in the Zoroastrian Literature," in the Dastur Hoshang Memorial Volume *(Bombay: Fort Printing Press, 1918), pp. 399–453 (see esp. pp. 419–424). For other accounts of Persian evil eye beliefs, see John DeCunha, "On the Belief in the Evil Eye among the Modern Persians,"* Journal of the Anthropological Society of Bombay, *1 (1886–1889), 149–153, and Eda W. Lindquist, "Rue and the Evil Eye in Persia,"* The Moslem World, *26 (1936), 170–175.*

The Iranians have a tradition which says that the evil eye puts the camel into the pot and mankind into the grave.[1] Undoubtedly fear of the evil eye exerts the greatest influence of all the superstitions that are common among the people. Their ordinary conversations are interspersed with *Má shá'llah* and *In shá'llah*, "What God wills" and "If God wills." These expressions are used to protect themselves against

* Reprinted from Bess Allen Donaldson, *The Wild Rue: A Study of Muhammadan Magic and Folklore in Iran* (London: Luzac, 1938), pp. 13–23.

the evil that may lurk behind a remark of appreciation or admiration. When they speak of illness, such words as *nazar*, "a spell cast by a malignant eye," *chashm zakhm*, the "eye that wounds," and *chashm zadah*, "struck by the evil eye," are frequently used because so much of their illness is attributed to this influence.

But what is it that they regard as the evil eye? Those who have proffered information agree that it is a power in some eyes to bring evil to whatever they look upon. These eyes are variously described as *chashm shúr*, the "salty eye"; *chashm zakhm*, the "eye that wounds"; and *chashm tang*, the "narrow eye." This last term refers to the eye that casts a spell through covetousness.

The majority of the common people hold all of the general beliefs regarding the evil eye, but there are others who acknowledge only those which can be traced to the Koran, or to one of the Prophets, or to one of the Imams. They find their chief authority in Sura 68: 51: "Almost would the infidels strike thee down with their very looks when they hear the warning of the Koran, and they say, He is certainly possessed."

There is a story that at the time of Muhammad a woman from an opposing faction attempted to bring calamity upon him. She tied seven knots in a piece of rope and on each of these she blew her breath. She hoped by this magical rite to ruin his influence among men and to bring to naught all his efforts. The rope and its intended use were discovered, and then it was that the *chahar kaul*, "four promises," were revealed to Muhammad,[2] so that he might not fear such women, but put his trust in God. Naturally these four suras are considered most efficacious against the evil eye. They are written and worn by anyone who thinks he has fallen under the spell of evil, or they are read repeatedly until the effects of the evil are removed.

The use of talismans against the evil eye was permitted by the Prophet. Asma', the daughter of Umais, relates: "When I said to him, 'O Prophet, the family of Ja'far are afflicted by the baneful influence of an evil eye, may I use spells for them or not?' then he replied, 'Yes, for if there were anything in the world which would overcome Fate, it would be an evil eye.' "[3]

The measure that is often employed to ward off the evil eye is to utter *Má shá'llah*, "What God wills!" The authority for its use is found in Sura 18: 37: "And why didst thou not say, when thou enteredst the garden, 'What God wills'? There is no power but in

God." All complimentary remarks should be prefaced by this expression, and failure to say it before admiring or praising a child will certainly be considered to be the cause of any illness or misfortune which may befall it in the near future.

When a person speaks of his intention to do something, he has no right to make a simple, direct statement, he must say *In shá'llah*, "If God wills," for the future is with God. To omit this would very likely result in the failure of the undertaking. The authority for this precaution is found in Sura 18: 23: "Say not thou of a thing, 'I will surely do it tomorrow,' without saying, 'If God wills.' " As Rodwell has remarked, "Muhammad had omitted this qualifying statement when, in reply to the Jews who had asked for the history of the seven sleepers, he simply promised to give it on the morrow,"[4] but we find it explicitly enjoined by example in Sura 12: 100, where we read, "And when they came unto Joseph, he took his parents to him and said, 'Enter ye Egypt, if God will, secure.' "

The Koran further suggests the advisability of avoiding circumstances which would cause wonder or surprise. When Jacob sent his sons to Egypt for corn, according to Sura 12: 67, he advised them: "O my sons! enter not by one gate, but enter by different gates. Yet can I not help you against aught decreed by God." The shaikh who furnished the information regarding this verse explained that eleven grown sons of one father would arouse admiration anywhere. He added that Iranians, to avoid being too conspicuous, will not go in groups, but will separate and go singly or two by two, so as not to excite wonder. They are alarmed when people are surprised on account of a large family or great wealth or large flocks. It is at such times that covetousness and jealousy, with their "narrow eye" and "short glance," enter with dire results. If one is dressed attractively when he goes into the street he is in danger; therefore, before going out, he should read two of the four promises,[5] so as to protect himself from the possible evil.

There are, however, many verses from the Koran which are believed to afford protective power against the evil eye. Two that are widely used are Sura 10: 81, "And when they had cast them down, Moses said, 'Verily God will render vain the sorceries which ye have brought to pass: God prospereth not the work of evildoers' "; and Sura 12: 65, "And when they opened their goods and found their money had been returned to them, they said, 'O our Father, what more can we desire? Here is our money returned to us; we will provide corn for our families, and will take care of our brother, and shall receive a camel's burden more of corn. This is an easy quantity!' " These and many other verses are mentioned in the numerous books of magic that are in general use.

It matters little by what name this baneful influence is called; everyone knows exactly what is meant, but all do not agree as to the way the power is exerted. Some say that the power of the look alone is but slight, and that words must accompany the look to make it really dangerous. Others claim that the evil is in the glance, and that the accompanying remark only tends to increase or lessen its malignancy.

The possessor of an evil eye may or may not know that he has it. He may have been born with it, in which case it is because of the sign of the zodiac into which he was born, or because of the star that was rising at the hour of his birth. It exists in various degrees of power in different people. It is said by some, however, that there are few who actually do have it, and that perhaps most of them do not realize that it is in their possession. One Shaikh expressed the opinion that most of the fear of the evil eye has been created by the imaginations of the people, and that the real causes for it are not nearly so numerous as they think but the fear of it is certainly general, and so many ills and misfortunes are ascribed to it, that most people have been suspected at some time of being the cause of calamities that have come to those with whom they have had contact.

If a person knows that he has the power of casting a spell he may be able to control it, for he can then gauge it according to his desires. Should it, however, be so strong that he cannot direct it, his only escape, if he be moved by kindness, is to avoid looking at anything that is beautiful or striking in any way, so as to remove the possibility of danger. There are but few, whether among the upper or lower classes, who do not have a dread of the look of admiration.

There is a man in Meshed who claims to know that he has this uncontrollable power in his eye. He warns people not to bring anything which is good or beautiful into his presence. He is generally shunned, for people think that if there is such danger when he is in a sympathetic frame of mind, what might he not be able to do in anger or jealousy!

To instance a particular woman, also of this city, who has claimed to have the ability to cast spells, one incident will illustrate how she has sometimes employed this power or art to her own advantage. As she was going out of her house to the public bath, she noticed a fat sheep that belonged to a neighbour who lived in the same courtyard. Jokingly she said, "Have some soup from that sheep ready when I come home and I'll help you eat it;" and with a laugh she passed into the narrow street. Shortly after she had gone, the animal, when nibbling the leaves from a small mulberry tree that grew in the yard, got its head caught in a sickle that had been hung on one of the branches. In its struggle to get free, its throat was cut and it soon bled to death. When the woman returned, after the usual several hours at the bath, the soup was ready.

There is a well-known story of a shopkeeper who said to his apprentice, when a caravan of camels was passing his shop, "Go and buy some of the meat of that camel," indicating a particular animal. The boy took the money and followed the caravan. When they reached the place of loading and unloading, near the city gate, the animal fell down and died. The boy rushed up to buy the meat. The camel driver asked him who had sent him to buy meat, and the boy replied that his master had sent him. The camel driver asked to be shown the master's shop. The boy led him to the shop and as soon as he saw the shopkeeper he said *Chashm básh!* which, idiomatically translated, is equivalent to "What eyes!" The shopkeeper's eyes burst from their sockets and fell to the ground! Evidently the camel driver's eyes possessed more of the evil power than his.

Another story tells of a man with an evil eye over which he had no control. Some of his acquaintances were digging a well, and they struck a stone which they could neither dig through nor break. One of them remembered the power of this man's eye and went to him, asking him to come and see the strange stone they had found in their digging. When they showed him the unusual hardness of the stone by striking it with their picks, he remarked, "That is a remarkable stone," and immediately it cracked in several places. The workmen then went on with their work and removed the stone piece by piece.

Much as the women of Iran love to adorn themselves and to look attractive, yet they are in fact afraid of admiration. A charming lady took her small daughter to enroll her in a school. After all the arrangements had been made, one of the older students was asked to show her over the school building. As they descended the stairs, she caught her heel on a step and fell. Her face and arm were bruised, but they were promptly cared for by the Principal and the visitor seemed to be grateful for the solicitation that had been shown. As she left the building, however, she told the student that she couldn't think of sending her daughter to that school, because her fall had been the result of the evil eye. It would be too dangerous to leave an attractive child in a place where it was so evident that the evil influence was working.

Evil results may follow at once, as in the above cases, and there are some who claim that people have fallen dead immediately when looked upon; but the power may also work slowly, as in the following instance. The child concerned was a little boy who was strikingly beautiful and the most attractive in any group. Iranian women of the middle and lower classes almost always take their babies with them when they go calling. This mother realized the danger to her child and had named him *Ma shá'llah*, thus every time his name was spoken he would be protected from harm. One day a woman took him in her arms and fondled him rather extravagantly, but did not mention his name, so a few days later the child was stricken with fever. Every known charm was used for his recovery but day by day he grew worse. The mother then took him to several doctors but all to no avail, and at last the child died. Ever afterwards the mother spoke of him as her child who was given the evil eye by a jealous woman who would not speak his name.

Women often say that their children are ugly or that they are not very smart, when it is evident that they are unusually pretty and bright. They will deliberately allow attractive children to go unwashed to make them unattractive, or they sometimes give the names of animals to especially clever children, thinking that by calling a child "Donkey" it will be kept from harm. If a precocious child has done intelligent or amusing things, the very superstitious mother will spit upon it. Spitting is believed to overcome the evil consequences of admiration, for the Prophet spat upon Ali when he sent him forth to fight the *dívha* or demons. If a child has been greatly admired, a piece of the admirer's garment will be requested and will be pinned upon the child's clothing as a talisman.

When a family moves into a new house they should by all means give a party to their friends, or better than that, they should sacrifice an animal and give the meat to the poor and spread the blood of the victim over the door. This will protect them from admiration or jealousy. "Your eyes to the soles of your feet, say *Ma shá'llah*," is commonly said to a person who has admired something and has not protected it. If, however, one wishes to express praise, he may do so safely by first saying *Allah akbar*, "God is great."[6]

Covetousness is feared as much as admiration or surprise, and is held to be responsible for as much bad fortune. Special circumstances seldom fail to cause anxiety. One of two or more wives of the same man may be childless and may look upon the child of her *vasni* or rival wife with such longing that she is feared, and any illness the child may have will probably be blamed upon her; or a woman has a frail child while her neighbour's baby is robust, and the latter fears the look of her neighbour upon her healthy child. Likewise any misfortune which may come to the child will be attributed to the look of longing or covetousness of the mother of the frail child. A man may own an animal that is in excellent condition, a donkey, a sheep or a cow, and is constantly uneasy for fear some one will cast a look of desire for possession upon his healthy animal. To protect it an iron key will be tied to a cow's horn, or a blue bead or a cowry shell will be fastened around the neck of a donkey or into the wool of a sheep. A tree bearing choice fruit may become the cause of envy, and lest evil come upon it and its fruit fall or become wormy, or lest it be injured by hail, the owner will bind a prayer, which is usually a verse from the Koran, to one of its branches; and while a courtyard that can boast a well of clear, cold water is much to be desired, yet its owner may not be at ease, for he has a neighbour who owns a well of hard, bad-tasting water. Lest his good well fail as a result of his neighbour's covetousness, he will throw a written prayer into it and try to cease his worry. And beautiful girls, especially when they become brides, may be looked upon in a way that is dangerous by mothers who have less comely daughters or by other girls who are not so favoured. Should oriental boils or smallpox, if they have thus far escaped, mar their beauty with lasting scars, it would be on account of some spell cast upon them, consequently each one will wear about her neck a tiny Koran in a golden box. Also women who weave the cord shoes that are commonly worn in dry weather are so afraid to have their work praised that they seldom make the two shoes alike. One is almost always a trifle smaller than its mate, and this is to avoid perfection; in fact it is not uncommon to find in rugs, even in those of superior quality, some slight irregularity in pattern or colour. The weaver has done this intentionally, so that the article may be considered imperfect, for the evil eye is believed to be strongly drawn to perfection and with disastrous results.

As has been suggested, perhaps the Iranians do not restrict themselves to the preventive and protective measures that are found in the Koran and in the Traditions. They have worked out many devices to meet their especial needs. Something rare or strange, something that bears a resemblance to an eye and attracts their attention, sooner or later becomes a talisman. Some of the most common of these charms are shells, stones, mother-of-pearl, and various parts of animals.

Cowry shells are frequently observed. This shell is called *bibín tarak* (eye-cracker). One of them may be sewn to a child's garment, and it is often the only visible charm; or great numbers of them may be sewn in patterns onto the tape or leather bands that are used in the trappings of animals. When the eye of envy or admiration is cast upon the wearer, these innocent-looking decorations have the power to cast back the evil upon the dangerous eye and *cause it to crack!*

The agate stone, in the form of beads, bars, or ring-settings, is considered to be highly effective against this evil power. A bead of grey agate performs the same services as the cowry shell. Long bars, with holes drilled in them, are strung or tied onto the necklaces of charms, which are still frequently seen on village women. A piece of agate will be cut so that the layers of colour form a series of circles so as to resemble an eye. This is a common type of jewelry. Rings and other ornaments that are fastened to necklaces are often set with these polished agates. The onyx is called *bábá gaurí*, "father of avarice," and is considered to be extremely dependable to send back the evil glance.

Mother-of-pearl is also thought to possess power against the evil influence. It is generally cut into fancy shapes, a fish, a tooth, or a dagger; and it is worn for ornamentation as well as protection, and a panther's claw is used by many to ward off the evil power. Pieces of the horn or of the skin of the deer are also regarded as exceedingly potent. Deerskin is used instead of paper or cloth on which to write prayers, but the dried eye of a sacrificed sheep[7] is of all things the most highly esteemed, for almost invariably one dangles from the cap or shoulder of the Iranian baby; and some say that if the eye has been stolen from another woman's baby's cap, then its effectiveness is enhanced.

Incantations play an important part in the efforts to remove the influence of the evil eye. When an afflicted person is thought to be a victim of *nazar*, or the glance of the evil eye, a particular kind of incense, which is made of seeds of the wild rue, mixed with leaves of myrtle and frankincense, is burned at sunset; and while the smoke is curling about the head of the victim, the following incantation is repeated:

Isfand, kí kásht?.................. Muhammad.
kí chíd?.................... Ali.
kí dúd kard?............ Ḟatima.
az baraya kí?.......... Az baraya Ḥassan was Ḥussain.

Wild rue, who planted it?...... Muhammad.
who gathered it?.... Ali.
who burned it?....... Ḟatima.
for whom?............ For Ḥasan and Ḥusain.

The names of the "Five"[8] are all in this incantation, combining their power with that of the incense. The Iranian women call this incantation *'átil wa bátil*, or "offensive and defensive." These words may be chanted during the process of burning the incense:

Isfand, isfand dánah,
Isfand, sí yáh sah dánah,
Bi-tarakh-a-chashm-i-hasúd yáh bigánah,
Hamsáyaiyi dast-i-rást,
Hamsáyaiyi dast-i-chap,
Hamsáyaiyi pish-i-rúh,
Hamsáyaiyi pusht-i-sar,
Kad-i-buland, kad-i-kutáh,
Chashm-i-durusht, chashm-i-ríz,
Chashm-i-sabz, chashm-i-síyáh.

Wild rue, seeds of wild rue,
Thirty or three seeds of wild rue,
Crack the eye of jealousy or hostility
In the neighbour to the right,

In the neighbour to the left,
In the neighbour across the way,
In the neighbour behind the house,
Whether tall or whether short,
With large eyes or with small,
With eyes of green or eyes of black.

Or on a Tuesday night, seven girls, under fourteen years of age, will be chosen to sit under a drain from the roof, and with their faces turned towards Mecca. They pound some lye to powder in a mortar and pestle, then each girl puts her hand under her dress and allows it to come out at the neck, and thus handicapped, in turn they pound the substance and repeat:

Har ki kard átil,
Man kardam bátil.

Whoever cast the spell,
I have made it vain.

When the lye is all powdered it is put into a vessel, when it is mixed with vinegar and placed upon the roof, where the stars may shine upon it. In the morning some of this mixture is poured over the head of the one who is thought to be under the spell; a drop is also given him to drink, and some is sprinkled on the wall nearby, and all the while the person who is performing the rite keeps reciting:

Whoever cast the spell,
I have made it vain.

If, however, the evil influence does not yield to any of the foregoing measures, a shaving may be taken from the door that leads to the street. This is bound with seven pieces of blue homespun cloth. One piece is used for each of seven persons who may possibly have cast the spell of the evil eye. This shaving is then burned along with the seeds of the wild rue. With the ashes spots are made between the eyes, on the palms of the hands, and on the soles of the feet of the victim, while the following words are spoken:

In shá'llah raf'-i-nazar shudah.

God willing, the spell has been removed.

Ordinarily there is apt to be only a suspicion that the attack of illness is the result of a spell, but there are several methods of determining whether or not a spell has actually been cast. Until the complete removal of the veil in 1936, the following simple method was much used by the women. If a woman repeated one of the verses of the Koran which had been previously mentioned, she would stretch out her arm to the corner of her head-kerchief. If the arm and kerchief would prove to be of the same length, then no spell had been cast. If, however, they should be uneven in length, then this is a sure sign that evil has been done. If the arm should stretch farther, then a woman is the evil-doer; but if the kerchief should be longer, then the witchcraft has been performed by a man.

When it has been proved that the evil eye has been given, steps may be taken to detect the guilty person. A common expedient is to hold an egg between the two palms and to press upon it as the name of each suspect is spoken. At the name of the guilty one the egg will break.

Another method is as follows. A conjecture is made as to the probable time the spell was cast; then there is an effort to recall everyone who was present on that occasion. When this has been done, someone procures a brick, then dips her finger into castor oil and makes as many oil spots on the brick as there were people present at that time. She speaks the name of each one with great solemnity as she makes each mark; then she puts a burned match on each corner of the brick, and in the centre she places a piece of new cotton, a crystal of rock candy, some salt, an egg, and again the seeds of the wild rue. Now the brick is taken carefully, with all these things upon it, to some place where roads cross, and it is left there. When the woman who took away the brick returns from her errand, her confederates inquire, "Salaam, where have you been?" She replies, "I have been to the house of an enemy." "What did you do there?" they ask. "I saw him die and I buried him," she says.

The idea is that by this ceremony the evil is made to return upon the doer and at the same time it reveals who did it, while in the meantime the victim of the glance is left to recover. But there is scarcely any limit to the variety of beliefs and practices that are connected with the evil eye,[9] the whole conception has for so long a time dominated the daily life and thought of the people.

NOTES

1. Majlisi, *Hilyatu'l-Mullakín*, p. 88.
2. Koran, Suras 109, 112, 113, 114.
3. Hughes, "Dictionary of Islam," quoted from the *Mishkat*, book xxi., ch. i., part 2.
4. Rodwell's translation of the Koran, p. 182, note 3.
5. Majlisi, *Hilyatu'l-Mullakín*, p. 88.
6. Majlisi, *op. cit.*
7. *Cf.* Index of *The Wild Rue* under "Sacrifices on *'Aid-i-Kurbán.*"
8. *Rawdat al-Shuhadá*, p. 24, The "Five" are Muhammad, Ali, Fatima, Ḥasan and Ḥusain.
9. *Cf.* Westermarck, "Ritual and Beliefs in Morocco," vol. 1., ch. viii., which gives a comprehensive account of these practices in other countries.

The Shilluk's Belief in the Evil Eye

*Rev. D. S. Oyler**

The evil eye remains a powerful force in the Mahgreb, that is, Arabic north Africa. In Algeria, Morocco, Egypt, and Tunisia, one can find countless instances of belief in the evil eye. In sub-Saharan Africa, in contrast, one finds relatively few occurrences of the evil eye except in those areas where Islamic influence is strongly felt. The evil eye has been reported in Ethiopia and also among the Shilluk, a people living in Sudan. It is likely, though not easily demonstrable, that the Shilluk as a Nilotic people possess cultural traits in common with peoples past and present far to the north, e.g. Nubians. In any case, however it may be explained, the Shilluk do seem to have a constellation of beliefs and practices almost certainly cognate to the evil eye complex found throughout the Indo-European and Semitic world.

In this account by a missionary, we find a number of ethnocentric, condescending statements beginning with a reference to the collective "animistic mind" of the Shilluk and ending with the concession that ancestors of the English believed in witches "even after they had reached a much greater development than the Shilluk has attained." But despite this deplorable tone—found unfortunately as often in the writings of many early anthropologists as in those of colonial administrators and missionaries—Reverend Oyler manages to communicate a usefully detailed description of the Shilluk version of the evil eye. The reader may remark, for instance,

* Reprinted from *Sudan Notes and Records*, 2 (1919), 122–28.

that one of the techniques allegedly employed to cure a case of the evil eye entails sticking a red-hot nail into the eyes of a sheep, a seemingly striking parallel to the use of a "dried eye of a sacrificed sheep" reported in the preceding essay as an amulet in Iran.

To the animistic mind of the Shilluk, the occult powers are always near, and the fact that they can not be seen makes them none the less real. Around, about him everywhere are the spirits, and daily he comes in contact with people, who are the possessors of occult powers. They recognize five classes of people, who are in possession of hidden powers. They are:

> The servants of the king, that is the people in whom
> is the spirit of one of the kings;
> The beneficent medicine men or witch-doctors;
> The malignant medicine men or witch-doctors;
> The people with the power of the evil eye, and
> The people possessed of the evil spirit.

Some say that the class of people with the power to cast the evil eye receive their power from the evil medicine men, and would class them together, but very few make that classification. However, in talking about the evil eye, it always brings up the subject of the malignant medicine men. The powers claimed for the two classes are very similar.

Many say, with good reason, that the people possessed of the evil spirit should not be so called, but that their affliction is merely a disease. We would call it insanity.

These articles do not exhaust the subjects, but a little has been gleaned from the contradictory tales of the Shilluks. Often the ideas of the natives are hazy as to the powers which animate the different classes, but they have no doubt as to the power of the people who make the claims.

The Shilluks believe firmly in the power of the evil eye. A few claim that the people who cast the evil eye belong to the evil medicine men, and receive their power from them, but the people are almost unanimous in saying that they have their power separately, and they think that it comes from God. The fact that the power is inherited tends to prove that they are really a separate class.

When one person in a family has the evil eye, the house is spoken of as the house or family with the evil eye, though all the members of the family may not have that power. A man may have this power, and his wife be all right, or it may be the wife that is affected, but in every case all their children are affected, though the unaffected husband may have untainted children by another wife. This taint is carried by their descendants, and theoretically at least is supposed to extend to the end of time.

A girl who has the power of the evil eye is not sought in marriage, and while the man afflicted in this manner is not desirable as a husband, yet he does not have so much trouble in getting a wife. This is not because they differentiate between the sexes, but because a man pays a heavy dowry for his wife, and he does not want to buy a tainted wife, whose children will also bear the taint of a hidden power. If the afflicted man has the price, the father is very often willing to accept him for a son-in-law, and that is especially true, when the daughter is not very desirable. As a class the people with the evil eye try to keep their neighbours ignorant of their powers.

In addition to those who inherit the evil eye, others suddenly receive the power. It suddenly falls upon them, or comes on them. They know not how it comes, but suddenly they find themselves with that dread power.

A person possessed of the evil eye can not always be distinguished. The fact that a certain person has that power is known in his own village, and the stranger coming in soon enquires about it, and is told. However one mark can be relied on to some extent, and that is if a person has eyes in which the whites are small, and the iris is large in proportion, and the iris is very dark. This test is not sure as some people of the class do not have this mark, and others, who do not have the power have the mark.

The possessed is conscious of the fact that he has the power and may even mention the fact. The power is made operative by looking fixedly at the person to be made the victim. The person exercising the power is usually in anger when the deed is done. The person who is bewitched says the eye went into me, and if the person who did the deed speaks of it, he will usually say that his eye went into the person.

The evil eye does not always take effect in the same part of the body. If the curse falls on the eye, the person will have sore eyes terminating in blindness. They recognize three causes of blindness, other than accidents. Blindness may follow the small pox, or measles, or else it is the result of the evil eye. When the evil eye strikes the ear, deafness is the result, and when it is on the head, sores and swellings appear on the head. When the body is affected, it is covered with sores. The intestines or the liver may be the part afflicted, and they swell to unnatural size, and the worst part about it is that the swelling is permanent. One young man, who was a very fine looking child, was afflicted thus, and ever since he has been out of proportion. The doctors called it enlargement of the spleen. A man who is a very swift runner may have the evil eye take effect in his feet, and in that case the feet swell, and the victim has trouble in walking. The curse may fall on the teeth, and they decay. The evil eye may strike the unborn babe, and it disappears. The most dangerous place to have the evil eye take effect is in the heart, and in case it does the victim can not live through the day.

The evil eye is not confined to the body, but it may also affect the domestic animals belonging to a person. When a person drinks the milk of a cow that has been touched by the evil eye, it causes his insides to swell. A very fine appearing cow is not permitted to go into the village by herself but is kept with the herd, and she is to be kept in the middle of the herd so that she may not be seen, and the curse come on her. A very fine calf is always kept hidden. Sheep may become the victims of the evil eye.

The power extends beyond animate things to the inanimate. A blacksmith may make a very fine bracelet, and it breaks as he is putting it on the wrist of the owner. The bracelet was bewitched by the evil eye. When a very fine spear breaks when it is being polished just after it is made, it is because of the evil eye.

As can be seen from some of the effects of the evil eye, the Shilluk's idea of sickness has much to do with the increasing of their belief in the evil eye. They do not think of a disease as being contagious so much, as they think of it being spread by some hostile agency. Some people carry their views to such lengths, that they are inclined to think that every accident, and every case of sickness is caused by some occult agency. The power may be exercised by some other agent than the person with the evil eye.

When a person is taken sick, all the symptoms are very thoroughly discussed by the people of the village, and if some mysterious features or circumstances are brought to light, it is immediately looked upon as a visitation from some occult power. Most cases of sickness present some puzzling features, and so it is easy to give credit to the evil eye for much of it. Most accidents occur not because someone was careless, but because some hidden power was invoked against the person. The patient is then taken to the good medicine man. He goes through certain forms to determine the source of the evil charm. He may decide it is from the evil eye, or from an evil medicine man.

When a medicine man undertakes to cure a case of the evil eye, he aims to do two things. The first is to cure the person suffering, and the second is to put that particular charmer with the evil eye out of business. A sheep is brought, and the medicine man heats a nail red-hot. With the nail he blinds the sheep. He then tells the patient that he is cured, and at the same time the burning out the eyes of the sheep is a type of what will happen to the person who cast the spell. His eyes will waste away. If the eyes of the person who cast the spell do not become inflamed, the cure does not take effect. When the person who casts the charm hears of the cure performed by the medicine man, he hastens to him at night, and beseeches him to spare his eyes. The medicine man exacts a good fee from him, and then assures him that he will save his eyes, but warns him not to do it again, and threatens to kill him if he sees him casting the evil eye on another person.

A person with the evil eye can cure a person who is suffering from the evil eye. Of course he gets a good fee for it. Before he takes the case he gets a small fee, such as a sheep or a hoe, and after the case is cured he demands a large fee, usually a cow. The patient sits down near the person who is to treat him. The latter says: "You have come near me, therefore you will not die." He then grinds up a bit of wood, and putting it in water, makes the patient drink it.

The spell of the evil eye may be cast in the presence of people, and all present even to the victim may be ignorant of what is being done, though it may be known. The man with the evil eye may be seen staring at the victim. For that reason the Shilluks do not like to have a person look them in the eye. When a person stares at a Shilluk, he usually averts his eyes, or protests.

When the evil eye has been cast on a person, he very seldom tries to discover the identity of the person who bewitched him. Should the person boast of having done it, he will be fined as though he had killed a man. The victim may have seen the person staring at him, and directly accuse him of the act, but that is not always safe, as the case is brought before a medicine man. If the person accused of casting the evil eye shows fear he is guilty, and must pay a fine equal to that paid for killing a man. If he shows no fear, it was a false accusation, and in that case the accuser must pay an equal fine for his false charge.

The motive for using the evil eye is usually envy or jealousy or anger, for the evil eye always picks a shining mark, it does not fall on poor people, nor is a poor thing bewitched. A poor man may occasionally be the victim of the evil eye, but it is always an accident, as he has eaten food that has been bewitched to catch a richer person. They take some precautions to avoid the evil eye.

If a person has some very choice food, it is covered so that the evil eye may not fall on it. Food is very often bewitched, but it is usually meat or fish that is tainted, and it is very seldom that food made from grain is affected. Food that has had the evil eye cast on it can be made fit to eat by giving some of it to a dog. They say that the dog takes off the eye. The milk of a cow that has been affected can be cleansed by taking some of it in a vessel, and pouring it on a fire. The fire is put out, and from that time the milk of that cow is safe to use. If these precautions are not taken, the food will cause nausea. After the nausea has passed, evil consequences may remain, or a person may be all right.

The natives weave their hair into fantastic shapes. If a person has very fine hair, he puts a few thorns in it to keep off the evil eye. Should the evil eye fall on his hair, his head would break out in sores.

When a person has his body well oiled or covered with some fine ashes, he is very likely to have the evil eye cast on him. To escape that misfortune he takes a cucumber like pod from a wild plant, and takes out the seeds. Some of the seeds are put on the temples, and some on the neck, and others on the tip of the shoulder blade, or the entire fruit may be worn suspended from the neck.

When butter is boiled to clarify it, the work is usually done at night so that the evil eye may not be cast on it.

The Shilluks will not say that they are in good circumstances, lest it be heard by some envious person, and he should cast the evil eye on their possessions. When a rich man is asked in regard to his property, he usually says I have one or two cows, but they are very poor cows.

The parents of a very fine looking child do not like to let people see it for fear someone will cast the evil eye on it, and the parent is very angry when someone comments on the good appearance of the child.

Should the child be taken sick, the parents call on the person who made the remark, and demand that he pay the fine required when a person is killed. The accused usually holds out, and a compromise is effected. He brings a sheep, and one of its ears is cut off. The sheep then is a witness against the man, and by doing that, he assumes the responsibility for the child. If it dies, he pays the fine as though he had killed it. Even if the child reaches maturity and dies, the man is responsible and must pay the fine.

Frequently people have hard knots in their flesh. These are really stones that have been put there by someone with the evil eye. The swellings do not disappear.

The Shilluks have a custom that when a person is threshing his grain, they go to beg from him. Sometimes they go in such numbers that the man has very little left for himself, but he does not dare to refuse for fear someone in the party may cast the evil eye on him. He gets even by going to beg from some other person.

They give a few warnings as to conduct when with a person who has the evil eye.

If you walk with a person who has the evil eye, let him walk in front, for if you go in front you give him a good chance to cast the evil eye on you.

When a person with the evil eye begs from you, grant his request, because when he accepts your present his power over you is broken, and he can not injure you. He may regain his power if he comes again and is refused, for if you refuse him, he becomes angry and casts the evil eye on you.

When eating, let the oldest of the party take the food first, so that if the evil eye has fallen on the food he may detect it, and the food can be cleansed.

When eating with a man who has the evil eye, do not eat much or he will kill you.

When you are angry at a certain village, do not enter that village or you will get the evil eye.

Do not speak harshly to a man who has the evil eye, or he will cast the spell on you.

Once a man gave his daughter to the king to be his wife. The girl had the evil eye, and when the king learned that fact, he gave the woman to another man lest she kill his other wives.

At the present time a chief is suffering from the evil eye. The people of another village had stolen his cow. He went to the village in anger, and talked harshly. While there he felt a chill run through his body. He went home, and took sick. His body has sores on it that have come from the evil eye.

The man with the power to cast the evil eye is feared by the people, but he is not feared as much as the evil medicine man. When he causes death, it is usually sudden, though it may be lingering. When a person with the evil eye dies, the people of the village rejoice, though they do not show their joy openly.

The possessors of the evil eye are deceived even as the people who fear them. They go through life apart from their fellow men in many respects. They believe in their own evil powers, and while their claims sound childish to us, yet we must consider the fact that the history of the English speaking world reveals the fact that our ancestors were afraid of witches, even after they had reached a much greater development than the Shilluk has attained.

The Evil Eye and Infant Health in Lebanon

*Jamal Karam Harfouche**

In this remarkable investigation of the evil eye in Lebanon, we find quite a contrast with most anecdotal reports from other areas. First of all, Jamal Kamal Harfouche is a professor of maternal and child health in the school of public health at the American University in Beirut and the focus of the research was upon infant care and the maternal attitudes towards such care. The data was systematically obtained from 379 expectant mothers through interviews and questionnaires. These mothers were essentially a self-selected group insofar as they all elected to avail themselves of the facilities of the prenatal clinic at the Outpatient Department of the American University Hospital in Beirut between August, 1960, and February, 1962. The selections presented here were taken from a book which treated such topics as: Breast-feeding and maternal attitude in the prenatal period, Maternal diet during pregnancy and birthmarks, Maternal diet in the postpartum period, Breast-feeding during early neonatal period, Dietary, emotional and other factors affecting lactation, etc. The reason why the evil eye was included concerned its undeniable influence in the maternal nursing situation. The reader will see that looking at the evil eye from the perspective of a professional in the public health field provides a different picture. Moreover, the evil eye as a critical factor in maternal care reminds us of its continuing importance in the modern world. It is not merely

* Reprinted from Jamal Karam Harfouche, *Infant Health in Lebanon: Customs and Taboos* (Beirut: Khayats, 1965), pp. 81–106.

a quaint superstition but a folk belief with serious implications with respect to how individuals perceive the world and their place in it.

Another praiseworthy feature of Professor Harfouche's account consists of the ethnic differentiation of the interview sample. The sample included 131 Armenians, 130 Maronites (Christians) and 118 Sunni (Moslems). Thus instead of simply generalizing about Lebanon in general, Professor Harfouche is able to distinguish differences in belief among different ethnic/religious groups. In addition, the numbers of responses to a given question afford some statistical indication of the frequency and perhaps degree of belief in various facets of the evil eye complex.

The information presented in this section was obtained by home visits, talking to mothers during their repeated visits to the clinic, and largely by asking these questions during the prenatal or early postnatal periods.

1. Does the evil-eye affect your milk supply?
   Yes .... *No* ....
   If yes; how? ....
2. Does the evil-eye affect your baby's health?
   Yes .... *No* ....
   If yes; how? ....

Effect of Evil-Eye on Lactating Mothers

Of the 379 mothers interviewed, 208 or (54.9%) expressed belief in its harmful effects. Of these, Sunni and Maronites led, as shown in Table 1.

Most mothers expressing belief based their credence on personal experience, or on that of others. Only three percent said they learned of it in their community. Regardless of whether the effect was experienced or related, the common practice was to counteract the harmful effect by repellents. Of the latter, the physician, and other health workers, are thought to be ignorant. Many prevent the evil-eye by using charms, relics and other protective measures described in the following chapter.

TABLE 1
Harmful Effect of Evil-Eye on Milk Supply

Type of Answer	Armenian No.	Armenian %	Maronite No.	Maronite %	Sunni No.	Sunni %	Total No.	Total %
No opinion	37	28.2	87	66.9	84	71.2	208	54.9
Yes	93	71.0	43	33.1	32	27.1	168	44.3
No	1	0.8	—	—	2	1.7	3	0.8
Total	131		130		118		379	

What Invites The Evil-Eye? In this instance, the person accused of having an evil-eye, (often referred to by Sunni and Maronite mothers, as an "empty-eye") is an envious woman. She is not necessarily blue-eyed, and is not usually aware of the harmful effect of her "empty," or "envious eye." "If aware, she cannot help it." Such a woman may be a neighbor, friend, relative, a mere childless stranger, or even one with a poor milk supply. However, these two characteristics are not always a reason for having an envious or an evil-eye.

The affected mother is usually reputed to have large breasts, and a milk supply that arouses jealousy or envy in others. She can be spared the ill-effect if the evil-eyed observer, the mother, or any person present, mentions the Deity, while the envious comment is being made.

It is not considered advisable for a mother to nurse in public for her own protection and safety. However, her presence is not necessary for the evil-eye to work. An exclamatory remark expressing surprise at the abundance of her milk by an envious person can exert an adverse effect on the milk even in her absence.

Other Invitations:

Bragging or boasting: A lactating mother, family members, neighbors, friends and admirers, can also invite the evil-eye by boasting about a mother's good milk supply in the presence of others.

Nagging: In-laws or any trouble-making member of the family may cause the milk to decrease, or dry up completely; this through envy or dislike of the lactating mother.

Types of Effect:

The effect of the evil-eye is sudden and immediate. "It hits like a bullet." The affected person is incapacitated without previous warning, apparent cause, or explanation. The harmful effect on mother's milk, as described by interviewees, may be of a direct or an indirect nature.

a. The direct effect may be quantitative, or qualitative.

   The quantitative direct effect: The most widely experienced (36.4%) quantitative direct harmful effect is "drying up" or "complete suppression" of the milk. In this instance, the evil-eye is said to "snatch the milk from the lactating mother." This was held mostly by Maronites and Sunnis, to a lesser degree by Armenians. If the suppression is complete, the effect is usually irreversible and the mother is thought to lose her milk throughout the lactation period.

   The next widely experienced quantitative direct harmful effect is a "decrease" in the milk supply, or a "partial suppression," as indicated by 25.4 percent of the answers. This may be reversible or irreversible. If reversible, a mother expects a return of her milk shortly after the beginning of the adverse effect. This may take place either spontaneously, or by resorting to the use of evil-eye repellents.

The qualitative direct effect: Belief in this effect is held mostly by Sunni and Maronites (13.1%). In this instance, the milk is said to become "lighter," "watery," "poisonous or harmful to the baby." "It spoils and changes into pus and blood."

b. The indirect effect: was described by 24.4 percent of answers expressed by all mothers. The milk undergoes a quantitative or qualitative change as a result of sickness which affects the mother and her breast.

If the evil-eye hits the breast, it becomes "painful," "swollen," "inflamed," "develops a boil or abscess." The mother is incapacitated, her milk supply decreases or dries up completely. The affected breast "ceases to function and an operation may be needed." Three mothers (two Maronnites and one Sunni) stated that an eye-shaped patch appears around the nipple.

When the evil-eye affects the mother, she "gets sick," "develops fever," or "loses weight." As a result, her milk decreases or dries up completely. It "becomes poisonous," and "harmful to the baby" who also "gets sick," "vomits," "develops boils" and "fever."

Effect of Evil-Eye on the Infant

Of the 379 mothers, 308, or (81.3%) expressed belief in the harmful effect. Of these, Sunni and Maronites were in the lead (Table 2).

Of the mothers who expressed belief in the evil-eye effect on the infant, 23 percent of the Maronites, 10 percent of the Sunni and 4 percent of the Armenians stated that they had seen their own child, or the child of a close relative, neighbor or friend, go through such an experience. Only 11 percent of Maronites, 9 percent of the Sunni and 0.8 percent of the Armenians stated they had heard women in their community speak of the evil effect. The remainder did not specify.

TABLE 2
Harmful Effect of Evil-Eye on Infant

Type of Answer	Ethnic Group							
	Armenian		Maronite		Sunni		Total	
	No.	%	No.	%	No.	%	No.	%
Yes	97	74.0	109	83.8	102	86.5	308	81.3
No	34	26.0	21	16.2	15	12.7	70	18.5
No opinion	—	—	—	—	1	0.8	1	0.2
Total	131		130		118		379	

On the whole, women are thought to be more possessed of the evil-eye than men, although both sexes may exert a harmful effect on the infant. A woman exerts her "evil-effect" by watching the infant nurse, playing with it, touching it, or speaking of it in a boastful manner without mentioning the name of the Deity or the Cross. A woman who exerts a harmful effect through her words, rather than her look or touch, is described by Armenians as having "a bad breath." "When her breath reaches the baby he gets sick."

Type of Infant Most Frequently Affected: A common belief among interviewees is that nursing infants and small children in general are more subject to the evil-eye than older children and adults. Of these, the most vulnerable are male infants who enjoy perfect health and good looks. Such infants may even fall victim to their own mothers' evil, or empty-eye, in as much as they are thought to be perfection. In one instance, an Armenian mother (when her infant case No. 75 was brought to the clinic for his 18-months check-up) had an extensive first degree burn covering her neck and the upper part of her back. When asked about the burn, she said that the infant had developed fever and swollen glands in the neck, shortly after his 15 months visit. A diagnosis of "evil-eye disease" was made by the maternal grandmother. She poured hot melted lead (commonly referred to as *sakbeh,* by Arabic-speaking mothers) into a deep plate filled with water to detect the suspect and repel the evil-effect. The mother held the plate over the infant's head. The melted lead was poured into the water three times. The third time the lead separated into granules making a loud noise "like a bullet." Some hot granules scattered and struck the mother on the neck and upper back as she bent over the water to look for the image of the suspect. To the grandmother the noise was indicative of the "evil-eye disease" and the burned neck was positive proof that the "mother was the suspect." This diagnosis very likely made the mother feel guilty and refuse the proposed laboratory tests necessary to arrive at a proper diagnosis.

Type of Effect: The harmful effects of the evil-eye on the infant, as described by interviewees, carry a wide range of severity. If the hit happens to be light there may be mild illness and if it is severe there may be sudden death. The severe effect producing disability or death is by far the most common of the two.

The onset of evil-eye disease is often sudden and dramatic. The evil-eye is said to hit "like a bullet." Prior to its effect the infant has no complaints and appears usually to be in perfect health.

Some of the symptoms of evil-eye disease are commonly indicative of serious illness and may be alarming to the physician (i.e., tremors, convulsive seizure, severe spells of crying, refusal to nurse, color changes, as becoming blue, or black etc).

In classifying the various effects according to the frequency of answers, central nervous system manifestations occupied the third place, gastro-intestinal tract symptoms occupied the sixth place, with sudden illness and death occupying the first and second order respectively (Table 3).

TABLE 3

Harmful Effect of Evil-Eye on Infant

Type of Effect	No. of Answers	%
1. Sudden illness	166	33.1
2. Instant death	81	16.2
3. Central nervous system (restless, irritable, drowsy, listless, unconscious, tremors, convulsions, paralysis, crippled, deformed, headache, severe crying)	78	15.6
4. High fever	71	14.2
5. Stunted growth (withers, loses weight, grows weak)	37	7.4
6. Gastro-intestinal tract (diarrhea, dysentery, colic, vomiting, poor appetite, stops nursing)	30	6.0
7. Skin (boils, rash, abscess, turns pale, blue or black)	20	3.9
8. Others: (blindness, poisoning, ceases walking, etc.)	18	3.6
Total	501	

Since belief in the harmful effect of the evil-eye on infants is widespread, whenever a diagnosis of the ailment is made by the mother or someone else, evil-eye repellents are first tried before seeking medical advice. This order of priority in dealing with sudden and severe illness among infants is based on the following reasons:

1. The physician is thought to be ignorant of the illnesses caused by the evil-eye.

2. Medicines prescribed by physicians do not help evil-eye disease or diseases.

3. If the evil-eye is not detected (or remains unknown) and is not repelled immediately by those who know, then the sudden and severe illness may lead to immediate death or a disability.

During one of our home visits, a three-months-old Sunni baby (case no. 149) was revealed to have a first degree burn on the arm for which the mother sought medication. When asked about the burn, the mother stated that two days previously the baby had a sudden, severe and continuous crying spell which she attributed to the evil-eye. While pouring hot melted lead into a vessel over the baby's head, a few drops fell on his arm and burned it. In this instance the mother made her own diagnosis of evil-eye disease. She treated the baby independently although she was instructed to visit the clinic whenever she felt the baby needed examination by the attending physician.

The art of healing an evil-eye disease is a reality in the lives of the Lebanese mothers with whom we dealt. This art is an institution with ardent advocates and sponsors who uphold its established concepts and practices. Within its system the role as well as the characteristics of the suspect (or the person possessed of an evil-eye), the patient, the diagnostician, and the druggist are easily defined.

The suspect is the envious person who unconsciously exerts the evil-effect on others. The effect is transmitted by a look, a touch, an expression of envy, or a "bad breath."

The patient is the envied healthy, handsome child.

The diagnostician is the shrewd and experienced one who inspires confidence and is endowed with special insight. Like the physician, he is also a healer or a performer who counteracts or removes the evil-effect with his drug or performance once the diagnosis has been made.

The druggist dispenses herbs, incense, lead, charms and special preparations in the correct proportions. Like the pharmacist in a Western setting, he has a shop[a] from which he makes a living.

Evidence obtained in this study indicates that the healing art of the evil-eye in Lebanon has a cross-cultural pattern with an informal type of schooling to disseminate its concepts and practices. Apprenticeship in the art is perfected within the family circle; the sons and daughters learning from their parents.

Like Western medicine, the healing art of the evil-eye has a preventive and a curative aspect. The devices used in each case depend upon a proper understanding of the cause, effect and mode of transmission by an intelligent specialist with adequate training and perseverance in his art.

On the whole, it may be said that the preventive and curative devices known to interviewees combine witchcraft with religious practices. Whereas the witchcraft devices have a cross-cultural pattern, the religious devices have a limited use with ethnic specifications to a varying degree.

The witchcraft devices, whether curative or preventive, rest largely upon two fundamental principles which constitute the roots of magic.[1]

1. The devices based on the law of similarity which may be termed "homeopathic, or imitative magic," whereby "like produces like," or "effect resembles cause."

2. The devices based on the law of contact, or contagion which may be termed "contagion magic," whereby the things which have once been in contact continue ever afterwards to act on each other.

Both principles derive from a false conception of natural law.

The system of sympathetic magic based on the laws of similarity and contagion is composed of positive as well as negative precepts. It tells one what to do and what not to do.

The positive precepts: Positive magic or sorcery says "Do this in order that so-and-so may happen." Its aim is to produce a "desired event." Charms or amulets constitute a good example of the positive precept in magic.

The negative precepts: Negative magic prohibits. It says "Do not do this, lest so-and-so happen." Its aim is to avoid an undesirable event. Taboo is a negative application of practical magic.

The devices used by interviewees, either to prevent or to avert the effect of the evil-eye, once it has taken place, represent the positive precepts of magic because they are meant to produce a "desired event." Each of these categories will be considered separately.

Preventive Devices

Charms (or amulets) and relics: In contrast to relics, charms have no religious value, but are believed to have a magic power and consist of what we commonly refer to as witchcraft. The known types of charms may be divided into two varieties.

Spells or verbal charms such as an incantation, a magic formula, a song or verse which is chanted or repeated in a low voice, over the affected jointly with a special act performed by the exorcist to drive out the evil-effect. Verbal charms are largely used by interviewees for cure, and will be considered under the curative devices.

Amulets, or object charms (visible, or encased and concealed) are worn to avert ill or to secure good fortune. They are largely used for preventive purposes, especially among infants and children noted for their proneness to sorcery. The use of amulets by Lebanese mothers seems to have a cross-cultural pattern, and the same type, or types are used by mothers in the three ethnic groups. Amulets may be used alone or jointly with relics for their synergistic effect.

Only 104 (or 27.4%) out of 379 interviewees (Table 4) stated that they use charms to protect their infants from the evil-eye. However in actual practice almost every baby in each of the observed ethnic groups was seen with a set of charms either pinned over the shoulder or hanging on a golden chain around the neck or wrist.

TABLE 4
Use of Charms to Avert Effect of Evil-Eye

Type of Answer	Ethnic Group							
	Armenian		Maronite		Sunni		Total	
	No.	%	No.	%	No.	%	No.	%
Yes	23	17.6	47	36.2	34	28.8	104	27.4
No	107	81.7	80	61.5	82	69.5	269	71.0
No opinion	1	0.7	3	2.3	2	1.7	6	1.6
Total	131		130		118		379	

Some of the amulets or charms most commonly used were given to us by mothers while others were purchased at a special shop which also carries evil-eye disease repellents and drugs.

The blue bead is the amulet most widely-used by the three ethnic groups. It is smooth and round, a symbol of the full moon "the increaser," "the multiplier," "the giver of life, of growth and of fertility." It secures good luck and averts the ill-effects brought about by the dark phase of the moon. In the absence of the moon the powers of sorcery and black magic may be evoked to work their mischief unchecked, "for Hecate, the dark moon, was captain of the horde of ghosts and mistress of black magic."[2]

The soft blue color represents the mild and refreshing light of the moon which invites the dew, initiates vegetation, promotes growth, and generates life. The blue color may also be symbolic of the sky in which the moon rises.

In ancient civilizations the full moon was thought to have a special bearing on mothers and children. Diana was famed for blessing women with children. She presided over childbirth and was called "opener of the womb." Artemis, the Greek prototype of Diana, "would not even speak to childless women." Anahita purified the milk of nursing infants and the womb of females. She was also invoked by marriageable girls and by women in childbirth.[2] Aristotle taught that the course of a disease was influenced by the moon cycle. Galen believed that infants born between the last and first quarters of the moon were weaker and more susceptible to infections than those born during the waxing phase and the full moon.

The horseshoe is also widely used by the three ethnic groups. It may be symbolic of the crescent or the waxing phase of the moon, "the power of growth, and patron of all things that grow."[2] It secures good fortune and averts the ill-effects brought about by the waning moon which was conceived by primitive peoples as being overcome by the dragon or eaten up by a dark and destructive power. Under the waning moon it was said that all things were diminished and brought low. By natural deduction, this phase was considered unlucky for any enterprise, such as sowing grain that needed growth. Many ancient kings wore a horned head dress emblematic of the "horned moon."

The crescent has been used through the ages as a charm to bring increase of flocks, herds, corn and more particularly increase in the family; a greatly desired blessing. The flags of some Middle Eastern countries still bear the crescent as emblem of power and national pride. The horned crescent rises high over minarets and the domes of mosques. It is still felt lucky, by many peoples, to see the new moon. "Take money and turn it over for the moon, and the increaser will multiply it for you."

In Lebanon, belief in the increasing and decreasing effects of the moon on growth is widely held by farmers in all sectors of the country. The agricultural pattern is largely dictated by the moon cycle. The Lebanese farmer watches for *al-hillat* or *al-hilal* (the waxing moon) to sow and reap the crop, to trim and graft the plants. The eleventh day of the lunar month is considered the day of choice for breeding cattle. Lebanese Muslims fast and feast with the rise of the new moon. With the waning phase, or *al-naksat,* even the human mind is thought, in some localities, to wane. Man's sanity and insanity, as well as his mood and behavior are believed to turn in cycles like the moon. With *al-naksat,* the sane is apt to become jittery, and the insane "becomes agitated and out of control."

The hand of Fatima is almost as widely used as the blue bead and the horseshoe. It may be made of blue glass, of wood, or of metal (silver or gold). Its use is consistent with the well-known verbal charm "Five in the eye of the devil," which is used for protective purposes, especially by Sunni mothers.

The hand of Fatima is thought to represent the stretched hand of the dead, with sharp and pointed fingers, directed like spikes to pluck out the evil-eye, or to make it blind. For just as the dead can neither see, nor hear, nor speak, so one may on homeopathic principles render envious people blind, deaf and dumb by the use of dead men's bodies, or of anything that is tainted by the infection of death. In Europe, properties of the dead were ascribed to the "hand of glory," a dry and pickled hand of a man who had been hanged. "It rendered motionless all persons to whom it was presented, they could not stir a finger any more than if they were dead."[1]

A Glass Eye, round or heart shaped, with a black pupil surrounded by a halo of blue, is used by three ethnic groups, but less commonly than the blue bead. Its use is consistent with the common saying "an eye for an eye," and is in accordance with the law of similarity in imitative magic, whereby "like produces like," and the evil-eye is thought to be repelled by an eye of a similar nature.

Alum is usually cut in a triangular shape to be used as such, or with a set of blue beads trimming the edge. It may be pinned on a place where it shows, or it may be wrapped in a piece of paper or cloth and pinned to the underwear of the infant where it does not show. In either case, alum is thought to act like a shield, when the infant is hit with the evil-eye the alum cracks and the infant is spared. Alum is also thought to burn or to cauterize the evil-eye just as it cauterizes a wound.

Wood: a piece of wood from *al-mais* tree (known also in Arabic as *lotos* or *al-nasham-el-abyad*) round, elongated in shape, and pierced in the middle to hang on a thread, or to be pinned on the infant (with a piece of alum, and a blue bead, for their synergistic effect), is commonly used by the three ethnic groups, especially Sunni, to avert ill or to secure good fortune. If *al-mais* wood is not available, a piece of wood from an old armchair may be used as a substitute.

Al-Mais tree (Celtis Australis, Fam. Urticaceae) derives its Arabic name from the verb *mayasa (mayasan)* which signifies the libration of the moon. It is thought to grow in the moonlight, and bears a small fruit which is round like the moon. In English, it is called lote or nettle tree. To nettle means "to fret, to sting as with nettles, hence to irritate," or to produce urticaria.

The tree (Zizyphus lotus, Greek lotos) is reputed to bear the lotus fruit represented in Hindu and Egyptian Art. The Indian lotus (Nelumbo Nucifera) was considered sacred. The Egyptian lotus was used as the floral emblem of Egypt. In the Odyssey, the lotus eaters who subsisted on the lotus fruit lived in the dreamy indolence it produced. The lotus is also related to "lot," a word of Teutonic origin, meaning "fortune," "the fate which falls to one by the powers overruling man's destiny." From it also derive the words "lottery" (an affair of chance), and "lotto" (a game of chance).

The use of wood as an amulet is consistent with the verbal charm "touch wood," which is almost universally known, and finds its roots in magic, as well as in ancient religious beliefs.

The use of wood in homeopathic magic is based on two principles.[1]

The principle of animated trees and plants, whereby the tree is conceived as the "embodiment, or the abode of the life-spirit," "tree-god" or "a vegetation spirit" credited with the power of causing the rain to fall, flocks and herds to multiply, and women to bring forth easily.

The principle of the transference of evil, whereby the plant "can infect man just as much as man can infect the plant." "Action and reaction are equal and opposite." Because it is possible to shift a load of wood from our own back to the back of another, primitive man also believed that the evil of which he seeks to rid himself may well be transferred to a person, a tree, or a piece of wood which acts as a vehicle to convey the evil to the first person who touches it.

Relics, or Religious Charms

The most widely used relics by Sunni mothers are: *ayat-el-kursi, masha'a-allah, masshaf kareem, hijab* or *hirz* (that which is written and hidden to protect and fortify without being seen). Maronite, and Armenian mothers used a cross, a medal (Madonna, or patron saint), *dakhira* or *thakheera* in which a relic from a patron saint is concealed (i.e., hair, piece of clothing, wood, etc.). They also used a *hijab* or *hirz,* but less commonly than the Sunni, Armenians referred to it as *nusga* or *nuskha* (a copy).

Curative Devices

The devices known to interviewees used in their community to avert the ill-effect of the evil-eye also have a cross-cultural pattern. These combine witchcraft and religious practices to a varying degree.

Of all informants in the three ethnic groups, 86.0 percent (93.2% Sunni, 90.0% Maronite, 75.6% Armenian) knew of such devices. 65 percent gave the names of the devices with a detailed description of the procedure. The rest stated they had only heard of the device and were unable to specify details.

The practiced, or heard-of devices, fall into six major categories (Table 5). Any one of these may be used alone or with devices falling under other classifications.

TABLE 5

Curative Devices

Types practised or known	No. of Answers	%
1. *Rakwi (Al Rukyat)*	124	26.3
2. Fumigation (incense)	119	25.2
3. *Sakbeh* (melted lead)	90	19.1
4. Charms	53	11.2
5. Prayers (read over the head)	52	11.0
6. *Takbees* (exerting gentle pressure over the head)	34	7.2
Total	472	

Al-rukyat is commonly referred to as *al-rakwi* or *rakwi* and the performer is known as *raki* or *al-raki* or *al-rakyat* for a female. It was mentioned most by Maronites (42.7% of answers) and least by Armenians (14.2%) with Sunni between the two (16.7%). It is based on the claim that a *raki* by resorting to supernatural forces becomes endowed with the power of controlling, or changing the course of an event. The procedures used for performing a *rakwi* have a cross-cultural pattern with some variations in combining witchcraft with religious practices.

The most common procedure consists of citing an incantation, or repeating a secret prayer over a liquid medium, such as water, olive oil, milk and orange blossom held in a small vessel (usually a bowl, *tasset al-ra'abi*) over the head of the affected infant. Of the liquids, water is the most popular. Olive oil is used only by Christians (Maronites and Armenians).

Following the incantation, or prayer, the infant is given the liquid to drink. Part of the water may also be used to wash the face and/or, other parts of the body. Armenians discard some of the water on the cross roads, in a flower pot or in the garden. Olive oil is used by Maronites and Armenians to paint the sign of the cross on the forehead, or to rub the baby on the affected site.

If the incantation is repeated over salt instead of a liquid, the salt is wrapped in a piece of cloth and pinned on the baby.

The prevailing belief among the informants is that an incantation, or a secret prayer, fit for use in performing *al-rakwi* is known only to a few people in the community. These are usually women, more often than not Druze or Sunni, (as stated by Maronite mothers) who yawn several times while citing the incantation. If the performer sheds tears over the liquid while yawning, it is a strong indication that the infant is hit by the evil-eye. Tears of the yawning performer are also capable of repelling the evil-eye, especially if they fall on the body of the affected infant. Some Maronite mothers stated that incantations for performing *al-rakwi* were available for sale at special shops in Beirut city. They are also of the opinion that such incantations often include a mention of "Allah," "Jesus" and "*Mariam-bint-Amran,*" "*Issa,*" "*Musa,*" "King Solomon." When Maronite mothers perform their own rakwi, the Lord's prayer is cited 3[b] or 7[c] times in the reverse order. Passages from the psalms of David and other parts of the Holy Bible, may also be used, with or without the Lord's prayer.

Armenians also make extensive use of prayers from Narek,[d] and less commonly from the Bible and Gyprianos or Cyprianos.[e] Sunni read an *ayat* from the Kora'n or a passage from *al-hadith.* Some stated that an incantation may be taught by a man to a woman, but not by one woman to another.

The following variations in procedure were mentioned by Armenians only.

The use of matches: While repeating the Lord's Prayer, 3 times, 3 matches are burned and thrown into the water. Both water and matches are later discarded in a corner.

The use of bread and a sharp object: A loaf, or a piece of bread is poked with a knife or scissors, making the sign of the cross over the baby's head while repeating the Lord's Prayer. Pins, needles or a comb may be put in the water.

The use of metal is based on the belief that not only by certain acts can the soul be imperilled, but the danger extends to bringing it into contact with certain material objects deemed potentially noxious. Especially noxious and dangerous are objects made of iron. The disfavor in which iron is held by the Gods and their ministers is so great that its use as a charm for banning ghosts and other dangerous spirits is well known. The Jews used no iron tools in building the temple at Jerusalem or in making altars. Scottish Highlanders refrained from putting iron in the ground on Good Friday, since fairies who lived underground might resent having the roof pulled from over their head. In Morocco it is considered a great protection against demons, hence it is usual to place an iron knife, or a dagger, under a sick man's pillow. After a death various peoples refrain from the use of sharp instruments so long as the ghost of the deceased is supposed to be near, lest they might wound it.[1]

The use of charcoal: The mother burns 3, or 7 pieces of charcoal, and says a prayer from Narek, or repeats the Lord's prayer 3 or 7 times, as she puts the burning pieces of charcoal in the water, one by one. Fire is known to have a purifying effect. Charcoal is dark like the head of "Hecate" goddess of the night; when lighted it is thought to burn the evil-eye and to purify.

Another alternative is to list the names of the visitors who called on the family the day the baby was struck by the evil-eye. A charcoal fire is started, and the burning pieces of coal are dumped into a basin of water, piece by piece. During the process, the names of the visitors on the list are read, one by one. When the name of the suspected person is read, the dumped piece of charcoal floats instead of sinking to the bottom. When this happens and the suspected person is identified, the floating piece of charcoal and the water is thrown away in the middle of the crossways where the accused is likely to pass and his (or her) ill-effect is repelled.

Fumigation by incense or other substitutes: Several mothers made extensive use of incense, and/or other substitutes, either to prevent or repel the evil-eye by fumigation as indicated by 25.2 percent of their answers (15.8% Armenian, 24.8% Maronite, 36.2% Sunni).

This device bears four different explanations, each claimed by the informants to be effective.

a. The incense is used in sacred places, hence it pleases the Gods and is capable of repelling evil.

b. Fire burns evil and has a purifying effect.

c. The fumes obscure the path of evil and thus deter it.

d. Evil is incompatible with the pleasant odor of burning incense.

Fumigation may be used alone or with other devices, especially a *sakbeh* (or melted lead). This is usually followed by burning a piece of clothing of the suspect, without his or her knowledge.

Incense is readily available to all three ethnic groups. It may be brought from the church (by Armenians and Maronites), or given by a *sheihk* to Sunni mothers. It is usually burned in an open charcoal fire and the baby is waved over the fumes, 3 or 7 times, while a prayer or an incantation is said.

As an alternative, the burning incense is put in the charcoal fire in a small metal plate, or in a *majmara* (a copper burner with a wooden handle). This is passed over the infant's head, or over his body several times. One Sunni mother stated that the burning incense may be waved near the breast of the mother when her milk decreases or dries up, after a *kabsseh,* a *ra'abi,* or if she is struck by the evil-eye.

Some mothers fumigate their infants regularly for preventive purposes. Others fumigate only when the need arises. Various mixtures are used for this purpose. Directions for their use may be given to the mother by a special shopkeeper. Mixtures familiar to the informants in the three ethnic groups are listed below:

Mixtures Used by Sunni:

Ither (a piece of clothing, a thread, or a hair taken from the suspected and identified person without his or her knowledge).

Incense + *Ither.*

Incense + salt (if salt makes a crackling sound when burned over an open fire, it is highly indicative of the evil-eye. It is also believed that this sound simulates the noise made by a bullet and thus shoots the evil-eye.

Incense + salt + coriander (coriandum savitum).

Incense + salt + dry mint + onion shell + a piece of paper. While fumes are rising, the fire is poked several times, and the performer says, "May this pierce the eye of so-and so."

Incense + salt + *habet-el-barake* (black cumin) + *Ither* from 7 different persons (if the suspect is unidentified). The baby is waved 3 times over the fumes as the healer reads an *ayat* from the Kor'an.

Incense + salt + *Ither* + a head of garlic pricked with a pin. While waving the baby 3 times over the fumes, the healer says, "Five in his, or her eye."

Incense + salt + a thread from the clothes of the suspect + dry garlic roots + dry onion roots.

Lint or splinters from the four corners of the rug or mat, from the child's sleeping room + a thread, or a piece of cloth, from all those present. The baby is moved three times over the fumes while the performer repeats an *ayat* from the Kora'n.

Incense + Alum.

Incense + 3 *ayat* from a *sheikh.* Incense and one *ayat* are burned 3 times daily to fumigate the sick child.

The following is a translation of an incantation given to us by an informant.

"May Mariam, the daughter of Amran, fumigate you with her incense, during her presence and in her absence."

"While passing by the rock, the green herb she picked, fumigated *Issa,* and *Musa* with the spirit of the Almighty."

"In the name of Allah, master of the two universes, I ask the sun not to set on you an evil-eye, or an envious look."

Mixtures Used by Maronites:

Incense alone: One mother stated that she fumigates her baby with burning incense weekly to protect him from the evil-eye, or the harmful effect of a *ra'abi.*

Incense + *Ither* + mention of Allah.

Incense + splinters from four corners of the mat.

Incense + salt.

A sacred relic from the church (i.e.: dried flower, or a live branch distributed on Palm Sunday, or on Good Friday. These are kept all year round to sanctify the house, fumigate babies and prevent or repel the evil-eye). These may be used alone or with incense and salt.

Incense + soil from the street where the suspect may have trod.

Mixtures Used by Armenians:

Incense alone is the most widely used as in the case of Maronites. If the mother is sick she inhales the fumes. The infant is merely passed over the fumes three times, or until he ceases crying.

Incense + thyme + salt + onion shell + garlic shell.[f]

Ither + sugar sprinkled over it. The ash is rubbed on the forehead or on the skin.

Incense + alum.

Incense + thyme.

Incense + soot from a blackened pan + salt + onion shell + garlic shell.

Sakbeh (or a *rakwi* with melted lead poured over a liquid medium) is used to detect the suspect and avert the ill-effect of the evil-eye. Maronites use it more frequently than Armenians and Sunni (26%, 17%, 12.6% of answers respectively).

The most common procedure consists of melting a piece of lead in a spoon while saying a prayer. Once the lead is melted, it is poured into a small vessel (bowl, cup or deep plate) containing water. This is held over the head of the affected infant. When the melted lead reaches the cold water it solidifies in the shape of an eye, a face, a hand, or simulating some other feature of the suspect. For proper identification, the pouring of melted lead is usually repeated 3 times, less commonly 7 times. If lead is poured more than once, only the last *sakbeh* is usually used for identification. The preceding ones are discarded.

Modifications of this procedure were described by mothers in all groups. Some pour the lead on the floor. Others add to the water; scissors (to poke the eye), a comb (to comb it away), or a green leaf. Armenians put the melted lead in a piece of salted cloth and then discard it in the middle of a cross road. Other objects are also put in the water; a pin, onion or garlic husk, bread, old slippers, green thyme, charcoal, a needle, salt or a knife. The bread is given to the dog. The salt, thyme, onion and garlic husks are burned. The scissors and knife are not used for twenty-four hours. The pin and needle are buried in the soil. Part of the water is used to wash the baby's face or to sprinkle the house while saying a prayer. The remainder is discarded.

Al-takbees as a healing device, was only mentioned by Sunni (28.8% of answers). The infant is taken to a *sheikh*, a *sheikha*, a *hajji*, or an elderly woman known to have a healing touch. An *ayat* from the Kora'n is read by the healer while pressure is put on the infant's head or other parts of his body. At the end of the prayer he blows in the infant's face indicating that the evil-eye is extinguished by his (or her) breath.

BIBLIOGRAPHY*

1. Frazer, J.G., Gaster, T.H. The New Golden Bough. New York: Criterion Books, Inc. 1959.

2. Harding, E.M. Woman's Mysteries, Ancient and Modern. New York: Pantheon Books, Inc. 1955.

3. Sarafian, K.A. St. Gregory of Narek and Narek. Fresno, California, 1951.

NOTES

a. Dabbous chain stores found in Beirut carry evil-eye disease repellents and drugs.

b. The odd number 3 may be related in its use to the old Babylonian cult which conceptualized Sinn, god of the moon as triune composed of three persons. These three persons, or gods, are Anu, Enlil or Bal, and Ea. They represent the three phases of the moon. Ishtar, like Sinn her predecessor, is also triune. She is goddess of heaven, goddess of earth, and goddess of the underworld (thus the 3 worlds). The statue of the moon goddess was often crowned with a turreted head-dress, or symbolised by three pillars, or three buds, with the crescent moon above them. In the combined form, the moon goddess was composed of Artemis (the crescent or waxing moon), Selene, (the full moon), and Hecate (the waning and dark moon). The rites of this goddess were performed at night in order to turn aside her wrath and the evil she so often wrought. She is "Dea Triformis of the cross-ways" who leads travellers astray. As queen of the ghosts, she sweeps through the night followed by her "dreadful train of questing spirits." She is goddess of storms, of destruction and

* This bibliography is greatly reduced from the fifty-one item bibliography found in the original book. Most of the items concerned pediatrics and maternal care. Only those few references actually used in the evil eye discussion have been reproduced here. However, the reference style of the original source has been preserved. Ed. Note.

of the terrors of the night. She brings sickness and death. Even as late as medieval times witches were "seen" flying through the air headed by Hecate herself. The idea of the threefold nature of the feminine divinity was present in the legends of the three Maries in the Christian Faith. Islam, has accepted these three holy virgins and incorporated them into the religious system of the prophet as the "three daughters of Allah." They retain the ancient names of the three aspects of the Arabian moon goddess. *Al-Ilat, Al-Uzza* (the black stone which is still venerated) and *Manat* (stands for time, in the sense of fate. It is equivalent to the Hindu concept of Karma and is commonly used in the sense of luck).

c. The odd number 7 and its relation to supernatural forces is known to us through many ancient myths and legends. The "Seven Tablets of the Creation" date from the seventh century B.C. In the Babylonian account of the Great Flood, the storm and the deluge were calmed on the seventh day. In Tantric diagrams the transition of the souls of the dead carried by the moon over the waters to the sun where they lived a redeemed life, is represented by the "Seven Stages of Consciousness." In the Vishna Purana (a creation myth), Varuna caused the cosmic ocean to be churned. The solid coagulum which appeared gave the "Seven Gems" of which Chakra, the moon was the first that arose and Soma the last. The goddess in the form of a golden cow covered by a black robe, was carried around the shrine of the dead Osiris seven times, representing the wanderings of Isis (the moon goddess of Egypt) who journeyed over the world searching for the scattered parts of his body. The pilgrims in *Mecca* pass round the *Ka'ba* seven times. The seven-fold course between the two low hills, *Safa* and *Marwa* is performed in remembrance of Hagar, who ran desperately back and forth, calling to heaven for water for her dying son. During *Idu-L-Qurban* or *Qurban Bairam* seven stones are cast at three pillars of masonary known as "Great Devil," "Middle Pillar" and "Little One," recalling Abraham's meeting with Satan, whom he repelled with stones.

d. St. Gregory of Narek, author of the prayer book Narek, was born 951 A.D. in the village named Narek near the city of Van in Armenia, in the district of Rushduniantz. He died in 1011 at the age of sixty. His mother was a niece of Anania, the abbott of the monastery of Narek where St. Gregory received his education and thereafter served as a teacher. The book was written at the request of his pupils and the monks of the Monastery. It was not only used as a prayer book in the Monastery, but also outside, and during the past ten centuries has been widely used among the Armenian people as an ideal prayer book of the nation. The prayers of Narek are conversations, or familiar talks with God. The main idea in the prayers is a perpetual struggle of the spirit of man to obtain his salvation. Narek can be compared with St. Augustine's "Confessions" and Thomas à Kempis' "Imitation of Christ."

e. A prayer book.

f. An old wives' tale still current in England, that the best way to prevent a cold is to wear a piece of garlic around one's neck (Gelfand M., Medicine and Custom in Africa. Edinburgh and London E. & S. Livingstone Ltd., 1964. pp. 57–58).

The Evil Eye in Some Greek Villages of the Upper Haliakmon Valley in West Macedonia

*Margaret M. Hardie (Mrs. F. W. Hasluck)**

The documentation by classicists of the belief in the evil eye in ancient Greece is paralleled by contemporary field work investigations by ethnographers and folklorists in modern Greece. One of the valuable features of this representative sample of such scholarship by Margaret Hardie is her detailed reporting of curative spells. It is not always easy to elicit folkloristic data in cases where informants are genuinely afraid of the consequences of misusing such data. Informants often feel that revealing magical medicinal formulas may do harm to themselves or to their charges. In this instance, Margaret Hardie noted that since the counteractant spells had to be spoken to be effective, she found it was sometimes possible to persuade reluctant informants to write them out for her. In any event, we must be grateful for the excellent rapport Margaret Hardie evidently had with her informants and for the interesting spells she was able to record.

For other accounts of the evil eye in modern Greece, see Edward Dodwell, A Classical and Topographical Tour Through Greece, *Vol.*

*Reprinted from the *Journal of the Royal Anthropological Institute* 53 (1923), 160–171. Reprinted by permission of the Royal Anthropological Institute of Great Britain and Ireland.

II (London: Rodwell and Martin, 1819), pp. 30–37, John C. Lawson, Modern Greek Folklore and Ancient Greek Religion *(Cambridge: Cambridge University Press, 1910), pp. 8–15, Bernhard Schmidt, "Der Böse Blick und Ahnlicher Zauber im Neugriechischen Volksglauben,"* Neue Jahrbucher für des Klassische Altertum Geschichte und Deutsche Literatur, *31 (1913), 574–613, J.K. Gubbins, "Some Observations on the Evil Eye in Modern Greece,"* Folklore, *57 (1946), 195–197, Robert A. Georges, "Matiasma: Living Folk Belief,"* Midwest Folklore, *12 (1962), 69–74, and Regina Dionisopoulos-Mass, "The Evil Eye and Bewitchment in a Peasant Village," in Clarence Maloney, ed.,* The Evil Eye *(New York: Columbia University Press, 1976), pp. 42–62.*

Introductory

To the investigator of Greek folklore no superstition is so useful as the all prevailing belief in the evil eye (Βυσκανία). Greeks, both men and women, readily admit its existence and their own fear of it, for it is abundantly warranted by scripture, in particular by Solomon, notorious as an authority on magic.[1] The investigator can therefore arrive in a village and at once, without danger of being baffled by shyness, suspicion, or stupidity, ask who suffers from overlooking. A little adroit playing on the belief that the more attractive a person is, the more he must fear the evil eye, will work wonders in the way of establishing sympathy between the investigator and the villagers. Otherwise much time may have to be wasted in trivialities in order to establish this essential sympathy. Questions on such a subject also instruct the villagers in the burning topic of the investigator's business and save annoyance from the ignorant suspicions which arise so easily in a Macedonian mind. Further, they frequently discuss it among themselves and are primed with numerous stories of its manifestations and cure. This familiarity of theirs with the subject enables the investigators, as they pour out their information, to instil into their minds ideas of orderly presentation of their knowledge and of clear enunciation in speaking. In dealing with a topic so safe and so familiar there is no risk of losing information by administering this necessary and useful training.

Nature and Prevention

Overlooking may be voluntary or involuntary. The former is produced by spreading all the fingers wide and moving the hand, palm downward, with a quick, slanting gesture towards the person to be cursed; one or both hands may be used. But this type is in practice little more than a jest, the known consequences of overlooking being too serious for a person to burden himself lightly with them. It is rather the involuntary variety which is the object of Macedonian fears and the subject of my paper.

In the Upper Haliakmon valley it is not known who has the evil eye. Blue eyes and meeting eyebrows inspire none of the fear they do in Old Greece, presumably because blue eyes are portentously rare in Old Greece and frequent in every Macedonian village, where 30 per cent of the population is blue-eyed according to my anthropological lists. It is known, however, that if a new-made mother suckles her infant from both breasts without an interval between, her glance will be baleful to the first thing on which it rests afterwards. Again, should a mother weakly yield to the tears of her newly weaned son and resume feeding him, he will, in later life, have the evil eye.

Those who are found by experience to have the evil eye seem to take a regretful pride in its possession. The horse-and-rider story told me in every village with local *dramatis personae* is typical. According to this, a villager claims to have such power; and, to convince his rather sceptical friends, expresses admiration of a stranger who happens to ride by at that particular moment; the stranger inevitably falls. Or it may be that a stranger casts doubt on the reputed skill of a villager; the latter's friends summon him to prove it at the expense of the stranger as he leaves, and the result is a triumphant vindication of the villager's claims.

Overlooking is known to be seldom due to spite, and no rancour is cherished against a person who has the unfortunate gift. He (or she) is simply avoided for the future. It is advisable to turn back and make a fresh start if you meet such a person going to your work in the morning.

It is difficult to say what attracts the evil eye. Beauty is, of course, a great danger to its owner, but any one, young or old, ugly or beautiful, may be attacked. Only those born on a Saturday are exempt, but on Saturday afternoon, be it understood; for it was on

Saturday afternoon that Christ was born, and it is from Christ that the Saturday-born derive their exemption. New-made mothers have much to fear from it until their purification, forty days after the birth of their child. Beasts and inanimate objects suffer no less than men; young children suffer most of all, although infants are safe until they are baptized or their mother celebrates her purification, I think, because the infant is scarcely regarded as an entity until those events take place.

Any illness which is obviously not due to organic disease, a breakage, or a chill, is set down to the evil eye. The ordinary symptoms are discomfort, headache, whining, sleeplessness, and peevishness. Usually the trouble yields to one or other of the remedies given below, but sometimes it is severe enough to bring death within forty days. An extreme case was that of an infant of Kastoria (the ancient *Keletron*), which was taken to visit its grandmother when two months old. Its swaddling bands had just been undone when a neighbour called. She admired the fine child, with the result that it fell ill at once, and in spite of every conceivable remedy being tried it died in twenty-four hours.

Prevention, even in Macedonia, is thought better than cure, so amulets (βασκαντοῦρες) are generally worn to keep the evil eye at bay. Adults often have a cross or sacred picture or piece of incense concealed about their person. New-made mothers have a variety of prophylactics under their pillow or on their head, such as a red string, incense, bread, salt, garlic, indigo blue, a nail, gunpowder, a black and white thread, a ring, a pair of silver buckles. The ring and the silver buckles divert the visitor's attention to themselves, silver having in itself an additional power over evil magic, as in our own silver bullet. The black and white thread I do not understand: I have found it again in a prophylactic spell said over a new-made mother by a Vlach woman. Gunpowder is a potent killer of men, so may reasonably be expected to destroy any evil eye that glances at the mother. A nail is the symbol of strength and will occur in a spell I give later on (No. 1). The power of the indigo rests presumably in the intensity of its blue. Garlic has recognizedly caustic properties (τὸ σκόρδο εινε καυστικὸ). Salt strengthens and preserves. Red is in some obscure way potent because it is the colour of Christ's blood. Bread because of its use in the communion mass has a well-known religious significance: the bread which has been used during morning service in the church of Our Lady Made Manifest (Παναγία Φανερωμένη), of Kastoria, has a great reputation as an amulet in such cases.

Children wear round their necks a cross or a picture of Christ or the Virgin, but they may discard their amulet in Kastoria when three years old. An infant may wear on its bonnet a clove of garlic, a few white beads, a cheap pearl cross, a scrap of coral, or the gold (gilded) coin known as a *flourí*.

A remarkable necklace was worn by a Bogatsko baby. The foundation was of alternate blue, white, and silver beads, all alleged to be without prophylactic value. At intervals were suspended a vulture's claw set in silver, a roughly shaped lapis lazuli bead, a small packet of alum, a picture of St. Stylianos, a cross, and a packet containing a snail inside a walnut shell. The claw is a very favourite child's amulet among all creeds and languages of Macedonia. The power of the snail I do not understand; the alum presumably derives its efficacy from its well-known fixing properties in dyeing. St. Stylianos—whether his name is derived from στύλος, *a column*, or from στηρίξω, *I support*, according to the Macedonian pronunciation, Styrianos—is a well-known patron of weakly children. The lapis lazuli bead's colour is effective, but, in addition, the bead has been found useful in preventing miscarriages, and is hence called σταματόπετρα ("stopping-stone"). I therefore now think it probable that several elder brothers and sisters of the infant had died, presumably from overlooking, so the mother hung St. Stylianos and the "stopping-stone" on this child in the hope of "stopping" the sequence of deaths, but I have not yet returned to Bogatsko to inquire.

Shops have a horseshoe or a clove of garlic suspended over the door. A Shatista man has particular confidence in a French horseshoe he picked up during the war; it is, of course, twice the size of an ordinary Macedonian shoe. Calves wear necklaces of bright wool tassels, as does even a young donkey of my acquaintance—adult donkeys, as is known, are unworthy even of being overlooked. Horses wear a tuft of badger's hair on the forehead, but never the blue bead necklaces so familiar to the tourists of Athens and Smyrna.

The spoken word may also effectively ward off the dreaded evil. As is well known, the pale skins of North Europeans are much admired by the dark-complexioned children of the South. As a result, on my removing my glove one day in Shatista, a woman screamed "Garlic!" and kissed my hand, exclaiming, "It is as white as a saint's." Another in Kastoria remarked that I was "milky-white" (by no means true), whereupon her friend turned up the hem of my dress and exclaimed ἔχει ἀστὰρ τὸ φουστάνι της ("Her skirt has a lining"), meaning, I suppose, that I had also defects.

I have so far found no Greek prophylactic spell said over a new-made mother, though I have no doubt that such spells exist, like the Vlach one I have mentioned above. To protect an infant, undo his swaddling bands and pass the hand upwards to the crown of his head and down again over the trunk, saying, "If his *pudenda* are evil eyed, then may his face be evil eyed!" (Θὰ πάρῃ ἡ φύσι τον ἀπὸ μάτι, τότε νὰ πάρῃ ἡ μούτρα του ἀπὸ μάτι). The spell is from Shatista.

In these prophylactic measures two principles are discernible. The pictures of the saints, the cross, the incense, and the bread make a direct appeal to religion for preservation, while such amulets as beads, garlic, horseshoes, and badger's hair belong to a lower level, to secular rather than to religious magic, according to a distinction made by my husband and elaborated by him in his forthcoming book, *Transferences from Christianity to Islam*. Apart from the confidence they give—it will be noted in how many there is a suggestion of power and permanence and stability—their main purpose is apparently to divert to themselves the attention of any possible overlooker. Thus, a Kastoria small boy, who was frequently overlooked, was never allowed by his mother to leave the house until she had daubed some coffee grounds on his cheek, in order that the first remark made on him by passers-by might be a comment on his dirty face, *i.e.,* on something extraneous to his personality. Similarly, in the village of Serbia, South of Kozani, women for a similar reason dye small spots on their cheek—but here I suspect that the ladies are quite aware of how these "patches" enhance their charms. Another small boy of Kastoria habitually wore stockings that were not a pair, or, if they matched, one was outside in. An incautious person admired a string of twelve horses he saw one day; at once the bells on the two foremost horses shivered into a thousand pieces but the horses themselves remained unhurt, the bells having attracted all the evil to themselves. The amulets, in short, are a species of lightning conductor, just as the power of overlooking is thought popularly to be a kind of electricity which resides in the eye.

Remedies for the Evil Eye

Sometimes, however, all preventive measures prove in vain, and the evil eye has fallen on some one. Recourse is then had to various well-tried remedies. A woman of Kastoria, who is noted for her magic touch, takes a thread from the patient's clothes, mutters a spell, and heals the patient. A Greek gipsy in the same town massages the patient's forehead and presses upwards his eyebrows. In Bogatsko bear's hair is burned, and the child held in the fumes, a curious remedy which is based on a still more curious custom. In autumn, dancing bears are led round the villages, and not only entertain the villagers but also walk over the bodies of sick men, women, and children to cure them, much as do the dervishes of Constantinople. Mothers make a point of buying some hair from the bear to store against future need.

Like their amulets, their remedies for overlooking fall into the two categories of religious and secular magic. Of the religious the most obvious is summoning a priest to read a prayer over the sufferer; in his service book he finds one ready to hand called "A Prayer for Overlooking" (Εὐχὴ εἰς βασκανίαν). If an animal has been evil-eyed, a cross made of pitch may be hung round its neck, pitch being used in both white and black magic because of its supposed presence in the nether regions. A horse fell sick once at Kastoria and was unable to rise. Its owner and his friends by main force dragged it to its feet, and then beat it three times round the church of Our Lady Made Manifest; the horse was immediately visibly better, and next day they loaded it for a successful journey to Shatista, ten hours away.

The most prominent church at Shatista is that of St. Menas, the finder. Hanging on his *eikon* in the church is a big silver model of an eye, with which a cross is signed over an animal ill of overlooking; failing to cure is, I am told, unknown.

Similarly, a little oil may be taken from the sacred lamps in a church and placed in water in three plates. If the child has been overlooked, the oil mingles with the water, otherwise not. Apparently nothing more is necessary to cure the child.

A famous religious remedy is the μονόκερο. This is one of the small crosses with equilateral limbs which the monks of Athos carve with a figure of Christ and sell all over the Levant. It is reported to be made of the horn of an animal which has only one, μονόκερο signifying literally "unicorn." Mr. G.F. Abbott accepts this derivation and explanation,[2] and it is certainly true that most of the μονόκερα now sold are made of horn. But the monumental *Greek Dictionary*, which is in process of compilation, is sceptical of both explanation and derivation; rightly I think, for I note that the older μονόκερα in Macedonia are carved wooden crosses set in silver, and not made of horn at all. In addition, three times out of seven I hear the word pronounced *monokyro* (μονόκυρο), such confusion of *y* and short *e* being frequent in popular Macedonian pronunciation. I would, therefore, suggest that the older form is μονόκυρο—the word seems known only in Macedonia and Thrace, and not to have reached Old Greece. The meaning would then be μόνος ὁ Κύριος ("The Lord alone [cureth]"), an explanation I was, as a matter of fact, offered by a native of Velvendo near Serbia.

Be the meaning of the word what it may, the μονόκερο is much employed to cure overlooking. An old woman takes a glass of fresh water, and with the μονόκερο in her hand signs the cross three times across the water, whereupon she plunges the μονόκερο into the water. If bubbles rise to the surface of the water, as they usually seem to do, the patient is certainly suffering from overlooking but will now recover without more ado; plunging the μονόκερο into water being both for diagnosis and cure.

Curative Spells for the Evil Eye

It is never difficult to learn the religious remedies for overlooking, but spells are more difficult to obtain. For one thing, the old women who know them earn a few pence by them, and are naturally unwilling to divulge their secrets to a possible rival, a scientific reason for their acquisition being neither understood nor believed; only when old enough to "retire from business," do they communicate them to a younger woman. Some are afraid that imparting their knowledge will bring their own death, though exception may be safely made in favour of the eldest born of a family, a condition I am fortunate enough to fulfil. There is also a general belief that the spell acts for only one person at a time; when the "wise woman" is, as often, a harassed mother who soothes her peevish child to sleep by her spell, it is a serious matter to surrender her power. Fortunately, the words must be *spoken* either to act or to break the spell, so that women who can write can usually be persuaded into writing down the words. There is no difficulty about learning the ritual part of the spell. I have nowhere in Macedonia found, as I did in the island of Keos, that the spells may be told by a woman only to a man and *vice versa*.

The *bona fides* of my informants may be suspected. Unnecessarily, I think. Apart from the character of the spells themselves, which conform to the usual rules of magical procedure, the circumstances in which I obtained No. 7 renders its forgery impossible. Its narrator is a young girl of Bogatsko, to whose father's house I was unexpectedly taken on my first morning in that village. She was very willing to go through the ritual part with me, but extremely reluctant to communicate the words in case she broke the spell, which she used every night to send her nephew to sleep. Finally, after banishing all her relatives from the room, she produced a well-thumbed piece of paper on which she had written down the words as dictated by the old woman who had taught her the exorcism. She wrote them down in my notebook from this piece of paper, but pulled me up short when I inadvertently repeated aloud one of the sentences. She had no time to concoct and write down the words, and her terror of breaking the charm was painfully real. As several of the others are apparently broken down versions of this one, it is of some importance to have established its genuine character.

The charms I have so far collected are as follows:—

(1) From Kastoria:

If a visitor has overlooked a child, take three nails, three live coals, and three splinters from the door by which the visitor left. Put them in a shovel and hold the shovel a few minutes in the fire. Then lay the child on the ground, pour a little water on the shovel, and let the resultant smoke envelop the child. If the nails leap about in the shovel, the trouble is due to the visitor's evil eye. Finally, give the child a little water to drink from the shovel and its crying will cease.

It is scarcely to be doubted that the woman says a spell (λόγια) but my informant, being a man, did not know it.

(2) From Kostaradja above Bogatsko:

A woman takes a dish of water and makes a cross over it. She then drops a live coal into the water. As it falls to the bottom, it takes the evil eye with it. She next signs the cross three times over the water and then takes a little dust from the coal, sprinkles salt on it, and rubs the sufferer's head with the mixed coal and salt. She concludes by throwing three pinches of salt into the fire to banish the evil eye.

Here again the woman doubtless says a spell.

(3) From Bogatsko:

A "wise woman" is summoned. She first says forty "πατερημοί," which apparently means saying the words "Our Father" (πάτερ ἡμῶν) forty times. Then she takes a glass of water which has been newly fetched, in silence (νερὸ ἀσμπόρστο), from three fountains. Into it she drops five coals in succession, repeating for each the following "narrative charm":—

Γέννσε ἡ γελάδα ἕνα μουσχάρι
Γλίφουντας ἡ μάνα μὲ τὸ σάλ τὸ ξεβάσκανεν.
Γλίφουντας καὶ'ϝῶ ἡ μάνα τὸ ξεβάσκανα.
Νὰ ξήσῃ στὸν κόσμον καλά, νὰ μὴ παθένῃ τίποτε.

The cow gave birth to a calf.
Its mother, licking it, undid the evil spell with her spittle.
And I, the mother, have undone the evil spell by licking.
May the child live and prosper and not suffer any harm!

This said and done, the woman gives three pinches of salt to the patient and sprinkles water on his face. Any remaining water is to be thrown out at cross roads. The old woman is given a penny for her pains, but tramples it under foot before pocketing it in case it should have been infected by the patient's trouble.

(4) From Sarakina, 12 hours south of Shatista:

Take three live coals and a glass of fresh water. Sign the cross with each coal across the water and plunge it in after saying:—

Λιάρα γελάδα,
λιάρα μοσχύρα,
πάει στὸ μπαζάρ καὶ δὲν βασκάθηκε.
Ἔτσι νὰ μὴ βασκαθῇ καὶ τὸ μικρό.

Dappled cow,
Dappled calf,
Went to market and was not evil-eyed.
Thus may the child not be evil-eyed!

This and the foregoing spell are evidently related. I hope later to give elsewhere a fuller version which I obtained from the Greek-speaking Moslems of the same area.

(5) From Kastoria:

Break a live coal into three pieces. Take three pinches of salt, give one to the child, throw a second over your shoulder, and cast a third into the fire. Then sign the cross, saying Χριστὸς καὶ Παναγία ("O Christ and the Virgin"), and drop the first fragment of coal into a glass of fresh water. Pick up the second fragment, saying νὰ σκάσουν τὰ κακὰ τὰ μάτια ("Down with evil eyes"); and drop it into the water. Drop the third fragment in. Then give the child three sips of the water to drink and three times touch its forehead with the water, saying:—

Νίβγω τὰ κακὰ τὰ μάτια
καὶ τὰ ἀποφθεμάγματα
καὶ αἱ κακὲς τῆς ὥρας.

I am washing away evil eyes
and curses
and evil days.

Then with the open hand sprinkle the child eight times with the water, your five fingers multiplied by eight making the magic number forty. Any water left is to be thrown out into the street, the usual repository of rubbish in Macedonia.

My informant's ten months old child is reported to require this treatment every night before it can go to sleep.

Several poorer versions of this spell have been given me elsewhere, and at Kastoria itself.

It may be noted that the lady's Greek is not above reproach, the syntax of the last line being dubious, and ἀποφθεμάγματα apparently a Mrs. Malaprop rendering of ἀποφθέγματα.

(6) From Kastoria:

Take a glass of water and three grains of salt. Make a cross three times with the salt across the water, saying each time, εἰς τὸ ὄνομα τοῦ πατρὸς καὶ τοῦ υἱοῦ καὶ τοῦ ἁγίου πνεύματος ("In the Name of the Father and the Son and the Holy Ghost").

Then throw one of the grains of salt into the fire, and the second into the water. With the third, sign the cross in front of the patient three times, afterwards putting it in his mouth.

Next pick up three live coals with the tongs. With each make a cross over the water and drop it into the glass, saying to the first and second, εἰς τὸ ὄνομα τοῦ πατρὸς καὶ τοῦ υιοῦ καὶ τοῦ ἁγίου πνεύματος. To the third say, instead, ὅποιος τηράει μὲ κακὸ μάτι, νὰ σκάσῃ τὸ μάτι του ("Death to the eye of whoever has the evil eye"). If the coals do not sink to the bottom of the glass, the *malaise* is not due to overlooking; if they do, it is. If all sink to the bottom, the overlooker is a man; if only one sinks, the overlooker is a woman.

Now sprinkle the water on the patient with the open hand, the back being towards the patient and the fingers pointing downwards. Continue the sprinkling so long as it takes to mutter the creed (τὸ "πιστεύω"). After this give the patient three sips of the water and then wet his cheeks, forehead, and hands with it. Finally throw any that remains out of the window, but with averted face, saying, ἔξω τὸ κακὸ, μέσα τὸ καλό ("out with evil, in with good"). Turn the empty glass upside down and leave it so overnight.

This exorcism can be handed on only to the eldest born of a family, men as well as women being eligible to learn it if the first-born of their family.

(7) From Bogatsko:

Take a metal coffee-cup and make nine indentations in the ashes of a charcoal brazier (μαγγάλ). Take a glass of water in the left hand and a black-handled knife in the right; with the knife take a little ash from each of the nine marks, sign the cross with it over the water, saying, 'Ιησοῦς Χριστὸς νὰ νικάῃ τὰ κακὰ τοῦ τάδε ("May Jesus Christ destroy the ills of So-and-So"), and let the ash fall into the water. Obliterate the nine indentations.

Now with the same knife draw a large cross in the ashes of the brazier, saying, 'Ιησοῦς Χριστὸς καὶ 'Ανάργυροι οἱ Θαυματουργοί, νὰ νικάῃ τὰ κακὰ τοῦ τάδε καὶ αὐτὰ τὰ κακὰ ἔργα τοῦ ἀρρώστου ὀπίσω νὰ γυρνοῦν. ("May Jesus Christ and the Unfeed Saints [Cosmas and Damian] conquer the ills of So-and-So, and may the evils that have befallen the sick child go back the way they came"). Then take a little ash from the four arms of the cross and say, 'Ιησοῦς Χριστὸς νὰ νικάῃ τὰ κακὰ τοῦ τάδε, as you drop it into the water. Obliterate the cross, saying, Χαλνῶ τὰ κακὰ μάτια, τὰ κακὰ ἔργα ("I am blotting out evil eyes and evil deeds"). Three times altogether this large cross is to be made and obliterated.

Next, pick up three live coals from the brazier with the tongs, make a cross with each over the water, and let it fall into the water. Each coal represents one of the three possible sources of overlooking, viz., woman, man, or that vague thing, half ghost, half shadow, called ἴσκιον. On making the cross say, Ἰησοῦς Χριστός. On dropping in the first coal, which stands for women overlookers, say, σβοῦν τὰ κάρβουνα, σβοῦν τὰ σίδηρα · νὰ σβοῦν καὶ τὰ κακὰ τοῦ τάδε · νὰ σκάσουν τὰ βυξιά της ("The coals are quenched, the iron [tongs] is quenched, may the ills of So-and-So also be quenched. Destruction to her breasts"). As the second coal, representing men, is dropped in, say σβοῦν τὰ κάρβουνα, σβοῦν τὰ σίδηρα · νὰ σβοῦν καὶ τὰ κακὰ τοῦ τάδε · νὰ σκάσουν τὰ κάτω του ("The coals are quenched, the iron [tongs] is quenched, may the ills of So-and-So be quenched.") As the third, representing the vague ἴσκιον, falls into the water, say only σβοῦν τὰ κάρβουνα, σβοῦν τὰ σίδηρα · νὰ σβοῦν καὶ τὰ κακὰ τοῦ τάδε.

If a coal sinks to the bottom of the glass, it reveals that the man, the woman, or the ἴσκιον, which it represents, overlooked the child.

After this take a pinch of salt and three times sign the cross before the patient's face, saying, Ἰησοῦς Χριστὸς νὰ νικάῃ τὰ κακὰ τοῦ τάδε ("May Jesus Christ conquer the ills of So-and-So"), put a little of the salt in the child's mouth, and throw the remainder on the fire, saying, ὅπως σκάξ τοὺ ἅλας, νὰ σκὰξ καὶ τὸ κακὸ ἀπὸ τοὺ παιδὶ ("As the salt 'bursts' so may the child's trouble 'burst' "). Take a second pinch of salt and forty times stroke the child's forehead with the inside of the thumb, with an upward slanting movement, saying, σαράντα 1 πατερημοί, σαράντα 2 πατερημοὶ up to σαράντα 40 πατερημοὶ (forty, 1, "Our Father": forty, 2, "Our Father": . . . : forty, 26, "Our Father": forty, 27, "Our Father": . . . : forty, 40, "Our Father"), that is, counting up to forty, at each number prefixing "forty" and adding "Our Father."

A third pinch of salt is now taken and the child's forehead stroked as before, while the operator counts backwards from forty.

Next dip your hand in the water and from close at hand sprinkle the patient, the back of the hand being kept towards him and the fingers pointing downwards. Sprinkle him three times, twice from right to left, and the third time from left to right, so as to begin and end on the right. Each time say, νίβω τὰ κακὰ μάτια, τὰ κακὰ ἔργα ("I am washing away evil eyes and evil deeds").

Then sprinkle him from a distance three times, saying, ἄν το ἔφερεν ἡ μέρα νά το πάρῃ ἡ νύχτα ("If it came with the day, may it go with the night").

Wet your finger in the water and touch the child's lips with the words, ἄν το ἔφερεν ἡ νύχτα, νά το πάρῃ ἡ μέρα ("If it came with the night, may it go with the day"). Any water left in the glass is to be poured out into the gutter, while you say πῶς τρέχ τὸ νερὸ ἀπὸ τὴν ὑστραχιά, νὰ τρέχῃ τὸ κακὸ ἀπὸ τὸ τάδε ("As the water runs away in the gutter, so may the evil run away from So-and-So"). Conclude by turning the glass upside down (to prevent any remaining, I think).

It is throughout essential to say the patient's name.

(8) From Sarakina:

Take a glass of fresh water and three grains of salt. Drop them one by one into the water, saying, κίνσε ὁ Ἔηλιος καὶ ἡ Ἔηλιανα νὰ παιὲν στὰν ἐρμιά, στὰν ἀποριά, καὶ βρῆκαν τὴν 'Αθανὰς καὶ το βάσκαναν · καὶ ἔτυχα ἐγω ἡ Μαρία καὶ σὲ ξεβάσκανα μὲ τρὶα σπειρὶα ἅλας ("Mr. and Mrs. So-and-So set out to go to a lonely, desert place and found Tommy and overlooked him. And I, Jane, happened to come along and have cured you of your overlooking with three grains of salt").

Next drop three coals into the water, one by one, counting each time backwards from forty and saying ἄν εἰνε ἀπὸ ἄντρα, νὰ βγοῦν τὰ μάτια του καὶ νὰ σκάσουν τὰ πουπούλια του · ἄν εἴνε ἀπὸ γυναῖκα, νὰ βγοῦν τὰ μάτια της καὶ νὰ σκάσουν τὰ βυξιά της ("If a man did it, may his eyes fall out. If a woman did it, may her eyes fall out and her breasts burst").

The Nature of the Spells

The first of these exorcisms bears little or no relation to any of the others, relying, as it does, mainly on the superstitious value of the number three and the medical effect of "smoking" the child. The six exorcisms which follow are, as will be seen, closely interrelated, while the eighth again stands by itself.

In the six the familiar mixture of religion and superstition confronts us both in formulae and ritual. Thus, in Nos. 2, 4, 5, 6 and 7 the operator sanctifies the water she uses by signing the cross over it. A further religious element is added to No. 5 by saying "O Christ and the Virgin," and to No. 6 by invoking the Father, Son and Holy Ghost and by repeating the Creed. In No. 7 the words "Our Father" are murmured forty times, as in No. 3, their potency in No. 7 being enhanced by prefixing the superstitiously valuable word "forty." The same spell invokes Christ as the conqueror of evil, and appeals to the healing saints Cosmas and Damian.

On the superstitious side salt and live coals are used in all the exorcisms, the symbolism being apparently that the evil eye is to "burst" with a sound like that of a live coal hissing in water or of salt crackling in the fire. The latter is indeed explicitly stated in one formula of No. 7: ("As the salt 'bursts,' so may the child's trouble 'burst' "). The admitted virtues of salt as an antiseptic, a strengthener and a preservative, account for its choice as a weapon both of defence and offence against the evil eye. We ourselves, it may be added, believe, at least on Saturdays, that evil is averted by throwing salt over the shoulder, as in No. 5.

Apart from the mimetic symbolism of a live coal hissing in water, it is not easy to understand why a coal should have power attributed to it. No explanation has ever been offered me by the people themselves. It may possibly derive from their knowledge of the cleansing and disinfecting properties of charcoal ash. As their usual fuel is wood, the "coal" is always a piece of charcoal. Educated Greeks have suggested to me that the coals sink or float according as they are very porous, and therefore absorbent of water or not, a scandalously rationalistic interpretation of their alleged "testing" powers.

Passing from superstitious ritual to superstitious formulae, we find that these are at once more varied and more interesting than the religious. In the latter no explanatory ritual accompanies the spell, in the former such an accompaniment is the general rule. Thus, in Nos. 5 and 7 words and actions alike suggest washing away evil; as the exorcizer in No. 7 destroys the cross she made in the ashes, she claims to destroy the evil. Water is to be poured out into the gutter in No. 7 that the trouble may vanish as the water vanishes. In the same exorcism the patient's sickness is supposed to be ended by the extinguishing of the coals and tongs in the fire. At the end of this spell, however, occurs a formula divorced from any explanatory ritual, when both day and night are invited to remove the spell; it is no more than an attempt to exhaust the contingencies in which the evil befell the child, and is only one more example of the foolish meticulousness which characterizes many "old wives' remedies." A few mere imprecations conclude the list of superstitious formulae.

It will have been noted how many of the *motifs* found separately in Nos. 2, 3, 5 and 6, recur in No. 7. The connection between them is so close that No. 7 may almost be considered as the parent of the others.

The remnants of a "narrative charm" are found in No. 3, and again in No. 4. As already stated, I possess a fuller version, collected from a source outside the scope of this paper. No. 8 is a separate and complete "narrative charm," chiefly remarkable for its confusions of thought and gender.

A striking feature in the exorcisms is the use of "lucky" numbers. *Three* is found in the ritual of No. 1 (3 times), No. 2 (twice), No. 3 (once), No. 4 (once), No. 5 (four times), No. 6 (five times), No. 7 (six times as *three* and once as *nine*, its multiple), and No. 8 (twice). *Forty* occurs in the ritual of No. 3 (once), No. 5 (once), No. 7 (twice) and in the formulae of No. 8 (once), of No. 7 (three times). Exceptionally, *five* coals are used in No. 3. Numerically *three* appears more prominent than *forty*, yet it is the latter which has given its name to exorcisms (σαραντίσματα) and exorcising (σαραντίξειν).

A word remains to be said on No. 7 where the exorciser strokes the child's forehead with her thumb. This is evidently rudimentary massage, and it is certainly very soothing, as this particular girl does it. Differences in the touch of people's hands are popularly recognized, while another form of head massage is still in backward Bogatsko required of young wives if their mothers-in-law find it difficult to go to sleep: it is the ἔλα νά με ψειρίσῃς and *pire tchiqar* which alarm our modesty at intervals in Greek and Turkish folk-tales, but are seldom to be literally translated.

This slight scientific element of cure being admitted, there seems nothing more of scientific value in the spells. The words are generally a patter of mere nonsense, a fragmentary spell being as potent for healing as the complete edition. It is by their suggestion of help and healing that the spells work, exercised, as they are, on people extremely susceptible to suggestion, whether it be for good or ill, for sickness or health. And so even the men who in health affect to despise such "old wives' remedies" (γυναικεῖα πράγματα) have glad recourse to them in sickness and find frequent healing.

NOTES

1. The references are collected by Elworthy, *Evil Eye*, note 7A.
2. See his *Macedonian Folklore*, p. 142.

The Evil Eye in Roumania, and Its Antidotes

*A. Murgoci**

From the eastern Mediterranean we move to eastern Europe. Again we find the same familiar evil eye pattern. In Greece, for example, according to the preceding essay, if a mother were to "weakly yield to the tears of her newly weaned son and resume feeding him, he will, in later life, have the evil eye." Similarly in Roumania we shall learn that being "weaned twice over" may be a cause of the evil eye. What is not so clear is why a feature of infant care should be thought to be causally related to the evil eye and why specifically a return to the maternal breast.

Another interesting detail among many in this relatively brief but extremely informative account is the personification of the evil eye in a counteractant spell. The reader may recall that the Sumerian text cited earlier also depicted the evil eye as an independent entity capable of approaching or withdrawing from human victims.

The first point which was impressed on me when living in Roumania was the precautions I must always take to avoid casting the evil eye. As babies are fascinating objects, my natural instinct was to look at them rather intently, and even to murmur some complimentary remark. I was invariably interrupted by my husband or maid, who began spitting repeatedly, saying "*Să nu-i fie de deochiu!*" (Let it not

* Reprinted from *Folklore*, 34 (1923), 357–62.

be a cause for the giving of the evil eye), and dragging me away. I had not realised that I was bringing the poor baby into danger. Any observation and any praise would have been enough to cast the evil eye on the baby, but the danger was much intensified by the fact that I had green eyes—a rare thing in Roumania, where most eyes are brown. The only things wanting to make the danger almost fatal were that my eyebrows should have been joined, or that I should have been born in a caul, or have been weaned twice over. That my intentions were eminently benevolent did not make things any better, as the casting of the evil eye is not intentional. It is, however, possible to take precautions to avoid casting the evil eye—namely, spitting three times and saying "*Să nu-i fie de deochiu!*" The Roumanian habit of calling a child *urîtule* (ugly thing, horror) as a term of endearment is nothing but a precaution against the evil eye. But I have seen the word lead to strained relations, possibly as undesirable as the evil eye, when inadvertently used towards the children of Westerners.

The symptoms caused by the evil eye are broken sleep, or loss of sleep, headache, constant yawning, buzzing in the ears, any kind of digestive pain or derangement, fever, depression, and general weakness. Even death may result.

Although children, and more especially young babies, are most exposed to suffering from the evil eye, all kinds of living beings, and even inanimate objects, may suffer. Domestic animals, more especially the new born, show the effects of the evil eye by pining away, flocks of sheep by diminishing in number, fowls by pecking at one another, bees by deserting their hives, fruit-trees by drying up, milk by not giving butter, houses by falling in pieces, and money by diminishing in quantity.

There are various methods of gauging the mischief caused by the evil eye, whether it is likely to be fatal or not. These methods generally form part of the rites performed in breaking the spell of the evil eye. Thus in Mehedinti, after the sacrament given to the person *deochiat* (afflicted by the evil eye), the priest puts a crumb of the sacred bread into a glass of water. If the bread floats, every one becomes cheerful as if the sun had come out from behind a cloud, for the sick person will get well again; if it falls to the bottom, the sick person is no longer for this world, and the women at once begin the death lament, a fact which does not exactly improve the patient's chances of recovery.

Another method is to melt a piece of lead or of yellow wax, and pour it into a glass of water. The lead or wax, cooled down rapidly by the water, is supposed to take the form of a human figure. If the head is upwards, it is a sign that the evil eye has not been fatal, and the child will live. If the head is downwards, the child will die.

With the evil eye, as with everything else, prevention is better than cure, so precautions are taken by parents that their children shall not be *deochiat*. Among the Serbs a red thread is worn by a mother on her middle finger for a long time before her baby is born; in Macedonia a twisted red and white thread is worn round the neck. In Bukowina, during the birth of a child, the midwife makes a red tassel and nails it over the door; in Moldavia she puts a needle with a red thread on the threshold; and in Macedonia she puts a twisted red and white thread over the door and a knife at the threshold. The nail, needle, and knife, being of iron, keep off evil spirits in general, not the evil eye in particular.

If the baby should be born in a caul, the caul is preserved. It is spread on sweet basil to dry, and kept as a charm against various forms of evil. If it is possible to obtain water in which a white goose has been washed, it is advisable to bathe the baby in this as a charm against witchcraft in general. Salt in the bath protects against the evil eye and evil spirits. After the bath a spot of white ashes (*benchiu*) is put on the baby's forehead, as a special protection against the evil eye. A similar spot of mud or of ashes can be put on the forehead at any period of childhood to protect the child, and to be a warning to visitors of the danger of evil eye, so that they may say "*Să nu-i fie de deochiu!*" to themselves. In Välcea, saliva is placed on the navel as a protection against the evil eye. Till a child is at least a year old, it must never look into a mirror, or it will cast the evil eye over itself. Hence all mirrors are removed from the room where the baby is, or, if not, they are carefully covered up. Protection against the evil eye is also obtained by dressing a child so as to avoid observation, or even dressing it so badly as to call forth unfavourable comment only. The most general form of protection is, however, to wear something red, and after birth both mother and child go on wearing red ribbons or bows for a long time.

The red is not used for children only, but also for young animals. Once a calf was born in the yard of a peasant cottage in Transilvania where I was staying. Before I even saw it, it had bits of red flannel tied to its horns, to the root and tip of its tail, at intervals down the tail, in fact everywhere where red flannel could by any means be got to stick on.

In the case of older babies the red bow is considered specially necessary when the baby leaves its own home. My eldest baby had hair so very short and fair that it was almost invisible. My maid used to prepare her for a visit by getting three or four hairs in the centre of her head to stick together by licking them, or waxing them, and then attaching to them a big red bow. The effect produced by the red bow, apparently springing from nothing on the head of the smiling unconscious child, was certainly ridiculous enough to ward off anything other than a laugh.

It is to be noted that the Turks, who also believe strongly in the evil eye, guard against it by putting on something blue. The significance of red is of great interest. Does it represent the colour of blood in sacrifice, as the blood on the doorpost to ward off the destroying angel in the tenth plague would seem to suggest, or does it represent fire as a purifying agent?

Another method of guarding against the evil eye is to wear an amulet. The most complicated of these amulets are made by the Transilvanians, and contain 3 bulbs of garlic, 3 grains of pepper, 3 of spring wheat and 3 of autumn wheat, 3 pieces of incense, 3 grains of salt, 3 crumbs of bread, and, lastly, 3 pieces of the caul of a child. Other amulets to tie round the neck of the child are a little bag with some charcoal, some garlic gathered at Trinity, or a piece of the bark of a fir-tree. Often the customary red ribbon round the neck of a child has garlic fastened to it. A bulb of garlic may also be tied to the tail of domestic animals.

As money may be *deochiat* by counting it, or a flock of sheep by saying how many sheep are in it, obvious precautions against the evil eye in such cases are that tradesmen should never count their money till the evening, so as not to spoil business, that card players should never count their gains till the close of the game, and that shepherds should never tell how many sheep they have.

If, in spite of all precautions, a child has been *deochiat*, the obvious thing to do is to remove the spell. Sometimes a *baba* (an old woman skilled in removing spells) is called in. She puts some glowing charcoal into water, repeating, if she knows one, a powerful incantation; if not, saying the Lord's Prayer. Then she washes the face of the child with this water and gives it some to drink. More often those in charge of the child carry out the same proceeding themselves; in fact it seemed to me to be a matter of routine in my household to give my babies water into which glowing charcoal had been put if they cried much. If a child seemed in any way to have had a fright, it was given fresh water (*apa neînceputa*) to drink. This, however, so far as I understood, was a form of charm against evil influences in general rather than against the evil eye in particular.

In Välcea, the spell of the evil eye is also removed by a *baba* with water and glowing charcoal, but the ceremony is altogether more complicated. A new earthenware pot is taken and filled with water, and into this are thrown as many pieces of glowing charcoal as there are persons under suspicion of having cast the evil eye. If a piece of charcoal sinks to the bottom of the pot, this means that the person it represents has cast the evil eye. The *baba* says a charm to remove the spell, and the child *deochiat* is sprinkled with the water, and also drinks some. A quite similar proceeding is adopted if, instead of a child, a domestic animal has been *deochiat*.

Among the Jugoslavs two bits of charcoal are supposed to tell what is to be the fate of the person *deochiat*. The *baba* takes two bits of charcoal, and one she calls "life," and the other "death." She puts them into a pot, and pours water on them. If "life" falls to the bottom, the person *deochiat* dies; if "death" falls he lives.

It is thus seen that the great charms which protect against the evil eye are something red, garlic, and salt. The great charm which breaks the spell, when it has been cast, is glowing charcoal—and it seems not impossible that the protecting influence of red may be due to red representing in a weakened but permanent form the glowing of the charcoal.

In the incantations which break the spell of the evil eye, the evil eye is personified and addressed as if he were an evil spirit, thus:—

"Avaunt, oh evil eye, from the eyes,
Avaunt, oh evil eye,
Or the breath from the mouth will get at you.
Avaunt, oh evil eye,
Or a blast of breath will get at you.
Avaunt, oh evil eye, from the eyes,
Or the sun will get at you,
And cut off your feet.

Avaunt, oh evil eye, from the cheeks,
From the gristle of the nose,
From the shoulders and the neck,
From the brain in the head,
From the spleen and from the heart.

. . . .

Come out and go away,
For I have broken your spell with my words.
I have taken you by the hand,
And I have thrown you to the winds,
That ——— may remain clean, holy, and with a
 clear mind
Like the flowers of the meadow,
Like the dew of the morning."

It is clear that the evil eye, in spite of its terrible effects, is conceived of as a singularly childlike and docile spirit, if the recitation of the above be sufficient to get rid of him forever.[1]

NOTES

1. References: Gh. F. Ciausanu, *Superstitile Poporului Român*, cap. xxx; T. Stratilesco, *From Carpathians to Pindus*, pp. 248–9.

The Jettatura and the Evil Eye

*Giuseppe Pitrè**

Nowhere in the world is the evil eye more a part of daily life than in Italy. Malocchio, *as it is termed, has been the subject of numerous treatises by Italian scholars from the late eighteenth century to the present day. Of all those who have written about the evil eye in Italy surely none did so with more knowledge than Giuseppe Pitrè (1841–1916), one of the founders of the field of folklore as an international discipline.*

Pitrè, despite the demands of his practice of medicine, devoted most of his life to the collection of folklore in his native Sicily and elsewhere in Italy. His indefatigable collecting resulted in literally dozens of volumes of folklore placed on record. His twenty-five volume Biblioteca delle tradizioni popolari siciliane *represents the fruits of a lifelong attempt to document every conceivable aspect of Sicilian folklore and life. This monumental work includes four volumes of proverbs and four volumes devoted to customs, beliefs, and superstitions. It is from one of the latter volumes that the present essay on the evil eye has been translated.*

In his essay Pitrè expands upon a distinction made by the folk, especially in Sicily and southern Italy generally between the malocchio *and the individual who is responsible for causing it, namely the* jettatore. *Most reports of the evil eye say comparatively*

* Translated from Giuseppe Pitre, *Biblioteca delle Tradizioni Popolari Siciliane*, Vol. XVII, Usi e Custumi, Credenze e Pregiudizi del Popolo Siciliano, vol. IV (Palermo, 1889), pp. 235–49. I am indebted to Ms. Lynn Gunzberg for translating this essay from Italian into English.

little about the supposed characteristics of the agent of this power. Yet in Italian scholarship there has always been an avid interest in the jettatura. Nicola Valletta in his Cicalata sul fascino volgarmente detto jettatura *of 1787 even included specific inquiries in his proposed questionnaire asking whether the jettatore might be likely to wear glasses or a wig and whether there were any gestures, voice quality, or eye and facial characteristics by which a jettatore could be positively identified. Pitrè attempts to answer several of these questions by describing jettature in some detail. Accordingly, Pitrè's essay gives the reader not only an idea of the mechanics of the evil eye in Italy, but also a vivid picture of the jettatura including some sympathy for the individual who rightly or wrongly is labelled by his fellows as a jettatore.*

For additional material on the evil eye by Pitrè including a discussion of protective amulets, see "Jettatura e Malocchio. Scongiuri, Antidoti ed Amuleti," Biblioteca delle Tradizioni Popolari Siciliane, *Vol. 25 (Palermo: Libreria Internazionale A. Reber, 1913), pp. 193-211.*

For other representative treatments of the evil eye in Italy not mentioned by Pitrè (who possessed a knowledge of folklore bibliography nearly unmatched in his own day), see Filippo Valla, "La Jettatura (Ocru malu) in Sardegna (Barbagia)," Archivio per lo Studio Delle Tradizioni Popolari, *13 (1894), 419–432, Frank Jewett Mather, Jr., "The Evil Eye,"* Century Magazine, *80 (1910), 42–47, Max Leopoldo Wagner, "Il Malocchio e credenze affini in Sardegna,"* Lares, *2 (1913), 129–150, S.A. Callisen, "The Evil Eye in Italian Art,"* Art Bulletin, *19 (1937), 450–462, Sara Stocchetti, "Interpretazione Storico-Critica di una Diffusa Superstitione Popolare,"* Lares, *12 (1946), 6–22, Clara Gallini,* Dono e Malocchio *(Palermo: S.F. Flaccovio, 1973), Willa Appel, "The Myth of the* Jettatura,*" in Clarence Maloney, ed.,* The Evil Eye *(New York: Columbia University Press, 1976), pp. 16–27 and Edward Foulks, Daniel M.A. Freeman, Florence Kaslow, and Leo Madow, "The Italian Evil Eye: Mal Occhio,"* Journal of Operational Psychiatry, *8(2) (1977), 28–34. For considerations of Pitrè's contributions to the study of folklore, see Giuseppe Cocchiara, "Giuseppe Pitrè,"* Convivium, *6 (1934), 219–240, Giovanni Gentile,* Giuseppe Pitrè *(Firenze: Sansoni, 1940), Giuseppe Cocchiara,* Pitrè, la Sicilia e il folklore *(Messina-Firenze: Casa Editrice G. D'Anna, 1951), and*

Antonio Pasqualino et al., Pitrè e Salomone Marino *(Palermo: S.F. Flaccovio, 1968).*

A sort of malevolent spell practiced by certain men and women, *jettatura* or, as some say, *mursiana*, is one of the most dangerous aspects of our life. Cataldo Carducci, the Neapolitan poet, wrote:

> Non suona altro jettatura
> Che malìa, fulmin, contagio,
> Un malanno, una sciagura;
> Tal si norma or per adagio,
> Che con lei va tutto insieme
> Il peggior ch'uom fugge e teme.

Trans: You can't call *jettatura* by any name other than sorcery, thunderbolt, infection, a misfortune, a disaster; For so the adage warns, That whatever goes along with it is the worst of what man shuns and fears.

The person who practices *jettatura* is the *jettatore* (*gittaduru* in Nicosia), he who *casts* (*jetta*) the spell, either because he envies the well-being[1] of others or because he desires that evil befall them. And he has the power within himself to invoke both natural and supernatural misfortunes and misadventures upon a person, a family or a household.

He has particular signs and characteristics which distinguish him from every other human being: a thin face, dark, sallow; small, deep-set eyes; a hooked nose; a long neck like those who swallow saliva: he's altogether unpleasant and burdensome, offensive, repugnant. Antipathy is his constant companion and there's only a short distance between it and *jettatura*; it's so short, in fact, that without thinking some people call a particularly unlikeable person a *jettatore.* Likewise they say *facci* or *occhi di jittaturi* ("jettatore face" or "jettatore eyes") about someone with such a horrible expression that he disgusts and repels all those who see him or come near him. Nature has been provident and wise to accentuate the features of the *jettatore* and to give him a repellent appearance, so that everyone can watch out for him.

The *jettatore* is pernicious in every respect, occasionally even to himself. Until 1883, there lived a man in Messina whose glance was considered so fatal that at his death the rumor spread that he died because, while walking down Corso Garibaldi, he just happened to look in a large mirror displayed in a storewindow. People say that since he could not save himself from the harmful influence of his own eyes nor, on the other hand, bear anyone else's gaze (since his own powers overcame everyone else's), he just stopped living.

The presence of the *jettatore*, or the fear that he might appear, or even if his name comes up in conversation, is cause for public disaster or private harm. If you are playing cards and he comes by and speaks to you, luck will turn her back on you. If you're in a carriage and meet him, your horse will rear, the carriage turn over and you yourself will dislocate your foot or break your collarbone. If you have to speak or sing at a public gathering, all of a sudden you lose your voice or, if it's at night, the lights go out; a window opens and your papers are either messed up or blown away or else you are attacked by near-fatal pain. If you are in love and your love is returned, the *jettatore* can easily cool your girl's passion. If you depend on a friend for some important business, you can be sure he'll get sick just the day you need him while until yesterday he was ready to help out. If you have a case in court, the dossier will arrive late and then once it does arrive, you'll find that an important document is missing, or your lawyer has a speech impediment or the judge, the one who understood the problem and was favorable to you, will suddenly get the dry colic. And then there's the hitch that since it's just before vacation time, you're condemned to pay damages, costs and interest. Want more? A storekeeper or any salesman on whom the *jettatore* "sets his sights," as the common people say, will begin to notice customers avoiding his shop. A child, under the influence of an occult and inexplicable illness, will begin to waste away. All the troubles of this poor world rain down upon the house and the family on which the *jettatore* has gazed, as the poet of Caltanissetta says:

> Cavaddi estinti, carriaggi rutti,
> Denti caduti e morti repentini,
> Arvuli sicchi ccu tutti li frutti,
> Troia incenniata ccu tanti i ruini.
> Casi arrennati, mindici ridutti,
> E siminati cuperti di spini:
> Un jittaturi d'unni 'ncugna e passa.
> Un gran fituri vi spargi e vi lassa;[2]

Trans: Dead horses, broken-down carriages, Fallen teeth, sudden deaths, Dried up trees with all their fruit, Troy burnt with all its ruins. Houses buried in sand, shrunken beggars, Sown fields covered with thorns: A *jettatore* from that place draws near and passes by. He spreads a great stench and leaves it behind;

and as another illiterate poet of Palermo in his *Ragiuni pirchì lu cornu è contra la jettatura* (Reasons why a Horn is Effective against *Jettatura*) observed, he who has had *jettatura* done to him

Si mancia, lu manciari cci fa pesti;
Si vivi, si cci rumpi lu bicchieri;
Siddu camina, cu li genti 'mmesti;
E s'havi a ghiri avanti, va 'nnarreri,
Si dormi, così si 'nsonna funesti,
Si discurri. è pigghiatu pri sumeri;
Si scrivi si cci scàncara la pinna,
E si voli addattari 'un trova minna.

Trans: If he eats, his food becomes putrid; If he drinks, his glass breaks; If he walks, he pushes people; And if he needs to go forward, he goes backwards, If he speaks, he is taken for an ass; If he writes, the pen breaks, And if he wants to nurse, he finds no breast.

The least you can get is a headache and it's the evil eye rather than *jettatura* which causes such intense pain (Nicosia).

This may seem a rather exaggerated picture, but it isn't really, if you consider that especially the eye of the *jettatore* is morbific for everyone and his nose is a sure measure of his maliciousness.[3]

He who believes in *jettatura* believes all this and keeps his distance from the *jettatore* just as he would from the pestiferous breath of a poisonous reptile. The steps taken to prepare oneself against him and to nullify his powerful and terrible influence stem from this.

The daily life of the people is rich in amulets and *phalli*, supreme defenses against *jettatura*. The principal charm is iron in any form, and the best is the horseshoe attached to the walls of a stall or certain doors of the house. Iron is the generic name for any metal which one uses as an antidote to *jettatura*: steel, lead, silver, gold. And so a man who encounters a *jettatore* or hears one spoken of, immediately touches his watch chain or a key in his pocket or a coin or metal buttons if he has any on his coat. And just to be sure he touches certain organs which, to ward off *jettatura*, are worth all the chains, keys, coins and buttons in the world. This touching of metal or flesh is represented by the phrase: *Tuccari ferru* (touch iron). In cases in which this antidote is ineffective, the *jettatura* must be particularly malicious.

Horns are also an effective remedy and as a result men and women wear little horns made of coral as charms on their watch chains and they are used as amulets around the necks of newborn babies. Large, clear, shiny ox horns are used as decoration in certain great or middle-class homes, the same as deer's heads with tree-like antlers hung in a hall, and the longer and more twisted the horns, the better they serve this beneficial purpose.

In addition there are small kerchiefs and braids or red wool which are considered excellent safeguards when hung at a window, on a railing, at the gate. And that's why in the Cìvita section of Catania until a short time ago, red (*'ncarnata*) women's shoes were worn against *jettatura* and *gastìma* (curse).[4] That is why when one decorates a horse, a mule or a dray donkey he uses lots of red wool lace, and the carters attach it and wrap it all around the wood on top of the yoke (*sidduni*) of the cart itself.[5] That's why the cabmen attach it to the ring over the headlamp of their carriages and the butchers to some carcasses of billygoats with their rough and twisted horns. The peasants attach it to the canes planted in the middle of fields, orchards and gardens, the city-dwellers to the bellpulls at gates or doors or to the small trees on the balcony or to the potted plants on the stair. And certain loose women attach it to their bed frame, to the trestle, the curtain, the pillow. Wherever you go, you'll always or almost always see a small piece of red canvas or wool or cotton which carries with it the tacit understanding that the evil eye, sorcery, witchcraft, wizardry and such spells should stay far away from that place.

I know people who, not knowing to which saint to pray to avoid *jettatura*, tie a ribbon to their pipe, to their house-spectacles case, even to the handle of the coffee pot. And we all know about country people who have a ribbon, or a little cross or a star of red wool sewn into the lining of the vest or jacket next to their shirt.[6] The fiercest enemies of *jettatura* tie the ribbon—red, of course— to [their] horns to multiply the protection a hundredfold. Others use a plumerial leaf (*agone americano*), salt, red pepper, bone (*fuso*). But the most sceptical have no faith in these; they consider them ineffective, good only for certain silly women who feel absolutely safe when they've sewn a salt crystal (*uogghi di sau* in Nicosia) inside their underwear or hidden some powdered salt under their hair (*s'agghiummunìanu un pugniddu di sali sutta lì capiddi*, Alcamo).[7]

We have plenty of words to avert or exorcise *jettatura* as well as the evil eye: one of the most common is a formula recited as one extends the index and little fingers of one or both hands while bending the others inward, to resemble horns. The formula goes like this:

> Cornu, gran cornu, ritortu cornu;
> Russa la pezza, tortu lu cornu,
> Ti fazzu scornu:
> Vaju e ritornu,
> Cornu! cornu! cornu!

> Trans: Horn, big horn, twisted horn; Red the cloth, crooked the horn, I mock you: I go and come back, Horn! horn! horn!

and it is accompanied by spitting vigorously three times: *ppu! ppu! ppu!*. . . .

The formula against the evil eye, which when you get right down to it, is *jettatura*, goes like this:

> Occhiù e malocchiu!
> E fuiticci l'occhiu.
> Crepa la 'nvidia,
> E scatta 'u malocchiu!

> Trans: Eye and evil eye! And break his eye. Let envy die, And the evil eye explode!

It must be noted here that spitting is less effective than the devices mentioned above, but I repeat that spitting three times is especially effective against the evil eye. My good friend, Salamone-Marino, writes: "It often happens that you see one of our people, on a visit to a sick person, spit three times on the doorstep; or a relative of a woman in labor stand at the window and spit three times glancing around her with a stern look. One sees a man spit when a lady of easy virtue stares at him, just as, viceversa, a woman will do when a man who is known as a depraved night-prowler sets his sights upon her. One also sees anyone who meets a hunchback, or a wizard, who are unpleasant in their features and their reputation, spit behind their backs. And, finally, one sees mothers who catch some dubious woman kissing their babies, spit energetically in her direction as soon as they see her turn her back. . . ."[8] There are those who wear rue or *erba caccia-diavuli* (the devil-chaser herb), those who wear garlic or onion, and those who wear the tail or some of the skin from a wolf's forehead.[9] Some wear pigs' teeth (Pietraperzia), some wear images of the saints inside small bags, some a cross made from needles sewn in the lining of their clothing (Nicosia), some a little Saint Anthony's pig which is tied around children's necks (Palermo); but these are all minor remedies and are not always strong enough against the evil eye or a *jettatura* of a certain strength.

Instead of spitting, one gestures like Vanni Fucci in Dante's *Inferno*, together with the exorcising exclamation: *Pampini e ficu!* (vine leaves and fig!) *Pampini e ficu!*, a gesture which the coral workers make into trinkets, charms and amulets of coral.

With this shameful act there are the strange words of the most famous conjuration of Palermo against *jettatura*, which is said at the corner formed by two walls as soon as the *jettatore* has gone away:

> Spatricu, spatricu!
> Ovu di tunnu 'n Francia,
> Chista è 'a pampini è chista 'a ficu:
> Ossu mal'ossu supra 'u pittinicchiu,
> Fora fattucchiara,
> Fora di casa mia!

Trans: Away with you, Away with you! Tuna eggs in France, This is the vine-leaf and this is the fig: Bone bad bone over the little comb, Out sorceress, out of my house!

or with fewer words:

> Spaticu, spaticu, spaticu!
> Ovu di tunnu 'n Francia,
> A mari vaja la mala vintura!

Trans: Away, away, away! Tuna eggs in France, Let bad luck go to sea!

And they spit three times.

Urine is considered to be a considerable remedy for neutralizing the sinister effects of the *jettatore*'s eye; there are persons who are not embarrassed to sprinkle the ground where the evil one has stood for they are convinced that in this way they inure it against his dangers. It's hardly a clean remedy, but there it is.

During card games, and other games, a good charm against *jettatura* is the usual horns gesture with one or both hands on the table, accompanied by these words which have been hallowed by custom and which recall three very black things:

> Inga!
> Mascarò!
> E natiche di schiava! . . .

> Trans: Ink! Black spot (or substance used to blacken things)! And a female slave's buttocks!

And how many times have we heard these words from the mouth of a gentlewoman who would otherwise never say such indecent things! while one hand extends tapered and attractive fingers, bejewelled with a splendid ring, which repeat the horns gesture.[10]

Now, turning the page, one can't not feel sorry for the poor wretch who, because of some painful coincidence observed by someone, or because of some cruel person, is labeled a *jettatore* by the public. This man is morally lost and not only himself but also his family, for often *jettatura* is considered hereditary, and in that way it becomes subtle and powerful. The *jettatore* has no name, no friends, nor the possibility of a social life. No one speaks of him, and no one wishes to incur the dislike of acquaintances by walking with him. His servants work for him only out of their need to eat. And, incredible as it may seem, on his tomb—as long as his need be distinct from others—rather than invoke merciful rest, one puts the harmful motto: *toccaferru* (touch iron) as if he were there alive and speaking.[11]

At this point I ought to give the names of some famous *jettatore*s in Sicily, but for the same reason that the *jettatore* is never mentioned, I am forced to withhold them. The Sicilian readers of this article would touch every key and chain in their houses.

I remember that when a pious bishop of Girgenti was visited at home by a certain Cip......, the building was soon deserted and was expected to collapse as a result. —Woe to him who would have anything to do with that man from Aff.... whom the cultivated public accused of the worst kinds of *jettatura*!—Very few congregants were usually present at the masses said by the aforementioned N.; his sermons (since he did have a weakness for preaching) were avoided and his greeting not returned or shunned, his smile met with clenched teeth and unspoken curses. People speak about services which ended badly, about candelabra falling down the steps of the altar endangering the altar boys and the church wall hangings catching fire because of his presence.[12]

I know another priest much like N., a certain B., who is the sacramental chaplain of the most populous zone south of Palermo. His parishioners don't want to be married by him, they don't want him to baptize their babies or bless their dead. They even claim that the certificates of poverty, birth and marriage signed by him in the parish archive will have no effect. Lastly, I recall that the most famous *jettatore* of this half-century in one of our large cities takes or gives his name to a Sicilian town and whoever arrives there on the train trembles when they call out the name. The agent who goes along the cars to invite the passengers to disembark, names the station in a low voice, as if he had a lump in his throat, as if *jettatura* were really hanging over his head. No one speaks and no one looks at the nine enormous letters which some poor artist painted on the station wall. In the country, one kilometer from the unmentionable town, is a poor hovel where no one goes and where the remains of that man rest in eternal sleep. He had left Palermo and gone to find his death in that small town, and his bones which have endured a true odyssey, remain unburied. They can't be brought to the village because the inhabitants won't allow them and they can't be taken to Palermo because under some article of the Health Code, the Government refuses them.[13]

NOTES

1. In fact, there is a proverb which says: Casa 'nvidiata/ O iddu è povira, o iddu è malata. (Trans: An envied house/ Either it's poor or there's sickness within.) because, at best, a household, a family which is envied by bad people, begins little by little to become impoverished or soon will fall victim to all sorts of illnesses.

To look upon an object or an individual with an envious eye, can bring great harm to it, most often as an accident, If someone shows us a handsome animal and we don't want it to fall prey to the evil eye, we must take care in touching it; if not, the evil eye will strike.

2. Pasquale Pulci: *Poesie siciliane,* fasc. I, p. 30 (Caltanissetta: Tip. Scarantino, 1864.

3. After the eyes, the nose is held to be characteristic. At the Villa of the Philippan Fathers in Palermo, where children, youths and adults from the city go to spend a few hours with wholesome games and pastimes, he who plays ball, for example, or quoits or surdateddu (little soldiers) in order to win, can weaken his oponent's game (*mal giuoco*) by drawing a cross on the ground with his finger and saying: *Nasu N......a!* The ghostlike nose is considered among the most dangerous because it recalls a poor priest who joined the Olivella (of the aforementioned Philippan Fathers) with the reputation of a dangerous *jettatore.*

4. G. Borello: *Poesie siciliane,* p. 100.

5. See my *Catalogo e descrizione di costumi ed utensili siciliani mandati alla Esposizione industriale di Milano 1881 (Gruppo VIII, Classe 50) per cura del Municipio di Palermo,* pp. 6–7 (Palermo: Tip. P. Montaina e C. 1881) in –4°.

6. In some small towns the cross is called a *S. Caloìru* (Saint Calogero), and it also helps keep one from other dangers which do not come from the evil eye. Those who carry this cross sewn inside the doublet (*ciliccuni*) recite to it three Ave Maria.

7. When part of this chapter, which had been first published in Hungary in an elegant pamphlet edition of only one-hundred copies (Koloszvàr, *Sumptibus Editoris Actorum Comparationis Litterarum Universarum,* 1884. In –12° pp. 12), was republished in the *Giornale di Sicilia* anno XXVIII, n. 36 (Palermo: 5 February, 1888), many letters came to the editor expressing astonishment that I don't believe in *jettatura.* One of them, from Riposto near Giarre in the province of Catania, deserves to be quoted here:

> "Distinguished Editor: Since I am one of those who respect *jettatura,* though they may not believe in it, and since I read in your paper a marvelous article about it, signed P., allow me to suggest another very ancient recipe which I have permitted myself to transcribe here.
>
> "Please feel free to pass this on to Mr. P. if you wish, thereby enriching the vast collection of remedies, in order to guard against the evil influences of something which will, in time, become a science.
>
> "Please accept the regards of an assiduous reader."

And here is the recipe:

Corna e curnicchi picculi,
Curaddu lavuratu,
Spilli e pindenti d'àmbira
'Na pezza russa allatu,

Un ferru senza tèmpira,
'Na chiavi masculina
'Na testa d'agghiu frivula
'Na pezza cilistrina,

Ma quannu poi, a lu massimu,
Ca non cci giuva nenti,
'Na stritta di tis. . . .
E passa certamenti.

Trans: Horns and little horns, Carved coral, Amber brooches and pendents, Next to a piece of red cloth, Untempered iron, A key without a hole, A head [brain] like weak garlic, A piece of blue cloth, But then when, at the worst, None of this helps at all, Squeeze the [tes]ticles, And it will surely pass.

8. It would be helpful here to mention that in Sicily we say *pigghiari ad occhiu* (keep one's eye on someone) for *bewitch*. But as Professor Castelli (*Credenze* p. 25; (Palermo: 1878) observes, one can bewitch with the tongue as well as the eye, which is why praise, good wishes and especially kind words which one hears about one's good health, even if they come from a friend, are considered a spell. (Cf.: *Archivio delle tradizioni popolari,* vol. III, p. 133) As Pliny said, there were some families in Africa who could thus cause the death of things they praised, make the trees dry up and children die.

A particular spell is occasionally attributed to certain hunchbacks and their families. When one sees one of them who is unfortunately considered a bewitcher, or even when one hears his name, one makes horns with the fingers, as mentioned above. In addition men do other things which decency does not permit me to describe or they touch certain parts of their bodies.

9. *Archivio delle tradizioni popolari,* vol. I, p. 133.

10. At this point it seems fitting to relate what a Sicilian often quoted in this work has written on the subject and in that way corroborate what I have written about it:

"*Jettatura* is a Neapolitan word which in Tuscany corresponds to bewitchment. Among the many different members of society, among the many and diverse beings in the human race, are some whose moral and physical make-up does not fit well with ours. Their appearance does not penetrate to our hearts, they more often than not wound our eyes and leave an unpleasant sensation. Their ideas and their manners disgust and repel us. From this antipathy is born and it's only a short distance from antipathy to *jettatura.* One need only discern in him the slightest gloomy feature or a phlegmatic or boring nature to declare him a *jettatore.* (The *jettatore* par excellence is he who has a dark and melancholy physiognomy, is of poor mind and won't leave you alone.) Now one would have you believe that this person called *jettatore,* who is practically surrounded by an atmosphere of misfortune, really causes calamity, misadventures and troubles, and holds open Pandora's box to the detriment of any one nearby. Does this feared basilisk of society draw near while you are playing? you will lose in abundance. Does he greet you while you are in your carriage? the horses will shy. Is he at table with you? the bottles will break. But by touching a piece of metal or a horn, they wish you to believe that like a pentacle it will rob *jettatura* of its power so that it no longer works." (Cacioppo: *Cenni statistici,* pp. 125–126).

11. Among the poems against the *jettatore*, is the cruel and brutal one of Borello, whom I have already cited here, on page 54 of his *Poesie siciliane,* a close imitation of the *Delatore* of Prati.

12. I met him more than once on the street and soon found myself abandoned by whomever I was with just because N. greeted me, or sometimes, politely came up to me. One of my friends even went so far as to threaten to break off our friendship if in the future when we were together I would allow that *jettatore* to approach me!

13. On the subject of *Jettatura* in Italy, see: — for Naples — Valletta: *Cicalata sul*

Fascino, volgarmente detto Jettatura (Naples: 1777 and 1787, 1814, 1819, 1834, 1881); Schioppa: *Antidoto al Fascino detto volgarmente Jettatura per servire d'appendice alla cicalata di N. Valletta,* (Naples: 1830); Marugi: *Capricci sulla Jettatura.* (Naples: 1815); (Carducci): *La Jettatura a Fenicio Pimene dedicata,* (n.d.); C. Flandini: *Etudes et souvenirs de voyages en Italie et en Suisse,* I, 26 (Paris: 1838); Bidera: *Passeggiata per Napoli e contorni,* v.I, p. 204 (Naples: 1845); Robello: *Cenno critico intorno ad alcuni costumi ed usi napolitani,* Cap. XII (Florence: 1850); Monnier: "Naples et les Napolitains", ch. VII in *Tour du Monde* (Paris: 1861) second semester; L. Du Bois: *Lettres sur l'Italie et ses musées,* pp. 29, 194 (Brussels: 1874); Dumas: "Impressions de voyage: Le Corricolo", I, ch. 15 in *La Jettatura* (Paris: 1878); Jaccarino: *La Jettatura collocata fra le scienze naturali; poemetto bernesco in ottava rima,* (Naples: 1876); Gabrielli: "La Jettatura" in *Napoli Letteraria,* new series, vol. III, n. 30 (Naples: 24 July, 1886); Mezzanotte: "Don Michele Gargano jettatore" in *Gazzetta Letteraria,* vol. X, n. 38 (Torino: 18 September, 1886). — For Calabria — Pigorini-Beri: "In Calabria: stregonerie; In Calabria: Fra i due mari" in *Nuova Antologia,* vol. XVIII, n. 18–21 (Rome: 1883); Dorsa: *op. cit.*, p. 119. — For the Abruzzi — Pansa: *Saggi di uno studio sul dialetto abruzzese*, pp. 75–78 (Lanciano: 1885). — For The Marches — Castellani: *op. cit.*, p. 14. — See also — Pardi: *Scritti vari,* vol. III, p. 233 (Palermo: 1873); Vannucci: *Storia dell' Italia antica,* 3rd. ed., vol. I, pp. 94–95 (Milano: 1873); Pico Luri di Vassano (L. Passinari): *Modi di dire,* p. 232 (Rome: 1875); Robba: "La Jettatura secondo Democrito" in *Rivista di Filosofia scientifica,* vol. VI (Torino: February 1887); Tuchmann "La Fascination" forthcoming in *Mélusine* vols. I, II, III, IV (Paris: 1886–88), The notes regarding Italy are to be found in Chapters 1, 2, vol. II, columns 385–391; Grossi: *Il Fascino e la Jettatura nell'antico Oriente* (Milano: 1886); Mancini: "Jettatura e scongiuri" in *Nuova Antologia,* vol. XII, 3rd. series, (Rome: 16 December, 1887), p. 656 and ff.

Scoring Aboon the Breath: Defeating the Evil Eye

*Thomas Davidson**

The intensity of the belief in the evil eye in Italy and Greece and elsewhere in the circum-Mediterranean area is fairly well known. What is not so often realized are the longstanding traditions of the evil eye in other areas of Europe including northern and western Europe. The occurrence of the evil eye in Scotland is well attested, for example. R.C. Maclagan's excellent book, Evil Eye in the Western Highlands, *published in 1902, provides ample documentation of its presence in this part of the world. In the following brief essay, Thomas Davidson samples the Scottish traditions, calling special attention to one in particular: the drawing of a wet forefinger across a victim's forehead or drawing blood from the same area as a means of combatting the adverse effects of the evil eye.*

For an indication of the extent of the evil eye in northern Europe, see H.F. Feilberg, "Der böse Blick in nordischer Überlieferung," Zeitschrift für Volkskunde, *11 (1901), 304–330, 420–430, Ragnar Hemmer, "Det onda ögat i skandinavisk folktro,"* Brage Årsskrift, *7 (1912) [1913], 52–75, Åke Campbell, "Det onda ögat och besläktade föreställningar i svensk folktradition,"* Folkminnen och folktankar, *20 (1933), 121–146, Gunnar Landtman, "Tron på det onda ögat i svenska Finland,"* Budkavlen, *18 (1939), 34–42, and Toivo Vuorela,* Der Böse Blick im Lichte der Finnishchen Uberlieferung *(Helsinki: Academia Scientiarum Fennica, 1967). For*

* Reprinted from *Chamber's Journal*, (1950), 308–311.

additional illustrations of the Gaelic tradition besides the Maclagan book mentioned above, see William Mackenzie, Gaelic Incantations: Charms and Blessings of the Hebrides *(Inverness: Northern Counties Newspaper and Printing and Publishing Company, 1895), pp. 34–43, George Henderson,* Survivals in Belief Among the Celts *(Glasgow: James Maclehose, 1911), and Lady Gregory,* Visions and Beliefs in the West of Ireland, *Vol. I (New York: G.P. Putnam's Sons, 1920), pp. 127–152.*

> Against the blink of evil eye
> She knows each antidote to ply.
>
> Train, *Strains of the Mountain Muse* (1814)

James Napier, in his book on folklore (1879), recounts an interesting experience he had when he was a child. He fell ill, and nothing the doctors could prescribe appeared to do him any good. The old skeely-wife of the village therefore was called in, as it was suspected he had got a blink of the uncanny een. She set to work on the patient and her *modus operandi* was as follows. A sixpenny-piece was borrowed from a neighbour, a good fire was kept burning in the grate, the door was locked, and the patient placed upon a chair in front of the fire. With the sixpenny-piece she lifted as much salt as it would carry, and placed both in a tablespoonful of water. The water was then stirred with the forefinger until the salt was dissolved. Next, the soles of the sufferer's feet and the palms of his hands were bathed thrice with the solution, and after these bathings he was made to taste the solution three times. The operator now drew her wet *forefinger across his brow*. The remaining contents of the spoon she cast right over the fire into the back of the grate, saying as she did so: 'Guid preserve frae a'skaith.' These were the first words permitted to be spoken during the ceremony. Thereafter, the patient was put to bed.

Such was the cure. What about the cause of the *ailment? This*, we are told, was due to a suspected blink from an uncanny ee, or, as it might have been expressed in certain parts of the Borders, the subject had been 'overlooked.' Now, the belief in the existence of the evil eye, or, as it was called in the south of Scotland, the ill or uncanny ee, was without doubt on the topmost rung of the ladder of diablerie. It was confidently held that this power was granted in most cases by the devil to the more favoured of his followers, although it had to be admitted—but very grudgingly—that to some people it came as an unfortunate natural endowment. In this latter case it was very often a curse to the unhappy possessor. For example, we hear of a man in Nithsdale, who, possessing een of unsonsy glance, and having no wish to avail himself of its potential power, found life very difficult. His eyes blasted the first-born of his yearly flocks and spoiled his dairy. He went so far, indeed, to prevent trouble, that he never looked a man or woman full in the face. Such instances, however, appear to be the exception rather than the rule.

Generally, too, we find that this particular field of the diablerie was left open to the old women, who, if tradition tells true, made the most judicious use of their precious gift, and when they found how much their uncanny een were dreaded made the most of the situation. Does not Galloway's folksong inform us:

> Kimmer gets maut, and Kimmer gets meal,
> And cantlie lives Kimmer, right couthie and hale;
> Kimmer gets bread, and Kimmer gets cheese,
> And Kimmer's uncannie e'en keep her at ease.

From the same quarter, Cromek being our informant, we learn that, before markets were so fully attended, the lowland wives would go at the sheep-shearing times into the uplands, taking pieces of cloth, sugar, and tea for barter in the wool traffic. The *pawky auld dame* trusted to her far-known character, going always empty-handed—yet she returned with the heaviest and fairest fleeces. The Bute Session Records gravely relate that Marget McKirdy, who was accused of charming, confessed that she used the following charm for 'ane evill ey':

> I will put an enchantment on the eye,
> From the bosom of Peter and Paul,
> The one best enchantment under the sun,
> That will come from heaven to earth.

The ill ee was dreaded by the peasantry because a mere glance was sufficient to cause grievous harm to mankind and all kinds of property; it deprived cows of their milk, and milk of its nutritive qualities, so that it could not be churned into wholesome butter. The people who had the most to fear from the witch with the uncanny glance were the farmers and dairymaids. They had, as we can well imagine, as many antidotes—equally superstitious of course—to apply in defence against the witch's evil glance. Train catalogues some of the dairymaid's remedies as follows:

Lest witches should obtain the power
Of Hawkie's milk in evil hour,
She winds a red thread round her horn,
And milks thro' rowan-tree night and morn,
Against the blink of evil eye
She knows each antidote to ply.

The use of rowan-tree was noted by King James I. in his *magnum opus* on witchcraft. There he says: 'Such kind of charmes, as commlie dafte wives use for healing forspoken goodes, for preserving them from evill eyes, by knitting roun-trees or sundriest kind of herbes to the haire and tailes of the goodes'; and as late as the 18th century this practice was carried out in the Borders. A certain Mr. Mabon in the town of Selkirk faithfully adhered to this old superstition by always ensuring that a new cow, before entering his byre, had one of her ears pierced and decorated with a rowan-tree pin and red thread or ribbon.

When the Border farmer's wife found the cows had been 'overlooked' and their milk bewitched, she applied this remedy. On the return of the milkmaids from the loaning with their milkpails upon their heads, and when the foremost took down her vessel in order to pass under the doorway, the farmer's wife dropped a horseshoe heated red-hot into the milk. It was necessary that the ceremony should be performed at the instant when the milkmaid was lowering the pail, and it was further required that no one should be aware of her intentions.

A slightly different technique was adopted in an instance which occurred in Auchtergaven, Perthshire. A farmer, having bought a cow whose milk at first upon churning seemed to refuse to yield butter, called in the old women of the neighbourhood who were reputed to be skilled in such matters. The women met together in solemn conclave and unanimously decided that it was a sign of something, and that Hawkie had got the *blink o' an ill ee*. By order of the conclave a bottle full of the milk was thrown over the former owner's house. The churn was taken out of the door empty, and brought in at the window full—still with no effect. At last, the cow was walked away a hundred yards, brought back, and tied to a new stake in the byre, after which her milk yielded abundance of butter, the owner and others concerned remaining quite satisfied of the virtue of the charm.

Going back to the opening tale, we noticed there that the skeely-wife drew her wet forefinger across the patient's brow. Now, this action is but a variation of what was probably considered the most efficacious remedy that could be applied against the evil eye. The Border name was 'scoring aboon the breath,' and consisted of drawing a blunt instrument across the forehead to the effusion of blood. To be really effective, it was necessary to make two scores forming a cross. In cases where the scoring was to be carried out on the 'victim,' it was sufficient, as in the example cited, merely to draw the forefinger across the forehead. When the witch was scored, however, more drastic methods were resorted to, and generally a small pin or rusty nail was used. Nails from a horse's shoe were particularly efficacious. In this connection, we find the following record. In April 1747 Helen Irvine, spouse to George Grierson of the Parish of Bowden, appeared in the Kirk of Selkirk and complained to the Presbytery there assembled that 'Robert Speedin came to her house a month ago about seven in the morning, and reviled her by calling her a base blade and saying "what have we to do with you?" to which she only answerit, "Robert! I never did you harm," after which he gripped her in a violent manner by the side of her head, and as she apprehended, scored her above the eyes to the effusion of blood, with some instrument which he had in his hand; then went off to the smiddy where the blacksmith was at work and said to him and his son that now he had succeeded in scoring Nell Irvine's brow.'

In 1704 Archibald Lawson of Stow quarrelled with Marion Wilson. When he went home, he found his child took 'a greeting,' which continued for some days and nights. Convinced that Marion was the cause, he went to her and bled her with his nails, and forthwith the crying stopped. Marion had the reputation of being a witch, and it would seem she had been held down and bled with an awl on a previous occasion.

Finally, an instance of scoring above the breath is recorded about a farmer in Wigtownshire as late as 1825. He had some cattle which died, and there was an old woman living about a mile from the farm who was considered no very canny. She was heard to remark that there would be "mair o' them wad gang the same way." So one day soon after, as the old woman was passing the farmyard, one of the farmer's sons took hold of her and got her head under his arm, and cut her across the forehead. We are not told, however, whether this antidote or remedy was effective or not.

This belief in fascination by the eyes is as old as time itself. Virgil alludes to it, and says: *Nescio quis teneros oculus mihi fascinat agnos.* The Rev. Robert Kirk in his *The Secret Commonwealth* (1691) speaks with conviction about the destruction of animals whereon the eye glances first in the morning, and goes on to cite the case of a man in his parish "who killed his own cow after commending its fatness, and shot a hare with his eyes." Joseph Glanvill, also, was a firm believer, and in his *Sadducismus Triumphatus* (1681) writes: "I am apt to think there may be a power of real fascination in the witch's eyes and imagination, by which, for the most part, she acts upon tender bodies. For the pestilential spirits, being darted by a spiteful and vigourous imagination from the eye, and meeting with those that are weak and passive in the bodies which they enter, will not fail to inflict them with a noxious quality."

That the superstition was so widespread and generally accepted in Scotland becomes very apparent when we find the eminent legal authority Sir George Mackenzie including it in his *Laws and Customs of Scotland* (1674, etc.). There he says: "Witches may kill by their looks, which looks being full of venomous spirits, may infect the person whom they look. I know there are those who think all kinds of fascination by the eyes, either an effect of fancy in the person affected, or else think it is a mere illusion of the Devil, who persuades witches that he can bestow upon them the power of killing by looks, or else the Devil really kills, and ascribes it falsely to their looks; whereas others contend that by the received opinion of all historians men have been found to be injured by the looks of witches: and why may not witches poison this way as well as the Basilisk doth?" He goes on to state that "though witches confess that they did kill by their looks, their confession and belief may, if they be otherwise of a sound judgment, make a very considerable part of a crime when it is joined with other probabilities, yet *per se* it is hardly relevant."

Why the malignant powers of the evil eye should have been so universally believed in and accepted may seem remarkable to us now, but in that dark reign of superstition and ignorance, where casualties, misfortunes, and griefs, due mostly to violation of natural laws, were put down to the dreaded powers of evil spirits, demons, and witches, it is not strange that special significance should have been given to the human eye. It is the only physical organ which can truly express the innermost workings of the mind, whether they be pity and compassion, or envy and hate. At one instant it flashes fiery, full of scorn and rage; at another, its glances, envenomed with hate, can seer the very soul; and last of all it can melt in compassion and love, pity and sorrow. And according to the fragment, *Wag-at-the-Wa'*, we are told:

> Whenever the e'en holes wi' low shall he fou'
> Then is the time come, that ye may dread the pow—
> For Hell's e'en are firelike, and fearfu' to view;
> Their colour they change oft frae dark red and blue:
> They pierce like an elf-prick, ilk ane that they see,
> Then beware of their shimmer, if ye're seen ye will
> die,
> Your heart pulse will riot, your flesh will grow
> cauld;
> And now happy's the wight, that draws breath till
> he's auld.

As for the ridiculous remedies applied, we can only say that where all rational conception of the causes of disease and of medicine is completely absent, and where every illness is superstitiously attributed to demoniac sources, it is not surprising that the use of magical or supernatural ceremonies as a panacea for these ills led to an eager credulity in their efficacy, no matter how absurd and anomalous in themselves. For, after all, if the witch could kill, she could also cure.

The Evil Eye Among European-Americans

*Louis C. Jones**

When immigrants from the Old World came to the New, they brought the evil eye belief complex with them. Not all folklore survived the ocean passage. Some was apparently too localized, too closely associated with the beloved topography left behind. Thus, for example, the Irish leprechaun and the Scandinavian troll remained in the old country. But most of the diverse evil eye traditions: the Jewish, the Italian, the Greek, etc. were successfully transplanted to some extent. No doubt one reason for this was the continuing fundamental importance of the evil eye in the worldview and belief system of the new immigrants struggling to adapt to the demands of a strange and sometimes anxiety-producing environment.

American folklorist Louis C. Jones, mostly on the basis of 170 reports made by college students enrolled in his folklore classes in the early 1940s surveyed various evil eye traditions. The preponderance of Italian (90) and Jewish (48) informants in his sample may have affected the breadth and reliability of his composite account of the evil eye. Still, one can appreciate the authenticity of many of the details by comparing them with analogous ones mentioned in the substantial scholarship devoted to the evil eye in the Old World.

Interest in the evil eye among immigrant groups has continued. For Greek-Americans, see Robert A. Georges, "Matiasma: Living Folk Belief," Midwest Folklore, *12 (1962), 69–74; for Syrian and*

* Reprinted from *Western Folklore*, 10 (1951), 11–25.

Lebanese-Americans, see Alixa Naff, "Belief in the Evil Eye among the Christian Syrian-Lebanese in America," Journal of American Folklore, *78 (1965), 46–51; for Italian-Americans, see Richard Swiderski, "From Folk to Popular: Plastic Evil Eye Charms," in Clarence Maloney, ed.,* The Evil Eye *(New York: Columbia University Press, 1976), pp. 28–41, and Edward Foulks, Daniel M.A. Freeman, Florence Kaslow, and Leo Madow, "The Italian Evil Eye: Mal Occhio,"* Journal of Operational Psychiatry, *8(2) (1977), 28–34.*

Belief in the evil eye did not survive among the early immigrants to this country; even among the Negroes, where many seventeenth- and eighteenth-century British beliefs have flourished, there appear to be almost no traces of it. I have no evidence of its survival among English or Scottish stocks, although English and Scottish folklore contain frequent references to "overlooking," as the English call the act. It is then among the later immigrants that we find the belief in the evil eye intact, most vigorously among Italians and Jews.[1] It is almost always true that the first generation born in this country puts no stock in the evil eye: the second generation never heard of it. It survives for the life span of the immigrant and only in urban areas where there is a large number of people from the same or similar background in Europe. The *Encyclopaedia Britannica* remarks that "one of the most striking facts about superstitions in the New World is that the evil eye seems to be foreign to the whole hemisphere. Its absence is often cited as a good example of the occurrence of unexpected human divergences."

Fear of the evil eye is based on the belief that certain people possess eyes whose glance has the power to injure or even kill. Origins of the belief can only be guessed, but they have been traced back to the earliest of human records and the references in Deuteronomy indicate that the evil eye was known early in the Hebraic world. Usually its possession coincides with a malevolent spirit, but not always, for, as we shall see, some possess it unwillingly.

Who Possess the Evil Eye

All witches possess the evil eye, and that is one of the ways they produce their maleficia, but many other people whose lives are only modestly vicious are similarly cursed. This is a power with which individuals are born; it is never acquired, except by those who have been fed by a wet nurse. Frequently possessors are persons whose eyes are different from the common run: Germans look with suspicion on those with red eyes; the Irish, on those with a squint or those whose eyes differ in color. Often it is a glaring or piercing eye that is to be feared. It may not be the eyes at all, but the eyebrows that give us the key to their owner's power. Some Italians have it that heavy eyebrows which come together like, say, John L. Lewis', are the telltale trait. There is no indication that any particular class or group in the community is more liable to possess the evil eye than any other.

Preventives

While the removal of the effect of the evil eye is frequently a rather complicated matter consisting of well-patterned rituals, there are a multitude of everyday devices used as preventives, warding off tragedy before it can get its grip. Babies, especially, must be protected, since they are peculiarly liable to attack. There are general prophylactics, consisting of colors, objects, and miniature objects to provide protection at all times; then there are special actions and phrases to be used when a given situation is fraught with danger.

In Mohammedan countries, blue is considered the most potent color of protection, probably because in the same lands, among dark-eyed people, the blue eye is a suspect eye and therefore blue would attract the evil glance to itself, rather than to the person or object which is thus adorned. I recall seeing horses and camels in Morocco and Algiers with great blue buttons on their harnesses. The same color is used in countries like Greece and Armenia where there has been contact with the Turks. In those countries children wear blue "eye beads" conspicuously on their clothing. Elsewhere in Europe, among both Jews and Christians, the favorite protective color is red. Red ribbons are tied around a baby's throat, hair, or leg; in Italy, sometimes with a religious medal attached. In Greece, where both conventions are honored, a mother still in childbed will tie a red ribbon around her arm. In Ireland, a red thread is woven into a horse's tail where it cannot be seen but where its effectiveness will be great. A Jewish device for preventing the sterility in fruit trees which might result from being overlooked is to paint the trunk of the tree with red paint. Red is sometimes combined with other charms, as when it is the color chosen for the embroidering of a cross on a child's underwear or for a bag containing garlic to be worn around the neck.

Among the Italians there is a custom which survives vigorously in this country, as any stroll through a Little Italy on a sunny spring afternoon will prove; that is the use of miniature charms or a red coral necklace. Young American mothers of Italian parentage will laugh when you ask about these charms or beads their babies wear and say that the child's grandmother gave it to him as a present, and it's a cute ornament, and if the old lady thinks there's more to it than that, what harm can it do—this last a bit defensively. Then you talk to the old lady herself, sometimes with the help of a friend who speaks Italian, sometimes in a lame and uncommunicative English. You gather that these young mothers are a well-meaning but ignorant crowd who make a lot of hocus pocus over things they learn in school, like tooth brushing, and vitamins, but they are criminally negligent of their children's real welfare. Take her daughter-in-law, for example, a fine girl in many ways, but does she remember to keep the string of red coral on little Joseph's neck, day and night, every day? She does not! And the old lady has assured her that if she did, there would never be any trouble from *malocchio*. And what happened? The baby was taken to his mother's aunt's house one day last winter and the charms were left at home. Everybody for blocks around knew her aunt, Angela Trepasani, had the evil eye. And Angela made a great fuss about what a beautiful baby, and so on and so on—all the time wishing to herself she could have had a child of her own years ago. And what happened that night? Little Joseph nearly died of the colic, and his foolish mother didn't even know what caused it and called in an American doctor!

Little Joseph's grandmother might have given him any one of numberless minute charms for his protection, but coral has the double advantage that it is both red and in the horn shape which appears in many forms as a prophylactic against the evil eye. Sometimes a child will wear a single little horn, about three quarters of an inch long, fastened to a silver chain. Other possibilities are wrist charms with tiny fish, anchors, keys, hearts, a little hunchbacked man, scissors, or a string of thirteen coins. Rarely in America does one see, although they may be hidden in the clothing of children more often than we think, phallic-shaped charms, ancient symbol of the life force, to oppose the death force of the evil eye. There are little silver charms in the shape of a hand; frequently these make the sign of the fig or *fico* (thumb between the first and second finger) which is, of course, a phallic sign; indeed, one that is used still to ward off the evil eye when a special danger is present. The double fig, or horned hand (the extension of first and little finger from the closed fist), is another form into which these charms are made. Undoubtedly in the old country some were to be worn on the outside of a child's garments to attract the glance from the child itself, while others were to be worn underneath the garments to offset its power once it had been given. These distinctions have been lost in the New World, as near as I can discover.

The charms I have just been discussing are all in miniature, but such full-sized objects as knives, scissors, keys, crossed safety pins, salt, and *mozzoh* are to be found in baby carriages as protectives. Another Jewish protective, which I dare say is rare in this country, is made by removing and drying the eyes of three mice and wearing them in a bag about the neck. Easier to come by, but worn in the same way, is three-sided garlic. It goes without saying that crosses and religious medals are also widely acknowledged to be safeguards against the evil eye, and, with the more religious, sufficient safeguards in themselves.

The talismans mentioned so far are for the protection of the individual; there are a few recognized as potent in the defense of a whole house. Italians use horseshoes, cow, goat, or deer horns, and stuffed heads on which there are horns. Jewish people scatter salt about the house and tack the *mazzuzah* to the front-door frame with the evil eye in mind, among other things.

Besides these talismans, there are manual and verbal charms used for protection, some of these are religious, many of them are distinctly pagan. These differ from the talismans, too, in that they are used when a particularly dangerous situation arises, such as the presence of one known to possess the evil eye, or undue compliments or praise. Inherent in the belief in the evil eye is the pagan fear of the gods who are ever jealous and quick to cut down the man who forgets his place.

For another to praise him or his too much is to encourage him in thinking himself secure or especially favored. Whom the gods would destroy, they first raise up. This whole concept is implicit in the fear of the evil eye; here the possessor of the eye becomes merely an agent for the jealous gods who are ever around us. During the centuries the emphasis has been shifted so that the blame falls upon the overlooker, and the fear of the gods is transferred to him. While some will object to this oversimplification of a highly complex and historically beclouded matter, it helps us see with some perspective the customs of muttering, "God bless it," or "God save the mark," or "God love it," as the Irish and Italians say, or "*Keinahora*" (no evil eye), as the Jews do, when a child or treasured possession is being praised. Thus the God of Christianity or Judah is called upon to protect the child, or calf, or whatever is being praised, from the jealous wrath of the pagan gods. These acts, naturally, are done with none of this in mind; they are done instinctively and without historic pondering, just as you or I might tip a hat, or say "God bless you," when somebody sneezes.

Gestures of defense are also made in these dangerous situations. The fig, which has already been mentioned as it appears in the miniature charms, is found among both Jews and Italians. Since very early times the fig has been recognized as an insult and defiance to both men and demons. It is made by inserting the thumb between the first and second fingers, as a symbol of the sex act; a variant called the double fig consists of holding the right thumb in the closed left fist and the left thumb in the right fist; this symbol of the child within the womb survives, so far as I can discover, only among Jews. The important fact to be remembered about the fig is that while it is a gesture of insult to men, and presumably to demons, it also immobilizes the latter, making them incapable of harming the maker of the fig. It is for this reason that it survives as a prophylactic against the evil eye. There is a Jewish belief that the descendants of Joseph are immune to the powers of the evil eye, which accounts for the custom of making a double fig and repeating, "I am the seed of Joseph whom the evil eye may not touch," upon entering a strange city where one is unfamiliar with the local characters of supernatural disrepute.

Certain other motions are considered efficacious. One may, according to the Jews, glance down the left side of the nose, as an act of protection, and a bridegroom, who is especially liable to the envious, evil glance, should walk backward as much as possible just before his wedding. Spitting is held useful by both Italians and Jews, among whom it is frequently thought advisable to spit, or make the pretense of spitting, whenever one is complimented. One earthy, big-hearted Italian woman has a preventive charm which would have delighted the Wife of Bath: if someone tells her she is looking well or younger than ever, she scratches her behind and says,

Fo sangue mio fratello
Sempre e buona una gratella.

(Even if it is my brother,
I will scratch myself anyway.)

Bestowal

There is general unanimity in the belief that the effect of the evil eye is brought about by staring at the victim. The direct, long-held, piercing stare is what people fear and recognize as the one which carries malevolent power. This feeling is so pronounced in Poland that they are disturbed when anyone looks overlong at a baby or new-born animal; just to be safe, the parent or owner should spit over his shoulder and say, "Na psa uroki," meaning, approximately, "May the evil fall on the dog." Some Italians feel that it is unwise for one who has recovered from a long and dangerous illness to leave the house for some time, lest people stare at him and among them will be one with *malocchio*. From New York City comes the advice that one should never stare into anyone's eyes in the subway, lest he be the possessor of the evil eye, a rare instance of the absorption of beliefs about the evil eye into American mores.

Staring, then, is the physical method by which the evil passes from the eye to the victim, but usually back of this act is an emotional state which generates the desire to harm: envy, jealousy, anger, and these are disguised behind a facade of praise and compliments. Two or three examples will be sufficient to clarify the situation.

An Italian baby was suddenly and inexplicably taken sick, and its mother went to an old healer in the community who told her that someone had put the evil eye on the child during the day and asked who had visited the house. The child's mother said that she had had only one visitor, a kindly soul who had praised the baby, and said, in a heartfelt manner, that she envied the parents having so lovely a child. Having made her diagnosis and discovered the cause, the healer made an herb bath, the ingredients of which she refused to disclose, and, while she mumbled a charm, bathed the baby in the brew. After a little while a scum came to the surface and the healer showed it to the child's mother, pointing out that the evil had now left the baby and it would be better directly. [Elizabeth Hansen: Camille Agosta.]

From a man who grew up in the ghettos of Warsaw and fought in the abortive revolutionary movement of 1905, eventually coming to America indirectly by way of Siberia, comes a story of what was suffered by a young seamstress whose work was greatly admired. One day a girl came to her to make a bridal gown and the seamstress worked day and night until the dress was finished; the result was beautiful. The morning after it was done another girl came to the seamstress' house; she too was soon to be married and wanted a wedding gown. When she saw the one that had been finished, she wanted that one—it was so lovely, so suited to her figure, a perfect dress in every way. But the seamstress could only say no, and promise that she would make her one very like it. In anger and annoyance, the second bride-to-be left the house, dissatisfied with the decision she had to accept.

No sooner had the girl left than the seamstress felt unaccountably tired, then sick, until shortly she went to bed, screaming with pain. Her mother could do nothing to help her and so it was with a sense of relief that she listened when a neighbor told her of a man seven miles away who could help the girl. She went immediately to this man's house and when she entered, even before she could say a word, he took a dish of water and looking into it,said, "You have a daughter who is very sick." Then he gave the mother the same dish of water and told her to run back with it as fast as she could go. When she arrived home she was to wash the sick girl with it and give her some to drink.

The mother did exactly as she had been instructed, and as she washed her daughter's body the pain went out of it and the girl felt better immediately. She completely recovered except for a single spot on her body which her mother missed—that was one finger, on which big black spots long remained. Everyone, of course, knew that the second bride had given the seamstress the evil eye, and afterward many other people suffered from her glance. [Sylvia Greenblat: her father.]

The pattern repeats itself over and over again. You are fortunate, the mother of a beautiful baby or possessor of a fine cow, a healthy brood of chicks, a handsome lover, new clothes, or you are old and have a good appetite, brisk health, then along comes one who has only praise, only glowing words, but underneath there burns jealousy, envy, anger at your luck. The newcomer seems to be taking in every detail of your good fortune: you think nothing of it until he is gone and the baby gets sick, or the cow will give no milk, or your head aches, or your appetite is gone. Then you know. Once in a while it is someone you have angered, a girl whom you have deserted, or an old beggar woman you have refused, but this is less frequent.

Occasionally people bestow the evil eye without malice. Such a person has this affliction and tries to control it, but when he sees something he envies, the eye works against his will. Consider the case of the Italian woman who called in a neighbor to see her beautiful silk worms and the wonderful spinning they were doing; but the man said no, that he possessed the evil eye and whether he willed it or no, he might harm her worms. But she said that didn't worry her and she insisted. And so he looked at them and as he looked they began to die. [Mary Scuderi: Mrs. Anthony Patone.] Or the Jewish woman who went to visit a friend who had just had a baby and soon after she left the house heard a great deal of confusion, with running about and sending for the doctor. She came over as fast as she could because she knew that only she could help her friend. She had been fed by a wet nurse as a baby and so possessed the evil eye, but was always careful to say *keinahora* when she praised or admired something; this time she had forgotten to do that and her friend's relapse was the result. She "swore off the curse" and so the young mother was quickly cured. [Estelle Engelhardt: Alice Abelove.]

Effect

Perhaps the variety of effects which a glance from the evil eye may produce has not yet been sufficiently emphasized. It should be remembered that while any human is liable to these attacks, children, and especially babies, are particularly susceptible. Sometimes they cry and none can tell why, others get colic, or convulsions, or hiccoughs, or a fever, or their skin gets red and dry, or their throats hurt, or their heads ache. Some who go through life with hunched back or crossed eyes are told by their parents the story of how they were "overlooked" when they were beautiful babies. Sometimes those afflicted die.

Most frequently the effect upon adults is a piercing headache—and this appears over and over again in the record. But other results are to be found: some people are tired and sick, another gets a fever, or a nervous breakdown, eyes may become sore, stomachs may get out of order. Women in childbed are in particular danger because of the envy they arouse, once they have come through their labor successfully.

Animals are liable to attack from the evil eye—cows will go dry, pigs will squeal, horses will rear up and run away. Crops may be spoiled, or baking, or cheese when it is being made. Indeed, the effect of the evil eye may, presumably, be felt in any aspect of human life or any aspect of life which affects human beings.

Diagnosis

If one is suffering from one of these well-known effects of the evil eye—a severe headache, let us say, his first problem is diagnosis. There is no sense in going to a doctor if what you need is a healer with a "good eye," or *upshprecher* (literally one who can "talk off" the evil eye), as the Jews call him. Now keep in mind that at this state all that the healer is doing is determining whether or not the ailment is organic or is a result of "overlooking." The cure comes later.

There is an Irish method which, apparently, requires no special powers, and can be done by any friend or relative of the afflicted. You make the sign of the cross over his forehead, yawning while you are doing this. If he yawns in return, you may be sure that it is the evil eye from which he suffers. [Margaret Seyffert: Angie Sutterley.] There is a feeling among the Italians, too, that if a person enters a room and others begin to yawn, it is a sure sign that the newcomer has been afflicted by one with an evil eye. A woman suspects that her ailing baby has been so cursed, and she takes it to her mother-in-law's house; no sooner do she and the child enter the room than the older woman begins to yawn; then the mother and grandmother know how to proceed. [Ann Monaghan: Marie Trapasso.]

Syrians also recognize the yawn as a diagnostic aid. If a Syrian thinks he is suffering from the effects of the evil eye, he goes to a wise woman or healer. She takes a green leaf from some kind of mint or, lacking that, a needle. With either of these articles she bends her body over the patient and makes the sign of the cross. She then repeats certain secret charms, and certain prayers, continuing the making of the cross while she is doing this. If the patient has been "overlooked," the woman will begin to yawn and her eyes will water. If the pain of the patient does not let up after the third repetition of the prayers, the wise woman must proceed to a more drastic cure. [Lillian Abraham: her parents.]

Another method of diagnosis, most frequently found among Jews, depends upon the dropping of objects into water and from their reactions analyzing the situation. One can take hot, melted beeswax or melted lead and drop it into a basin of water held over the head of the afflicted person—if the wax or lead forms the figure of a human, then the evil eye is to blame. Among Roumanian Jews a related technique is used, but with a difference; salt, bread, and a hot coal are thrown in a glass of water; if the bread and coal rise to the top, the evil eye is responsible for the discomfort; if neither rises, the person is physically ill. An old Italian woman used to drop grains of wheat into a saucer of water; if they floated, the evil eye was to blame; the pattern they formed could be read to aid in the cure which followed.

Another method of diagnosis is closely related to the commonest Italian cure, using oil and water, of which much more will be said shortly. With infinite variation in the procedure—sometimes using the finger, sometimes a silver knife, or an iron rod, sometimes blowing on the surface or stirring the drops—the basic ritual remains the same: take a basin of water and let a few (usually three) drops of olive oil fall onto the surface, then read the result. There is no unanimity in the interpretations, but a large majority believe that if the oil forms, or even can be encouraged to form, a single circle, that is, "an eye," then the patient has been "overlooked." If it remains in separate little globules, the problem is organic and not supernatural.

Cures

Having made our diagnosis, we now should consider the cures for the evil eye; these display great variety, exhibiting strong racial and regional peculiarities. Throughout, it will be noticed that the basic principles are most frequently founded upon sympathetic magic, and only occasionally upon contagious magic. It will also be observed that the cures are frequently extensions of the diagnostic tests mentioned above.

By and large it is believed that these cures can only be achieved by one who is specially endowed or trained for the work. This is a person with a "good eye," an *upshprecher*, a healer, or white witch. Their position in the community is invariably excellent, although many of them, especially among the Italians, make no other claim to supernatural powers. A good friend of mine, Thomasina Pallotta, whose parents were born in a mountain district south of Naples, and who now is an unusually successful social-studies teacher in a New York State high school, is greatly sought after during vacations when she goes home because she is known to have a "good eye." The interesting fact is that while she can cure the headaches of her friends who are suffering from being "overlooked," she herself has absolutely no belief in the evil eye nor her own cures. Her attitude is that if she can help her friends, she is glad to do it, but for herself, she takes an aspirin.

She was taught the ritual she uses on Christmas Eve, the only time of the year it can be passed on, according to Italian tradition. The only woman (and among the Italians it always appears to be women who remove the evil eye) who can learn the ritual at any time of the year she chooses is the mother of twins, who belongs to a special and privileged class. As near as I can determine, it is considered bad luck for either an Italian or Jewish healer to take any money for her services, an attitude which coincides with that of many white witches and healers of this country who feared that they would lose their God-given power to heal if they accepted money for it. Some people will tell you that evil witches are capable of both inflicting and taking off the effect of the evil eye; in that instance, pay of some sort is expected.

The cures themselves are based upon the use of herbs, water, or salt, the use of the clothing of the "overlooker" or the "overlooked"; by the use of licking and spitting; the use of oil and water. Many cures combine these elements into a fairly complicated ritual as we shall see; many of them combine religious signs and prayers with more pagan techniques.

The only reports I have of the use of herbs come from the eastern Mediterranean area. In Greece they take three whole cloves and burn them in the flame of a candle. The ashes are put in a glass containing about an inch of water; this should be swallowed in three swallows; a few drops should be left in the glass so that it can be thrown over the left shoulder to the pavement where people are walking by. An Iranian living in New York reports that among her people the spell of the evil eye can be broken by picking certain herbs at midnight. The herbs are then burned; when the sufferer steps into the smouldering fire, the spell is broken. Many people pick the herbs at the proper time and dry them so that they will be at hand when the need arises. (It is also possible to cast the spell of the evil eye by burning the same herbs and concentrating on the person you wish to harm.)

So far as I can determine, the use of salt as a cure is now confined to the Jews. In one ceremony, of which I have a number of examples, salt is thrown into the four corners of the room. One *upshprecher* placed a piece of bread and salt in each corner, while another put salt in one corner and a twig, placed in some particular position, in another—this is, of course, in the room in which the sufferer lies. When a child is sick, the salt can be poured three times around the baby's head, then a little is thrown into three corners of the room, the remainder going into the fire. With this ritual goes a verbal curse, the words of which I do not know, to the effect that the tongue of the person with the evil eye should be burned, just as the salt was burned.

We have already seen that water is used to diagnose the effects of the evil eye; it is also used, with various other items, as a cure. The Syrian healer, who has, for example, used the diagnostic ritual mentioned above and discovered that the patient is indeed suffering from the evil eye proceeds then to the cure, which consists of taking a piece of charcoal and breaking it into small fragments. As she tosses these into a basin filled with water, she calls out the names of the people with whom the patient has associated just before the attack. When one of these pieces of charcoal sinks, she knows the responsible person. That particular piece is taken out of the basin and crushed to a powder, with which she makes a sign of the cross on the forehead, chin, and near the ears of the patient.

Hungarians, Poles, and Russians all seem to put faith in the use of water for their cures. Hungarians cure a child by taking hot coal ashes, or anything burned (a match or candle will do), and dipping it four times into a glass of water. After each dip, they make the sign of the cross over the water and rub some of the water on the forehead of the child. After the fourth dipping and rubbing, the water is sprinkled in the four corners of each room in the house; this not only removes the curse from the afflicted but returns it to the one who was responsible for it in the first place.

A Russian cure for the evil eye, which seems to attack in the form of fevers, chills, and headache, relies upon breaking pieces of bread into a glass of water, and pretending to spit into the glass three times; then the fingers are dipped into the glass and passed over the forehead. A little of the water should be drunk, followed by a good slug of whiskey. Then let the patient go to bed and in the morning he will be cured. [Mary Honcharik: Mrs. Walter Honcharik.] (The last item in this ritual by itself has been known to produce remarkable results, even in persons who do not believe in the evil eye.)

Poles throw hot coals into holy water, counting by threes while they add salt. They drink some of the water and rub some on the face. The remainder is taken outdoors by the victim and thrown on the roof. In Galicia Jewish people appear to have borrowed the customs of their Gentile neighbors, for there they drop crumbs of bread into a glass of water while reciting special prayers.

Spitting is, of course, an ancient and widely used device for keeping off all forms of evil; it is especially used to remove the curse of the evil eye among Jews. A variant, used mostly in curing children who have been "overlooked," consists of having the mother lick the eyes or forehead of the child. Sometimes she turns her head after each lick and makes a sound which is taken to be "Poo!" but which originally, at least, must have been a polite spit.

Expectoration has long borne a relationship to magic spells and rituals, often being used at the beginning and end of the ritual. We have already noticed that it may be used as a preventive, and the very approach of one suspected of possessing the evil eye will cause the careful person to turn his head and either spit or make the pretense of spitting—usually three times and to the left side. I have some evidence that it could also be used by the one who cast the spell to dismiss it. There is a tradition in a Kingston, New York, family of Jewish friends of mine concerning a grandmother who in her youth was once "overlooked" and had the spell removed in this way. Not feeling very well, she had lain down one day when a visitor was announced, for they were a family of some means back in Russia. There entered the poorest woman in town, one known to possess evil powers; she sat down and spoke for a little while with the ill woman, and then left. No sooner was she gone than my friend's grandmother became violently ill; in the delirium which followed she kept calling the old woman's name. Her husband went out and brought the woman back to the house, and when she came into the bedroom the sick woman was quiet and appealed to her to remove the evil eye. The old one seemed to grow angry, turned and spat on the floor and left. Immediately the pain ceased and the woman became well again. [Blanche Navy: Mrs. David Navy.]

Another Jewish cure, which has nothing to do with the one who casts the spell, requires that the sufferer go by himself and take either an undergarment which he has recently worn or his nightclothes and spit on it three times; he then makes as if to wipe his face with it. This is ineffective if anyone sees it being done.

There are two distinct methods involving the use of clothing; one centers around garments of the "overlooked"; the other, around those of the possessor of the evil eye. The first assumes that if you burn clothing which has been in intimate contact with the "overlooked" one, you destroy the effect, burning the power of the evil eye out of him. On the other hand, if you destroy or injure an article of clothing belonging to the possessor of the evil eye, you will injure, by way of contagious magic, the possessor himself, forcing him to remove the curse.

The latter method is reported from the Irish, Jews, Italians, and Syrians, being, of course, a common device to counteract any kind of witchcraft. The former method, the burning of the victim's clothes, also used widely in the counteraction to witchcraft is, so far as I know, used only among Italians.

Some Italian white witches boil a piece of the afflicted one's clothing, pricking it with a long fork. Another is reported to have asked for a handkerchief which had recently been used by the afflicted woman; this she burned, saying certain magic words. Another similarly used the cap of a boy suffering from headache and said prayers over it, thus relieving the pain.

From a Jewish woman who grew up in Poland comes a remedy which utilizes both methods. If a child cries and will not sleep, she suggests that first you lick his eyelids and spit. If this doesn't work, go to the person you believe to be responsible and obtain a small particle of clothing; when you get it home put it on a pot cover, place a burning coal on the cloth, and fan the smoke so that it blows across the baby's face. The method of last resort, these first two having failed, requires that you take an article of the child's clothing to an *upshprecher* who holds it in his hands and yawns, saying, "That was a bad spirit," and when you get home the child should be cured. [Marilyn Warshaw: Hannah Markowitz.]

From an Italian source come very explicit requirements for the size of the garment to be taken from the possessor of the evil eye; it may be any article of clothing, but must be long enough to measure from the elbow to the fingers of the afflicted one, at least two and a half times. The white witch to whom you take this garment will measure it three times, saying prayers each time. The sufferer should then wear the garment until his headache or other pain has disappeared. [Vera Kosak: Rosaria Trusco.]

Syrians have it that the garment or piece of material to be used in the countercharm must be stolen from the overlooker; that unless it is stolen the charm is useless. Once more, it is taken to a white witch who burns it, holding it over the victim's head, praying while she does it. The remnants of the garment should be buried immediately, thus completing the cure. [Abraham: *ibid.*] From a woman born in Ireland comes a similar charm except for the element of burial.

An interesting Italian charm which is related to these requires that one take a lock of hair from the person afflicted and give it to the possessor of the evil eye: that returns the curse to its source; quite understandably a certain amount of ingenuity is required, for no overlooker wants to taste his own medicine. Others look through the pillow on which the sufferer sleeps to see if there are any feathers in the shape of a cross; if there are, the feathers are removed and burned, then a cure can be effected. There is another Italian belief that if one sleeps after having been overlooked, it is harder to remove the effect of the evil eye than if it can be cured before he sleeps.

This brings us to the cure for the evil eye which outnumbers all others among Italians; I have no evidence that it is to be found among other groups in America. In its simplest terms it consists of letting drops of olive oil fall in water while prayers are being said, but the variations rung upon this simple ritual appear to be manifold. I shall describe at some length three methods which contain the principal variations within this ritualistic pattern, and then comment on further variations observable from a score of informants, many of them from women capable of removing the curse of the eye themselves.

Take a medium-deep dish and make the sign of the cross over it, saying, in effect, "May the Lord heal your suffering and help in removing the Devil's curse; may his curse return back and injure the one who gave this curse of the evil eye." A spoonful of olive oil and a knife should also be at hand. The afflicted person sits in front of you while you take a drop of the oil on the end of your middle finger and drop it into the water in the dish. Let about five drops fall into the water; if the oil spreads out into a large circle until it seems to disappear into the water, then the person has the evil eye, and badly. (So much we have already had before, under the subject of diagnosis; now we go on to the next step.) The oil on the surface of the water is then cut with the knife in the shape of a cross, whereupon the dish is emptied and the whole process is repeated to the number of three times. If this shouldn't work, the sufferer's only recourse is to go to the one who overlooked him and beg to have it taken off. [Thomasina Pallotta: Mrs. Elizabeth Serio.]

The second method relies more upon religious elements than the first; not only are there prayers, but the use of the key, symbol of the papacy, is surely not a matter of accident. This is especially notable since the informant said that the only substitute for the key was a saint's medal, which could be used. Again you take a deep dish and fill it with water, then set it on a table or some other level surface where the water will not move. Take a teaspoonful of olive oil and a key; with the key cross the sufferer three times, repeating the Lord's Prayer each time you do this. With the key still in hand, repeat this process over the oil and over the water. Now dip the key into the oil and let drops of it fall into the water. (If it remains in small globules, do not continue after the seventh drop, for the suffering does not come from the evil eye, but from some other cause.) The larger the circle of oil formed in the dish, the more serious is the effect of the evil eye upon him. You continue dropping the oil into the water until the circles get very small, repeating the Lord's Prayer to yourself all the while the oil is dropping. When the oil begins to form small circles, it indicates that the spell is being broken; the "eye" which first was formed is destroyed and in its place we have a multitude of little eyes. You are now ready for the last phase of the ritual, which consists of crossing the person's forehead seven times with the oiled key, repeating to yourself the Lord's Prayer each time. If the first healer gets no results, a second, and even a third may be consulted, but no more than that. [Ida Occhino: her mother.]

The third example comes from a middle-aged, gentle Italian woman living in Canastota who learned it, it is worthy of note, from a man who once cured her baby years ago. She collects a soup dish, water, a spoon, a knife, and olive oil. First she crosses herself three times, being careful not to say amen. Then she makes the sign of the cross three times over the dish of water, saying the following prayers to herself, in this order, an Our Father, a Hail Mary, and a Gloria. She then drops three drops of oil in the water with her index finger and says, "I offer these prayers to blessed eternity. Drive away from (the person's name) the evil eye, all sickness and curses whatsoever." (Yetta fodda tutti (name) la malocchio, la maladia, i invermi.) This entire procedure must be followed three times, at least once after sunset. The oil is then dropped in the water and cut with the knife, moving vertically from top to bottom and horizontally from left to right. One other fresh detail from this informant concerns the importance of the healer keeping her spiritual life in good repair; she must pray every day until her death, saying three Our Fathers, three Hail Marys, and three Glorias. [Concepta Zumbo: Mrs. Angeline Cerio.]

There is some disagreement as to what should be done with the oil and water after it has been used. One would have it thrown where none may walk on it, another would have it drunk by the one who is suffering; a third variant, which adds salt to the water, requires that when the water is thrown out the window the healer should repeat these words.

Aqua e sali
Soco fanno limaari
Non chi pozza giovaro.

(Water and salt
I hope that whatever
The witches devise will fail.)

Following this the victim of the evil eye says the following prayer:

San Anna, San Anna sia
Cu ava fari mali a (name)
Bene sini sia.

(Saint Anne, Saint Anne
Whoever wish harm to befall (own name)
I only wish you well.)

This last is based on the belief that there is no hope of getting the spell removed unless the person who has cast it is reassured that his victim will not retaliate; the naming of Saint Anne, of course, gives it the validity of a vow. [Josephine Valente: Antonina Scaduto.]

Today one could probably go into any large Italian settlement in the United States and find women who know rituals for the removal of the evil eye; similarly in other groups of Europeans who are somewhat isolated culturally from the mainstreams of the land in which they live. But for the most part these women are over fifty and another twenty-five years will see the belief almost completely lost sight of in this country—unless, of course, there comes a fresh tide of immigration. Our land seems to be a dead end for a belief which has had a long run down through innumerable centuries.[2]

NOTES

1. This study is based on 170 reports collected between 1940 and 1946 by the author's students in American folklore at New York State College for Teachers, Albany, New York. The distribution of information is as follows: Italian 90, Jewish 48, Irish 9, Polish 6, Syrian 4, Greek 3, Armenian 2, Russian 2, German 1, Hungarian 1, racially unidentified 4. In the more important contributions the names of the collectors and informants are indicated within parentheses, collectors first. Materials filed in Folklore Archive, Farmers' Museum, Cooperstown, New York. This study is part of a longer work written in 1946–1947 under the terms of a Guggenheim Fellowship.

2. The standard work in English on this subject is still Frederick Thomas Elworthy, *The Evil Eye* (London, 1895).

The Evil Eye in Its Folk Medical Aspects: A Survey of North America

*Wayland D. Hand**

In this survey by Professor Wayland Hand of UCLA, we find another view of the evil eye in the United States. Rather than relying upon the limited data afforded by those students who happen to enroll in one's class, Professor Hand has utilized his extensive bibliographical knowledge of published as well as unpublished sources mentioning the evil eye. Scholarship clearly requires both *fieldwork and library research. There would be no printed sources if fieldwork at some point were not carried out, but once field materials are housed in folklore archives, included in dissertations or theses, or published in some format, one needs to be able to retrieve such materials, often selectively. In this case, Professor Hand has chosen to concentrate upon the folk medical aspects of American evil eye practices. Accordingly, he searched his many sources for details concerning diagnosis, symptoms, and preventive and curative agents.*

Belief in the evil eye is as pervasive in many parts of the world as it is ancient. In compiling his classic two-volume work, *Der böse Blick und Verwandtes* in 1910, the well-known Hamburg ophthalmologist

* Reprinted from the *Actas del XLI Congreso Internacional de Americanistas,* Mexico, 2 al 7 de septiembre de 1974, Vol. III (Mexico, 1976), pp. 183–189.

S. Seligmann consulted over 2,100 bibliographical sources.[1] A sequel volume which was published a dozen years later and which dealt with the magic power of the eye and the phenomenon of fascination brought responses from scores of fellow practitioners all over the world,[2] including oculists and optometrists. In connection with the great work of Seligmann it is interesting to note that after the baneful power of the eye had been studied for centuries by scholars in anthropology, ethnology and folklore, workers in literature and the arts, students of religion, geographers, travelers, and a host of other investigators, the evil eye finally claimed the attention of eye specialists themselves. A recent American writer on the subject, Dr. Edward S. Gifford, for example, is a Philadelphia ophthalmologist.[3]

In Europe, belief in the evil eye is most pronounced in the Mediterranean countries, an area that is part of the vast geographical continuum extending along a central axis from India westward through the Middle East and all the way to Spain and Morocco. The spread of the belief in the evil eye to the New World, and particularly to Latin America, proceeded along an extension of this same central axis, as the New World was opened up to colonization and commerce after the fifteenth century.[4] A secondary route of transmission, and one more important for North America, came with the settlement of the St. Lawrence and Lower Mississippi river basins by the French, and the colonization of the Spanish Southwest by explorers and colonists from Mexico. As an admixture to the basic Anglo-Saxon colonization of the eastern seaboard, which set in by the beginning of the 17th century, there came later—particularly during the 19th century—ethnic components from all parts of Europe, including strong representations of the Romance and Slavic, as well as of the Germanic peoples. The interplay of these various cultures, as seen in the transmission of folk beliefs and superstitions concerning the evil eye, represents an historical development that is as intriguing as it is impossible to unravel.

The antiquity of beliefs in the power of the human eye is seen in the prevalence of fear of the evil eye in Old Testament times.[5] Besides being attested in the Bible itself, the evil eye is mentioned in the Apocrypha, in the Talmudic writings, and at a much later period, in the Koran.[6] References to the power of fascination go back to the 7th century B.C. in Assyrian and Accadian documents,[7] and myths concerning it are to be found in Sumerian sources in Mesopotamia dating from the third millennium B.C.[8] Seligmann has traced the belief in the evil eye to all peoples of the Middle East, Southern Asia, and the Extreme Orient, as well as to the inhabitants of most other parts of the world.[9] In this useful survey he has supplied a table of designations of the evil eye, by countries and language groups, together with the verb forms used to denote casting of the evil glance, the names of possessors of the harmful power, male and female, designations of the person harmed, a list of amulets and other apotropaic measures to deal with the malady, and the names of special healers invoked.[10]

Belief in the evil eye is attested in Northwest Europe in early times. The mythical Irish giant, Balor of the Evil Eye, for instance, was celebrated for his lethal gaze which could strike whole armies dead.[11] There is also mention of the "glance of eye" in Beowulf, Old English epic poem of about the year 1,000 A.D., as one of the dark and evil forces to confront the warrior.[12] Feilberg has traced in convincing fashion the belief in the evil eye in Nordic tradition from early times to the present,[13] and Vuorela has written a monograph on the prevalence of old beliefs and practices concerning the evil eye that are encountered in present-day Finland.[14] In the Anglo-Saxon countries the belief in the evil eye appears to have been better preserved in Scotland than elsewhere.[15]

From this brief historical and geographical survey it will be easy for the student of these matters to trace out North American manifestations of the evil eye and to connect them with their most immediate European sources and antecedents. In surveying so vast a field, however, the investigator, while recognizing local oikotypal differences in beliefs and traditions concerning the evil eye, will nevertheless be aware of certain basic notions encountered everywhere. Briefly summarized, these involve the possessor of the power of the eye, and the unusual nature of, or reasons for, his baneful gift, the manner in which the evil glance is cast on the victim, measures used to prevent, counteract, or repair the mischief, and special healers and functionaries who dispose over these magico-religious medical gifts.

Since it is impossible to deal with the manifold aspects of the evil eye, I have been obliged to confine myself in this paper to matters that come under the purview of folk medicine rather than entering upon the broader field of magic. Even though the magical component is not as rich and hardy as it is in the European homeland, there is nevertheless a reasonably representative body of folk beliefs and customs to be found in the United States and Canada. Despite the fact that I know the Latin American tradition much less well, I venture the guess that elements of the general European stock-in-trade, not found north of the border, are certain to be found somewhere in the Mexican tradition itself or elsewhere in Latin America.

Diagnosis of the evil eye involves not only the symptoms as observed in the victim, but is also determined by some knowledge of the person causing the affliction. Admiration of a child by childless widows,[16] for example, or even a childless man,[17] particularly if the praise is fulsome, is a good indication of the jealous and designing person that is likely to possess the power of the evil eye. The case for suspicion of intended harm to the child is strengthened if the visitor is deformed in some way,[18] cross-eyed, possessed of eyes of a different color, or if his or her eyebrows should happen to meet.[19] Gypsies, Negroes, and other minorities are often singled out as bearers of the evil eye, as in Ohio, for example.[20] In some traditions persons born on Christmas day are thought to be bearers of the evil eye.[21] In the Mexican-American tradition one member of a set of twins is thought to have the power to harm people through his glance.[22] In New York State it is believed that persons are usually born with the evil eye.[23] Similarly, there is a notion in the northeast of Scotland, and elsewhere, that the evil eye is inherited, but I have not come upon this view in the United States.[24] In the Mexican-American tradition a person born with the *vista fuerte* may unwittingly bring harm to his fellows by a mere glance.[25] In the Jewish tradition it is believed that a child acquires the power of the evil eye by being suckled by a wet nurse.[26]

The symptoms of being "eye bitten," "blinked," "overlooked," or "forelooked," as this malady is variously described in vernacular terms,[27] generally involves the appearance of fatigue and discomfort, as in Pennsylvania,[28] or incessant crying on the part of the afflicted child, as in the Jewish tradition of Ohio and the Latin-American tradition.[29] Even such a common ailment as colic, in which a child is costive and fretful, may be taken as a symptom of the evil eye.[30] Generally, however, the attack is associated with more sudden and violent onslaughts.[31] Chills and fever, coming on suddenly, are suspected to be magically induced,[32] particularly if the child vomits.[33] Cramps and convulsions fall into this same category of sudden and unexplained seizures.[34] Hiccoughs, with its jerking and uncontrolled spasms, is particularly singled out as an indication that the victim is suffering from the evil eye.[35] Perhaps the malady most often regarded as being caused by the evil eye is the common headache. This belief is encountered in the Italian, Jewish, and Russian traditions of New York State.[36] It is also found in Pennsylvania and Ohio,[37] among the Italians in West Virginia,[38] and in the Latin-American tradition in Texas and New Mexico.[39] An unusual sign of being a victim of the evil eye is found in the Polish tradition of Ohio, where it is believed that a person with long, silky hair that becomes matted, has been smitten by the heated eye.[40]

Ritual diagnosis of the evil eye is a rarity. In the polyglot cities of Ohio drops of olive oil are eased onto water in a flat container. If the oil mixes with the water it is generally believed that the person is under a spell. However, some people believe that if the drop of oil remains intact, the person being investigated is under the power of the evil eye.[41] In the Latin-American tradition throughout the American Southwest there is a wellknown European ritual involving the breaking of eggs on the body of the supposed victim, or placing the broken egg in a dish near the bed. In New Mexico, for example, if the child has *el mal de ojo*, the image of the eye will appear in the yolk.[42] There are various other indications, including a sure sign of possession when the raw egg yolk at the head of the bed is magically cooked, as it were, overnight.[43] Among American immigrants from various parts of central and northeast Europe bread is used in a ritual to detect the evil eye. The bread is broken and put into a glass of water. If the bread does not sink, this is taken as evidence that the patient has been eye-bitten.[44]

Ailments caused by the evil eye range from the general malaise to wasting and decline, and other unspecified maladies;[45] also a whole range of diseases in addition to headache, fever, convulsions, cramps, and the like, mentioned above. Impairment of sexual capacity and function is also associated with the evil eye,[46] as are impotence and sterility in man,[47] and even nocturnal pollutions.[48] The evil eye also figures prominently in female complaints, menstrual disorders, and problems of pregnancy and childbirth.[49] In the Romance countries abortion is likewise associated with the evil eye.[50] Most heinous of all in connection with the birth cycle is the casting of the evil eye to dry up a mother's milk or to make a child refuse the breast.[51] I have not come upon these beliefs in the United States. In light of this wide range of folk beliefs and superstitions it is not surprising that the evil eye should also be credited with causing mental and emotional disorders, all the way from nervous breakdowns,[52] to imbecility and insanity.[53]

As in other magical diseases, the evil eye does not respond to the ministration of the usual medical practitioners.[54] Special healers are pressed into service[55]—powwow doctors, Jewish *Upsprechers* who know how to "talk off" the spell,[56] and the *felcher*, the doctor without a licence.[57] Many women in South Philadelphia, for instance, know the proper prayers against fascination, and are willing to remove the accursed evil eye without remuneration.[58] Among the Genoese of central California the secret words used by the healer of the evil eye can be divulged only on Christmas Day.[59]

It is difficult, of course, to differentiate between natural and magical cures with regard to the evil eye since most cures, as befits the nature of the malady, often themselves contain magical or religious aspects. In keeping with the principles of natural medicine, of course, special herbs are pressed into service, and are dried and held ready for use.[60] In 1905, Emil Berdau, writing on Mexican folk medicine along the Texas border, tells of the bathing of a child in a decoction of *Yerba de Cristo* as a preliminary to the disenchantment from the evil eye in an involved ritual employing eggs.[61] The use of garlic is principally apotropaic, although it is widely believed that the cloves possess absorptive power.[62]

The bathing of ailing children with herb baths was practiced,[63] but I find no mention of salt baths, for instance, which were used as an apotropaic ablution in Scotland, among other places.[64] In Maryland, however, salt was sprinkled in every corner of the room and on the threshold to disenchant a child stricken with the evil eye.[65] Licking a child with the tongue is encountered in curative procedures for the evil eye in New York State.[66] A most unusual ritual, met with only in the Latin-American tradition in the Spanish Southwest, involves finding the culprit who had inflicted the evil spell, forcing him or her to drink a mouthful of water, and then making him empty it directly into the suffering child's mouth.[67] Berdau's account of the ritual specifies the use of water drawn in the moonlight outside one's yard.[68] A water ritual in New York, formerly practiced by South Italians, involved placing a saucer of water on the victim's head preliminary to the mumbling of a verbal charm.[69] In New Mexico around 1910 the sweepings from the four corners of the sufferer's room were boiled in water, taken into the healer's mouth and then spewed into the child's face. It was not specified as to whether the person performing the disenchantment had herself inflicted the spell.[70] The fiery element is resorted to in ritual cures just as is the use of water. Glowing coals, ashes, charcoal, and various fumigants are used to counteract the effects of the evil eye,[71] and the burning of a hole in the garment of the person communicating the evil will turn the harm upon the perpetrator himself.[72]

Time will not allow more than a listing of the usual kinds of preventive and curative agents employed against the evil eye in North America. In the main they are well known. Wherever excessive praise is heaped upon a child by a jealous or designing person, the child's mother, or anyone near, would customarily spit upon the child to prevent *el mal de ojo*.[73] Also, it was widely thought that touching the child after it had been unduly praised would somehow counteract the intended harm.[74] Sometimes the remark about a "beautiful child" is offset by the statement that "it's an ugly child," or some other disparaging remark, as in Ohio.[75] If, on the other hand, the admiration is sincere, the person must add "God bless," or some other religious remark to the same effect.[76] Because of the constant fear of enchantment mothers carefully guard their children,[77] cover their faces, or even hide them.[78] In the New Mexican Spanish tradition, a mother taking a young child with *el mal de ojo* from the house, must be sure not to cross rivers or ditches with it, in the fear that once she did so the child would become permanently afflicted.[79]

Preventive gestures of "the horns" or "the fig" are made with the hands,[80] and crosses are inscribed on the child's forehead.[81] In Brooklyn this is done with laundry bluing.[82] Perhaps the most common means to avert the evil eye, or to cure it, is the use of amulets. These range from bracelets and necklaces of various materials such as jet and coral,[83] to chains and crosses,[84] and beads of various kinds, including red and white beads as well as those of coral.[85] These latter were the favorites. Horns of various kinds, or amulets made of horn, are widely used.[86] Often they are mounted in silver, as in Toronto.[87] A favorite amulet is a miniature hunchback.[88] The familiar *gobbo*, is often carved from mother of pearl or from stone of some kind, but this Italian charm is also made from almost any durable substance, including, of course, coral.[89] In a shop in South Philadelphia in the late

1950's, Dr. Gifford was able to buy small gold figures and other kinds of amulets of hunchbacks, crescent moons, fish, and other votive pieces to counteract the evil eye.[90] Curio shops in almost every large American city carry trinkets of this kind. Horseshoes, common in witchcraft, are also used to protect the house from the evil eye.[91] They are nailed to the wall, or to doors, in the accustomed manner. Knives, scissors, and other bladed instruments employed in witchcraft, are also pressed into service against the evil eye.[92] Finally, among several other kinds of objects employed, red ribbons were fastened to the child, often around the neck.[93]

It is difficult to summarize a paper as diffuse and wide-ranging as this. I hope, however, that these representations will convey some notion of the prevalence of folk beliefs and customs connected with the evil eye that are to be found in the United States and elsewhere in North America. More systematic work is needed, of course, to depict these interesting traditions in their variety and fullness, and even in their present-day vitality.

NOTES

1. S. Seligmann, *Der böse Blick und Verwandtes. Ein Beitrag zur Geschichte des Aberglaubens aller Zeiten und Völker* (2 vols., Berlin: Hermann Barsdorf Verlag, 1910). (Unless otherwise noted, all references are to this parent work.)

2. S. Seligmann, *Die Zauberkraft des Augens und das Berufen. Ein Kapitel aus der Geschichte des Aberglaubens* (Hamburg: L. Friederichsen & Co., 1922).

3. Edward S. Gifford, Jr., *The Evil Eye. Studies in the Folklore of Vision* (New York: The Macmillan Company, 1958). The reader should also know of the earlier standard work on the evil eye in English: Frederick Thomas Elworthy, *The Evil Eye. An Account of this Ancient and Widespread Superstition* (London: J. Murray, 1895).

4. George M. Foster's notions of the transmission of the evil eye to the New World from Mediterranean areas generally coincide with my own. See George M. Foster, "Relationships Between Spanish and Spanish American Folk Medicine," *Journal of American Folklore*, 66 (1953), 203, *passim*. (Hereinafter cited: Foster, Spanish Folk Medicine.)

5. J.D. Rolleston, "Ophthalmic Folk-Lore," *The British Journal of Ophthalmology*, 26 (1942), 484. Cf. Deuteronomy XV: 9; XXVIII: 54–56; Proverbs XXIII: 6.

6. Rolleston, p. 484.

7. *Ibid.* Cf. Benjamin Lee Gordon, "The Evil Eye," *Hebrew Medical Journal*, 34 (1961), 292.

8. Edward S. Gifford, Jr., "The Evil Eye in Pennsylvania Medical History," *Keystone Folklore Quarterly*, Vol. 5, No. 3 (1960), 3. (Hereinafter cited: Gifford, Pennsylvania.)

9. Seligmann, I, 12–47.

10. *Ibid.*, I, 48–64. This Appendix contains a bibliography of dictionaries and special glossaries.

11. Rolleston, p. 485; Alexander Haggerty Krappe, *Balor With the Evil Eye* (Institut des études françaises, Columbia University, New York, 1927).

12. Rolleston, p. 484.

13. H.F. Feilberg, "Der böse Blick in nordischer Überlieferung," *Zeitschrift des Vereins für Volkskunde,* 11 (1901), 304–330, 420–430.

14. Toivo Vuorela, *Der böse Blick im Lichte der finnischen Überlieferung* (Folklore Fellows Communications, No. 201, Helsinki, 1967).

15. John Graham Dalyell, *The Darker Superstitions of Scotland* (Glasgow: Richard Griffin & Co., 1835); Robert Craig Maclagan, *Evil Eye in the Western Highlands* (London: D. Nutt, 1902).

16. John R. Crosby, "Modern Witches of Pennsylvania," *Journal of American Folklore*, 40 (1927), 308.

17. Gifford, Pennsylvania, p. 6.

18. Crosby, p. 308.

19. Newbell Niles Puckett Collection of Ohio Popular Beliefs and Superstitions (unpublished; hereinafter cited: Puckett, Ohio); Foster, p. 207; E. and M.A. Radford, *Encyclopaedia of Superstitions* (ed. and rev., Christina Hole, London: Hutchinson & Co., 1961), pp. 155–156; Gordon, p. 267; Walton Brooks McDaniel, "The *pupula duplex* and Other Tokens of the Evil Eye in the Light of Ophthalmology," *Classical Philology*, 13 (1918), 336; Phyllis H. Williams, *South Italian Folkways in Europe and America. A Handbook for Social Workers, Visiting Nurses, School Teachers, and Physicians* (Institute of Human Relations, Yale University, New Haven: Yale University Press, 1938), p. 153

20. Puckett, Ohio (unpub.); Radford and Hole, p. 156; Ella Mary Leather, *The Folklore of Herefordshire, Collected from Oral and Printed Sources* (Hereford: Jakeman & Carver, 1912), p. 51.

21. Williams, pp. 142, 155.

22. William R. Holland, "Mexican-American Medical Beliefs: Science or Magic," *Arizona Medicine*, Vol. 20, No. 5 (May, 1963), 93.

23. Louis C. Jones, "The Evil Eye Among European Americans," *Western Folklore*, 10 (1951), 11. Cf. Franz Boas, "Current Beliefs of the Kwakiutl Indians," *Journal of American Folklore*, 45 (1932), 224.

24. Dalyell, p. 22; Rolleston, p. 485.

25. Holland, p. 93.

26. Jones, pp. 11, 17.

27. Gifford, Pennsylvania, pp. 3, 7; Dalyell, p. 45.

28. Gifford, Pennsylvania, p. 7.

29. Puckett, Ohio (unpub.); Ozzie G. Simmons, "Popular and Modern Medicine in Mestizo Communities of Coastal Peru and Chile," *Journal of American Folklore*, 68 (1955), 62.

30. Jones, p. 17.

31. Benjamín S. Moya, *Superstition and Beliefs Among the Spanish-Speaking People of New Mexico* (M.A. thesis, University of New Mexico, Albuquerque, 1940), p. 34.

32. Jones, pp. 17, 21; Gifford, Pennsylvania, p. 6; Moya, p. 36; Aurelio M. Espinosa, "New Mexican Spanish Folk-Lore," *Journal of American Folklore*, 23 (1910), 409.

33. Dorothy J. Baylor, "Folklore from Socorro, New Mexico," *Hoosier Folklore*, 6 (1947), 149; Simmons, p. 62.

34. Seligmann, I, 123 (USA); 200 (Germany, Ireland, Scotland); Jones, p. 17; George M. Foster, *Empire's Children: The People of Tzintzuntzan* (Smithsonian Institution. Institute of Social Anthropology, Publication No. 6, Washington, D.C., 1946), p. 267.

35. Jones, p. 17; Gifford, Pennsylvania, p. 4; Claudia de Lys, *A Treasury of American Superstitions* (New York: The Philosophical Library, 1948), pp. 312–313.

36. Jones, pp. 17, 19, 21; *New York Folklore Quarterly*, 21 (1965), 185.

37. Gifford, pp. 4, 7; Puckett, Ohio.

38. *West Virginia Folklore*, 12 (1962), 29.

39. Moya, p. 37; Florence Johnson Scott, "Customs and Superstitions Among Texas Mexicans on the Rio Grande Border," *Publications of the Texas Folklore Society*, 2 (1923), 83.

40. Puckett, Ohio (unpub.).

41. Puckett, Ohio (numerous attestations), *West Virginia Folklore*, 12 (1962), 29; Foster, *Spanish Folk Medicine*, p. 208; Williams, p. 155; Antonio Castillo de Lucas, *Folkmedicina* (Madrid: Editorial Dossat, S.A., 1958), p. 56.

42. Moya, p. 37; Espinosa, p. 410; Foster, *Empire's Children*, p. 267, Foster, *Spanish Folk Medicine*, p. 209; Simmons, p. 65; Scott, p. 83; Josephine Elizabeth Baca, "Some Health Beliefs of the Spanish Speaking," *American Journal of Nursing*, 69 (1969), 2174; Servando Martínez and Herry W. Martin, "Folk Diseases Among Urban Mexican Americans," *Journal of the American Medical Association*, 196 (1966), 162.

43. Ruth Dodson, "Folk Curing Among the Mexican," *Publications of the Texas Folklore Society*, 10 (1932), 84–85.

44. Jones, pp. 18, 21. Serbo-Croatians in eastern Nebraska still practice this test.

45. Rolleston, p. 484; Seligmann, I, 201; Jones, p. 17; George D. Hendricks, "Superstitions Collected in Denton, Texas," *Western Folklore*, 15 (1956), 9; Rodney Gallop, *Portugal: A Book of Folk-Ways* (Cambridge: Cambridge University Press, 1936), p. 59.

46. Rolleston, p. 484; Gifford, Pennsylvania, p. 4.

47. Seligmann, I, 197, 199; Leonard W. Moss and Stephen C. Cappannari, "Folklore and Medicine in an Italian Village," *Journal of American Folklore*, 73 (1960), 98.

48. Seligmann, I, 200.
49. Rolleston, p. 486.
50. Castillo de Lucas, p. 434; Moss and Cappannari, p. 98.
51. Seligmann, I, 93, 197, 200–201.
52. Jones, p. 17; Moss and Cappannari, p. 98.
53. *Anuario de la Sociedad Folklórica de México*, 3 (1942), 109; Seligmann, I, 200.
54. Seligmann, I, 200.
55. Jones, p. 19.
56. Jones, pp. 18–20.
57. James R. Foster, "Brooklyn Folklore," *New York Folklore Quarterly*, 13 (1957), 88.
58. Gifford, Pennsylvania, p. 7.
59. Jane Voiles, "Genoese Folkways in a California Mining Camp," *California Folklore Quarterly*, 3 (1944), 213.
60. Jones, p. 20; Foster, *Spanish Folk Medicine*, p. 209.
61. Emil Berdau, "Der Mond in Volksmedizin, Sitte und Gebräuchen der mexikanischen Grenzbewohnerschaft des südlichen Texas," *Globus*, 88 (1905), 384.
62. Puckett, Ohio (unpub.).
63. Jones, pp. 15–16.
64. James Napier, *Folk Lore, or Superstitious Beliefs in the West of Scotland Within This Century* (Paisley: Alex. Gardner, 1879), p. 30.
65. Annie Weston Whitney and Caroline Canfield Bullock, *Folk-Lore from Maryland* (Memoirs of the American Folklore Society, Vol. 18, New York, 1925), p. 83, No. 1704.
66. Jones, p. 20.
67. Moya, p. 37; Espinosa, pp. 409–410; Baca, p. 2174; Martínez and Martin, p. 162; John G. Bourke, "Popular Medicine, Customs and Superstitions of the Rio Grande," *Journal of American Folklore*, 7 (1894), 126; Scott, p. 83.
68. Berdau, p. 384.
69. *New York Folklore Quarterly*, 21 (1965), 185–186.
70. Espinosa, p. 410.
71. Alixa Naff, "Belief in the Evil Eye Among the Christian Syrian-Lebanese in America," *Journal of American Folklore*, 78 (1965), 50; Jones, pp. 20–21; Napier, p. 39.
72. Folk-Lore, 14 (1903), 83; Jones, pp. 20–21.
73. Moya, p. 35; Puckett, Ohio (unpub); Eugene S. McCartney, *Folklore Heirlooms* (Michigan Academy of Science, Arts, and Letters, Vol. 16, 1931), p. 130. Since envy is a common cause of the evil eye, I have not done more than mention it here. The reader would be well advised, however, to consult the excellent article of George M. Foster, "The Anatomy of Envy: a Study in Symbolic Behavior," *Current Anthropology*, 13 (1972), 165–202, esp. p. 174, *passim*.
74. Dodson, p. 84; Hendricks, p. 4; Martínez and Martin, p. 42; Scott, p. 82; John Q. Anderson, *Texas Folk Medicine*, 1,333. *Cures, Remedies, Preventives & Health Practices* (Austin, Texas: The Encino Press, 1970), p. 30.
75. Puckett, Ohio (unpub.).

76. *Ibid.*

77. Helen M. McCadden, "Folklore in the Schools: Folk Beliefs, Current Report," *New York Folklore Quarterly*, 3 (1947), 337.

78. John H. Bushnel, "Medical Folklore from California," *Western Folklore,* 6 (1947), 273, No. 3; Charles Wagley, *The Social and Religious Life of a Guatemalan Village* (American Anthropological Association, Memoir Series, No. 71, Menasha, Wis., 1949), p. 26; Ruth Bunzel, *Chichicastenango, A Guatemalan Village* (Locust Valley, New York, 1952), p. 101.

79. Moya, p. 38.

80. Puckett, Ohio (unpub.); *Pennsylvania Folklife*, Vol. 14, No. 3 (Spring, 1965), 44; Williams, p. 95; *Keystone Folklore Quarterly*, 14 (1969), 113; Castillo de Lucas, p. 56.

81. Moya, p. 36.

82. James R. Foster, p. 89.

83. Moya, p. 35; Espinosa, p. 410; *Journal of American Folklore*, 4 (1891), 35 (Nicaragua); Puckett, Ohio (unpub.); Foster, Spanish Folk Medicine, p. 208.

84. Puckett, Ohio (unpub.).

85. O.H. Hauptmann, "Spanish Folklore from Tampa, Florida," *Southern Folklore Quarterly*, 2 (1938), 12; Puckett, Ohio (unpub.); Napier, p. 36.

86. Jones, pp. 13–14; *Pennsylvania Folklife*, Vol. 14, No. 3 (Spring, 1965), 44; Puckett, Ohio (unpub.).

87. *Journal of American Folklore*, 31 (1918), 134.

88. Jones, pp. 13, 17; *Pennsylvania Folklife*, Vol. 14, No. 3 (Spring, 1965), 44; Puckett, Ohio (unpub.).

89. Fanny D. Bergen, *Animal and Plant Lore* (Memoirs of the American Folklore Society, Vol. 7, Boston and New York, 1899), p. 131, No. 133.

90. Gifford, Pennsylvania, p. 8.

91. Jones, p. 14; Teresa Slamick *et al.,* "Sign of Spring," *West Virginia Folklore*, 10 (1960), 43; Puckett, Ohio (unpub.); Napier, p. 139.

92. Jones, pp. 13, 19; *Pennsylvania Folklife*, Vol. 14, No. 3 (Spring, 1965), 44; Moss and Cappannari, p. 98; Radford and Hole, p. 25.

93. Bushnel, p. 273, No. 3; Puckett, Ohio (unpub.); Anderson, p. 30; Foster, Spanish Folk Medicine, p. 208.

Reflections on the Evil Eye

*Richard G. Coss**

Having generously sampled some of the farflung descriptive literature devoted to the evil eye, the reader may have become increasingly curious about the possible reasons why the evil eye should exist in the first place. While the number of theoretical speculations about how and why the evil eye should have developed in the way that it has is admittedly limited, these attempts at explanation do not lack a certain boldness of imagination.

One approach to the evil eye entails considering hypothetical connections to more general gaze or stare behavior. Professor Richard G. Coss of the University of California at Davis has sought to examine the evil eye against the background of psychological studies of eye contact and aversion. His lively discussion of experiments carried out with an impressive variety of forms of animal life does give one pause, regardless of whether or not one accepts the premise that the evil eye can be fully explained in this fashion. It can, after all, scarcely be denied that eyes are a physical characteristic of many animals other than man and it seems reasonable enough that eyes are used to communicate fear, anger, and other emotions among many of these non-human animal forms. Readers should also keep in mind that different theories of the evil eye are not necessarily mutually exclusive. One theory does not automatically rule out another. Several theories may be equally persuasive and perhaps even correct. (Or two competing theories may both be wrong!) Here at any rate is one of the most ingenious speculations to date.

*Reprinted from *Human Behavior,* 3, no. 10 (October, 1974), 16–21.

The eye has been treated as a powerful symbol in a wide range of cultures for thousands of years. Incised staring eyes peer blindly from neolithic Chinese and Bronze Age Celtic funerary pottery presumably to protect the grave from tampering people and imagined spirits. The Greek kylix drinking cup often depicts two painted staring eyes that may act as a protection device. In addition to the eyes being displayed on a wide variety of human artifacts, pagan folklore in many cultures has sustained the myth of the "evil eye." The Greek legend of Medusa refers to her ability to turn men to stone with a single glance. Small, grotesque amulets were worn conspicuously by Egyptians, Phoenicians, Etruscans and Romans to protect the wearer from the evil eye. The Greeks placed talismans in their homes to catch the eye of the "fascinator" and wore amulets that appeared to deflect the envious glances of passing people.

The origin for the belief in the evil eye within the Western culture has been attributed to the ancient Greek theory of visual perception where the eyes were thought to emanate rays that struck objects and people with sufficient power to produce physical harm or even death. The late 19th century investigator of the evil eye myth, Frederick Elworthy, reported that many unrelated languages throughout the world manifest reference to the evil properties that are exhibited by the fixed stare.

Recent preliterate societies in Africa and the Far East have employed props to accentuate the provocative aspects of the stare. Facial paint enhancing the eye shape and masks with eyes portrayed by brightly painted concentric circles have been displayed by men in secret society rituals as protective devices to suppress the evil activity of suspected spirits and inhibit the intrusions of women and children. One West African tribe occasionally substituted baboon skulls with cavernous eye sockets for masks. Perhaps as a cultural parallelism in today's industrialized societies, fearsome monsters with exaggerated eyes have been developed by filmmakers to thrill movie theater audiences.

With or without applied decoration, the eyes are a provocative source of social stimulation, and this may account for the intense fascination with the eyes by many cultural groups. The direction of an affiliate's gaze is a powerful signal expressing interest in establishing contact or sustaining social interaction.

Among close friends or lovers, brief bouts of eye contact lasting a few seconds can be satisfying emotionally as long as the accompanying facial expressions are appropriate for generating pleasant moods. Conversely, prolonged eye-to-eye contact is invariably considered unpleasant, even among close associates. The unyielding stare of an approaching stranger is especially unnerving, but this also depends upon the social setting and the duration of the stare.

It has been suggested by several researchers that eye contact between strangers may be provocative because it violates the taboo of mutual looking without a proper introduction and, of course, it does act as an invasion of privacy. More important, however, the gaze receiver cannot anticipate what events might follow and, therefore, would be in a vulnerable position. Becoming the target of another person's interest often heightens the alertness of the observer who may attempt to minimize the visual intrusion by looking away. In public places filled with strangers, looking away—or gaze aversion, as it is labeled by researchers—is common. People deliberately line up their bodies in public areas, such as subway stations, to avoid inadvertent eye contact with unfamiliar people. Curiously, they also play the game of trying to watch people without letting their eyes get caught. Most of us are skillful users of the "fractional glance," that momentary scanning of other people to see where they are looking.

Sometimes deception is employed to conceal the viewer's interest, such as placing the edge of a magazine just below the line of regard. Window reflections and mirrors provide oblique viewing angles that permit casual or covert monitoring of other people without revealing the viewer's intentions. If eye contact occurs inadvertently, gaze aversion can occur in less than one-fifth of a second, making it one of the faster body reflexes.

The intensity of gaze aversion, which varies considerably between people and within the same person depending upon the social situation, has been used as an indicator of certain behavioral disorders, such as infantile autism. Autistic children and, frequently, psychotic children with autistic symptoms rarely engage in eye contact with another child or adult for more than a few seconds. These children also persistently avoid looking near the facial region around the eyes. In an experiment that I performed with John Richer at an English hospital specializing in autism, we observed that severely autistic children will look at an unfamiliar adult face three times longer when the face is covered up with both hands than when the eyes are uncovered. These children also displayed a marked decrease in body movements indicative of fear when the eyes were covered. Normal children were also examined, but they displayed little difference in gaze toward the strange adult.

On the other hand, normal children in more natural rather than laboratory settings will show evidence of wary and shy behavior toward unfamiliar adults or angry parents. Gaze aversion, when it occurs under these conditions, is often accompanied by turning the head and body away.

This type of timidity in children when they are stared at briefly may, in part, result from frequent corrective lectures where the errant child is told to look at the parent's face. A childhood filled with negative experiences associating the fixed stare of a parent or playmate with aggressive activity may partially account for the sensitivity that adults display toward prolonged eye contact. But further, the similarities of child-rearing practices in many cultural groups, where the fixed stare accompanies hostile behavior, could partly account for the widespread fascination with the eyes in various forms of art and mythology.

There is, however, another factor that could account for the sensitivity toward eye shapes. By the fourth week of age, many full-term infants will vigorously attempt to establish eye contact by visually searching for the eyes of another person. The duration of eye contact between mother and infant has been observed to last for several minutes if the mother deliberately sustains eye contact. Conversely, those same infants, when in a fussy mood prior to being changed or fed, may actively avoid eye contact by looking away or closing their eyes.

The observations of both intense eye contact and less frequent gaze aversion by month-old infants raise an important point concerning the origin and nature of the human sensitivity to eyelike shapes. The higher centers of the brains of infants less than three months old are not well developed, according to the findings of anatomists. As a result of this slow maturation process, the ability of young infants to see and recognize complex shapes, in addition to coordinating their eyes, would be somewhat restricted. However, many month-old infants will either seek or avoid eye contact with nearby adults. Based on available research, which is limited in scope, it appears that this form of visually guided behavior is controlled by central nervous system components functioning soon after the infant's birth.

Several researchers have proposed that the infant would learn rapidly to identify the human face and certain facial features with rewarding caretaking activities. The problem with this proposal is that it fails to account for why the eyes alone are selected by the infant as "high intensity stimuli" rather than other features of the body and face, such as the hands and mouth, which are equally conspicuous. Furthermore, if early learning does play an important role in mediating the infant's gaze behavior, one would expect a more random selection of salient facial and body features for visual pursuit or avoidance by the infant. Without the apparent effect of specialized reinforcement that could induce early learning of the eye schema, why do the eyes become a provocative source of stimulation so early in infancy? The desire to seek social stimulation through prolonged eye contact by young infants is suggestive of an innate behavior pattern operative soon after birth that could exhibit survival value for the vulnerable infant by enhancing the mother's feelings toward her baby. Similarly, the smiling response, triggered by the frontal view of a human face or even a schematized face comprised of only two eyelike spots, appears to be directed by innate recognition and motor mechanisms because it generally occurs during the 44th week after the infant's conception, irrespective of the length of gestation period.

Gaze aversion by some infants already disturbed by central nervous system disorders or momentary inattention by the caretaker could exhibit the maladaptive property of reducing the intimacy of face-to-face interaction, which could further deprive the infant of needed social stimulation. In this context, however, eye-contact avoidance could increase the infant's general level of comfort by blocking the perception of a potent arousal-increasing stimulus. Interacting people employ the same strategy of avoiding eye contact when they formulate their thoughts prior to speaking in an apparent attempt to eliminate the powerful distraction offered by this type of social stimulation. Several researchers evaluating gaze aversion in laboratory situations have found that social stress generated by a change in interpersonal dominance or the closer proximity of a dominant person increases the subject's tendency to gaze avert.

The deliberate use of the fixed stare to intimidate others often occurs in established social hierarchies, such as work environments where an office manager or a shop foreman will give hard glances to errant subordinants. As mentioned above, the human sensitivity to the fixed stare may have partially innate components complemented by experience with aggressive social encounters. This innate portion could be a vestigial remnant of survival-oriented behavior deeply rooted in man's evolutionary history. For several years, I have been interested in tracing the evolutionary development of the fixed stare and concomitant avoidance behaviors in a wide range of animal species when they encounter their own species or predators face-to-face.

The most primitive vertebrate animal examined, the African jewel fish, displays one large concentric eyelike spot on each gill cover that resembles the jewel fish eye. During territorial fights, jewel fish will rush a rival and suddenly flare open widely their gill covers, thus presenting the illusory image of two staring eyes from a larger, closer and more formidable opponent. Fighting is often less intense when both fish present their eyespots frontally in full view rather than less visible oblique angles. Therefore, it is possible that this type of threatening eyespot diplay evolved as a protective behavior pattern to discourage intense territorial fighting that could be physically damaging to the species as a whole. Of course, this hypothesis assumes that jewel fish are inherently sensitive to eyelike patterns and that these eyespots evolved as a parasitic by-product capitalizing on the fear generated by two staring eyes. In tests of eyespot recognition conducted in France, I presented jewel fish with a variety of flat models shaped like the frontal view of a jewel fish with fully spread gill covers. Each model exhibited a different number of painted eyespots and specific types of swimming behavior were measured when a model was presented rapidly in a manner simulating an attacking jewel fish. The model depicting two eyespots in the same configuration as an aggressive jewel fish triggered the greatest swimming response.

More advanced animals, such as birds and mammals, show evidence of fear when presented with two staring eyes. English ethologist Robert Hinde has reported that an owllike model with eyes evoked a greater vocal disturbance in chaffinches than a similar model without eyes. More recent studies of predator recognition by German ethologist Eberhard Curio support these observations in other species of birds. There is evidence to suggest that recognition of eyelike shapes by some birds is a partially innate response. David Blest found that hand-reared yellow bunting and great tit birds, isolated from frightening experiences with predators, avoided a butterfly with large eyespots conspicuously displayed on its hind wings.

Gaze aversion, indicating sensitivity to the eye schema, is also observed in birds. Certain species of gull perform a ritualized type of gaze aversion during courtship activity called "head flagging," which appears to make both birds more comfortable and improves the chances of successful mating. Crowded barnyard chickens also gaze avoid by turning their heads and bodies away from the nearest chickens. Mammals, such as rats confined in small cages where escape from close-range encounters with more dominant rats is limited, perform bouts of gaze aversion that restrict the disturbing perception of the adversary's face and, at the same time, remove from view any counterthreatening facial features that could elicit an attack. To the human observer, gaze aversion by the submissive animal appears as an appeasement display inhibiting aggression, but this is probably secondary to its primary role of blocking the input of disturbing facial stimuli.

In recent years, researchers interested in the origin of human social behavior have examined primates in their natural habitat. Their observations consistently refer to the aggressive role of the fixed stare and the appeasement properties of gaze aversion. Lemurs and lorises, for example, will gaze intently at a rival as a signal of threat intention. The closer proximity of a staring opponent can induce extreme gaze aversion in a submissive adversary, such as lowering the head and covering the eyes with the tail. Gaze aversion is especially apparent in zoo-kept ring-tailed lemurs.

Recently, I had the opportunity to examine the gaze behavior of the lesser mouse lemur, the smallest and perhaps most primitive living primate, in an attempt to determine if the eye schema elicits visual avoidance behavior during face-to-face encounters. A series of models was designed to depict different numbers and spatial arrangements of concentric circles. It was anticipated that the model presenting two spots in the horizontal plane, which schematically resembled staring eyes, would be looked at less than the models with fewer eyelike features. The findings of these experiements lend support to the contention that two staring eyes are the facial features responsible for eliciting gaze aversion in lemurs.

Many species of Old and New World monkeys and the larger apes engage in gaze behavior not unlike the more primitive lemurs and lorises. Among the primates in general, both staring and gaze aversion are protective behavior patterns limiting the intensity of aggressive and potentially damaging encounters. Dominant males deliberately employ the fixed state to intimidate rivals who either flee or display submissive gestures. This type of competitive social behavior tends to sustain certain favorable genetic traits, such as the motivation to form protective hierarchies by suppressing the breeding rate of less successful members of a primate group.

Human beings show gaze behavior patterns similar to even the most primitive primates. Several studies of the emotional impact of provocative pictures have shown that unpleasant or erotic pictures, disturbing to the viewer, generally receive less visual inspection because they elicit mildly unpleasant emotions. Scaled-up versions of the models used in the lemur experiments, discussed above, were presented by a special viewing apparatus to psychotic children with high levels of gaze aversion and to normal children. Both groups of children looked less at the model exhibiting the most eyelike features. The results obtained from the psychotic group were surprisingly similar to the results obtained from the tiny mouse lemurs, a species separated from man by at least 50 million years of evolutionary development. These findings suggest that the most eyelike pattern was looked at less because it elicited slightly unpleasant feelings in both groups of children.

In controlled laboratory settings, the perception of the fixed stare of a stranger can elevate the viewer's central nervous system arousal, as represented by galvanic skin and brain-wave responses, significantly higher than when the stranger averts his gaze. Similarly, I conducted several experiments using projected images of eyelike patterns in place of real faces in order to isolate the perceptual aspects of the fixed stare responsible for eliciting arousal increases. Using models with different arrangements and numbers of concentric circles—and measuring the increase in pupil dilation, another attribute of arousal—I found that slides of two concentric circles were the most potent arousal-increasing stimuli and that the horizontal placement was more provocative than either the vertical or diagonal arrangements. Moreover, groups of two horizontally placed circles with multiple concentric rings and darker interiors evoked proportionately higher increases in arousal as compared with groups of two circles with less contrasting contours. This latter finding offers support to the observations that the conspicuousness of the eye schema, as related to size, proximity and overall clarity, plays an important role in affecting the viewer's response. Myopic people without their eyeglasses have reported to this investigator that eye contact is easier to sustain during social encounters when they wear glasses. Perhaps, in the same fashion, eye contact at a distance is less disturbing because the image of the eyes is blurred.

Large eyes, on the other hand, may trigger the opposite effect. Architect James Lennon developed a series of large vertically hung transparent panels displaying a single column of abstracted frowning eyes. These panels, which appeared to the casual observer as "super graphics," were placed perpendicular to the entrances of several stores in an attempt to reduce shoplifting. According to Lennon, potential shoppers were observed to walk briskly into the interior of the test store without loitering near the merchandise adjacent to the panels. Shoplifting dropped markedly during the test period when the panels were hung, while the volume of merchandise sold remained constant.

Studies of eyelike patterns displayed on human artifacts imply that ancient and recent preliterate people were intuitively correct in capitalizing on their own sensitivity to staring eyes. They assumed that exaggerated eyelike designs adorning masks, shields and helmets would terrify their real or imagined enemies.

As can be seen from the research on eyespot patterns, which suggests that these patterns suppress predation or aggressive activity, the human use of this type of display is not without precedent. In addition to eyespot patterns displayed by a variety of lower animals, many vertebrate species have evolved conspicuous coloration surrounding their eyes, which increases the impact of gaze behavior by deceptively increasing the apparent size of the eyes. The function of these "eye-rings" is not well understood, at present, but they could act as a special signaling device to improve species' recognition or to augment the intimidating properties of the fixed stare under conditions of poor visibility in heavy foliage and at night, depending on the species.

A few species of fish, birds and reptiles exhibit conspicuous eye-rings, albeit varying in intensity somewhat sporadically. Numerous mammalian species, on the other hand, exhibit circular eye-rings contrasting sharply with the facial hair. Eye-rings are especially apparent on the small marsupials, but perhaps the most notable examples are displayed by the familiar panda. Among the primates, a few species of lemurs and lorises display spectacular black eye-rings dominating their entire faces. In some species of African and Asian monkeys, eye-rings appear as large colored patches predominantly positioned above the eyes and varying in hue from light brown to bluish white.

African baboons and geladas disturbed by the fixed stare of an opponent may suddenly return the stare and raise their eyebrows, exposing two bright, light-brown patches in a spectacular counter-threat display. Under less threatening circumstances, these monkeys may close their eyes momentarily like a flashing beacon while continuing to raise their eyebrows, thus stretching the skin over the eyelids and presenting the illusion of two bright, enormous eyes.

In man, the eyebrow hair forming two prominent semicircular arcs above the eyes, which enlarge their concentric contours, could be considered partial eye-rings. Like the eye-rings of baboons, human brow hair certainly enhances the perception of facial expressions involving subtle changes in brow movements. Dark round sunglasses, on the other hand, block perception of eyebrow expressions and the direction of the person's gaze, in addition to providing two large, eyelike forms that could disturb nearby people.

Some people report that they feel more comfortable when they wear dark sunglasses, possibly because they can look at other people without revealing their interest. Without sunglasses to provide a partial shield, the orientation of the human gaze is relatively easy to detect because of the visible white sclerotic coating of the eyeball surrounding the iris. At further distances, the brow ridge and eyebrow hair can cast dark shadows that provide additional cues of the head orientation of other people.

Decorating the region around the eyes, as well as other areas of the face and body, appears to increase feelings of security and self-esteem in members of many different cultural groups; and it may well be one of the oldest forms of aesthetic expression. Iron-oxide pebbles, rounded apparently by the friction against a softer surface, have been found in a lower Paleolithic site in France tentatively dated at 300,000 years old. Contemporary Australian aborigines, who simulate the living conditions of Paleolithic man, often accentuate the eye region with feathers and paint. Ancient Egyptian men and women painted their upper eyelids with black lead sulphide and their lower eyelids with green copper carbonite. A different technique employed by European women during the Middle Ages to make their eyes more attractive was to take the narcotic belladonna, which darkened their eyes by strongly dilating their pupils. Presently, the cosmetic industry vigorously encourages Western women to aspire to greater beauty by painting their eyebrows and eyelids, gluing on false eyelashes and smearing variously colored powders above their eyes. With nature's precedent of many millions of years combined with several thousand years of human practice, how can they miss?

The Evil Eye: Forms and Dynamics of a Universal Superstition

*Helmut Schoeck**

A much more conventional theory of the evil eye argues that it is basically concerned with envy, specifically the fear that someone else's envy of one's own good fortune may bring about misfortune. Sociologist Helmut Schoeck articulates this view of the evil eye as a part of his more general theory of envy as a universal factor in human societies. Whether or not Schoeck, a Professor of Sociology at the Johannes Gutenberg University in Mainz, Germany, is correct in claiming that envy is universal, it seems quite clear that the evil eye is not. He is therefore in error when he asserts that "belief in the evil eye seems to be shared by all peoples at all times." Equating envy with the evil eye allows Schoeck to translate a Kikuyu (from Kenya) word which literally means "envious thought" freely as "evil eye." This strongly suggests that the a priori assumption of universality can lead to the distortion of data. Similarly, American Indians both in North and South America do not appear to have had an indigenous evil eye belief. Accordingly it is not *"likely that the native Indian population in precolonial times had equivalent notions about potential evil from envious eyes." (One of the reasons why students need to read more than one interpretation of a given phenomenon is precisely so they can develop critical faculties so as*

* Reprinted from *Emory University Quarterly*, 11 (1955), 153–161.

to evaluate for themselves the plausibility of a particular statement.) On the other hand, if the evil eye really is related to gaze and staring behavior found among non-human animals as well as man, why isn't it universal?

For a fuller account of Professor Schoeck's conception of envy, see Helmut Schoeck, Envy: A Theory of Social Behavior. *(New York: Harcourt, Brace & World, 1970).*

Fear of the Evil Eye is man's oldest and most universal superstition.[1] It is probably our most destructive one too, and it derives from elementary facts of human biological and social existence. Little wonder that this belief is still with us, hardly suppressed by whatever enlightenment our race has mustered of late.

First of all, what does the evil eye mean to the believer and where can we find him? In the United States he resides mostly in the Black Belt, in Southern states in general as well as in isolated mountain areas, in the Southwest with its Latin people and folklore, and in all communities with heavy immigration from the shores of the Mediterranean Sea.

A college student of Italian descent from Clarksburg, a town in the mountains of West Virginia, described the impact of the evil eye in a vein suggesting that she has not yet freed herself from the superstition:

> There is a certain spell you cast on people. In Italian they call it the "malukes" [apparently an Americanized version of Italian *malocchio*, evil eye]. A person may get the "malukes" from bad eyes of someone *who is envious of that person*. The effect may be mild and yet people have been known to almost die of this evil spell. You feel very tired and restless. Many people get very sleepy and don't eat. Some become so ill that a doctor can't help them. The only thing that will take the spell away is prayers of a certain type. You must take an article of clothing with you when you are having the spell taken away. Usually a woman takes her brassiere. They also say salt drives away evil spirits. You may also hold your fingers in a certain way. You usually have them horned. *I have seen some of these things work.* I don't know if it's true or not, but I guess if you have faith in something it will work.[2]

A survey of a wide range of different cultures shows that the phenomena connected with our superstition are well-nigh universal.

Everywhere, people fearing the evil glance behave similarly, although their actions may vary. Practically all languages seem to have a word for the evil eye. And the psychological dynamics, the emotional force behind the evil eye, points always to the same source, the same emotion, no matter in which society we find it. It is envy. In other words, it seems that the whole complex of evil eye beliefs is the cultural manifestation of man's oldest sin. Theological views of man's inherent badness are frequently clad in words and analogies which show the prime evil of human nature to be its capacity for malevolent envy.

There are countless references to the evil eye which prove that the underlying emotion or sentiment—the imputed motive—is envy. In *Matt.* 20:15 the employer chides the worker who has complained about the more generous treatment of fellow workers, "Is thine eye evil?" The Greek adjective for "evil" used in this context means, among other things, "harmful," "dangerous." From the situation it follows that the worker was envious. Therefore, the employer, in fact, asked: Will your eyes cast evil on the favored ones?

Our own word, *envy*, is linked to the evil eye. The Latin word *invidia*, from which *envy* derives, consists of the verb *videre*, "to see," and the prefix *in*, meaning "against" as well as negation. On the other hand, in German (even nowadays, especially in Bavaria) the casting of the evil eye (*der böse Blick*) is often called *verneiden*, which is an emphatic dialect form of the verb *neiden*, "to envy." However, the linguistic bridge between envy and the evil eye can be shown in primitive languages as well. The Lakher, a tribe in India, believe in *ahmaw*, a sort of vampire soul, which "on seeing any one prosperous and happy, tries to get hold of the property of the person he envies by entering his soul and making him ill, in the hope that the sick man will then make offerings to him." N.E. Parry, who studied the Lakher, thinks that the term *ahmaw* approximates the concept of the evil eye, and reports that the Lakher believe a person with *ahmaw* always to be of an envious nature. The African tribe of the Kikuyu for a long time was thought to have no equivalent of the evil eye. Eventually ethnologist discovered that the Kikuyu word *kita*, or *kithamengo*, means practically "evil eye," although linguistically it would mean "envious thought."

To sum it all up, we can go to Sigmund Freud, founder of psychoanalysis, who certainly was a competent judge of the dark sides of human nature. In his essay *Das Unheimlich* (The Uncanny), written between 1917–1920, Freud affirmed:

> One of the most uncanny and most universal forms of superstition is the fear of the evil eye. Apparently, man always knew the source of that fear. Whoever possesses something precious yet frail, fears the envy of others. He projects onto them the envy he himself would feel in their place. Such sentiments are betrayed by glances, even if we suppress their verbal expression. And if anyone is too different from other people, especially because of unpleasant physical marks, he is thought to harbor unusually strong envy and the ability to translate that envy into malevolent action.

Although belief in the evil eye seems to be shared by all peoples of all times, there are cultures and ethnic groups among which the superstition wields excessive power. The authors of Greek and Roman antiquity attest its existence, and more than twenty centuries later little has changed. The farmers of southern Italy are as firmly in its grip as ever. Spain and Portugal are no exception, and Latin America, notably Brazil, shows a corresponding attachment to the lore of the evil eye. Yet it is likely that the native Indian population in precolonial times had equivalent notions about potential evil from envious eyes. Here, as elsewhere, superstition of conqueror and conquered merged and reinforced each other. Belief in the evil eye to this day is found among the Irish and Scottish peasantry, and especially in those counties of England which have a substratum of Celtic population.

Who is most likely to be suspect of the evil eye? In many cultures, it is a personal affliction, a misfortune, not the result of evil volition. Where this belief prevails, the effects of evil eyes usually are not deadly. No evil intention is imputed, and damages are not sought by the victims. The evil-eyed person has merely to make ritual sacrifices in order to rid himself of his dangerous mark. If such purification is ineffectual or considered impossible, the person with the evil eye may try to protect his fellows by shielding his eyes with his own hands in critical situations.

The evil eye may be looked upon very much like a contagious disease. Among the Lakher tribe, the female *ahmaw*, carrier of an evil eye, cannot get a husband. It is considered defamatory, therefore, to accuse a woman of being an *ahmaw*. Interestingly enough, though, in several societies the evil eye seems to be almost an exclusive trait of the female sex, or it may run in one sex of a given family. The Azande tribe in Africa, for instance, believes that the carriers of an evil eye, the *boro mangu*, transmit it from generation to generation, but always from father to son or mother to daughter, never from female to male.

The Azande (or Zande), as Edward Evan Evans-Pritchard has shown in a famous study, are a tribe with most elaborate witchcraft beliefs. They recognize two types of evil glances. There is the occasional ocular throwing of a spell or charm. Any Zande can and will do that if provoked. A genuine Zande sorcerer, however, is one who has the true evil eye. Azande language has one word, *mangu*, to designate witchcraft, sorcery, and evil eye. Another African tribe, the Bantu, also believes that a person is definitely born with the power of the evil eye.

As we have seen, when people fear jaundiced glances, they actually associate their fellow man's supposed or real envy with the belief in evil eyes. Moreover, all men fearful of the eye also fear oral praise by someone who might be envious and therefore might cast "the eye." For this reason it is not surprising that at least in one instance the mouth is taken as primary anatomical symbol of envious intent. Among the Arabs in the city of Timbuctoo the fear of "hurt from peoples' mouths" is so strong that natives feel weak at their stomachs if they overhear compliments about themselves. Whoever believes himself harmed by "hurt from a man's mouth," under native law, can sue for damages.

Who and what is mostly threatened by the evil eye? In general, everthing that is vital yet incomplete—in the process of becoming; everything that is beautiful or precious yet easily harmed, animate and inanimate alike, can attract the envious look. Children, especially pretty ones, and healthy domestic animals are considered favorite victims. Pregnant women are endangered, usually for certain periods only. (At the same time, however, in the Amazon town Itá, as elsewhere, it is the pregnant woman who is often thought to possess the evil eye.) All objects and actions surrounding marriage and birth invite the evil eye: the marriage bed, wedding gifts, and the consummation of marriage. The veil worn at weddings originally served to avert evil eyes. In Italy wedding gifts must not be brought or sent in advance. For if such gifts should pile up in quantity for any length of time, envy would be aroused. Italians also refrain from weighing and measuring their children, lest their physical progress might draw evil eyes. For the same reason in many peasant societies live stock is not counted. Often fear of the evil eye keeps women from going to prenatal clinics. This poses a major problem to public health officials in most Latin American countries today. Sometimes we can infer the fear of the evil eye. The Maori, the native race of New Zealand, take it for an ill omen if anyone should look on when the *taniko*, a fine type of weaving design is being worked. Women of a tribe in India show the same reluctance to have anyone watch their weaving.

Many taboos in regard to hunting and fishing resemble or come close to the evil eye belief. In Itá, a small town of the Amazon, the ill will of a man's envious friend is called *panema*. For instance, envious neighbors may collect the fishbones from a fisherman's yard and give them to the pigs. This will cause his fish lines to become *panema* and his catches will almost cease. The danger of a panema is so great that many hunters and fisherman hesitate to sell meat or fish, especially when the latter are caught with a new fish line. As in so many other aspects, belief in the evil eye and related black magic hampers the emergence of an expansive economy, which requires free exchange of goods and division of labor.

In his ever-present fear of evil eyes man has invented countless protections. One scholar collected more than two thousand different amulets which are worn by evil-eye-conscious people. Despite the great variety, certain basic devices are in use all over the world. We find among them sexual symbols as well as horns, claws, and teeth of amimals. The color blue is considered of protective value. But in Latin America children often wear a *red* ribbon for protection. The same purpose is served by the image of a bird. Sensitive places and objects, such as doors to bedrooms and barns, stables and expensive dinnerware, are protected by painted symbols. It does not take long in Pennsylvania to locate a barn with symbols designed to ward off evil eyes.

But it can be dangerous to wear or make protective signs and gestures. Common belief has it that the person with the evil eye is made especially aggressive if he should see any sign of defense. The wisdom of folklore apparently discovered that nothing makes a man more resentful than the correct or unfair ascription of envy. Defensive gadgets therefore are often hidden, under sleeves, tied to the arm or wrist. Tribesmen in Ethiopia wear leather cases containing written magic formulae to cancel the effect of evil eyes. Italians believe that even to speak about the evil eye can incite a potential *jettatore*, as the carrier of an evil eye is called in Italian. For that reason Phyllis Williams in her study of Italian folkways in America found it hard to substantiate the belief in many instances, although she knew that its function cannot be overrated. But Italians never feel sure whether or not some *jettatore* is present, and rarely mention the subject. But whenever a friendly gathering of mothers with children, in Italy, Latin America, or an Italian neighborhood in this country, suddenly breaks up as soon as a childless woman joins the group, the wise observer knows what has happened. The frightened mothers just take it for granted that the barren woman must envy their happiness and therefore cannot help casting the evil eye.

Throughout this paper we have called belief in the evil eye a superstition. But this does not make the fear expressed in the belief unrealistic. Undoubtedly, individuals who believe in the spell often do get sick. The literature abounds with cases of illness and even death of such persons. This is not too difficult to understand. Modern medical science recognizes so-called psychosomatic disorders. These are bodily disturbances, sometimes quite serious and persistent, which are primarily caused by emotional troubles. The effect of evil eyes most likely operates along these lines. An enlightened executive in our society may suspect the encroachment of a subordinate who conceivably covets his job. Thereupon the executive develops stomach ulcers. In primitive culture our executive would believe that the envious subordinate shot the evil eye at him.

There is, of course, no real link, no physical process between victim and *jettatore*. The whole drama takes place within the victim. Perhaps one of the most dangerous results is the feeling of utter futility. Cases are on record where a patient suffering from an ordinary illness refused to follow the doctor's prescriptions, or did it only half-heartedly, because he knew better. His illness came from an evil eye. Infant mortality among ethnic groups with strong belief in the evil eye often remains high despite efforts of public health agencies. Instead of rational child care in case of routine disorders, parents apply magic to cure the child from the effect of evil eyes.

Cultural anthropology recognizes both realistic and unrealistic fears. Perhaps we should classify belief in evil eyes as a realistic fear, provided we keep in mind that it is basically the fear of our neighbor's envy and malice. Thus the fear of envious eyes is probably more realistic than many a tract on human relations written by our latter-day Rousseaus who think man is good and only a particular form of society makes him evil. The belief in the evil eye reveals man's deep knowledge that, no matter what our station in life, what our fortune or assets, there will always be someone who is less favored by life. And he is a potential enemy.

From this perspective, the evil eye belief appears to be one of the most dysfunctional social controls in human society. That means, the more effectively it functions, the greater its harm to the welfare of the society afflicted with it. If a society lets belief in evil eyes go rampant, it lets itself be ruled by the envious. Consequently, any innovation, improvement, all activities conducive to economic growth—better health, changes in farming methods, in short, everything which has a chance of making one man and his family a bit more successful than the average—will be killed in its seeds. It can hardly be mere coincidence that cultural and economic backwardness correlates with an extreme incidence of the evil eye belief.

The most critical social relationship, as far as the evil eye is concerned, in all societies at all times is the guest-host relationship. A psychiatrist, Robert Seidenberg, in an article titled "On Being A Guest," described how an ancient problem reflects itself in the standard behavior of some of our contemporaries:

> A guest compliments the host on his well-being or prosperity. If later the host should become ill or lose his property, it is felt that the guest, being envious of the apparent health and prosperity of the host, caused the latter to suffer reverses. It, therefore, becomes improper to become too effusive in praise or compliments. If the compliment is paid, the recipient attempts to stave off the consequences by minimizing his well-being in front of the inconsiderate guest. He would say: "I only appear to be healthy; I really have many troubles." The propensity for understatement about self, as seen in many individuals in our society, has its origin in this superstition [of the evil eye]. With some people, business is never good. Their flag is the crying towel.[3]

To the present writer it is of considerable significance that of all cultures, as far as he knows, only our contemporary American standard culture has developed enough indifference to evil eyes to make it obligatory for the guest to admire freely the host's good fortune and "conspicuous consumption," whereupon the host will simply say "Thank you," instead of enumerating all his invisible misfortunes. This little fact may be a better clue to America's unique economic growth than many volumes of statistics will ever offer.

NOTES

1. A preliminary form of this paper was presented at the eighteenth annual meeting of the Southern Sociological Society, in the section on cultural anthropology, under the title "Forms and Dynamics of the Evil-Eye Belief," in Nashville, on April 1, 1955.

A complete bibliography on the evil eye would fill a small book. One of the earliest monographs on the subject is *De Fascino*, by L. Vairus (Paris, 1583). To date the most comprehensive study is *Der böse Blick und Verwandtes*, by S. Seligmann, 2 volumes (Hamburg 1910, 1911). Seligmann was an oculist in Hamburg and his work suffers from the lack of adequate anthropological categories. Also useful are: William W. Story, *Castle St. Angelo and the Evil Eye* (London, 1877); Frederick Thomas Elworthy, *The Evil Eye, An Account of this Ancient and Widespread Superstition* (London, 1895); R.C. Maclagan, *Evil Eye in the Western Highlands* (London, 1902); Alexander Haggerty Krappe, *Balor with the Evil Eye,* Studies in Celtic and French Literature (New York, 1927); Phyllis H. Williams, *South Italian Folkways in Europe and America* (New Haven, 1938); Lyle Saunders, *Cultural Differences and Medical Care* (New York, 1954); Henry J. Cadbury, "The Single Eye," *Harvard Theological Review,* Vol. XLVII, 1954.

2. For this hitherto unpublished account I am indebted to Dr. Ruth Ann Musick of Fairmont, West Virginia, a folklorist currently recording witchcraft lore of West Virginia. (Italics added.)

3. Robert Seidenberg, "On Being A Guest," *The Psychiatric Quarterly Supplement,* Vol. 23:1–6, 1949.

The Evil Eye—Envy and Greed Among the Patidar of Central Gujerat

*D.F. Pocock**

One of the hallmarks of the anthropological approach to a problem is in-depth fieldwork, with the anthropologist often relying upon the data provided by one or more key informants. D.F. Pocock, Reader in Social Anthropology at the University of Sussex, carried out such fieldwork among the Patidar, a caste of central Gujerat in India. In the course of his fieldwork, he encountered najar, the Gujerat equivalent of the evil eye, and he learned how it functioned from repeated discussions with different informants. Pocock's reporting of his experience gives us a concrete illustration of the effect of the evil eye on particular actual individuals. Rather than simply extrapolating from individual mini-case histories to give a generalized account of the evil eye among the Patidar, Pocock succeeds admirably in conveying something of the intense interpersonal strains resulting from (and also causing) accusations that someone had the evil eye.

Yet Pocock does much more than provide a picture of the evil eye in context. He suggests a refinement of the general envy hypothesis by calling attention to the importance of such factors as social status. In his words, the evil eye "is most feared when those who should be equal are not so in fact." Pocock also confirms the projective aspect

* Reprinted from D.F. Pocock, *Mind, Body and Wealth: A Study of Belief and Practice in an Indian Village* (Totowa, New Jersey: Rowman and Littlefield, 1973), pp. 25–33, 39–40.

of the evil eye. Person A who has something desirable, e.g., a healthy baby, sufficient food, etc. may project his own anxiety about possessing health or wealth upon person B who does not have such desiderata. Whether or not B actually feels envy, A may accuse B of having the evil eye. Pocock's combination of sensitive reporting of field data and his insightful analysis of such data exemplifies the social anthropologist's approach to the evil eye.

Momad[1] put on my raincoat and a large 1930s style trilby hat, known as a double-crowned Terai, and looking to my eyes rather sinister, pranced up the lane to the village. Ten minutes later he was back, crestfallen and carrying the coat over his arm. "What happened?" I asked. "Oh it's Surajben" he said, "she told me to take it off." "But why?" I asked. "Well," he said, "people would think I looked too beautiful." I had scarcely been in the village a month at this time. Why on earth Momad should be thought beautiful in a hat and coat several times too large, and badly travel-stained, I could not imagine. "But why, Momad?" I persisted "Why shouldn't you look beautiful?" "People," he said, "people would think that these are fine things." "But so what if they do?" "Well," he replied, "some people believe I would fall ill—it is *najar*."

The word *najar*, which in this context I translate as the evil eye, is also in common use with less dramatic meanings such as a "look," as in "have a look," or "sight," as in "short-sighted." Before I discuss its malevolent significance any further let me give a more detailed example. This concerns the same Surajben, the wife of Momad's patron in the village, Kishor, and whom Momad, although a Muslim, addressed affectionately as *māsi*—mother's sister.

Some months after the incident of the raincoat Surajben gave birth to her fifth son, Bhailal. Very soon afterwards the baby came out in a rash, which made it fretful and wretched. Surajben took him to the dispensary in Petlad and followed the doctor's instructions about bathing, powdering and the like. Momad and I went for a walk the evening after she returned from Petlad. "You remember we were talking about *najar*?" he said. "Yes, of course." "Well, Surajben thinks that Bhailal has been struck by it." "Oh really—what's she going to do about it?" I asked. "She's done it already," said Momad. He told me that Surajben had put some chillies and a scrap of the child's hair into a small brass bowl. On to these she had put a hot coal and inverted the bowl on a flat metal eating dish. Over this she had poured liquid buffalo dung. The bowl could not then be lifted and this had proved to her that the child was suffering from *najar.* Apparently a less elaborate test would have been to wave chillies round the child's head and throw them into the fire. If the gas from the chillies had escaped there would have been no *najar*, and another cause for the sickness would have had to be found. "So the baby is suffering from *najar*?" I said, "what does she do now?" "We shall have to wait and see," said Momad.

Within two days things were a little clearer. Surajben's husband's second cousin, Chiman, had no children. It seems that he had visited Surajben shortly after the child was born and made some comment about the way it could already move its eyes and notice things. Surajben had decided that this was the source of *najar*. You do not accuse people to their faces in such matters and, indeed, it is usually assumed that the guilty party is unaware of the damage done. Surajben therefore embarked on the following course of treatment: she made a point of visiting more frequently with her husband's kinsman and of inviting him to her house as well. As often as possible she would give him the child to hold; he, frankly fond of children, was always happy to hold it. Surajben was very pleased with the results. She had put a black thread round the baby's neck, as most mothers do by way of added precaution, but by giving the child a daily dose, so to speak, of Chiman's *najar,* its power diminished. The baby was allegedly always very ill after each treatment, but progressively less and less so, until finally the rash disappeared entirely.

When I saw Bhailal three years later, he was a very healthy and remarkably well-built little boy. Like all mothers who fear the envy of others, Surajben had deprived him of the formal appearances of care. Apart from the black thread with its little brass amulet he wore nothing, and his bleached brown hair grew to his shoulders. Surajben said that he was five years old, and therefore it was five years since I had visited them. I did not argue; Bailhal certainly looked a healthy five-year-old.

Najar, the evil eye, is the eye of envy, and it is an inevitable feature of a world in which men set store by looks, or health, or goods, or any pleasant thing. Even if, as is likely, one sets no store by one's mere subsistence, the very deprivations of others give grounds for fear. Since there is no one who cannot find someone whose plight is in some way worse than his own, so there is no one who is completely immune to envy and so to *najar*. Let me describe some typical *najar* situations. Doors should always be closed while eating otherwise hungry men may look in. Thus if one is eating out of doors, for example in the fields, and someone passes, one should offer him food. If food is offered, and can be accepted on caste grounds, some, be it only a little, should be eaten to demonstrate good will. A man in the village once suffered a fever because when he was drinking tea outside his house a stranger to whom he offered some, had refused it. The fever was only cured after he had given a coconut to the goddess. The stranger in this case was presumed to be deliberately malevolent—*melo manas* (literally—a dirty man). A woman was once feeding her child and looked at it with great affection. Her mother-in-law, fearing for the child, suddenly directed the young woman's attention to the stone flour-mill, which immediately broke in half. Here there is no question of envy, but of permanent evil eye unconsciously exercised. Envy enters only when we realize that it was the mother-in-law who spread the story through the village![2] A man bought a new hookah of the portable kind and was walking back from the town with it. A passer-by asked him where he had bought it, and it broke at once. A woman had a child and another asked to see it. It died. Whenever you feel that someone is looking at you, immediately pretend to take great interest in some worthless object, and so direct his attention towards that.

Although *najar* can run freely wherever there are human values, it is to a certain extent limited by a kind of realism. My battered hat and stained raincoat together with other marvels such as my typewriter, were not dangerous to me, as far as I could understand, any more than a landlord who lived in a village nearby had anything to fear from his silk shirts. *Najar* seems to be apprehended more from those with whom one is, in most other respects, equal, or has reason to expect to be. In a society governed by hierarchical principles in which status is given by birth, some seem to be naturally in a more favoured position than oneself, and one would not regard their superiority as a deprivation. This seems quite reasonable to me. We also do not really envy, that is truly covet, something which is not within our reach. What affect us more closely are the things which seem to just elude our grasp—the things which are only just better than the things we have, and with which, therefore, we can compare them.

The range of *najar* is limited, therefore, by the nature of caste society, which accords a status to each group, and by the weakness of human imagination, which reduces the number of material desires to the scale of existing material goods. But clearly there are other human goods which are neither accorded by caste nor beyond the range of any human being to conceive, such as health, beauty, popularity and the like: to this extent all men are vulnerable to all men.

On the face of it this seems an absurd situation: it means that no one can enjoy the very simplest and common joys of life because of a constant anxiety that he is exciting the envy of someone else. Actually something like this can happen.

I was in another village, in the house of a relatively wealthy man who had been very good to me. I will call him Swāmidās because he was a devoted servant—*das*—of Swāmi Narāyan, the deified founder of a Gujarat sect. We were sitting outside his front door one evening, looking out on the small courtyard into which the door of a poorer kinsman's house also opened. After a pause in our conversation he suddenly voiced his train of thought and said, "I *would* like to buy that house, but it's difficult." "But what on earth do you want it for, Swāmidās?" I asked. "Well, you know, my children play out here, they play with the children from that house and it makes difficulties." I remained silent. "You see," said Swāmidās, "sometimes I give my boys something nice—like an apple from Bombay, and the other children see it and of course they would like an apple too."

Swāmidās was dreaming out loud because there was no real likelihood that his kinsmen would sell their ancestral home. I do not think that, even if it had been possible, he would have forbidden his children to play with their cousins. He was far too generous a man to make his children secretive about the little luxuries he gave them. He was also far too sensible to allow himself to be forced into dispensing apples from Bombay to all the children in the neighborhood. I never heard Swāmidās make a similar remark, and certainly he regarded beliefs about *najar* as ignorant superstitions. Nevertheless, he was expressing a real anxiety about his own affluence which was not large enough to cancel out the poverty of his children's playmates.

The sequel to the story about Surajben and her baby throws more light on the situation. Let me say something about her first. She was a tall, very fair woman, in her forties, but prematurely aged. She was, I think, rather conscious of her position as the wife of one of the most influential men in the village and a little over-concerned to stress her sensitivity in caste matters. I remember that she once told me how she had eaten at a railway station in a room where a Vaghari was present.

The sight so upset her, she insisted, that she had been sick all the way home. The Vaghari are very low-caste herdsmen in Gujarat and the word has connotations of extreme filthiness. Surajben had five children, all boys. Her husband, Kishor, was a partner and manager of a small irrigation works owned by Swāmidās and some others who lived in a nearby village. The family had a financial security unknown to the bulk of the villagers. They ate rice very day and used wheat where the majority used millet. In short this was a family blessed in every way.

I had often spoken with Surajben about the beliefs and practices in which women were said to be the peculiar authorities. Amongst other things we had spoken of *najar* and she had explained a great deal to me. *Najar* was usually unconsciously exercised and sprang from desire. If one was contented one did not feel desire and therefore one's eyes could not hurt others. But there were some who had a kind of permanent core of envy in them amounting to a hatred, and such people could be recognized from their eyes which were unusually big and burning. If I observed Choto, for example, I would see what she meant. Choto had walked into the house one day when she was frying *bhajiān*, fritters; he had only glanced at the pan, but the whole batch was spoiled.

Choto was, in fact, a distant relative of her husband. They were both members of the same descent group and they were linked at the seventh inclusive generation. There is a saying in Gujarat to the effect that a distant cousin is a near relative when he is rich, but a poor brother is soon forgotten. The section of the lineage to which Choto belonged was extremely poor. Their area of the village was a crowded, dirty shanty town: Choto lived with his grandfather, his still unmarried sister, his mother, the uncle whom she had married after his father's death and the baby born of this marriage—all in a "house" of two rooms, both of which would have fitted twice into Surajben's kitchen/dining-room.[3]

Choto's father and uncle had divided the property in the lifetime of the former; Choto now had a fragment of unirrigated land on which he grew chillies and a few other spices. His uncle/stepfather maintained the mother and baby and himself on his own share—Choto could scarcely support his grandfather, his sister and himself from his land; he relied mainly upon his employment at the irrigation works. He was paid in cash and also in kind in that he had an occasional meal at Surajben's.

Here by any human understanding was a delicate situation. However, whereas Momad accepted patronage and, except in a few asides, showed no resentment, Choto burned. Momad was a Muslim and was treated as a member of a lower, but not polluting, caste. He was used to eating Surajben's food aside from the rest of the family, and to washing up his own utensils afterwards. Choto was of the same caste as Surajben, a Patidar, and as such could eat with the family. As a kinsman he had a right to be regarded as an equal. But he was to all intents and purposes a house servant as well as an employee of the husband.

Choto's father had been a rake and had died young, it was said, from drinking illicit liquor. Choto enjoyed something of his father's reputation. At night he told outrageous stories of his love affairs to the group of us who slept down by the irrigation works. These stories, like his ghost stories, were so enjoyably rich in exaggerated detail that no one ever challenged their veracity. He did have impressive eyes, large and glowing under thick eyebrows; he was not unaware of what Surajben said of their power.

On my second visit I got to know Choto quite well. Momad had gone to teach in a primary school some miles away. My Gujarati had much improved and Choto spoke no English. He was in touch with a side of village life very different from that represented by Surajben and her immediate family, and I was made fully aware of their disapproval of this new friendship. With Choto I enjoyed the underworld of the village; whereas in Surajben's family I had learned how things should appear, with Choto I discovered a lot about how things are.

I employed Choto as my *sāthi*, my companion, and shortly afterwards he began to wear a black thread around his neck with a brass amulet attached. I never discovered whether this was to guard him against the envy of his new employment, or whether he spoke the truth when he said that it was because he had been ill. We spoke of *najar* one day and I mentioned the one case that I knew in some detail, that of Surajben's baby, Bhailal, and the suspicion that rested on Chiman.

Choto didn't let me finish my story. Chiman, so much older, was a friend of his. They went drinking together in the fields at night and Chiman knew how to cook the partridges that Choto occasionally killed.[4] "That's stupid," he said, "why should Chiman look at Surajben's baby? His own brother's got several sons and they've none of them ever been sick. If Chiman were like that, that is where *najar* would have struck." "I am sorry," I said, "I thought you knew, and anyhow I just took it for granted that Surajben knew what she was at." "Surajben," he almost spat the name out, "she thinks of nothing but *najar*. I couldn't count the number of times she's called me out in the night to make some offering to the goddess—*mātāji*, she's just mean that's all. Do you know I once dropped in when she was frying *bhajiān* and when she heard me coming she shoved the pan under a bed to hide it." The implication was clear: had Choto found Surajben preparing *bhajiān* she would have been obliged to offer him some. I remembered Surajben's own account some three years earlier of what I assume was the same incident. "It's the same with that whole damn family," said Choto, "their life is such, *najar* is bound to strike."

Choto's view of things is complicated. He certainly believed in *najar*, but had grounds to defend Chiman his friend from the accusation. *Najar* was not then the kind of innocent weakness I had supposed. There was an implication of a moral defect, short of conscious malice. Moreover it was attracted not by mere envy but by meanness and a refusal to share good things. That was Choto's opinion and this came close to making sense of *najar* to me. *Najar* situations came into being not simply when people had enjoyable qualities or goods, but when people having these things took pride in them, and enjoyed them, in some sense, as though they had deprived others of them. Thus a good-looking man would only be likely to accuse others of *najar* if he were himself vain.

• • •

Let me conclude with a summary note on *najar* and beliefs about ghosts. Both are clearly related to human obligations and the failure to meet them. Joyce Cary in *The Horse's Mouth*, talking of the secretive way in which tramps in a London doss-house cook their food, speaks of the "evil eye which is the eye of envy." Certainly, at one level, the belief in *najar* tells us something about the greed and avarice which can only be found in their purest form where people live on the breadline, have never lived anywhere else, and do not expect anything more. It also tells of the acute value placed upon the, for us, ephemeral goods of youth, good looks and vitality in a population where the average expectation of life is only thirty years, where women are soon prematurely senile, and young men show signs of muscle wastage at twenty-five.

At the level of the sociological, *najar* tells us of status and equality. *Najar* is not to be feared between equals, such as brothers, nor between people whose status is clearly different and defined. It is most to be feared when those who should be equal are not so in fact. From this point of view natural good looks, which might be the gift of all, may be envied by any. At the social level, however, *najar* bites deepest within the caste, especially in a large caste such as the Patidar, where, in one lineage, a man may live in contentment while his kinsman spends his life near to starvation. When some do accumulate wealth, the fear of *najar* defines the ways in which wealth may be enjoyed, that is with modesty; it requires all men to be generous according to their means.

The evil eye can be turned away, and its ill effects can be cured. The belief in ghosts speaks more of irremediable ills past, and of unavoidable evil in life itself. The wilful over-looker who is the embodiment of pure unmotivated malice, the practitioner of the black science and the barren woman—for these there are no remedies. Among the ghosts are also those who have been cheated of their dues just as, in a sense, the barren woman is cheated. Such beliefs underlie the value of a good death which leaves neither material nor moral debt or loan behind it.

NOTES

1. The name is a corruption of Mohammad. Momad is one of a small group of Muslims in the village known as Vora. This name is a corruption of Bohora, the name of a large Shia Muslim sect. The corruption of the name is symptomatic of these village Muslims' ignorance of their faith. They circumcise their male children and visit the mosque in town once or twice a year, at which time they also eat meat. For the most part they behave as a vegetarian caste of middling status and are so regarded by the Hindus.

2. J.C. Pratt, who has done field-work in Siena, draws my attention to over-simplification here. He points out that sickness can also be caused by excessive love, *volere troppo bene;* as he puts it, "we have to take jealousy into account as well as envy." This suggestion from the Italian material that jealousy, or possessiveness, can directly harm its object must be explored in future comparative studies. (J.C. Pratt, D. Phil. thesis).

3. The re-marriage of the widow by a younger brother of the deceased is an economical custom much condemned by people of good family and pretension. Choto's family was looked down upon by those who had relinquished this custom within living memory. Choto's sister, although past the age at which village girls are usually married, still shamefacedly wears the blouse and skirt of a maiden.

4. The Patidar are in principle vegetarian, but meat-eating is not unthinkable. The fact to note is that a man might eat meat, or drink alcohol, out in the fields; he would not dream of bringing such things home to pollute the house. Similarly, a man might have sexual intercourse with an Untouchable woman, but he would not take food or water at her hands.

The Evil Eye

*Géza Róheim**

Among the list of those who have attempted to unravel the mystery of the meaning of the evil eye are a number of psychiatrists. Although not all psychiatrists are psychoanalytic in orientation by any means, perhaps the most typical instance of a psychiatric approach to the evil eye is the one offered by Géza Róheim. Róheim (1891–1953) was originally trained in Hungary as a folklorist. After discovering psychoanalysis, Róheim became the first psychoanalytic folklorist. He later carried out anthropological fieldwork in Central Australia, on Normandy Island, and for a short time among the Yuma Indians of the American southwest. Most psychiatrists do not go into the field as Róheim did. Nor do they control the extensive scholarship devoted to European folklore. (Most psychoanalysts are content to interpret an item of folklore—generally from the Grimm collection of folktales, the Bible, or from classical Greek mythology—solely on the basis of a patient's or perhaps their own free associations.) Róheim, in contrast, had fieldwork experience and a knowledge of standard folklore bibliographical sources.

Despite Róheim's unique training and experience, he has had a negligible influence upon the academic study of folklore. (Not one of the recent essays included in this volume even so much as refers to his analysis of the evil eye.) Part of the reason for this is Róheim's somewhat chaotic and undisciplined way of presenting ideas. His writing has a choppy disjointed style which gives the appearance of being a somewhat random listing of source materials interspersed

* Reprinted from *American Imago*, 9 (1952), 351–363.

with fanciful Freudian interpretations. Often the interpretations seem farfetched—even to those sympathetic to a Freudian approach. Yet on occasion, there are passages of sheer unalloyed brilliance. Most readers, not necessarily favorably disposed to psychoanalytic theory to begin with, lack the patience or perhaps intestinal fortitude to plow through Róheim's maze of fascinating data and interpolations in search of his insights. In the following essay, Róheim suggests that "the key to the whole evil eye belief" is oral jealousy and oral aggression, and he brings together some intriguing details in support of his thesis.

For other psychiatric considerations of the evil eye, see Phyllis Greenacre, "The Eye Motif in Delusion and Fantasy," American Journal of Psychiatry, *82 (1925–1926), 553–579, Emilio Servadio, "Die Angst vor dem bösen Blick,"* Imago, *22 (1936), 396–408, Garfield Tourney and Dean J. Plazak, "Evil Eye in Myth and Schizophrenia,"* Psychiatric Quarterly, *28 (1954), 478–495, Samuel D. Shrut, "Coping with the 'Evil Eye' or Early Rabbinical Attempts at Psychotherapy,"* American Imago, *17 (1960), 201–213, J.L. Th. M. Vereecken, "A Propos du mauvais oeil,"* l'hygiene mentale, *57 (1) (1968), 25–38, Joost A.M. Meerloo,* Intuition and the Evil Eye *(Wassenaar: Servire, 1971), and Edward Foulks, Daniel M.A. Freeman, Florence Kaslow, and Leo Madow, "The Italian Evil Eye: Mal Occhio,"* Journal of Operational Psychiatry, *8(2) (1977), 28–34. For further discussion of Róheim's contributions to folklore and anthropology (including his lengthy bibliography and references to studies of his work), see Roger Dadoun,* Géza Róheim *(Paris: Payot, 1972).*

Perseus is sent out in true folk-tale style by the king who wants him to perish, to get the head of the monster with the petrifying glance, the Medusa. Her glance suffices to petrify any mortal. The origin and affiliations of Medusa are given by Hesiod as follows.

"And again Ceto bore to Phorcys the fair-cheeked Graiae, sisters grey from their birth: and both deathless gods and men who walk on earth call them Graiae, Pemphredo, well-clad, and saphron-robed Enyo, and the Gorgons who dwell beyond glorious Ocean in the frontier land towards Night where are the clear-voiced Hesperides, Sthenno and Euryale and Medusa who suffered a woeful fate: she was mortal, but the two were undying and grew not old. With her lay the Dark-haired One[1] in a soft meadow amid spring flowers. And when Perseus cut off her head there sprang forth great Chrysaor and the horse Pegasus who is so called because he was born near the springs (pegae) of Ocean; and the other because he held a golden blade (aor) in his hands.

Now Pegasus flew away and left the earth, the mother of flocks, and came to the deathless gods; and he dwells in the house of Zeus and brings to wise Zeus thunder and lightning.[2]

There are three Gorgons and one of them is Medusa with the glance that kills. Gruppe regards Medusa as an abbreviated form of Eury *medusa*, the wife of Poseidon or Eurymedon 'he who rules far and wide.' Her other name is Gorgopis, 'She whose glance is awful.'[3]

Perseus kills Medusa by means of a shield provided by Pallas Athene—herself a sublimated Gorgo. He surprises her while asleep, he sees her face but only as mirrored in his shield. He cuts her head off.[4] This head is a popular *apotropaion* against the evil eye. It is noteworthy that it is most frequently used in the inside of cups. This is a protection for the drinker against the evil eye. While drinking he would look at the image and this would avert the evil eye. The Gorgons are also called the Graiae, the Grey Ones, they are swan maidens who have but one tooth and the eye they keep passing from one to the other. Perseus takes both and thus compels them to show him the way to Medusa (or to the Gorgons).[5]

Again the myth has something to do with the eye—tooth and eye go together. But why are there three Gorgons or Graiai? We should not forget that Medusa or Gorgon is essentially a mask or a head. Onians has shown that the head is the male genital organ, displaced upwards.[6] I have collected abundant evidence to show that the Gorgoneion is the vulva.[7] The cut-off head or stolen eye (tooth) would then be the female phallos which the hero cuts off with one fell stroke of his "sword." We shall now give a brief survey of what European folklore has to say about the evil eye.

One of the traits of the evil eye belief in Europe is very widespread; praising a child means casting a spell on it. In Bessenyötelke it is dangerous to praise a child's beauty,[8] this means casting a spell on it. A child should be protected from the evil eye by something red on its arm or neck. If a few drops of his mother's milk are poured into his eyes the child will have good eyesight. At Göcsej, the evil eye is most likely to injure good-looking children. A person gazes at such a child with a fixed stare and then at the earth that is enough, the child has been hit by the evil eye. If the person who casts the spell looks skyward the child can be cured if down, death will follow. Taking the baby out of his swaddles in the open window is the same thing as casting the evil eye. First outing of the child; wash it in the trough used for feeding swine, then it cannot be hurt by the evil eye. If you have your own dried navel-string under the bonnet or on your neck, you are immune against the evil eye. Furthermore, if an iron-pot has been put on the child after birth or hogs' excrements or the father's stocking in its bath; that is also a guarantee of safety, Donkey's hair from a male donkey for a boy, from a female if a girl.[9]

Spitting three times or licking the child's eyes is also a protection. An adult will be steamed over water in which they have boiled his own pubic hair. Another typical cure against the evil eye is dirty water, i.e., water in which somebody has washed before.

A very typical method is water with "live" (i.e., burning) coals in it. Properly speaking this is not curative but oracular. The aim is to find the person who has cast the evil eye on the patient. When they throw the live coal into the water they say:

> If you have come from under a hat, go back under a hat!
>
> For the second: If you have come from under a *párta*,[10] go back under the *párta*!
>
> For the third: If you have come from under a bonnet, go back under the bonnet (i.e., married women).[11]

"Overlooking" or the evil eye is the most dreaded calamity for children. Mrs. Barát[12] says: It might come from anywhere, even the green twigs might do it! It seems, however, that those who practice the protective incantation and those who have the evil eye are always elder women.

In the evening any careful mother or loving aunt will lick the child's eyes three times. Each time she spits right, left, backwards and finally says, while so doing:

> Auntie Borcsa, Auntie Sára, all that have seen you, may they not harm you.

It is important that she should enumerate all those who might have seen the child, because nobody could know who has done the mischief.

A child died of the evil eye at Nyirmegyegy. A woman with the evil eye was in the house on Good Friday. She asked the child's mother for milk, but she had none to give. By the evening the child was sick and on Easter Sunday it died. The following treatment would have helped the child.

Put nine bits of coal, nine chips of nine thresholds into a glass of water. Then mention names, when a bit of coal sinks at the mentioning of a name, that is the person who has harmed the child. Then bathe the child in this water and that will cure the child.[13]

Pretty little Helen got overlooked only because she believed that everybody was looking at her and only at her. Splinters are taken from the lintel and threshold of the door, they are strewn into a shovelful of embers and the child is held over the coals with its stomach bare, the smoking may be done with nine bristles from the broom or with nine hairs from the nape of the woman suspected of overlooking. If this was of no avail, hair would be taken from the person suspected of overlooking the child and bound round the child's arm.[14]

At Nagyszalonta it is dangerous to say "what a beautiful child." Moreover one should not stare at it, this would be *looking into the child's heart and that might kill the child.*

However, if it has happened the following countermeasures are available:

1. To spit on the child.
2. To wash its eyes in water containing coal.
3. To put live embers in a glass of water, splash it into the four corners of the room, and make the child drink the rest.
4. To take a hair of the person whose evil eye has harmed the child and burn it holding the child with its head towards the smoke.
5. The person with the evil eye should wash and then the child should be washed in the same water. Then the mother wipes the baby with the bottom of her shirt (etc.).[15]

At Vép they say, don't praise the child, you are overlooking it. The cure is blowing on the child but it is not really blowing, it is more like emitting saliva from the mouth. Another way is to bathe the child in "coal water" (szenes viz) and dry it with the bottom of a woman's skirt.[16]

We might say that the belief in the evil eye is *the* most universal trait of Hungarian folklore. Anybody whose eyebrows meet is dangerous, he has "bad eyes," with which he can "strike" people.

When cows are driven to pasture they get a red tassel tied to their tail against the evil eye. Red ribbons on the horn or tail of the cattle are supposed to divert the "striking eye" (szemverés equals eye hitting).[17] At Nagylengyel, if a woman who is nursing a child looks at the one while she has her own baby at her nipple, the woman who had been "overlooked" will lose her milk.[18]

In this statement we probably have the key to the whole evil eye belief: oral jealousy, oral aggression.

In Ukraina, a person with an evil eye can injure a cow even without seeing the cow, just by a glance at its milk. Milk is therefore carefully hidden from strangers.[19] The Benu-Asad (Arab tribe) say that after three days fasting you acquire the evil eye. Similarly in Germany if you have not eaten that day beware of looking out of the window, your glance might blast the trees.[20]

In Sweden, if a person has been weaned and then taken to the breast once more he or she has the evil eye.[21] It is chiefly the witch who is supposed to have an evil eye. The eyes of the witch are fatal for milk and butter.[22] Children are endangered by a whore looking at them. If a whore sees the child's soles or the mother's breast that may be fatal and the only way to ward it off is to turn the child round and show the whore its bottom.[23] When a cow has its first calf and has been milked for the first time they protect the milk with an apron against the evil eye.[24] In Macedonia, persons who after having been weaned took to sucking again are especially endowed with the evil eye.[25] The counter-magic consists in spitting and uttering the appropriate incantation. India supplies the following data. When a mare foals, Muhammadans and Hindus keep the mare and the foal in the stable for seven days. A Hindu will not expose the udders of a cow at calving for seven days and for ten or fifteen days will not take out of doors the first butter made because the evil eye might hurt the cow.[26] Food and envy are the outstanding traits of evil-eye beliefs. Muhammadans are told to serve their guests the same quality of food as they take themselves to avoid the evil eye. The guest must always be served first, otherwise the evil eye or the evil wishes of the guest will be mobilized.[27] Gluttons naturally have the evil eye but so do barren women, pregnant women and childless old couples.[28]

In Morocco the danger of being affected by the evil eye is very great while eating. To take food in the presence of some hungry looker-on is to take poison. At Fez a person "eats the poison of the other man's eyes."[29] The eyes of women are more feared than those of men; and old women are especially dangerous.[30] Young children and women in childbed are in especial danger of being affected by the evil eye.[31] In the Western Highlands, if a person who has the evil eye gets a little milk from another, he or she will be able to injure all the milk and the cows.[32]

As usual we find in Palestine that children are especially subject to the evil eye. The mother and her friends never talk about how pretty their children are, they never caress them but they always mention what is wrong with them and give them names like "you donkey," or "excrements." It is interesting that the literal translation of the Arabic word for "overlooking" is "sucking."[33] One of the preventive methods used by Jewish women in New York is to kiss the child three times and then to spit three times.[34]

In Spain the nursing mother is in great danger of being hurt by the evil eye.[35]

We find that women and especially witches have the evil eye more frequently than men and that the victim is very often an infant or the nursing mother or milk or a cow.

We conjecture that the latent meaning is precisely the opposite; the infant devouring the mother's breast.[36] The oral quality of the evil eye is evident. In French we have the saying "Devorer des yeux,"[37] in Hungarian "His eyes are bigger than his mouth," i.e., he desires more than he can manage. The aggression of the sucking infant is projected and personified in the hostile devouring glance of the witch-mother. There is a fairly close parallelism in European folklore that makes the witch the chief wielder of the evil eye.[38]

Now let us examine the main trends in counter-magic used against the evil eye. The spitting method used by mothers and midwives is interesting, for it reveals that they themselves are identified with the evil one and they are now spitting the child out, instead of devouring him.

The main theme of counter-magic is phallic.[39] In Latin *fascinum* means both the evil eye and the penis as averter of the evil eye.

The *turpicula res* was so much in use amongst the Romans that it became to be known under the name of fascinum (Horace Epod VIII, 18). In fact, fascinum became the popular Latin word for *membrum virile* and survives as fascino in modern Italian (Hastings Encyclopedia V, p. 612, Elworthy, The Evil Eye). The fascinum was attached to the triumphal chariot of the emperor to ward off envy and the evil eye. Preller quotes Plinius Historia naturalis XXVIII, 4, 7 "fascinus imperatorum quoque non solum infantium custos—currus triumphantium sub hispendens defendit, medicus invidiae."[40] Liber and Libera, god and goddess of freedom, happiness and plenty were represented by the *fascinum* carried round in triumphal procession at the vintage.[41] The image of Priapus significantly carved of a fig-tree protects the herd, the garden, the grave against the evil eye.[42] The famous "obscene" inscription of Pompei with the red stone phallos *Hic Habitat Felicitas* does not mean as was first thought, that a prostitute named Felicitas lived there but "here dwells happiness" with the phallos to avert the evil eye.[43] The thumb stuck through the second and third finger "fare la fica" (to show a fig) and (or) with thumb and little finger fare la corna.[44] Greeks and Romans called the middle finger shameless because it symbolized the penis, but also the healer because pointing with it averted the evil. "The gesture called "fig" with the thumb stuck out between two fingers really symbolizes the union of the male and female sex organ" as both the Greek and the Latin fica mean the vulva.[45]

But why does a stone with a hole in it ward off the evil eye and witchcraft? They are hung behind the door on cradles, on the bed of the mother after childbirth. Yorkshire and Lincolnshire witch-stones are used against the evil eye. They are hung on a bunch of keys or dangle behind the door.[46] In the Western Highlands stones with holes in them are hung on houses to keep the witches away. Round stones with a hole in them are called serpent stones. A number of serpents congregate at a certain place and tie themselves up in a knot. Then they move round and round these stones till a hole is formed in them. They then pass and repass after each other through the hole, leaving a coating of slime around the hole which then becomes hard. This slime is supposed to contain the healing properties. Water is poured on the stone and the person or beast affected by the evil eye drinks the water.[47]

Helwig writing in Angerburg in 1719 says:

> Ut iam taceam superstitionem mulliereculam quae simulac vaccas lac cum cruore reddre observant per foramen lapidis fulminaris eos mulgere solent vel cunis infantum hos lapides imponere ne fulmine tangentur.[48]

In Brandenburg they milk a cow through a knothole if they find blood in its milk.[49] Perforated stones called Trudensteine were used for the same purpose.[50] The Rumanians believe that if someone finds a piece of wood with knotholes in it they should keep it in the cleanest place of the house. If there is blood in the cow's urine the farmer makes the cow urinate through this hole. That deprives the witch of her power. The wood with the knothole is called vagina of the witches.[51] In the northern counties of Scotland a stone with a hole in it keeps both the evil eye and witches away.[52] "Hagstones" are a protection against witches and the nightmare hags.[53] In Silesia milk that has been bewitched is poured through a wedding ring.[54] Ruthenians pour the bewitched milk through a heated horseshoe.[55]

The Roumanian belief mentioned above makes it quite clear that all these holes and rings symbolize the witches' vagina. The fluid poured through the hole is therefore an imitation of coitus but on a pregenital level (milk, urine) or more precisely coitus with the witch-mother or the witch-mother's intercourse with herself.

Especially in North Africa and the Middle East we find an open hand with five fingers stretched out as the typical antidote for the evil eye. In Algeria they say that the giver of the admiring glance should have five fingers thrust in his eyes.[56] However, we have reason to suspect that there is another unconscious meaning. The Danakil bridegroom immerses his hand in sheep's blood and leaves his imprint on the bride's face. In Algiers Jews paint a hand on the head of the child before circumcision.[57] In Morocco they often say "five" meaning the five fingers, the hand. However, the word five is considered indecent, and they will say "and four" or something similar.[58] The use of masturbation as a means of warding off anxiety is well known. I suspect that this is the meaning of the hand amulet. A similar interpretation would be valid for the use of excrements or objects representing excrements (coal, garlic or urine)[59] as counter-magic against the evil eye, defecation expells the evil substance and anxiety acts upon the bowels.

Counter-magic against the evil eye is essentially Libido against Aggression turned inward (Destrudo). The main form, however, is the *fascinum*. This represents several latent contents, (a) A denial of castration anxiety (the Gorgon biting mouth, the vagina dentata), (b) exhibitionism as a denial of voyeurism and (c) the symbolic representation of masturbation. And finally it means this "I am now an adult, not a child with body destruction phantasies and corresponding talio anxieties."

With reference to (b) a voyeurism-exhibitionism[60] it should be emphasized that exhibitionism is really a biologically determined mechanism in the animal world, probably the usual form of wooing. Ferenczi once commented on exhibitionism as a means of frightening the child.[61] In using it against a supernatural danger[62] we have reversal as a form of magic or defense mechanism, i.e., the mortal is behaving "as if" the supernatural being were the child. Applied to the evil eye this is even true, for the genital gesture is adult if weighed against oral retribution anxiety. *The answer to the eyes or the mouth*[63] *of Gorgo-Medusa is the sword of Perseus.* What jumps out when the head is cut off probably represents Perseus himself, Pegasus the horse, and Chrysaor, the sword, both phallic. Medusa has been made pregnant by Poseidon who assumed the shape of a stallion.[64] The flight of Perseus through the air is "like thought" just like the magic stallion of the folktale. The head cut off would then really be a primal scene between stallion and mare—and Perseus is the child who replaces the father but may not *look*. Was he not sent by the tyrant to get the Gorgon's head *or* the king would rape his mother? That is precisely what he does himself. Like many myths this may have been a dream first, hence the dream flight and Medusa represented *asleep* when attacked by Perseus.

NOTES

1. Poseidon.
2. Hesiod, *Theogony*, 270–284.
3. Gruppe, O., *Greichische Mythologie und Religion.* 1906, II, p. 1141.
4. Cf. for further details and references Róheim, G., "The Dragon and the Hero," IV, "The Gorgon," *The American Imago,* I, 1940, pp. 61–83.
5. Cf. "Gorgon and Graiai" in *Roschers Lexikon*.
6. Onians, R. B., *The Origins of European Thought*. 1951, p. 93.
7. Róheim, *op. cit., American Imago*, I, pp. 74, 75.
8. Berze Nagy, I., "Babonák, babonas alakok és kokások Bessenyöteklen" (Superstitions, Superstition Beliefs and Customs at Bessenyötelke) *Ethnographia*, 1910, pp. 24, 26.

9. Gönczi, F., *Göcsej*, 1914, pp. 284, 285.
10. Head-dress worn by unmarried girls.
11. Gönczi, *op. cit.,* p. 287.
12. Luby de Benedekfalva, M., "Treatment of Hungarian Peasant Children," *Folk-Lore*, LII, 1941, p. 109.
13. *Idem, op. cit.,* pp. 111, 112.
14. *Idem, op. cit.,* pp. 112, 113.
15. Zs. Szendrey, "Nagyszalontai népies hiedelmek es babonák," (Folk Beliefs and Superstitions of Nagyszalonta) Fōgimnazium Értesitöje Szallonta, 1913, 4.
16. Varga, I., "Vépi népszokások és babonák" (Customs and Superstitions of Vép) *Ethnographia*, 1920, p. 100.
17. Jankó, J., *A balaton melleki lakosság néprajza* (*Ethnography of the Balaton*), 1902, pp. 411, 412.
18. Gonczi, F., "A gyermek születése körül való szokások Göcsejben" (Customs at Childbirth in Göcsej), *Ethnographia*, 1906, p. 158.
19. Koenig, S., "Magical Beliefs and Practices among the Galician Ukrainians," *Folk-Lore*, 1937. XLVIII, 67.
20. Seligmann, S., *Der böse Blick*, 1910, II, p. 172.
21. Feilberg, H.F., "Der böse Blick in nordischer Überlieferung," *Zeitschrift des Vereins für Volkskunde*, 1901, XI, p. 307.
22. *Ibid.,* p. 322.
23. In the Hungarian witches' trials whore and witch are practically identical.
24. Feilberg, *op. cit.,* pp. 327, 329.
25. Abbott, G.F., *Macedonian Folklore*, Cambridge, 1903, 144.
26. Abbott, I., *The Keys of Power*, New York, 1932, pp. 123, 124.
27. *Ibid.,* p. 129.
28. *Ibid.,* p. 120.
29. Westermarck, E., *Ritual and Belief in Morocco*, London, 1926, p. 422.
30. *Idem*, p. 420.
31. *Idem*, p. 421.
32. Maclagan, R.C., *Evil Eye in the Western Highlands*, London, 1902, p. 89.
33. Canaan, T., *Aberglaube und Volksmedizin im Lande der Bibel.* Hamburg, 1914, pp. 28–30.
34. Campbell Thompson, R., *Semitic Magic*, London, 1908, p. 88.
35. Hildburgh, W.L., "Some Spanish Amulets Connected with Lactation," *Folk-Lore*, LXII, 1951, p. 431.
36. Cf. Fenichel, O., "Schautrieb und Identifizierung," *International Zeitschrift für Psychoanalyse*, XXI, 1925, p. 561.
37. Doutté, E., *Magie et Religion dans l'Afrique du Nord,* Alger, 1909, p. 319.
38. Cf. on witches and cows and milk, Róheim, G., "Aphrodite or the Woman with the Penis," *Psychoanalytic Quarterly*, XIV, 1945, pp. 350–390.
39. Cf. Servadio, E., "Die Angst vor dem bösen Blick," *Imago*, XXII, 1936, p. 403.
40. Preller, L., *Römische Mythologie*, Berlin, 1858, p. 205.
41. *Ibid.*, p. 441.
42. *Roschers Lexikon*, Priapus 2975.
43. Seligmann, S., *Der böse Blick*, Hamburg, 1910, I, pp. 198–200.

44. *Ibid.,* II, pp. 186, 221, 62.
45. *Idem*, II, p. 184.
46. *Idem*, II, p. 27.
47. Maclagan, R.C., *op. cit.*, pp. 169, 170.
48. Toeppen, M., *Aberglauben aus Masuren*, 1867, p. 92.
49. Kuhn, R., *Märkische Sagen und Märchen*, Berlin, 1843, p. 379; Knoop, O., *Volkssagen, Erzählungen etc. aus dem östlichen Hinterpommern*, Berlin, 1885, p. 171.
50. Andree, R., "Trudensteine," *Zeitschrift des Vereins für Volkskunde*, 1903, p. 297. Andree Eysn, *Volkskundliches aus dem bayrisch österreichischen Alpengebiet*, 1910, p. 10. Further data are given in paper "Aphrodite, or the Woman with a Penis," *Psychoanalytic Quarterly*, XIV, p. 366.
51. Róheim, G., *Adalékok a magyarnéphithez*, Budapest, 1920, p. 171.
52. Henderson, W., *Folk Lore of the Northern Counties*, 1879, p. 194.
53. Black, G.F., "Scottish Charms and Amulets," *Proc. Soc. Ant. Scot.*, VII, pp. 457–459.
54. Drechsler, P., *Sitte, Brauch und Volksglaube in Schlesien*, 1903, I, p. 109.
55. Kaindl, R.F., "Volksüberlieferungen der Pidhireane," *Globus*, LXXIII, p. 3.
56. Westermarck, E., *Ritual and Belief in Morocco*, London, 1926, I, p. 446.
57. Seligmann, *op. cit.*, I, pp. 447, 448.
58. Westermarck, *op. cit.*, I, pp. 447, 448.
59. Farmers sprinkling their cows with urine. Maclagan, *op. cit.,* p. 135.
60. Cf. Bergler, E., *The Basic Neurosis*, New York, 1949, pp. 176, 177.
61. Ferenczi, I., *Further Contributions to the Theory and Technique of Psycho-Analysis*, Hogarth Press, 1950, p. 329.
62. Cf. Róheim, "The Dragon and the Hero," *American Imago*, I, p. 75.
63. This includes oral anxiety, the vagina dentata, and the phallic mother (phallos equals breast).
64. Cf. *Roschers Lexikon*, Perseus, p. 1989.

Envy and the Evil Eye Among Slovak-Americans: An Essay in the Psychological Ontogeny of Belief and Ritual

*Howard F. Stein**

It is surely misleading to think that approaches to the evil eye or to any other issue for that matter can be neatly categorized as exclusively sociological, anthropological, psychoanalytic, etc. A particular investigator may, and in all probability certainly will, combine several perspectives in his approach to a problem. One such combination of approaches includes both anthropology and psychiatry. The so-called field of "culture and personality" or psychological anthropology attempts to integrate the theories and methods of these two disciplines.

This paper is based on a two-year (January 1970–December 1971) study of three- and four-generation Slovak-American families in mill town communities in western Pennsylvania. The study was supported by a Fellowship in Ethnicity, Racism, and Mental Health of the Maurice Falk Medical Fund. A wider ethnohistoric and psychodynamic contextualization of issues discussed in this paper appears in Stein 1972. Thanks are extended to the several anonymous Associate Editors of *Ethos* for their incisive observations and criticism of earlier drafts of this paper. Finally, I would like to thank Professor Stephen C. Cappannari of the Department of Psychiatry, Vanderbilt University, for his enthusiasm and encouragement in urging me to carry my analysis of the Evil Eye to its inexorable conclusion. His close reading of the manuscript was equally helpful to me in shedding some dross and in making the argument more tightly knit.

* Reprinted from *Ethos*, 2 (1974), 15–46.

Howard F. Stein, a professor in the department of community medicine at the University of Oklahoma Health Science Center, has employed techniques and concepts borrowed from anthropology and psychiatry in his extensive analysis of the evil eye among Slovak-Americans. Professor Stein's sophisticated essay includes both ample citations from field data which he collected himself and references to the psychiatric literature concerned with childhood socialization theory. Starting with the Slovak-Americans' own folk theory of the connection between weaning and the evil eye, Professor Stein attempts to use the evil eye belief complex as a means of understanding the complexities of Slovak-American ethos and worldview. In some ways, Professor Stein's study may be said to represent a refinement of some of the insights earlier suggested by Géza Róheim, but in its ambitious and meticulous delineation of the subtleties of Slovak-American child care with respect to its possible influence upon or at any rate parallelism to adult personality structure, it breaks new ground.

Introduction

In the anthropological scheme of things, the widespread Evil Eye phenomenon is a subset of the inclusive set "witchcraft." Although there exists a gargantuan literature on witchcraft, little attention has been given to the *ontogeny* of belief in the Evil Eye and its significance for later witchcraft phenomena. My analysis of the Evil Eye among Slovak-American peasant immigrants and their descendants focuses on the interpersonal and intrapsychic dynamics of the "acquisition" of the belief and its overdetermined and manifest functional implications for social relations in adulthood. Through an analysis of the Slovak and Slovak-American folk system in continuity and change, I hope to illumine what the Evil Eye *does, means* and how it *comes into meaning*. One can state what the Evil Eye *is* only in terms of a precipitate whose dynamics are known. The analysis is based on ethnographic research conducted between January 1970 and December 1971 in several mill town communities in western Pennsylvania. While I focus on the minute particulars of the Evil Eye among Slovak-Americans, I equally attempt to integrate this analysis with the wider phenomenon of the Evil Eye and its secure position in the cosmogony of witchcraft.

Compendia ranging from F.T. Elworthy's early work on the Evil Eye (1958/1895) to Lucy Mair's recent volume on witchcraft (1969) are rich in case material, witchcraft "dogma," and the "micro-politics" of accusation. Yet without the human developmental perspective, the "deep structure" of *why* the Evil Eye works will elude us. Parenthetically I might add that although the Evil Eye is frequently distinguished from destructive envy or covetousness (see Evans-Pritchard 1951, Middleton 1955), an exploration of this "deep structure" reveals an intimate connection between them.

George Foster's recent essay on the "Anatomy of Envy" (1972) goes far to bridge the often vigilantly maintained abyss between "cultural" and "psychological" explanation by exploring culturally constituted psychological dynamics. Foster writes: "psychological interpretation of symbolic behaviour tells a great deal about society and culture without in any way negating the importance of sociological analysis" (1972:200). In this essay I explore the relation between the jealousy/envy syndrome and the Evil Eye within an *epigenetic* framework (see Erikson 1959, 1963), hopefully to illumine and be illumined by the psychocultural "anatomy" that Foster has dissected. Commenting on Foster's paper, Judith Brown writes: "Foster suggests that envy is pan-human because 'the good things' are everywhere scarce and unevenly distributed. I would like to add that the uneven distribution of 'good things' first becomes obvious in earliest childhood, a time when the individual is particularly impotent and vulnerable" (1972:188).

Alfred Kroeber once wrote of culture: "perhaps *how it comes to be* is really more distinctive of culture than what it *is*" (1948:253). What is true of "culture" should be equally true for "culture carriers." More broadly, the present approach assumes a systematic "relationship between the organized values and institutional efforts of societies, on the one hand, and the nature of ego synthesis, on the other" (Erikson 1968:223). Through an exploration of a specific sequence of "the ontogeny of ritualization" in man (Erikson 1966), this essay attempts to relate culture to those myriad official and unofficial ritualizations (and their underlying anxieties) pervading early childhood which communicate to the infant what life is all about.

In his analysis of Ifaluk ghosts, Melford Spiro suggests that a common experiential frame of reference is necessary for the perpetuation of culturally patterned beliefs (1967). George Devereux has argued similarly in terms of an "ethnic unconscious" (1969). Ego mechanisms mediate to cathect, to invest in, cultural beliefs (values, etc.) that constitute "cognitive affirmation of experience" (Spiro 1967:248), and which are later confirmed and reaffirmed by experience. Heinz Hartmann pointed out that through a "change of function" (1958/1939), these beliefs themselves become the referents and building blocks of cultural elaboration and manipulation, rather than their psychogenetic precursors. The adaptive synthesizing ego mediates to symbolize and ritualize early conflicts and traumata without the early experiences themselves becoming *conscious* referents: for example, identification, repression, projection, displacement, rationalization, symbolization, condensation, isolation, and regression selectively operate to create and maintain new referents for the inchoate anxiety (cf. Homans 1941), reciprocally affirming the agents of socialization as they establish, confirm, channel these anxieties in those being enculturated. Devereux (1970) and Erikson (1966) have both emphasized the complementarity of the socializer and the socialized with respect to unconscious conflict.

However, behavior, affect, and cognitive patterning are not only (unconsciously) overdetermined, but multiply determined. Hence we cannot automatically infer unconscious dynamics from an item of behavior. We should keep in mind an ancient distinction made by Hartmann, Kris, and Loewenstein (1951) between "institutionalized" aspects of behavior (e.g., child care practices, witchcraft accusation) and the "noninstitutionalized" aspects of behavior (e.g., maternal affect in relation to her infant, projection), and the care that must be taken when attempting directly to link them.

Let me add a word of caution. We must avoid letting the poverty of language impoverish our empirical studies and our theoretical constructions, lest we allow our ethnocentric semantic "black box" to prestructure our observations and our interpretations. Thus I do not a priori know what "envy" or the "Evil Eye" are. Foster began retroductively with the concept of envy, and attempted to confirm his hypothesis by induction from ethnographic data, in the process, discovering envy everywhere. If Foster has already provided a universal "deep structure," then it is pointless to look "deeper," and needless to formulate a problem—because there already exists a solution. Rather than start with envy and the Evil Eye as "given," I wish to explore the dynamics of its "givenness." My starting point is a pattern of culture and its enculturation, and my end point is the elucidation of envy and the Evil Eye. This inquiry focuses on the clustering of words and meanings around the Slovak-American Evil Eye. What this Evil Eye *is*, its significance within the social structure and personality, will differentiate out of this context. I take the question of its "origins"—whether by diffusion, independent invention, or syncretism—to be a matter of indifference for the present analysis, since its psychodynamic and social structural functions act as "selective forces" for its pervasive presence and persistence. Finally, this study of the "epigenesis" and "physiology" of envy among one group might be seen as complementary to Foster's universal "anatomical" formulation (1972), exploring how the universal and the particular, the "theme" and the "variation," might reciprocally illumine—*and test*—one another.

If there are universal common denominators, then I suggest that we look for them in a common ontogenetic experience coupled with common functional prerequisites and implications. Thus I would suggest a basis in (a) the underlying experience of maternal hostility and ambivalence, precipitating deep frustration and rage in infancy; (b) its linkage with the psychodynamic and cultural elaborations of the jealousy/envy complex; (c) its proliferation in the sociocultural domain into witchcraft, counterwitchcraft, and curing; and (d) their relationship to the socioeconomic realities of scarcity and deprivation. Despite my difference with Foster over the "identity" of envy (which I hope to clarify), the fact that the "identical custom" of the Evil Eye is widespread and is closely affiliated with a common clustering of psychological traits ascribed to envy, suggests that an analysis of the ontogenetic transformations of envy into the Evil Eye in a single case *may* help illumine the dynamics of the universal. My insistence on configurationist integrity does not vitiate the need for functionalist comparison (cf. Goldschmidt 1966), but (it seems to me) makes it possible without vivisecting a cultural ethos into artificial "shreds and patches."

Weaning and the Ontogeny of the Slovak-American Evil Eye

In Slovak, several words relate to the Evil Eye. "*Oči*" literally means "eyes"; "*počarič*" translates "to cast a spell." The two words are used interchangeably to designate the English language gloss "Evil Eye," which gloss was specifically used by Slovak-Americans with whom I worked. Furthermore, the Slovak word for "witch" is "*čaravnica*" (literally, "one who casts a spell"/"one who casts the Evil Eye"/ "witch"). Although both male and female can intentionally or by accident cast the Evil Eye, none of my informants ever heard of a male "witch." Restated in anthropological terms: anyone can be a "witch," but only a female can be a "sorcerer." In addition, the proclivity to sorcery "runs in families," from mother to daughter.

From lengthy discussions and long-term relationships I have established with Slovak- and Ruthenian-born mothers now in their 60's and 70's, I can with certainty extrapolate a folk account or "dogma" of the etiology of the Evil Eye: There exists a direct causal link between the capacity for having (casting) the Evil Eye and having been allowed to return to the mother's breast after weaning. In the *folk model,* it is a simple matter of cause and effect; and, by extension, of prevention.

I would like to explore this relation from two perspectives: first, from within Slovak-American culture, and second, from a psychoanalytic-ethnographic frame of reference. For heuristic purposes, I shall focus on the Evil Eye within the wider *field* of enculturation (though *not* as an isolate), exploring and delimiting its specific dynamics. (For an analysis of the entire socialization-individuation process, see Stein 1972: chap. 6.)

With the beginning of the infant's second year of life (approximately), the absoluteness of the mother's will, heretofore experienced more through the rhythm of time and relation than the mere fact of feeding, is precipitously brought home to the infant through the relative coincidence of sudden weaning (exacerbated by its coincidence with teething) and the onset of severe toilet training (as one second-generation Lutheran Slovak-American male summarized it: "Shit or die!"). The infant "gets it" at both ends, and with a vengeance. The one-sidedness of mutual regulation that is based on modalities of giving and receiving, bestowing and accepting, incorporating and expelling, activity and passivity (etc.) now expands zonally to encompass newly relevant body zones and psychomotor modalities, and exacerbates the relational vicissitudes of earlier ones, generating new variations on old, and solidly established, themes (see Erikson 1963:72 ff.).

The cultural ethos pervades and permeates each new psychosexual and separation-individuative stage (see Mahler 1968) and infuses the infant's cumulative "hypothesis" about the nature of the world (Spiro 1967). Intrapsychic structuring emerges to assure self-esteem and ward off anxiety; through introjection and identification, a personal and interpersonal (transactional) style consolidates to link individual personality with the cultural community of egos (see Spiro 1967, Erikson 1963, Devereux 1969, 1970, Caudill 1962). I would stress here that severe weaning does not independently "cause" the Evil Eye; rather, the weaning experience is prototypic or *archetypal* of the mother-child relationship, for it weaves into a "condensation" the strands of the Slovak ethos, which together, as a Gestalt, "create" the readiness to accept a "cultural" belief that resolves conflicts created by the quality of mother-infant relations. The folk explanation, here, as elsewhere, functions as a post hoc rationalization and explanation for beliefs and behaviors that are intuitively accepted as "natural." Nevertheless, the folk explanation, as a cultural "memory screen," suggests the deeper issues by virtue of its partial translucence and partial opacity. It "leads" *as* it "misleads.'

Among the Slovaks, weaning is sudden and uncompromising. There is absolutely no going back once the decision is made, and the mother refuses the breast or (in America) the bottle once and for all. The following interview excerpts will clarify the issue. The first example is Mrs. B, a Ruthenian Byzantine Catholic woman in her late 70's, married to a Slovak Latin Rite Catholic from a nearby *župa* (county). In the earlier part of the interview, I had first begun to suspect that weaning and the Evil Eye were somehow related, and asked her to tell me about the Evil Eye.

> I don't know what's truth. Those kind of people—get jealous of you—that you have something. They say baby get evil eye if mother go back nurse the child after she take him off the breast. When mother weans baby nine to twelve months. When baby cry—went back and nursed it further. Then that child has bad eyes. You never say: 'That's nice' [about the baby], because it will turn bad. A fellow had beautiful oxes—he was taking them

to sell at market. Another fellow came up the road and say to him: 'That's nice oxes you have.' The yoke broke the oxes in two! He don't mean it—don't mean to do it. It's his eyes. Spit first and then say what you want. When you wean your baby, *don't ever go back! Finished! Done!* No matter how much it cries!

The second example is from Mrs. I, a Slovak Lutheran in her late 70's. We were talking about child rearing, and I asked her how she handled weaning.

Finished! Stop! [punctuated, emphatic] Then right to the table. No more breast. Quite final. Nine months, one year. 14–15 months breast feed. Once you stopped, you never go back. Evil Eye: *počarič* . . . I never thought it about the children.

In a later interview with Mrs. I and her daughter, Mrs. D, Mrs. I continued talking about weaning:

Weaning—one year. I give other foods before weaning—strained or mashed . . . vegetable soup . . . Milk dried up after I stopped feeding them. I feed them one year. They start bite and I take them off! [wince, laugh]. One year, that's enough feeding baby breast. Beside them I feed them by table.

The third example is from a discussion with Mrs. G, a Slovak Byzantine Catholic in her mid-70's.

I never gave my children the bottle. I feed them—just breast. About five months start giving soup, mashed potatoes, carrots . . . . .Give breast all the time until year, year-and-a-half. When I stop giving breast—I never go back [strong]. Never, no more. Even if they cry—cry two days and two nights, but have to get used to it. I took Mike [eldest son] nine months off the breast. He cried three nights and three days. When Paul [second son] came around, I took him off one and a half years. I told him I was sick—he understood [Mike is 18 months older than Paul]. I nursed Steve [the youngest] twenty-two months. I born Paul when I'm 40. I let him have one and a half years because I love him like baby. He comes here every Sunday with wife and children for the *čeregy* [Slovak pastry] . . . Go back to breast—baby later see something, destroy it. Superstitious. I never heard of anyone taking baby back where I come from [the village of Zubńe, in Zemplín *župa*]—let them cry. I don't believe the superstitions.

The fourth example is from Mrs. Ma, a Slovak Latin Rite Catholic in her late 50's, and her eldest daughter, Mrs. Hr. Mrs. Ma remarked on weaning:

> Weaning ten months to a year. Start giving food after a couple of months. Then stopped with breast. Drinking milk from a cup. Never go back to feeding after that.

In a later interview, Mrs. Ma elaborated on weaning:

> If she puts the baby back [i.e., gives the breast after she has weaned the baby]—something about the eyes. *Oči*—strangers shouldn't stare at babies. Stop once feeding baby breast—giving back causes *oči*. Baby gets sore eyes from staring. Baby could even die from it. I took her [eldest daughter, Mrs. Hr., with whom she lives] when she was a baby—a couple of months old. She was crying. Took hot pieces of coal from the stove and put them in [a container of] water. If they sink, you know they've been stared at. Dip your hand in the water [motions, backhand movement]. Rub baby's head with your hand. Throw the water over your shoulder . . . she doesn't sleep—cries. My husband lit three matches. Drop them in water. They sink—somebody must have stared. My [MoSiDa] died from that. If matches or coal stays on top, it's OK. If they go down, that happened.

The final example is from a discussion with Mrs. Z, a Slovak Independent Catholic in her late 60's, and her second eldest daughter, Mrs. T:

> Mrs. Z: Once you take the child off the bottle, never give it back. Weaning—as late as 14 months. Some weaned off themselves early. They wanted to eat [shrug shoulders, smiling]! This was the first. I never gave special baby foods. Mashed potatoes, mashed carrots, noodles, mother's oats. Let them suck on pork chop bone. When you wean them, they cry for awhile. Give them an excuse [laughs it off]. The bogeyman took it. It broke. Give him a story.
> Mrs. T: When you're weaning at breast feeding—stop at teething.

In a later interview with Mrs. T (American born, in her early 40's), she elaborated on the above:

> Most of the babies were nursed by the mother. With one of them, I remember hearing the mother scream: 'Oeee!' The baby

> must have taken a good bite out of her. The mother said: 'It's time—*uš čas!*' The baby was around a year old. The baby sometimes had walking shoes on. My mother was nursing the baby. I don't remember which one it was.

Teething and abrupt weaning coincide. The mother withdraws herself from intimate contact with the infant. Playing with the infant, although present even before, is at a minimum. From here on, giving is mediated through a deluge of things, food, and engulfing protection—substitutes for an omnipresent self whose very approaches are "avoidant." Giving never ceases to be a major theme, but becomes indirect—which does not diminish the intensity of mutual dependency. The mother never ceases lavishly to interpose and impose herself on the infant's oral intake (or, for that matter, throughout the life of her "children"). The temporal and affective quality of this pervasive theme is that the mother's will be *absolutely* done, for example, in her choice to respond or not respond to "demands" for feeding, evocations of crying, calls for "attention," and the like.

To summarize the general response to my questions about weaning: the infant cries and whines for a few days, but then it's all over with. Since in traditional Slovak life, however, the Evil Eye is of such importance as an explanation for the experience of misfortune and the divination of malevolence, and functions effectively as a means of social control, the fact that it is (allegedly) intimately connected with weaning suggests a far deeper importance to *the meaning of* weaning than the mothers give in their matter-of-fact accounts of how quickly the weaning experience is out of sight and out of mind. Their other associations with weaning attest to their deep concern that their child not develop the Evil Eye. In a sense, the Evil Eye is a "communicable disease," since giving the infant the breast after it has been weaned is likely to "give" the infant the dread "eye disease." All of this is communicated to the child, and this communication summated into a "formula." Weaning is decisive, final—the mother must not go back, "no matter how much it cries." Then comes the explanation, the opposite side of the "equation," that the capacity to cast the Evil Eye is directly traceable to the fact that a mother gave in, went back, which somehow *caused* the child's eyes to go bad. As a consequence, anything this person says admiringly (without spitting first, thereby breaking the spell) will cause immediate destruction to what is admired. It can kill oxen. An inadvertent compliment or stare will kill an infant.

"Jealousy" and the Evil Eye in the American Experience

The Evil Eye is not talked about much in America—even among the older people of the immigrant generation. It is denied even as it is vividly attested to. Many laughingly dismiss it as superstition, ideologically disowning it, though living as though it were devastatingly true. These same people continuously speak of the Slovaks as "the most jealous people in the world." "*Jealousy*" is a term that I have heard in virtually every Slovak household I visited. It is always used with reference to "the others." Numerous first generation (immigrant) and second generation Slovak-American businessmen (e.g., grocers, barbers, tavern owners, morticians) and steel mill workers achieving advancement (e.g., foremen, machinists, and other skilled and/or supervisory positions) are berated both by family and Slovak "constituency" alike for trying to get ahead at everyone else's expense, for regarding themselves as somehow better than and superior to others. Without exception, every Slovak businessman with whom I spoke complained bitterly that his own people would rather frequent the business establishments of those of other ethnic origins than support their own—even in such instances of convenience where the Slovak market would be closer.

Another form taken by this "jealousy" is the frequent refusal of the father even into the third and fourth generations to allow his children to advance. A typical expression would be: "I've taken care of you long enough. You're old enough to start bringing in something yourself." One father, a very successful businessman in an East/Central European ethnic-American enclave, moved his family into a stone home in the most wealthy part of the city. Yet when his eldest son, now 22, expressed his wish to go to college, the father snapped: "What do you need to go to college for? When I was your age, I already had a job. I wasn't even able to complete high school. The education I had was good enough for me. I did it—you can do it." At the core of the value of being "the provider" was a deep resentment against it which was inverted through reaction formation into a fundamental source of self-esteem, but which resentment nevertheless could not be hidden. The father had worked hard for what he had, and spent his life providing for his ungrateful children; now it was their turn to bring in some money. Why should they have it better than he—even though he himself had desperately sought, and succeeded, in having it better than his parents? (cf. Anthony 1970). In Slovakia, the worker/provider ethic was predominantly male, but in America, with the possibility of female employment (e.g., as domestics, secretaries, bank tellers, waitresses), the female offspring frequently were inducted into the exploitable family labor force.

Yet a converse and contradictory "value orientation" and motivation existed (and exists) in the United States, and even underlay the motive for migration: the image of the American Dream, in which America was imagined as a utopia with streets paved with gold, where one could be free of the constricting bonds of dependency and authority. One wanted and sought more and more of the "pie" (and more pies) for oneself. Nevertheless, the vicious "jealousy" persisted and infused the experience of an emerging (and imagined) plenty. In one largely multigeneration Slovak/Ruthenian/Hungarian-American neighborhood in a western Pennsylvania mill town, I witnessed the not infrequent phenomenon (and was reminded that the pattern had been present since the turn of the century) that when one household bought a new radio or remodeled its kitchen, a neighboring or kin-related household would immediately embark on "doing one better," with a long-term status/prestige war of conspicuous consumption being waged. The *centrifugality* that was kept within limits in the peasant village through gossip, accusations of "jealousy," and the reality of "limited goods," in America erupted and ran rife. One accuses another of "jealousy," yet makes a counter-response that guarantees the irruption and accusation of "jealousy" by the one originally accused . . . and so the vicious circle goes.

Similarly, just as a father or mother is deeply "jealous" of the possible success of his or her children (especially those of the same sex as the parent, overladened with Oedipal issues), their own impetus for the American ethos of success, achievement, mobility, and independence induces a narcissistic identification with the potential success of their offspring, thus enabling them vicariously to succeed through their children, even as they envy and resent that very success they were unable or unwilling to try for (see Stein 1972:chaps. 6 and 7). Thus the father discussed two paragraphs above finally relented, and sent his son to college, but only after the son had convinced him that higher education was the only way to get a decent job today. When I visited with the family (the son had already been in college for three years), the father proudly told me that he was putting his son through college; that he strongly admired anyone who sought to advance himself through education; and that, as part of his contribution to his son's education, he had given up drinking liquor, giving the money that would have been spent on it to his son as an allowance.

The vicissitudes of "jealousy" are inevitably built into the dynamics of sibling rivalry that run rife within the family and between families. Behind the severely strong ethic of cooperation and sharing is the constant *competition* for what seems to be demonstrations of love (that are rarely forthcoming), by *outdoing others* in demonstrations of love. Paradoxically, this ethic creates its opposite: hostility, resentment, and more intense competitiveness. Mrs. D (quoted above), a woman in her 40's, said to me:

> Whatever we did it was to try to please our parents. We got so very little praise for it. We were so hungry for the praise we never got [imploringly]. It was expected of us—to do our jobs. We tried all the harder to do right—to get their praise. . . . When we learned to scrub the floor, we were told how to do it. We didn't dare to do it any other way. Always more criticism than praise.

This competition for rare pittances of approval and confirmation has the reciprocal effect of "playing into" the mother's needs, since the children are contending all the harder for demonstrations or signs of her love, each outdoing the other. In adulthood, one continues to preach and practice the ethic of cooperation, giving, and sharing—while simultaneously protesting against it (e.g., through constant complaint, "suffering," and occasional negativistic "undoing").

As "giving" took on an overcompensatory quality, so does "sharing," being a subset of "giving." One must renounce wanting, and the transformation is made from: "What I want I cannot have," to "What I cannot have I do not want." Here, as a consequence of the repression of the desire of "wanting," the desire later emerges as a "symptom." The following episode was related by Mrs. D; she was speaking of the different kinds of work she did after coming of age—that is, when she was sent to work, around age 10.

> I was baby-sitting and scrubbing floors when I was 12 or 13. I was 10 years old when [my eldest sister's] first baby was born. And I took care of her. Just like my own baby. I bathed her, fed her. . . . I had to scrub floors for other people. I *hated* it [referring

> to one woman's floor]: It was a beautifully scrubbed floor. It was so clean that they could eat off it. They probably did. But. . . they were careless with their things. She told me her necklace was missing. I didn't take it. I felt very guilty about it. Very guilty. We, too, had guilt complexes. I felt guilty about it a long time after. I still feel guilty about it. I wanted to tell her it wouldn't have gotten lost if they had taken care of her things. We weren't allowed to tell what we thought . . . why we were so suppressed in our communication. Everyone else was right—no matter what they said. You didn't dare answer back. The respect for our parents was the most important thing. They were our authority at the time.

The authoritarian atmosphere of the home conspired to make this young domestic's guilt unbearable, for there was no option for her to express herself, save to deny that she had stolen the necklace—and silence. Her tenuous self-esteem contingent on being a super-domestic was shattered because a single item was missing (out of place). What she hated she performed dutifully, religiously. Part of her guilt reflects her inner rebellion against a compulsive perfectionism. Another aspect of the guilt is her need for punishment for secretly coveting (casting the Evil Eye upon?) what belonged to another, which guilt she attempted to deny by focusing on her employer's carelessness. Her insistent innocence is counterpointed by a gnawing and enduring guilt, which suggests a wish that is equally enduring, but whose referent extends far beyond the necklace. Furthermore, her recollection of this episode immediately follows her expression of resentment for having to do so much for, give so much to, others. She contrasts this orientation toward others with a secret craving to meet her own needs, and renounces the latter while protesting the former—which constitutes a major strand in the ontogeny of "jealousy." The "jealousy" now extends to her own children, to whom she gives nothing that they want, unless they first work for it, earn it. As she suffered for the little she has (although she and her family live a "middle class" life), so must they for their wants. Because she denies what she craves, she cannot minister to her own children except as mediated through her own repressed needs: consequently, what she repressed in herself, she "represses" in her children.

During an interview with this woman's elder sister (the eldest in the family, in her 50's), I asked about the statement that I had often heard that the Slovaks are a very jealous people. She leaped on it in assent:

> That's so true. There's a proverb what says: "A Slovak wouldn't help another one out of a ditch." A mother and brothers do stick together. The Slovak people stick together. In the family sticks together. . . . Your neighbor will be jealous if we have something more. They were jealous also in Europe.

The Slovaks are "jealous," but they "stick together." Within one's own family "jealousy" is denied. One is not "jealous" of others—including family members. It is the others who are "jealous" of what one has. One is constantly giving to others, sharing with others, and doing for others—all compulsively, resentfully. Manifestly, one affirms the solidarity of the group; latently, one defends against the possibility that one's "jealousy" may be found out. One loves, one gives, but hates it. One seeks love desperately, and never receives it. Yet one must love, because those who had parented them demonstratively insisted on their love for their progeny, even as they communicated the opposite (that they were unwanted, burdensome) along other bands of the communication spectrum. One cannot openly dislike, hate, or envy anyone with whom one is closely bound up. The adaptive solution is through denial, repression, and reaction formation. As one brother said of his envied elder brother who was the favorite in the household: "What the hell. What can you say? He's egocentric and that's it. All you can do is love him to death." Killing with love is the only viable solution where vapid envy ("jealousy") consumes but must be denied, or, using the metaphor of the Evil Eye, *spat out*.

The following quotation from a second generation Slovak-American Latin Rite Catholic in his 50's nicely incorporates many of the issues discussed thus far, and adumbrates the ensuing discussion of the psychocultural dynamics of "jealousy," including such foci as the separation-individuation process; the relationship between the American Dream and the traditional ethic of the "limited good" (Foster 1965); the relationship between hostility, guilt, and the "susceptibility" to the Evil Eye; and the relationship between the "bewitcher" and the "bewitched," both in terms of current reality and early experiences that influence the response to the "reality." I asked him to tell me what he remembered about the Evil Eye. He began:

> I don't know nothing about the Evil Eye. My mother and dad—they never talked about the Evil Eye. I never heard them mention it. But I know there are these women—*čaravnica*—who can put the whammy on you if they don't like you. Maybe it's only women—I never heard of a man being a witch. Somebody who can put the whammy on you, like a curse. I never believed in it until it happened to my father. I was just little then—but even my older brothers talk about it and remember it. My dad was in his twenties—around 28. He came to this country when he was 14. He went to the South Side [Pittsburgh] and got a job in the mill. In them days you just went to the mill and went right to work—not like today when you first got to apply. . . . He was a hard worker. You work for what you get. You work hard so you can make it yourself, so you can get out on your own. You want to better yourself, not stay there in the slum. Work your way out of the slum. . . . When my father came here [before World War I], he took a room in a boarding house run by a woman from his village. That's how they all did it. They came over here and find out who's from where they come from. She helped lots of people get started. She was here maybe 10–15 years before my dad came. She boarded 8–10 men. When my dad got married, after they started having 3–4 children, it was impossible for all of them to live in just these two rooms. The family just got too big, and we had to move out. So he bought himself a frame house on Josephine Street, near the mill [but up on the hill, rather than on the floodplain where he had originally rented]. It was an old, run-down house, but he'd work on it to put it in shape. This woman, she didn't like the idea of losing the money for rent. She was mad at him for leaving, and put the whammy on him. They couldn't think of anybody else that had hard feeling for him, and she was known for witchcraft in Europe, so that they thought it was her. She know he was a hard worker, and that's how she'd get back at him. She was jealous that he'd gone off and left her. I wouldn't have believed it if I hadn't seen it myself. He couldn't walk for six months—his legs were paralyzed. The only way he could get around was on his ass. I was five years old at the time. I remember him fixing the fence around the house on the seat of his pants. That's the only way he could move around, He pushed himself along on his back side. He couldn't go to work, to church,

> nothing. The old lady—she figured this is how she would ruin him. You wouldn't believe it unless you'd seen it. Finally some people from church told him of this other woman who might be able to help him. He went to her, and she fixed him some herbs—like a tea or soup, and he drank it. And right after that he could walk like nothing ever happened. That's what changed my way of thinking about it. This old witch really could put the whammy on him. I asked him how his father knew it was her: She was the only person he knew of who had some grudge against him. Here he had lived so long with her, and she helped him out—and now he left. She figured she'd get even—and force him to come back. She was the only one who would be jealous of him. So he figured it must have been her. He told us she was known for being a witch already in Europe. She'd done this sort of thing to people over there before she came. She never married—who would have wanted her! It runs in families—only girls, not the boys. A mother would be a witch, then one of her daughters would be one just like her, and so on down the line. I never heard of a man putting the whammy on somebody. Just the woman—maybe they figure that you're getting it better than them, and they try to take it away. This woman, she was already in her sixties . . .

The "Deep Structure" of the Jealousy/Envy Complex

Let me now attempt to "locate" the cultural experience (Winnicott 1967) of "jealousy" among Slovak-Americans. I have thus far enclosed "jealousy" in quotations to indicate that it is being used as a folk-term. The discussion to follow will give an analytic perspective on the folk model. If "jealousy" indeed mediates between childhood overdeterminacy and adult-cultural fear and practice of witchcraft, then the nature of the link must be explored.

In his discussion of antitherapeutic rituals, Anthony F.C. Wallace notes that one function of witchcraft is as a "general palliative for social conflict prompted by the emotional lesions left by traumatic child-rearing experiences" (1966:179–180). Furthermore, witchcraft anxiety in part reflects "neurotic guilt toward the suspected witch" (1966:178–179). Robert A. LeVine similarly writes of witchcraft accusation as reflecting the use of defense mechanisms to reduce guilt feelings (1973:254ff). In their discussion of the relation between child training and adult belief, Whiting and Child (1953) postulate a high correlation between witchcraft belief and intense socialization anxiety, illness "cause," and illness explanation in three areas: oral, aggression, and dependency. As I shall discuss below, it would seem that *all* three of these components are heavily weighted in the Slovak and Slovak-American Evil Eye *constellation* or configuration (e.g., verbal spells or incantations, aggressive thoughts, magically introjected foreign bodies, soul loss, and spirit possession).

Warner Muensterberger writes of the ontogenetic "predisposition" to witchcraft:

> The common belief in witches tells us something about the mother's quite open ambivalence toward her children and shows a predominantly orally oriented mechanism of defense, which splits the mother image into the good, devoted mother and the dangerous, treacherous witch. . . . The belief in devouring demons is a projective manifestation of ideas which are clearly preoedipal and are very often connected with food sacrifices to deceased ancestors. This ritual is rather widespread and is an institutionalized attempt to undo oral-destructive fantasies against the retaliating mother (cf. Klein 1948). Since the struggle cannot be mastered by repression, animistic and magical concepts are created which transplant internal conflicts onto a projective, delusory antagonist (1969:209).

Thoughts and feelings intolerable for the maintenance of self-esteem and which may be felt as endangering one's very survival are projected outward as ego-alien and become transformed into threats from without. Early infancy is prototypic for this enduring condition, since the infant's very existence is dependent upon the mother's beneficent countenance (Erikson 1966, Winnicott 1967, Mahler 1968, Guntrip 1971). Fantasies of biting, annihilation, devouring rage, cannibalism, and destruction intensified by the mother's ambivalence and the sharp pain of teething, create, in turn, the fantasied danger of retaliation and annihilation from the mother (see Klein 1932, 1948, 1957, Klein and Riviere 1962). As a consequence of the *quality* of object relations between mother and infant, the "potential space" between them becomes injected with "persecutory material" that the infant cannot reject (Winnicott 1967:371). This "potential space" constitutes the infant's first "environment" in the social world, and the quality of relation within this potential infuses the emergent awareness of the geography and environment of the larger world with *its* meanings—the referents of "it" being simultaneously the individual, the culture, and the environment. Out of an ambivalence-laden "dual unity" emerges what E. James Anthony has evocatively called the "deep, seething, scarifying Kleinian envy" (1973:15) that is manifested through the dual processes of projective and introjective identification, and which produces an ego-splitting and object-splitting that is simultaneously adaptive to the world within and without. The countercathexis is the substrate for the belief in the Evil Eye. In this perspective the Evil Eye can be understood metaphorically as a *spat out introject*, an externalized, repudiated "bad self" and "bad object" that derived from the relationship with the "bad mother." Conversely, the "good self," incapable of envy, is bound up with the self-esteem derivative of the relationship with the "good mother." Recalling Freud's aphorism that "Delusions of jealousy contradict the subject" (1957/1911:64), one might state the transformation as follows: It is not I who envy, but he or she who envies me.

The Slovak-American data richly elucidates the tenet that "jealousy" kills, injures, paralyzes, and brings on illness. As in witchcraft accusations generally, the Evil Eye becomes an *explicans* for virtually anything to which one wishes to attribute it. If the referents of symbolism provide clues to its meaning, then the referents of the Evil Eye—discernible in rationalizations, accusation, and remedy—suggest that what the Slovak-Americans label as "jealousy" encompasses both *envy* and *jealousy*. The context of the use of the term designates its meaning. Strictly speaking, jealousy denotes one's own covetousness of what belongs to (or is part of) another (cf. Foster 1972). Among Slovak-Americans, jealousy and envy operate as complements to one another. Given the "limited good" ethic, and the "limited goods" in current reality and in the dimly remembered childhood experience, one *jealously* guards (i.e., suspicion) what little one has, anxious that even this will be taken away, a fear that is "reasonable" and infused with the early "ecology" of the mother-child environment; conversely, one deeply *envies* (i.e., covetousness) what another has or seems to have, again both ecologically and overdeterminedly "reasonable" given the nature of the "average expectable environment" (Hartmann 1958/1939). The Evil Eye thus encompasses and condenses into a single, reciprocal system, the *watchful guardian* and the longing, *often destructive, desire*: it is simultaneously *protection* and *projection*. In a recent paper on the Evil Eye in the circum-Mediterranean area, Moss and Cappannari wrote of the

> inherent ambiguity to human interactions. The multivalence of feelings can be potentially disruptive in community interrelationships. Since the evil eye is commonly regarded as a magical and *involuntary* threat by its bearers, anger of retaliation can be replaced by a patterned response which provides an alternative to personal confrontation. This ambivalence is the basic social psychological theme which underlies the Evil Eye belief (1972:14).

The magical and involuntary character of the Evil Eye are of equal importance in its persistence and control. Included in magicality would be the omnipotence of the wish, the magnitude of the imagined danger to oneself and another, and the equation between the thought and percept. Included in involuntariness would be the ego alien character of the magicality, its displacement, denial and depersonalization. Through the disqualification or disavowal of intentionality, the dangers inhering in the Evil Eye can be contained. Speculating into the matter of "function" and "dysfunction" of the Evil Eye, one might say paradoxically that the belief in the Evil Eye simultaneously fosters and prevents limitless strife, and its analysis reveals the delicately balanced structure both of culture and personality.

In the everyday world of the chronic but low grade Evil Eye (as opposed to the flareup of witchcraft accusation), the magical potency of the Evil Eye is controlled and contained, not only through fear, but equally through the common consent that it is largely involuntary, that all people of good will can be struck by "attacks" of envy. Thus the danger of retaliation is controlled and lessened by a sense of common predicament, and hence empathy for the person casting the unintended spell. Compassion is due not only the one stricken by the Evil Eye, but equally the unfortunate who is unaware that he or she is casting it. The "preventative medicine" of spitting before uttering admiration (etc.) acts equally as a control on the spread of the Evil Eye. The "endemic" only becomes "epidemic" when the "magical" overwhelms the defenses that perpetuate the sense of reality, and hence the "involuntary" becomes "intentional." At this point personal confrontation is infused with the anger of retaliation. For the most part, however, each acts to *protect* oneself and the others, even as one *projects* upon others one's deepest envy. Through identification, one not only protects oneself, but helps others protect themselves as well.

The concept of identification is critical for understanding the nature of witchcraft. LeVine has suggested that witchcraft belief and accusation are dependent on one's "representation of himself as mystically interdependent with his neighbors" (1973:265), or, in analytic terms, "symbiotic representation of the boundary and relationship between self and others" (1973:265).

> A person with a symbiotic representation of self-other relations will have developed a superego in which the evaluation of actions and the activation of guilt feelings are primarily dependent on the maintenance of emotional and material transactions between himself and others; and interruption in the flow of transactions . . . that provokes ill feelings in a neighbor leads (through regression) to the judgment that her vengeful attitude alone—which is experienced as part of the self—is wreaking punishment upon him (1973:265).

I might add that the lack of distinction between self-other boundaries is isomorphic with the concomitant lack of distinction between thought and percept, or inner and outer sources of experience. Indeed, the confusion of the "mote" and the "beam" lies at the very heart of the Evil Eye, intentionally obscuring the difference between the envier and the envied (cf. Weidman 1968).

In a review of the literature essay on envy, Walter G. Joffe nicely delineates the parameters of the dynamics of envy, any of which can come to dominate within the clustering of elements, contingent on the nature of object-relations that underlie phenomenological structuralization.

> Envy is . . . one of a variety of responses which may occur as a reaction to the *pain* which accompanies a discrepancy between actual and ideal self. Thus envy can be conceived as a *reaction* to a painful subjective state. It is a response which may mobilize aggression, may involve hate and resentment, and may contain an element of admiration. The individual who envies develops a covetousness for that which he does not have in such a form that his narcissism and well-being is to some extent restored by the fantasy of one day possessing that which he does not have. In this sense envy may indeed be an adaptive response acting as a spur

> to development. However, when the component of admiration is minimal and the aggressive component is dominant, regressive and destructive consequences may occur (1970:16).

From the Slovak-American data, it would seem that the aggressive component predominates in the dynamics of envy, overwhelming the "component" of admiration. Through the process of idealization the bad mother/bad child introject is separated (isolated) from the good mother/good child equation, and the repressed ambivalence projected onto "witches" (sorcerers) and everyday casters of the Evil Eye. The Evil Eye thus becomes a "culturally constituted defense mechanism" (Spiro 1965) for handling the "return of the repressed." The Evil Eye becomes a *culture-syntonic* structuralization of the jealousy/envy complex of infancy, whereby a constellation of symbolism and ritual attains *relative* autonomy from its origins (Hartmann 1958). In response to the ever-imminent danger of the Evil Eye, an array of detection procedures proliferates and is followed by an equal proliferation of remedial maneuvers, during the course of which the repressed source is obscured through projection and through a concentration on divination and cure in the *outer* world.

The remedy for being stricken by the Evil Eye betrays the oral-incorporative zonal and modal foci underlying it. Whatever the specific meaning of dropping three (or any larger odd number) hot coals or burning matches into water to determine whether they float or sink, the remedy—if the Evil Eye is diagnosed/divined by sinkage—is either to rub the water on the forehead of the infant or to have the infant (or adult, if the victim is an adult) drink the medicinal solution. For the child the crying, and for the adult the "eye sickness" or "headache," that is brought on by the Evil Eye is assuaged, and the spell is neutralized. In its most general sense whatever the external source of anxiety that suggests the Evil Eye, the remedy (whether rubbing the forehead or drinking) is always incorporative/absorbative, suggesting the oral-incorporative nature of the "problem" to which the remedy is a homeopathic solution.

In the folk idiom, "jealousy" is an act of will, secretly wanting what is not yours, wanting something you cannot have. One covetously desires to possess what one should not even want; one ambivalently remembers that distant "object" one tenuously "possessed," which in turn generates a boundless rage against the ambivalent object. Thus the very act of admiration can destroy the object of admiration. The only way to neutralize the effect of "jealousy" is to spit before uttering admiration; or if you suspect someone has put the Evil Eye on you, to perform the flotation experiments.

The Slovak explanation holds that the first "jealousy" is wanting the mother's breast when she does not wish to give it—when it has been withdrawn. One wishes to take when one no longer is given. But one must absolutely not give in to another's will. One remains steadfast, resolute, strong. The mother's will prevails over the child's wish and pleading. The rationale: if you get what you want (even) once, you will think you can have what you want every time you want something. The child, as the mother, learns to be alternately *will-less* and *wilful*.

A theme pervading Slovak socialization is the need for the child to become *strong*, and the fear that it will be *weak* and *fragile*. It is assumed that the infant is inherently weak and fragile and that it is the task of socialization to *strengthen* the child so that it will become immune to accident and harm. This is one of the purposes of swaddling, to prevent the child from injuring itself by putting its hands in its eyes; from breaking its fragile neck, back, arms, and legs. To allow the child to move freely invites these disasters: for example, the baby's head must be rigidly supported lest the weight of the head break the neck. Swaddling strengthens and protects the child by forcing the bones to grow straight, preventing dreaded deformation and weakness.

Crying is another vital mechanism for strengthening the child. The *mother* knows when the child is hungry, needs a change of diaper, or is merely "crying for nothing" or crying for "attention." The mother responds always to her own needs (i.e., to give, to withhold), not to the child's evocations. Crying is good because it "builds strong lungs." When a child cries, it is left alone to cry itself out, or to cry itself to sleep.

Until the child is able to sit up by itself, it is only minimally handled by the mother for fear that she may harm it or that it may hurt itself. The swaddled baby is the secure baby. Until the infant can sit up unsupported, none of its siblings is allowed to handle it. When the infant is held, it is always held flat and in front of the person holding it: the eyes of the infant *must* always be in a position to look directly (forward) at the person. For a baby to see a person by looking backward is to invite the possibility that the infant become cross-eyed. Great care is taken that the child develop good eyes, and the mother is ever fearful that her child will develop bad eyes.

From infancy, through toddlerhood—through adulthood, for that matter—the mother is constantly on the watch lest something devastating or disastrous happen to her "child." The child is not let out of her sight, or out of the sight of a reliable surrogate. Almost constantly, the mother is snatching her toddler from disaster—after first allowing the child to get at least one foot in the abyss.

The intrapsychic structuring that underlies this "strengthening" derives from, and is an adaptation to, the frustration, rage, fear of weakness, and experience of isolation that have pervaded infancy. A central defense utilized is reaction formation, producing a hearty, resolute, "fiercely independent" personality who is forever dependent and indebted, submitting unquestioningly to authorities on Heaven and Earth. The "depressive position" characterizes the core of the personality: longing for what was never truly given, denying the wish, enraged at the one who denied early needs, guilty for the hostility and fearing retaliation, forever making unpayable reparations and resenting the eternal indebtedness—all in a vicious circle. Only through ego-splitting does "*mamička*" ("mother"-diminutive: "sweet mother") become separated from the persecutory witch (see Stein 1972:chap.6).

In his pioneering paper on "separation anxiety," John Bowlby offered several insights on the significance of maternal ambivalence which are directly applicable here: "the child's heightened anxiety over separation and loss of love is [a reaction] to the unconscious hostility and rejection that lies behind it or to the threats of loss of love his parents have used to bind him to them" (1960:107). "For each of these experiences—separation, threats of separation, actual rejections or expectation of rejection—enormously increases the child's hostility, whilst his hostility greatly increases his expectation of rejection and loss" (1960:108). The repression of hostility generates further anxiety, since the need for the object coexists with a simultaneous pull away from the object and the fantasied holocaust of the object. The dimly remembered source of pleasure is renounced as it is secretly sought (in magic and religion). One defends against future vulnerability, yet craves what was never given by the original object. The fear of loss vies with a fear of dependency, leading to a precocious independence and a chronic, low grade melancholia underlying an "emotional flatness" (cf. Rycroft 1968:48). Through the cumulative experiences of swaddling, feeding, crying, weaning, efforts at evocation, autonomy, and motility, a defensive structure emerges to maximize the illusion of independence (while surrounded and engulfed by kinfolk), yet coexisting with an incapacity to be alone (cf. Winnicott 1958).

In a sense, the direct association of the "bad breast" with Evil Eye is a case of misplaced concreteness, since the part-object is enlarged and distorted and isolated from the relational whole. The *zonal* fixation, however, reflects and is a (symbolic) condensation of the more general—and generalized—*mode* of object relation, the *quality* of mutual regulation between mother and infant (Erikson 1963:72ff.). Just as the *quality* of object-relations determines the nature of the experience of separation anxiety and its resolution, so equally it underlies the specific *quality* of envy and the Evil Eye, differentiating it from the similar constellation and relationship in other cultures, despite an underlying identity of functional prerequisites and consequences.

If ascribing the Evil Eye or "jealousy" to another (projective identification) reveals the projective system of the accuser, then what underlies the Slovak mother's fears that she will cause the Evil Eye in her infant if she nurses again after weaning? What in the mother is projected upon, located in, and eradicated from the child? I suggest that it is her wish to have more and better than she has (on her own terms), against which recognition she recoils by stamping it out in her infant. The child's "demands" reawaken her own unfulfilled cravings, which she must simultaneously repress in herself and her infant (cf. Benedek 1970). As she could not have "more," so neither will the infant have "more." As she could not have a will of her own, neither will the infant have a will of its own—which she wilfully impresses on the infant. The mother's resentment at giving (when she wants to *receive*), her resentment at being saddled with an unruly brood of children who are her justification and her torment, is repressed and transformed via reaction formation into an overgiving, overprotective domination that infuses the early mother-child relationship with hostility, even as she insists that it is all for the child's good. The child desperately wishes to "hold on" to a mother (preserve the symbiotic tie—see Mahler 1968) whose very giving is a demand for a gratitude for what is not freely bestowed. One learns that giving with a vengeance is the essence of life; that one can only "receive" by indebting others through giving.

The oral incorporative mode and the trauma associated with it becomes the fixated point and model for later behavior associated with wanting or admiring. Any act of admiration must be first qualified (and its latent intent, *disqualified*) by spitting—expelling as opposed to incorporating. One must do the opposite of one's wish in order to negate the envy behind one's admiring statement. Stated "retrospectively," one must reject the breast even as one wishes to have it back. Finally, one cannot actively wish for anything—one can at best accuse someone else of having gotten something through illicit means, or accuse them of being "jealous" of what little one has.

How does the Evil Eye come to be capable of destroying and killing? How can the very act of wanting or coveting precipitate the destruction of what is wanted? Here the interpretation at a cultural level recapitulates the interpretation at the infant-fantasy level: Having wanted "the breast" caused it to go away, and destroyed (in fantasy) the mother. To want is to alienate the very object of one's desire. One wants so ravenously that one wishes to destroy what or whom one covets. Hostility is so intense that one wishes the destruction of what or whom one would possess. Not only has the mother "abandoned" the infant, which fantasy portends one's own annihilation, and which rage is projected onto the mother; but furthermore, the infant has made the mother go away by *wanting* (or having secretly ravished) her. The later spurts of autonomy, exploration, and "negativism" are responded to with horror and punishment by the mother whose projected dependency needs demand that the child-become-toddler be kept within the "symbiotic orbit" (Mahler 1968). Thus the mother simultaneously "abandons" the child as she with even more determination envelops it, labeling virtually all expressions of "will" (from attempts at autonomous functioning to the refusal to eliminate feces at the mother's command) the pejorative term "*fanta*"—"stubbornness."

Dependency and rage, and the vicious circle that is created, binds the infant to the mother, even as it generates a centrifugal pull away from in order to avoid being engulfed in her ambivalent vortex. Following the establishment of a pervasive sense of guilt in the infant, adult life becomes filled with ritualized atonements for one's dimly remembered, but pervasive, badness.

The intimate connection between the Evil Eye of childhood and the struggle between dependency and independence of adulthood is illustrated by the following rich episode that links orality, envy, and self-esteem through the medium of food transactions. It occurred in a second-generation Slovak-American Lutheran family at whose table I had been feasted and stuffed weekly for nearly a year. Invariably after the second or third (forced feeding?) helping, either the husband (in his early 30's) or the wife (in her mid 20's) would come out with a last ditch warning: "If you go away from the table hungry, it's your own fault."

> It was now only several days before Christmas (1971), and I had just finished feasting at their table on Slovak pastries which I greatly enjoyed. The wife then packed a half-*Kolach* (nut roll) for me to take home to my wife. I started to thank them profusely, meaning every mouthful of it. Suddenly, this ever-talkative family became absolutely silent and sullen, and I felt I had done or said something wrong. Both husband and wife hung their heads. The husband then said quietly: "You don't say thanks for food. The food's just there and you are supposed to eat it. It's there to be eaten. But you never thank someone for giving you food." His wife continued: "Not just for food, but food and flowers both. You never thank someone for flowers. They say it puts a spell on them and they'll just wither and die." I asked them if this is a Slovak tradition. The husband replied: "This is an old Slovak belief. You just never thank someone for giving you food or flowers. Why should you thank them? They didn't produce the food or the flowers. God gives us food and flowers. Therefore it's God who we owe our thanks to for these things. As far as that putting a pox on flowers goes, that's an old wives' tale, that has nothing to do with it. Flowers are from God. In the old days, everyone used to have a garden and grow flowers. If you saw a particular flower you really liked, that person would cut the flower and give it to you or would give you some of the seeds so you could grow it in your garden next year. But you never thanked them . . . you just took it." His wife added: "This isn't just Slovak. All those people from Europe believed the same way."

What had I done wrong? I had expressed unbuttoned admiration for the food by having given profuse thanks. To do so would be, according to the mythos of the Evil Eye, to put a curse, a pox, on it. What you are given you take and be silent about it. The only thanks that may be safely (and genuinely?) given is to God, from whom all blessings flow, a distantly, and at least in this aspect, an idealized preambivalent figure. Significantly, the husband in the above episode is a Lutheran minister; hence, the ready superimposition of the theological explanation, a post facto rationalization, upon the folk explanation.

The question arises as to how flowers and food are related. In Europe, they were often placed on the graves of parents at their funerals, at the anniversary of their death, and at ritual times during the Christian calendar (cf. Muensterberger 1969:209, above). In America, only the flowers continue to be put on the graves. They are both (food and flowers) an offering, an attempted sacrificial placation to assuage guilt, a ritual dutifully performed.

A further, and deeper, meaning of the connection between food and flowers is that to acknowledge admiration and indebtedness for something of someone else's is to reawaken their own infantile dependency cravings, which they have massively repressed. Why? At the conscious level, a copious "thank you" in the above episode led to embarrassment, whose unconscious referent was the realization of their resentment at giving, which had obscured, through reaction formation, their repression of wanting. In one sense, I was paying for the "priceless"; in another sense, I was paying for the "worthless." I was attempting to repay them for something that can never be repaid, because something done out of duty is not a genuine gift. Thanking them brought out their guilt of not having wanted to give—that is, their "child side." Thanking them was perceived as my payment to them, which *reverses* their position from giving, overbearing parent, to the child who does not want to give. I was originally the "child," and they the "parents"; by *giving* thanks, I inverted the relationship, and they were now forced by virtue of the "thanks" into recognizing their guilt of not *wanting* to give, but being "forced" out of duty to give. Since the food was given out of duty, to gratify ego ideal and appease the super ego, I could never eat or take enough food to satisfy them; nor could I repay them save by becoming eternally indebted to them, never able to repay the debt. Both their self-esteem and their hostility were bound up with the unspoken assumption that I do not attempt to *undo* the bind in which feeding enveloped me. Thanking did precisely that—shattered their hold on me: to which they could only respond by disqualifying my thanks and reassuming the parental prerogative (cf. Wynne et al. 1967, Haley 1967).

Perhaps this accounts for the above couple's sudden silence and momentary depression. Food and flowers, like sex in later life, are there for the taking. One gets "snatch" of whatever variety, and avoids getting close enough to source to feel the pangs of intimacy of indebtedness. One keeps vigilantly on guard to maintain a safe emotional distance from anyone, although one is already "swallowed up" by them. Such pervasive mythologies as the Evil Eye assure that one's guard will hardly ever be let down.

Conclusion: The Limited Good and Its Discontents

The persistence of the jealousy/envy complex even in the "limitless good" and "limitless goods" of the Slovak-American image of the American Dream attests to the vital continuity of the traditional ethos. If one's neighbor buys a new radio, one must buy one even better . . . and so on. Because the referents of what is "really" sought are repressed and unconscious, the cumulative gains in the real world can never be enough. To see another's gain awakens one's own deficit—and the concomitant memory of *loss*: I would hazard that this is the unconscious dimension of Foster's (1965) "image of the limited good," that the pie is indeed perceived as limited, and that another can gain only at one's expense. The ubiquity of the Evil Eye phenomenon suggests an extension of the "limited good" ethos far beyond classical peasant society: perhaps from the tribal Nuer, to the peasant Slovaks, to the modern, conspicuously consuming Americans, whose exhibitionistic boasting merely conceals their deep sense of inferiority (see Slater 1970, Erikson 1963:chap.8).

The bleak existence of the Slovak peasants in the barren Tatra and Carpathian mountains, in isolated nucleated villages prior to and under feudal Magyar rule, punctuated by invasions in their "crossroads of Europe," were productive of a hardly appetizing "pie." As in all of cultural adaptation, a sense of "necessity" is elevated into "virtue," and a cultural ethos and "ethnic unconscious" was elaborated to cope with the fears from without and the anxieties from within (informed by the past as well), developing into a self-sustaining homeostasis wherein the culture became part of the anxiety-inducing and anxiety-reducing "environment." In terms of "reality testing," the existence of the Evil Eye reflects a worried concern for the continuity of a precarious ecological homeostasis (see Stein 1972: chap. 2).

A Slovak worries about his oxen; a Nuer worries about his cattle. As "economics" is never merely "rational" economics, it is bound up with status, self-esteem, identity, ethos, history—and childhood. The jealous watch over one's own, and the covetous gaze at that of another, suffuse and confuse technoeconomic, interpersonal, and intrapsychic issues. Finally, within the Slovak variant on the Slavic "*zadruga*" (see Stein 1972:chaps. 2, 6), the subordinate and subservient role of the Slovak female in relation to the arbitrary and dominating male, her constriction within the home and to the bearing of children, produced a specific quality of hostility toward her children that became manifest in the specific quality of the Slovak Evil Eye. From the vastly accumulating literature on family dynamics (see Anthony and Benedek 1970, Handel 1967, Stein 1973), it should be obvious that matters of "role allocation" and "division of labor" have a highly valent unconscious or latent dimension in addition to the more readily recognizable conscious or manifest dimension. The interpenetration of the two demands special attention for students of family structure.

Perhaps it is not too farfetched to link Foster's "image of the limited good" with Freud's metapsychology of civilization and its discontents. Foster suggested that the image of the limited good might not be limited to peasant society; and, to extend Freud somewhat, it might be suggested that "a balance of discontents" characterizes all of human "civilizations" ("designs for living") from the most "primitive" to the most "modern." The ubiquity of the Evil Eye attests to the interpenetration of "reality" and "fantasy" in human cultural adaptation, to the importance of early childhood object-relations in generating anxieties, and to the role of culture (whether in the origin or in the perpetuation of a symbol system) in the resolution of these anxieties through a decisive "change of function" into the "anxiety free sphere of the ego" (Hartmann 1958).

It is hoped that the present analysis of Slovak-American data will serve as a contribution toward elucidating the universal dynamics of the jealousy/envy complex and the Evil Eye in their firm rootedness in childhood and society. It is further hoped that envy will not be reified into an "essentialist" *explicans* in psychological anthropology, but will be investigated in an "existential" framework, as the semantic referent of a multitude of responses to varying and specifiable human *conditions*, and not reflecting something inherent in "the" human condition. Envy and the Evil Eye, like the Oedipus complex, are inextricably bound up with the vicissitudes of nature and nurture.

REFERENCES

Anthony, E. James. 1970. The Reaction of Parents to Adolescents and to their Behavior, *Parenthood: Its Psychology and Psychopathology* (E.J. Anthony and T. Benedek, eds.). Little, Brown and Co.

———. 1973. Tustin in Kleinianland, review of Frances Tustin, *Autism and Childhood Psychosis* 1973. *Psychotherapy and Social Science Review* 7:14–22.

Anthony, E. James, and Therese Benedek, eds. and contributors. 1970. *Parenthood: Its Psychology and Psychopathology*. Little, Brown and Co.

Benedek, Therese. 1970. The Family as a Psychologic Field, *Parenthood: Its Psychology and Psychopathology* (E.J. Anthony and T. Benedek, eds.). Little, Brown and Co.

Bowlby, John. 1960. Separation Anxiety. *International Journal of Psychoanalysis* 41:89–113.

Brown, Judith. 1972. Comments on George Foster, The Anatomy of Envy, *Current Anthropology* 13:188.

Caudill, William. 1962. Anthropology and Psychoanalysis: Some Theoretical Issues, *Anthropology and Human Behavior* (T. Gladwin and W.C. Sturtevant, eds.). The Anthropological Society of Washington.

Devereux, George. 1969. *Reality and Dream: Psychotherapy of a Plains Indian* (rev. ed.). Doubleday (orig. 1951).

———. 1970. Normal and Abnormal: The Key Concepts of Ethnopsychiatry, *Man and His Culture: Psychoanalytic Anthropology after Totem and Taboo* (W. Muensterberger, ed.). Taplinger.

Elworthy, F.T. 1958. *The Evil Eye*. Wehman (orig. 1895).

Erikson, Erik H. 1959. Identity and the Life Cycle, Selected Papers. *Psychological Issues* I (1) Monograph I. International Universities Press.

———. 1963. *Childhood and Society* (rev. ed.). Norton (orig. 1950).

———. 1966. Ontogeny of Ritualization, *Psychoanalysis: A General Psychology* (R.M. Loewenstein, L.M. Newman, M. Schur, and A.J. Solnit, eds.). International Universities Press.

———. 1968. *Identity: Youth and Crisis*. Norton.

Evans-Pritchard, E.E. 1951. Some Features of Nuer Religion. *The Journal of the Royal Anthropological Institute* 81:1–13.

Foster, George. 1965. Peasant Society and the Image of the Limited Good. *American Anthropologist* 67:293–315.

———. 1972. The Anatomy of Envy: A Study in Symbolic Behavior. *Current Anthropology* 13:165–202 (including comments and reply).

Freud, Sigmund. 1957. Psychoanalytic Comments on an Autobiographical Account of Paranoia (dementia paranoides), *Standard Edition* 12. Hogarth Press.

Goldschmidt, Walter. 1966. *Comparative Functionalism: An Essay in Anthropological Theory*. University of California Press.

Guntrip, Harry. 1971. *Psychoanalytic Theory, Therapy, and the Self*. Basic Books.

Haley, Jay. 1967. The Family of the Schizophrenic: A Model System. *The Psychosocial Interior of the Family* (G. Handel, ed.). Aldine.

Handel, Gerald, ed. 1967. *The Psychosocial Interior of the Family*. Aldine.

Hartmann, Heinz. 1958. *Ego Psychology and the Problem of Adaptation* (trans. David Rapaport). International Universities Press (orig. 1939).

Hartmann, Heinz, Ernest Kris, and Rudolph Loewenstein. 1951. Some Psychoanalytic Comments on "Culture and Personality," *Psychoanalysis and Culture* (G. Wilbur and W. Muensterberger, eds.). International Universities Press.

Homans, George. 1941. Anxiety and Ritual: The Theories of Malinowski and Radcliffe-Brown. *American Anthropologist* 43:164–172.

Joffe, Walter G. 1970. An Unenviable Preoccupation with Envy: Review of Helmut Schoeck, *Envy: A Theory of Social Behavior*, 1969. Reviewed in *Psychiatry and Social Science Review* 4:12–21.

Klein, Melanie. 1932. *The Psychoanalysis of Children*. Norton.

———. 1948. Mourning and its Relation to Manic-Depressive States, *Contributions to Psychoanalysis*. Hogarth Press.

———. 1957. *Envy and Gratitude*. Basic Books.

Klein, Melanie and Joan Riviere. 1962. *Love, Hate, and Reparation*. Hillary.

Kroeber, Alfred. 1948. *Anthropology*. Harcourt, Brace and Co.

LeVine, Robert A. 1973. *Culture, Behavior, and Personality*. Aldine.

Mahler, Margaret (with Manuel Furer). 1968. *On Human Symbiosis and the Vicissitudes of Human Individuation*. International Universities Press.

Mair, Lucy. 1969. *Witchcraft*. McGraw-Hill.

Middleton, John. 1955. The Concept of "Bewitching" in Lugbara. *Africa* 25(3):252–260.

Moss, Leonard W., and Stephen C. Cappannari. 1972. The Mediterranean: *Mal'occhio, Ayin ha ra, Oculus fascinus, Judenblick*; The Evil Eye Hovers Above. Paper given at Symposium: The Evil Eye, Meetings of the American Anthropological Association, Toronto, Canada (Dec. 1). Passage quoted includes authors' addenda to p. 14 of MS in preparation for publication.

Muensterberger, Warner. 1969. Psyche and Environment: Sociocultural Variations in Separation and Individuation. *The Psychoanalytic Quarterly* 38:191–216.

Rycroft, Charles. 1968. *Anxiety and Neurosis*. Penguin.

Slater, Philip. 1970. *The Pursuit of Loneliness: American Culture at the Breaking Point*. Beacon Press.

Spiro, Melford E. 1965. Religious Systems as Culturally Constituted Defense Mechanisms, *Context and Meaning in Cultural Anthropology* (M.E. Spiro, ed.). Free Press.

———. 1967. *Ifaluk Ghosts, Personalities and Cultures* (R. Hunt, ed.). The Natural History Press (orig. 1953).

Stein, Howard F. 1972. An Ethno-historic Study of Slovak-American Identity. Ph.D. dissertation, University of Pittsburgh; available through University Microfilms, Inc. Ann Arbor, Michigan.

———. 1973. Cultural Specificity in Patterns of Mental Illness and Health: a Slovak-American Case Study. *Family Process* 12:69–82.

Wallace, Anthony F.C. 1966. *Religion: An Anthropological View*. Random House.

Weidman, Hazel H. 1968. Anthropological Theory and the Psychological Function of Belief in Witchcraft. *Essays in Medical Anthropology* (T. Weaver, ed.). Southern Anthropological Society Proceedings 1. University of Georgia Press.

Whiting, John W.M., and Irvin Child. 1953. *Child Training and Personality: A Cross-Cultural Study*. Yale University Press.

Winnicott, Donald W. 1958. The Capacity to be Alone. *International Journal of Psychoanalysis* 39:416–420.

———. 1967. The Location of Cultural Experience. *International Journal of Psychoanalysis* 48:368–372.

Wynne, Lyman, Irving M. Wyckoff, Juliana Day, and Stanley I. Hirsch. 1967. Pseudo-mutuality in the Family Relations of Schizophrenics, *The Psychosocial Interior of the Family* (G. Handel, ed.). Aldine.

Wet and Dry, the Evil Eye: An Essay in Indo-European and Semitic Worldview

*Alan Dundes**

If one bothers to read extensively in the scholarship devoted to a given issue, one may well become discouraged both by the amount of material to be digested and by the sobering thought that probably everything worth saying about the subject has already been said by someone else. Perhaps this is one reason why relatively few students of the evil eye took the trouble to locate and examine much of the previous scholarship. On the other hand, it is surely an exciting challenge to try to say something new and worthwhile about a well studied topic. Having taken the trouble to review the earlier scholarship (and to present in this volume what I consider to be some of the highlights of this literature), I should like to present my own analysis of the evil eye. I have, I hope, profited from the insights offered by other students of the subject.

The reader is cautioned against thinking that this is the final word to be written on the subject. It is only the final word in this volume. If the reader has learned nothing else, he or she should realize that scholarship is a cooperative chain extending through time with each individual scholar forging no more than one link in that chain. Future investigators of the evil eye may choose to use this essay or more likely this volume in general as a stepping stone to

I should like to dedicate this essay to the memory of Ernest Jones whose brilliant application of pschoanalytic theory to the materials of folklore has served as a continual inspiration to me over the years. I must also thank Stanley Brandes, Robert Coote, Osama Doumani, George Foster, Steve Gudeman, Barbara Kirshenblatt-Gimblett, Wendy O'Flaherty, Felix Oinas, Saad Sowayan, and Tim White for valuable references and suggestions.

* Reprinted by permission of the English Folklore Society.

construct more rigorous and more accurate analyses of the various facets of the evil eye belief complex.

The evil eye is a fairly consistent and uniform folk belief complex based upon the idea that an individual, male or female, has the power, voluntarily or involuntarily, to cause harm to another individual or his property merely by looking at or praising that person or property. The harm may consist of illness, or even death or destruction. Typically, the victim's good fortune, good health, or good looks—or unguarded comments about them—invite or provoke an attack by someone with the evil eye. If the object attacked is animate, it may fall ill. Inanimate objects such as buildings or rocks may crack or burst. Symptoms of illness caused by the evil eye include loss of appetite, excessive yawning, hiccoughs, vomiting, and fever. If the object attacked is a cow, its milk may dry up; if a plant or a fruit tree, it may suddenly wither and die.

Preventive measures include wearing apotropaic amulets, making specific hand gestures or spitting, and uttering protective verbal formulas before or after praising or complimenting a person, especially an infant. Another technique is concealing, disguising, or even denying good fortune. One may symbolically disfigure good looks, for instance, by purposely staining the white linen of a new dress or placing a black smudge of soot behind a child's ear (Rodd 1968:160–61, cf. Crooke 1968:2:6), so as not to risk attracting the attention of the evil eye. This may be the rationale behind behavior as disparate as the veiling common in Arab cultures, the refusal in Jewish culture to say "good" when asked how one's health or business is—the safe reply is "not bad" or "no complaints"—the common tendency among millionaires in Europe and America to insist upon dressing in rags, and the baseball custom in the United States of not mentioning that a pitcher has given up no hits. (The mere mention of a possible "no-hitter" would supposedly jinx the pitcher and result in a batter's getting a base hit of some kind.)

In the event of a successful attack by the evil eye, there are prescribed diagnostic and curative procedures available. One may first need to ascertain whether or not it is a true case of the evil eye and second, if it is, who is responsible for it. Sometimes, the agent, who was perhaps an unwitting one, is involved in the ritual removal of the evil eye and its ill effects from the victim. He may, for instance, be asked to spit on the victim's face (cf. Dodwell 1819:35–36).

Although widespread throughout the Indo-European and Semitic world, the evil eye belief complex is not universal. In the most recent cross-cultural survey Roberts found that only 36 percent of the 186 cultures in his world sample possessed the evil eye belief (1976:229); and he suggested that the belief "probably developed in the old world, particularly in India, the Near East, and Europe" (1976:234). From this and other surveys (e.g., Andree, Seligmann), it is clear that the evil eye appears to be largely absent in aboriginal Australia, Oceania, native North and South America, and sub-Saharan Africa. The few rare reports of its occurrence in Africa, apart from the Maghreb where it flourishes, suggest Islamic influence. In Latin America, the evil eye was surely part of the general Spanish and Portuguese cultural legacy. Yet within the Indo-European and Semitic world, it is difficult to think of a more pervasive and powerful folk belief than the evil eye.

The scholarship devoted to the evil eye goes back to classical antiquity. Many of the ancients referred to it and Plutarch (46–120 A.D.) featured it in one of the dialogues in his Table Talk (V, Question 7) "On those who are said to cast an evil eye." This dialogue begins as follows: "Once at dinner a discussion arose about people who are said to cast a spell and to have an evil eye. While everybody else pronounced the matter completely silly and scoffed at it, Mestrius Florus, our host, declared that actual facts lend astonishing support to the common belief." Sometimes the passing references indicated belief in the evil eye, sometimes disbelief. In his insightful homily "Concerning Envy," written in the fourth century, Saint Basil remarked ". . . some think that envious persons bring bad luck merely by a glance, so that healthy persons in the full flower and vigor of their prime are made to pine away under their spell, suddenly losing all their plumpness, which dwindles and wastes away under the gaze of the envious, as if washed away by a destructive flood. For my part, I reject these tales as popular fancies and old wives' gossip" (Saint Basil 1950:469–70).

One of the issues often discussed was whether the evil eye was a conscious or unconscious power. The famed Arab historian Ibn Khaldûn (1332–1406) tended to consider the power of the evil eye as deriving from an involuntary act and, for this reason, to be distinguished from intentionally malicious sorcery. In section 27 of chapter

6 of the *Muqaddimah* (1967:170–71), Ibn Khaldûn commented on the evil eye, calling it a natural gift, something that is innate and not acquired, not depending upon the free choice of its possessor. He ended his discussion as follows: "Therefore it has been said: 'A person who kills by means of sorcery or a miraculous act must be killed, but the person who kills with the eyes must not be killed.' The only reason for the distinction is that the person who kills with the eyes did not want or intend to do so, nor could he have avoided doing so. The application of the eye was involuntary on his part." Ibn Khaldûn's distinction, somewhat analogous to the modern differences between first and second degree manslaughter, is not held by all writers on the evil eye. Some (e.g., Mackenzie 1895; Cutileiro 1971:274) suggest that some cases of the evil eye reflect an evil disposition on the part of the person possessing the power while others believed to have the power are "innocent of any ill design."

During the Renaissance a number of treatises were devoted to the evil eye. Representative are Enrique de Villena's "Tradado del Aojamiento" of 1422, Leonardus Vairus's "De Fascino" of 1589, Martinus Antonius Del Rio's "Disquisitionum magicarum" of 1599–1600, Joannes Lazarus Gutierrez's "Opusculum de Fascino" of 1653, and Joannes Christianus Frommann's "Tractatus de Fascinatione" of 1675. These and subsequent surveys often contain valuable data. For example, Nicola Valletta in his *Cicalata sul fascino volgarmente detto jettatura* of 1787 ended his discussion with a series of thirteen queries, designed very much like the modern questionnaire, about the evil eye and the *jettatura,* the casting of the evil eye. Valletta's queries were: 1) Is the evil eye stronger from a man or from a woman? 2) Is it stronger from someone wearing a wig? 3) Stronger from someone who wears glasses? 4) Stronger from a pregnant woman? 5) Stronger from monks and, if so, from which order? 6) If the evil eye does approach, after the attack, what effects must be suffered? 7) What is the range or limit of the distance at which the jettatura can be effective? 8) Can the power come from inanimate objects? 9) Is the evil eye stronger from the side, from the front, or from behind? 10) Are there gestures, voice quality, eyes, and facial characteristics by which jettatura can be recognized? 11) What prayers ought to be recited to protect us against the jettatura of monks? 12) What words in general ought to be said to thwart or escape the jettatura? 13) What power then have the horns and other things? (Valletta 1787:152). Valletta then asked anyone who had had experience with the evil eye to get in touch with him and added that he would be happy to pay for any information furnished.

The steady flow of treatises continued in the nineteenth century. Italian scholars in particular were intrigued with a phenomenon that flourished unabated in their country. Typical are Giovanni Leonardo Marugj's *Capricci sulla jettatura* in 1815, and Michele Arditi's *Il fascino, e l'amuleto contro del fascino presso gli antichi* of 1825, and Andrea de Jorio's *La Mimica degli Antichi* of 1832, which was especially concerned with the traditional gestures used to avert the evil eye.

Modern scholarship on the evil eye may be truly said to have begun with Otto Jahn's pioneering essay, "Über den Aberglauben des bösen Blicks bei den Altern," which appeared in 1855. It, like so many of the early treatises, concentrated upon ancient Greek and Roman examples of the evil eye, but it differed in its honest and erudite consideration of all facets of the evil eye complex, including the obviously phallic character of so many of the apotropaic amulets. By the end of the nineteenth century, numerous essays had been written on the evil eye, though most of them were limited to descriptive reports from one particular area. Among the more general surveys of the subject was Jules Tuchmann's remarkably detailed series of articles on "La Fascination," which began to appear in the French folklore journal *Mélusine* in 1884 and continued intermittently until 1901. Tuchmann's massive and impressive collection of citations on the evil eye drawn from a huge variety of sources in many languages (Gaidoz 1912) may well have been the inspiration for folklorist Arnold van Gennep's delightful parody of the doctoral dissertation writer who tried but failed to write the definitive work on the evil eye (van Gennep 1967:32–36). A better-known nineteenth-century survey work is Frederick Thomas Elworthy's *The Evil Eye,* first published in 1895.

The next major effort, perhaps the most ambitious of all, was the encyclopedic two-volume work by oculist S. Seligmann, *Der Böse Blick und Verwandtes,* published in 1910. This, or the 1922 version *Die Zauberkraft des Auges und des Berufen,* remains probably the best single source of information on the subject, at least in terms of sheer quantity of ethnographic data. Other landmark studies of the evil eye in the twentieth century include Westermarck's extensive consideration of the evil eye in Morocco (1926:414–78) and Karl Meisen's two comprehensive essays (1950, 1952) in the *Rheinisches*

Jahrbuch für Volkskunde, the first covering the evil eye in the ancient and early Christian eras and the second treating the medieval and modern periods. Also worthy of mention are oculist Edward S. Gifford's *The Evil Eye: Studies in the Folklore of Vision* (1958), classicist Waldemar Deonna's marvelously learned and brilliant *Le Symbolisme de l'Oeil,* posthumously published in 1965, psychiatrist Joost A. M. Meerloo's *Intuition and the Evil Eye: The Natural History of Superstition* (1971), and a collection of anthropological essays on the evil eye, *The Evil Eye,* edited by Clarence Maloney (1976). This latter group of fifteen essays consists primarily of ethnographic description and makes little reference to the voluminous literature devoted to the evil eye in classics, folklore, and psychiatry. It does, however, include a long, important paper by John M. Roberts, "Belief in the Evil Eye in World Perspective," which carefully canvasses 186 diverse cultures to see if the evil eye occurs and, if so, with what other cultural variables it might meaningfully be statistically correlated. Still another comprehensive study is Thomas Hauschild's dissertation *Der Böse Blick: Indeengeschichtliche und Sozialpsychologische Untersuchungen* (1979).

The works mentioned thus far are essentially overviews of the evil eye belief complex but it should be noted that there are a number of valuable books and monographs on the evil eye in a given culture. Among the best of these are investigations in Scotland, R.C. Maclagan's *Evil Eye in the Western Highlands* (1902); in Spain, Raphael Salillas's *La Fascinación en Espana* (1905); in Finland, Toivo Vuorela's *Der Böse Blick im Lichte der Finnischen Überlieferung* (1967); and in Sardinia, Clara Gallini's *Dono e Malocchio* (1973). When one adds to these the literally dozens on dozens of notes and articles that discuss the evil eye either en passant or in some depth, it is clear that one has an unmanageable number of sources available to consult for relevant information.

Despite the enormous bibliographic bulk of the evil eye scholarship, it is not unfair to say that there have been few attempts to explain the evil eye belief complex in terms of a holistic integrated theory. By far the majority of the discussions of the evil eye consist solely of anecdotal reportings of various incidents. Anthropologist Hocart summed up the situation aptly when he said (1938:156): "There is a considerable literature about the evil eye, but it does little more than add instances to instances." Unfortunately, the situation has not changed; and as Spooner puts it (1976:281): "Permutations of practice do not appear to lead to a satisfactory formulation of theory."

Formulations of theories of the evil eye do exist. Recent speculations about the possible origin and significance of the evil eye have included the suggestion that it is related to gaze behavior perhaps involving gaze aversion, common in many animal species (Coss 1974). With regard to gaze behavior, Erikson proposes (1977:50, 58) that an infant experiences the unresponsive eye of an adult as a rejecting, hostile environment or "Other" (as opposed to self). Thus, according to Erikson, "the unresponsive eye becomes an evil one." It has also been claimed that the evil eye is an ancient type of hypnotic phenomenon (MacHovee 1976). But probably the most widely accepted theory of the evil eye contends that it is based upon envy. In his celebrated *Folkways,* first published in 1906, Sumner argued that the evil eye depended upon primitive demonism and envy. According to Sumner (1960:434), "It is assumed that demons envy human success and prosperity and so inflict loss and harm on the successful."

There is no question that envy is somehow closely related to the evil eye. This is clear in the earliest Near Eastern texts we have. The word *envy* is etymologically derived from the Latin *invidia,* which in turn comes from *in videre*, thus ultimately from "to see" or "seeing" as Cicero first observed (Elworthy 1958:7; cf. Odelstierna 1949:72, n.1.). To see something is to want it, perhaps. A common reaction to seeing a desirable object is to praise it, to admire it. An expression of admiration or praise is understood to imply at least a tinge of envy. Envy can accordingly be expressed either by eye or by mouth (or by both). Schoeck considers the evil eye to be a universal expression of malevolent envy (1955), but Spooner has criticized the envy theory, noting (1976:283) that "although it is perfectly valid and necessary at one stage of analysis, the anthropologist should attempt to build models at a higher stage of abstraction." Spooner might also have realized that no theory can be persuasive unless or until it enables one to explain the particulars of a given custom or segment of human behavior. How does the notion of envy explain, for example, the specific details of fruit trees withering, the common symptom of yawning, or the various gestures, such as spitting, employed to ward off the evil eye. Spooner does ask why, since envy in some form is probably universal, it should give rise to the evil eye in some societies but not in others (1976:283). One can only conclude that whereas envy is surely a component of the overall evil eye complex, it is not sufficient in and of itself to explain the complex in all its concrete detail.

The same difficulties inhere in suggestions that the evil eye complex provides an outlet for the expression of aggression, or that it acts as an agent of social control. The question that must be addressed is: why does the evil eye manifest itself precisely in the forms that it does? Why are very young children and infants especially susceptible to the effects of the evil eye? Or, why is the butterfat content of milk in a churn magically removed?

Psychoanalytic interpretations of the evil eye have also been partial. Because many of the apotropaic amulets and gestures have unmistakable phallic elements (Valletta 1787:18–25; Jahn 1855; Michaelis 1885; Wolters 1909; Elworthy 1958:149–54; Seligmann 1910:II:188–200; Deonna 1965:180–81), it has long been obvious that the male genitals are involved in some way with the evil eye complex. Since phallic gestures like the *fica* (Leite de Vasconcellos 1925:92) were used to ward off the evil eye, and since males often touched their genitals upon seeing a priest or other individual thought to have the evil eye (Valla 1894:422n; Servadio 1936:403; n. 8) then it is not unreasonable to assume that the evil eye threatened to make men impotent (Seligmann 1910:199; Servadio 1936). But if the evil eye constituted a danger to masculinity, why was it believed that a weaned infant who has returned to the breast would grow up to have the evil eye, and why was the evil eye especially damaging to *female* animals, such as cows? Roberts attempted a factor analysis of various features associated with the evil eye in his cross-cultural survey; he found the highest correlation with milking and dairy production though he was unable to explain this linkage (1976:241, 258). Of course, psychoanalysts have also argued that the eye could be a female symbol (Reitler 1913:160) with "the pupil representing the vagina, the lids the labia, and the lashes the pubic hair" (Tourney and Plazak 1954:489). Is the eye a phallus, or is it a vagina, or is it both (or neither)? And how would this possibly relate to injury to cows and their milk supply?

Géza Róheim suggests (1952:356) that the key to the whole evil eye belief is oral jealousy and oral aggression. This would illuminate the apparent connection with nursing children as well as the appropriateness of the use of spitting or oral incantations to avoid the evil eye. But in this case, it would not be so obvious why phallic means should be equally effective. Róheim does not succeed, in my opinion, in reconciling the oral and phallic elements in the evil eye complex.

Freud himself, writing about the evil eye in his 1919 essay on the 'uncanny,' considered its origin to be fear of envy, coupled with the device of projection. "Whoever possesses something at once valuable and fragile is afraid of the envy of others, in that he projects onto them the envy he would have felt in their place" (1959:393). Tourney and Plazak follow this psychiatric tack by emphasizing the eye as an organ of aggression. They suggest (1954:491) that "with the utilization of the projective mechanism, fear of the evil eye may represent the manifestation of one's own aggressive impulses attributed as being apart from the ego and acting in turn against it. A need for punishment because of guilt over hostility and aggression can be realized in the suffering of a recipient from the influence of the evil eye." Through projection, the original would-be aggressor is spared feelings of guilt because "I hate you" or "I envy you" has been transformed into "You hate me" or "You envy me." By means of this projective transformation, the active becomes the passive, the aggressor becomes the victim. This may explain why the rich and powerful are so often thought to have the evil eye—popes and nobility have frequently been said to have it. The poor envy the rich and powerful, but this envy is transformed into the rich casting an evil eye at the poor. But this psychiatric notion does not really explicate all the particulars of the evil eye belief complex either.

A plausible theory of the evil eye must be able to account for most, if not all, of the elements in the complex, including the manifestly male and female components. Consider the following modern Greek cure for the evil eye, which involves the formula (Dionisopoulos-Mass 1976:46): "If it is a woman who has cast the eye, then destroy her breasts. If it is a man who has cast the eye, then crush his genitals." In a variant (Hardie 1923:170), "If a man did it, may his eyes fall out. If a woman did it may her eyes fall out and her breasts burst." In India, we find the same alternation of male and female attributes. According to Thurston (1907:254):

> When a new house is being constructed, or a vegetable garden or rice field are in flourishing condition, the following precautions are taken to ward off the evil eye:

a. In buildings—
   1. A pot with black and white marks on it is suspended mouth downwards.
   2. A wooden figure of a monkey, with pendulous testes, is suspended.
   3. The figure of a Malayali woman, with protuberant breasts, is suspended.

b. In fields and gardens—
   1. A straw figure covered with a black cloth daubed with black and white dots is placed on a long pole. If the figure represents a male, it has pendent testes, and, if a woman, well-developed breasts. Sometimes male and female figures are placed together in an embracing posture.
   2. Pots, as described above, are placed on bamboo poles.

Since the evil eye is as dangerous to female breasts (including cow's udders) as to male genitals, it is necessary for the magical countermeasures to defend against both threats. The question is: what theoretical underlying principle or principles, if any, can explain the whole range of phenomena believed to be caused by the evil eye, from the withering of fruit trees, to the loss of milk from cows to impotence among males. The striking similarity of evil eye reports from different cultures strongly suggests that whatever the rationale behind it may be, it is likely to be cross-culturally valid.

I suggest that the evil eye belief complex depends upon a number of interrelated folk ideas in Indo-European and Semitic worldview. I should like to enumerate them briefly before discussing them in some detail.

1. Life depends upon liquid. From the concept of the "water of life" to semen, milk, blood, bile, saliva, and the like, the consistent principle is that liquid means life while loss of liquid means death. "Wet and Dry" as an oppositional pair means life and death. Liquids are living; drying is dying!

2. There is a finite, limited amount of good—health, wealth, etc.—and because that is so, any gain by one individual can only come at the expense of another (cf. Foster 1965). If one individual possesses a precious body fluid, semen, for instance, this automatically means that some other individual lacks that same fluid.

3. Life entails an equilibrium model. If one has too little wealth or health, one is poor or ill. Such individuals constitute threats to persons

with sufficient or abundant wealth and health. This notion may be in part a projection on the part of well-to-do individuals. They think they should be envied and so they project such wishes to the have-nots. On the other hand, the have-nots are often envious for perfectly good reasons of their own.

4. In symbolic terms, a pair of eyes may be equivalent to breasts or testicles. A single eye may be the phallus (especially the glans), the vulva, or occasionally the anus. The fullness of life as exemplified by such fluids as mother's milk or semen can thus be symbolized by an eye and accordingly threats to one's supply of such precious fluids can appropriately be manifested by the eye or eyes of others.

I am not claiming that any of the above folk ideas or principles are necessarily consciously understood by members of Indo-European and Semitic cultures. They may or may not be. What I am proposing is that they are structural principles of thought among the peoples of these cultures. I hope to show that they explain not only the evil eye but a vast range of traditional behavior ranging from tipping to some specifics of burial customs.

Documentation for the folk idea that life is liquid is amply provided by Richard Broxton Onians in his brilliant tour de force, *The Origins of European Thought about the Body, the Mind, the Soul, the World, Time, and Fate,* published in 1951. Onians is able to explain one of the rationales behind cremation. Burning the dead expedites the "drying" process, the final removal of the liquid of life (1951:256). He remarks on the Greek conception of life as the gradual diminishing of liquid inside a man (1951:215). I would add that the metaphor probably made sense in light of what was empirically observable in the case of fruits, among other items. Juicy grapes could become dry raisins; plums could become prunes, etc. With increasing age, the human face becomes wrinkled and these inevitable wrinkles could be logically construed as signs of the same sort of drying process that produced the wrinkles in raisins and prunes. It should also be pointed out that this Greek conception is also a manifestation of the notion of limited good (Foster 1965, Gouldner 1965:49–51). Man is born with only so much life force and he is therefore ever anxious to replenish it. Milk and wine are obvious sources of liquid (1951:227), noted Onians, and he correctly observes the content of toasts in this connection. One drinks "healths." What Onians failed to understand is that healths are supposedly drunk to *others,* that is, accompanied by such verbal formulas as "Here's to you," "Here's to your health," or "Here's long life to you." What this means in terms of limited good, I submit, is: "I drink, but not at your expense. I am replenishing my liquid supply, but I wish no diminution in yours." The very fact that a drinker mentions another person's *health* before drinking implies that if he did not do so, that person's health might suffer. In other words, drinking without a formulaic prophylactic preamble might be deleterious to the other person's health. In an unusual volume published in 1716 entitled *A Discourse of Drinking Healths,* we find this thought articulated: "And what strange Inchantment can there be in saying or meaning, As I drink this Glass of Wine, So let another Man perish" (Browne 1716:19).

Lévi-Strauss, in a rare instance of ethnographic fieldwork, reports on a custom observed in lower-priced restaurants in the south of France (1969:58–60). Each table setting includes a small bottle of wine but etiquette demands that one does not pour the contents of the bottle into one's own glass. Rather the wine is poured into the glass of an individual at a neighboring table. This individual will normally reciprocate by pouring the contents of his bottle into the initial pourer's glass. Lévi-Strauss explains this custom in terms of a structural principle, namely the principle of reciprocity: "Wine offered calls for wine returned, cordiality required cordiality." This is not an implausible explanation, but this custom which reflects an attitude towards wine remarkably different from that towards food, as Lévi-Strauss himself notes, may also exemplify the special rules governing the incorporation of liquids among Indo-European and Semitic peoples. The notion of limited good—as applied to the essential liquids of life—requires one to offer beverages to others. If one drinks without regard to one's neighbors, one risks being envied and becoming the object or victim of an evil eye. The reciprocity of courtesy is demonstrated in a Gaelic incantation against the evil eye reported from the island of Skye in the Hebrides. When washing in the morning (Mackenzie 1895:39), a person may recite:

> Let God bless my eye,
> And my eye will bless all I see;
> I will bless my neighbor
> And my neighbor will bless me.

Numerous reports attest that eating in public is thought to be especially dangerous with respect to the evil eye. Westermarck (1904:211; cf. Gifford 1958:48–50), for example, notes that "the danger is greatest when you eat. To take food in the presence of some hungry looker-on is the same as to take poison; the evil—*i-bas*, as the Moors call it—then enters into your body. When you commence eating, everybody must either partake of the meal or go away." In Egypt, Lane (1895:262) reports that his cook would not purchase the fine sheep displayed in a butcher's shop because "every beggar who passes by envies them; one might, therefore as well eat poison as such meat." A report that appeared in the Russian paper *Ilustriravansk Mir* in 1881 (according to Gordon 1937:306) reflects a similar belief: "The Russian government turned over a convict sentenced to die to the Academy of Science for the purpose of testing the powers of [the] evil eye. The prisoner was starved for three days during which a loaf of bread was placed in front of him of which he was unable to partake. At the end of the third day, the bread was examined and found to contain a poisonous substance." Gordon (1937:307) observes that while the story proves nothing—the bread could easily have been spoiled by being kept in a damp cell for three days, the very fact that a newspaper could print the report shows the readiness of the public to believe in the power of the evil eye.

One technique used in restaurants to avert the dangers of the evil eye is to offer onlookers some of one's food. In Spanish restaurants, for example, any person waiting to be seated at a table is frequently invited by patrons already eating to join them or share their food. This formulaic offer is inevitably refused but the point is that the invitation is made. Foster (1972:181) has described this very well:

> In Spain and Spanish America—to this day in small country inns—a diner greets each conceptual equal who enters the room with "*Gusta [Usted comer]?*" ("Would you care to share my meal?"), thereby symbolically inviting the stranger (or friend) to partake of the good fortune of the diner. The new arrival ritually replies "Buen provecho" ("Good appetite," i.e., may your food agree with you), thereby reassuring the diner that he has no reason to fear envy, and that he may eat in peace. The entrant normally would not think of accepting the invitation, and the courtesy appears to have the double function of acknowledging the possible presence of envy and, at the same time, eliminating its cause.

After commenting upon the probably similar functioning of such ritual predining formulas as the French "bon appetit," Foster proceeds to discuss the necessity for offering something to a waiter in a restaurant. Since a waiter may also envy a diner, he needs to be given something to ensure his good will, namely, a tip. In a fascinating brief survey of analogues to the word *tip* in a number of European languages, e.g., French *pourboire*, German *Trinkgeld*, Spanish *propine*, Portuguese *gorgeta*, Polish *napiwek*, Swedish *drincs*, Finnish *juomarabaa*, Icelandic *drykkjupeningar*, Russian *Chaevye [den'gi]*, and Croatian *Napojnica*, Foster concludes that the English word *tip* must come from *tipple* which means "to drink." (This is obviously much more likely than the folk etymology often encountered that *tip* is an acronymic formation from "to insure promptness" or *tips* from "to insure prompt service.") While Foster is surely correct in stating (1972:181) that "a tip, clearly, is money given to a waiter to buy off his possible envy, to equalize the relationship between server and served," he fails to comment on the possible significance of the fact that the waiter is invited to *drink* (as opposed to eat). In the light of the present argument, it is precisely liquids which must be offered to avert the evil eye.

The use of a liquid bribe, so to speak, is also found in other evil eye contexts. For example, in Scotland,

> A well-informed woman, an innkeeper, said that in cases where a person possessed of the Evil Eye admired anything belonging to another, no injury could follow if some little present were given to the suspected person on leaving . . . In the case of churning the small present naturally takes the form of a drink of milk to be given to anyone suspected of the Evil Eye, and so a reciter said that one should always, for safety's sake, give a visitor a drink of milk, and stated further that the beneficial effect was added to if the one who gives it first takes a little of it herself before handing it to the stranger (Maclagan 1902:22–123).

The suggestion that the efficacy of the "tip" is increased if one first takes a little of the milk before offering it to the stranger is reminiscent of one of the folk theories of the evil eye, which claims a connection exists between breast-feeding practices and the evil eye. One notion is that an infant allowed to drink freely from both breasts (rather than from just one) will grow up to have the evil eye. Another notion is that an infant once weaned who is allowed to return to the breast will likewise grow up to have the evil eye. Representative ethnographic data includes the following. In India (Crooke 1968:1:2), "One, and perhaps the most common theory of the Evil Eye is that 'when a child is born, an invisible spirit is born with it; and unless the mother keeps one breast tied up for forty days, while she feeds the child with the other (in which case the spirit dies of hunger), the child grows up with the endowment of the Evil Eye, and whenever any person so endowed looks at anything constantly, something will happen to it.' " In Greece (Hardie 1923:161), "It is known, however, that if a new-made mother suckles her infant from both breasts without an interval between, her glance will be baleful to the first thing on which it rests afterwards. Again, should a mother weakly yield to the tears of her newly weaned son and resume feeding him, he will, in later life, have the evil eye." (This belief could function as a socially sanctioned charter or justification for mothers weary of breast-feeding and anxious to finalize weaning.) Similarly, in Greece, one of the things that can cause the evil eye is "if the baby resumes breast feeding after having been interrupted for a few days or weeks" (Blum and Blum 1965:186, 1970:146). Analogous informant testimonies concerning the presumed causal relationship between reversing the weaning act and the evil eye have been reported in the Slovak-American tradition (Stein 1974) and in Romania (Murgoci 1923:357). (The folk theory that weaning reversal can cause the evil eye would seem to offer support to psychoanalyst Melanie Klein's claim that the primary prototype of envy in general is the infant's envy of the "feeding breast" as an object which possesses everything (milk, love) the infant desires [Klein 1957:10,29].) In all these cases, the infant is displaying what is construed as greedy behavior. Either he wants both breasts (when one is deemed sufficient) or he wishes to return to the breast after having been weaned (perhaps thus depriving a younger sibling of some of the latter's rightful supply of the limited good of mother's milk). An infant who gets more milk in this way is likely to become an adult who also attempts to get other forms of material good in this same way, that is, at someone else's expense. Thus he will be an adult with the evil eye, a greedy individual who, craving more than he deserves, or needs, may seek to take from the bounty of others. (In this context, it might be more apt to say that *tip* derives not just from *tipple*, but ultimately from *nipple*.) One wonders if the yawning symptom of victims of the evil eye might not be reminiscent of weaning insofar as the mouth in the act of yawning is constantly opening without obvious material benefit.

Confirmation of the importance of weaning and sibling rivalry in the evil eye belief complex comes from a curious detail in a remarkable legend which itself serves as a charm against the evil eye.

The text typically involves the personification of the evil eye, usually as a female demon, perhaps a Lilith, child-stealing figure. A saint or archangel encounters the she-demon and forces her to reveal all of her names (through the recitation of which she may henceforth be controlled) and to return any infants she has already carried off or devoured (cf. Gollancz 1912; Hazard 1890–91; Naff 1965:50–1; Montgomery 1913:259–62; Gaster 1900; Fries 1891; and Perdrizet 1922:5–31). Gaster cites a Slavonic version of the legend (1900: 139–42) in which it is the devil who steals and swallows a sixth infant after having similarly disposed of five previous ones. The mother Meletia dispatches her brother Saint Sisoe to recover her infants. When he confronts the devil and demands the return of the infants, the devil replies, "Vomit thou first the milk which thou has sucked from thy mother's breast." The Saint prays to God and does so. The devil, seeing this, regurgitates the six infants, who are safe and sound. In two seventeenth-century Greek versions cited by Gaster, the same motif recurs. Two saints, Sisynnios and Sisynodoros, demand that the villain Gylo return the children of their sister Melitena. The she-demon Gylo replies, "If you can return in the hollow of your hand the milk which you have sucked from your mother's breast I will return the children of Melitena." The saints pray and "they vomited at once into the hollow of their hand something like their mother's milk." Gylo then brings up the abducted children and reveals her other names (Gaster 1900:143–45; cf. 147–48). If the brother's regurgitation of mother's milk equals the restoration of infants, then one might logically assume that swallowing mother's milk is symbolically equivalent to destroying infants. Since the protagonists are brother and sister, we appear to have a case of sibling rivalry revolving around the allocation of mother's milk. Incidentally, the name of the personification of the evil eye, Gylo, may, according to Perdrizet (1922:25) who has studied the legend in some detail, be related to the Arab *ghoul*, which may in turn be related to the Babylonian *gallou*, which means "demon." The root may possibly be related to a variety of Indo-European words associated with greediness in drinking. Consider French *goulu*, meaning "gluttonous," or *gueule*, meaning "the mouth of an animal," with *gueulee*, meaning "a large mouthful." In English, it may be related to such words as *gullet, glut, gulp, gully,* and possibly *gurgle, gobble, gorge,* and *gurgitation. Gulch* once meant "drunkard" or "to swallow or devour greedily" while *gulf* once referred to a voracious appetite (and may derive from the Greek for bosom). To engulf means to swallow.

Water *is*, of course, necessary for the sustenance of life, and life itself is empirically observed to begin in some sense with an emergence from a flood—of amniotic fluid, perhaps providing a human model or prototype for creation myths involving supposed primeval waters or floods (cf. Casalis 1976). But it is the metaphorical and symbolic quests for water that are most relevant to our consideration of the evil eye. Onians explains that the idea that life is liquid and the dead are dry accounts for the widespread conception of a "water of life" (1951:289). The search for the water of life in fairy tales (cf. motif E80, Water of life), which is found throughout the Indo-European and Semitic world, as well as the common quest for the fountain of youth (cf. motif D1338.1.1, Fountain of youth), certainly support the notion that liquid is life. Hopkins (1905:55) distinguishes the two motifs, arguing that the "fountain of youth" comes from India while the "water of life" stems from Semitic tradition. In any case, the magic liquid can cure wounds and even bring the dead back to life. It can also rejuvenate, making the old young again. If the passage of life consists of the gradual diminution of finite fluids, then the only logical way to reverse the process would be to increase one's fluid supply. Whether fluids were taken internally (by drinking) or externally (by bathing, baptism, or being anointed), the life-giving or -renewing principle is basically the same.

If increases in liquid mean health, then decreases might signify the opposite (Onians 1951:212–14). I think it is quite possible that the English word *sick* comes ultimately from the Latin *siccus*, which means "dry." The total loss of liquid, that is, loss of life, would mean death. And this is why in the Indo-European and Semitic world, the dead are specifically perceived as being thirsty. The following custom is typical (Canaan 1929:59): "Water is not only essential for the living but also for the dead. As in ancient days so also now the Palestinian is accustomed to place for the dead a jar containing water; the only difference is that we often find on the tombs a shallow or deep cup-like cavity. Some believe that the soul of the dead visits the tomb and expects to find water to quench its thirst; therefore they that visit the tombs of the dead fill these cups with water." Onians in writing of the thirst of the dead notes (1951:285) that in Babylonia the provision of water to the dead fell to the deceased's nearest kinsman. This kinsman was known as a man's "pourer of water." One Babylonian curse was: "May God deprive him of an heir and a pourer of water." The widespread distribution of the conception of the thirsty dead has been amply described (cf. Bellucci 1909 and especially Deonna 1939:53–77).

Certainly the presumed thirst of the dead is a major metaphor in ancient Egyptian funerary ritual. According to Budge (1909:34), one of the oldest of the ceremonies performed for the dead was called the "Opening of the Mouth." The deceased was told, "Thy mouth is the mouth of the sucking calf on the day of its birth" (Budge 1909:60, 156, 209). Various offerings of food and libation were presented to the deceased, most of them specifically said to come from the Eye of Horus. "Accept the Eye of Horus, which welleth up with water, and Horus hath given unto thee" (Budge 1909:147; cf. 117, 129, 185). The Eye of Horus as a breast or other body part containing liquid is understood to refresh the deceased by offering him the necessary additional "fluid of life" to replace the fluids lost before death or during the process of mummification (Budge 1909:46, 52).

In the light of the centrality of liquid as a metaphor for life, it makes sense for envy to be expressed in liquid terms. The have-nots envy the haves and desire their various liquids. Whether it is the dead who envy the living (as in vampires who require the blood of the living and who are commonly referred to as "bloodthirsty"), the old who envy the young, or the barren who envy those with children, it is the blood, the sap or vitality of youth, the maternal milk, or masculine semen that is coveted. The notion of limited good means that there is not really enough to go around. Thus an admiring look or statement (of praise) is understood as a wish for precious fluid. If the looker or declarer receives liquid, then it must be at the expense of the object or person admired. So the victim's fruit tree withers from a loss of sap or his cow's milk dries up. The point is that the most common effect of the evil eye is a *drying up* process.

There have long been clues revealing the desiccating nature of the evil eye. A thirteenth-century Dominican, Thomas of Cantinpré, claimed that if a wolf and a man meet and the wolf sees the man first, the man cannot speak because the rays from the wolf's eye dry up the *spiritus* of human vision, which in turn dries up the human *spiritus* generally (Tourney and Plazak 1954:481). At the beginning of the twentieth century, twenty-three informants in Spain mentioned *secarse*, "drying out," as one of the characteristic symptoms of the evil eye (Salillas 1905:44). An interesting clinical parallel is provided in a case of schizophrenia where a nurse believed a private eye (not a detective but an actual eye) was watching her and that it had the power to draw vital body fluids from her (Tourney and Plazak 1954:488).

One of the oldest texts extant that treats the evil eye is a Sumerian one; it too confirms the association with water. It begins, "The eye *ad-gir*, the eye a man has . . . The eye afflicting man with evil, the *ad-gir*. Unto heaven it approached and the storms sent no rain." The evil eye even takes away water from the heavens. The Sumerian text suggests the cure involves "Seven vases of meal-water behind the grinding stones. With oil mix. Upon (his) face apply" (Langdon 1913:11–12, cf. Ebeling). One may compare this with a Neapolitan charm from Amalfi (Williams, 1961:156), which is nearly four thousand years later: "Eye of death, Evil Eye, I am following you with water, oil and Jesus Christ." The protective power of fluids including water is apparent in many ancient texts referring to the evil eye. For example, in the *Berakoth*, a book of the Babylonian Talmud, we read, "Just as the fishes in the sea are covered by water and the evil eye has no power over them, so the evil eye has no power over the seed of Joseph" [Simon 1948:120(20a), 340(55b)]. On a portal plaque from Arslan Tash in Upper Syria, a Phoenician incantation text inscribed in an Aramaic script of the early seventh century B.C. (Caquot and Mesnil du Buisson 1971) urges the caster of the evil eye to flee. It begins, according to Gaster (1973, but cf. Cross 1974:486–90) with these words: "Charm against the demon who drains his victims." This suggests the antiquity of the idea that the evil eye constitutes a threat to the body fluids. In modern Saudi Arabia, a person who is accused of having the evil eye may be labelled by the adjective *ash-hab* which means "grey and desiccated." A person with the evil eye is thus one who is dried out, in need of liquid refreshment.

Once it is understood that the evil eye belief complex depends upon the balance of liquid equilibrium, it becomes possible to gain insight into various apotropaic techniques. For example, on the back of a large number of ancient amulets used to keep the evil eye away appears a Greek inscription meaning "I drink." Bonner (1950:213) and other scholars puzzled by this inscription felt that this meaning was inappropriate and suggested alternative translations such as "I am hungry" or "I devour." But if these meanings were intended, one might ask, why should "I drink" appear so often. Bonner even went so far as to suggest that "perhaps the 'error' occurred on the first specimen manufactured in some important workshop and was slavishly copied." The point is surely that the folk know (in some sense) what they are doing—even if scholars do not. In the light of the present hypothesis, "I drink" makes perfect sense as the inscription of an anti-evil eye amulet.

Or consider the following detail of a contemporary Algerian Jewish custom. Whoever removes the effects of the evil eye from someone afflicted evidently runs some risk of having the effects transferred to him. "Pour éviter que le 'mauvais oeil' enlevé au malade ne pénètre en lui l'opérateur après avoir terminé absorbe un verre d'un liquide quelconque (eau, anisette, vin, etc.) que lui offrent les parents du malade" (Bel 1903:364). Clearly, the incorporation of liquid—whether it is water or wine is immaterial—is thought to guard against the dangerous effects of the evil eye.

Structurally speaking, the various apotropaic methods employed to avoid or cure the evil eye ought to be isomorphic. But how is showing a phallus or the fica isomorphic with spitting? I would argue that all these amulets or gestures signify the production of some form of liquid. Whether the liquid is semen or saliva, it provides proof that the victim's supply of life force is undiminished. Spitting is also an act of insult and it is quite likely that spitting as a counteractant to the evil eye represents a devaluation of the victim. In other words, a beautiful baby whether praised or admired or not represents a potential object of attack by an evil eye. If one spits on the baby (or asks the possessor of the evil eye to spit on the baby), one is mitigating the praise or admiration expressed. It is as if to say this is not a beautiful, admirable object (and that it should not be subject to an evil eye attack). On the other hand, spitting involves the projection of liquid for all to see. Crombie (1892:252) was quite right in remarking that saliva seemed to contain the element of life, but he did not realize that saliva can also be symbolically equivalent to semen (cf. Onians 1951:233, n.5). The initial consonant cluster *sp* occurs in both *sputum* and *sperm*, suggesting the emission of liquid, but even more persuasive is the unambiguous metaphorical evidence provided by the idiom "spitten image" (or "spit and image" or "spitting image"), used to refer to a child who greatly resembles his father (cf. Jones 1951:63, 273). The symbolic equivalence is also attested in jokes. Legman (1968:584) reported the following abbreviated text collected in Scranton, Pennsylvania, in 1930: "Two twins are conversing in the womb. 'Who's that bald-headed guy that comes in here every night and spits in my eye?' "

The important role of saliva in the evil eye belief complex is confirmed by an interesting practice reported in Greece and Saudi Arabia. In the Oasim district in north central Saudi Arabia, in cases where someone is afflicted by the evil eye and it is not known who caused the misfortune, someone representing the victim, usually a small male child, stands in a public area, for example, outside a mosque with a small bowl half filled with water and asks each male passerby to spit into it. This is done so as not to embarrass anyone in particular by accusing that person of having the evil eye. After everyone or, at least, a good many individuals have expectorated into the container (or made a pseudo-spitting gesture), the container is taken to the victim who drinks half the contents and anoints his body with the other half. In eastern Greece in the beginning of this century, a village girl fell ill. Her mother, fearing that the cause was the evil eye, hired a curer (female) to go to the church to collect forty spits in a glass from people going into the church. The curer kept track of the number of spits by counting kernels of corn. When she counted forty kernels, she brought the glass to the victim who drank it. The victim recovered within a few days. However aesthetically unpleasing or hygienically unsound such a practice may be adjudged by nonmembers of the cultures concerned, the cure certainly does exemplify the principle of liquid intake as a counteractant to the evil eye.

As for the Malabar custom described earlier, the male figures with pendulous testes and female figures with protuberant breasts used to ward off the evil eye can also be understood as liquid-bearing symbols. The large testes and breasts presumably represent an abundance of semen and milk. (The overturned pot may suggest that the abundance is so great that hoarding is not necessary.) The symbolic equivalence of breasts and eyes is suggested by a variety of data. In ancient European iconography circles with short lines radiating from the circumference were used to symbolize both eyes and breasts (Crawford 1957:41, 48, 96, 98; cf. Deonna 1965:64; Meerloo 1971:36). In contemporary German folk speech, dozens of idioms support the fact that "Eine der merkwurdigsten Gleichsetzungen im Vokabular der Sexualsprache ist Auge = Brust" (Borneman

1971). The interchangeability of eyes and breasts is also obvious from an examination of different versions of the folktale or legend "Present to the Lover" (Aarne-Thompson tale type 706B). Its summary reads "Maiden sends to her lecherous lover (brother) her eyes (hands, breasts) which he has admired" (cf. Williamson 1932, González Palencia 1932). Further data come from contemporary tattooing. "Open eyes are tattooed on American sailors' lids or around their nipples because the sailors believe that such tattoos will keep watch for them when they are tired or asleep" (Parry 1933:136), a belief probably identical to the one that accounts for the widespread Indo-European custom of painting an eye on either side of the bows of ships and boats (Hornell 1923, 1938). But the important point here is that the eyes are sometimes drawn around the nipples, which would exemplify the breast-eye equation.

Similar folkloristic data suggests that testicles and eyes may be symbolically equivalent on occasion. In Irish mythology, we find motif J229.12, prisoners given a choice between emasculation and blinding, an alternative reminiscent of Oedipus' self-imposed punishment of blinding for a sexual crime. (For a discussion of blindness and castration as allomotifs, see Dundes 1962:102.) One may note the same allomotifs in another European narrative setting. The plot summary of Aarne-Thompson tale type 1331, The Covetous and the Envious, is as follows: Of two envious men one is given the power of fulfilling any wish on the condition that the other shall receive double. He wishes that he may lose an eye. Legman (1975:611) reports a version from New York City in 1936: "A Jew in heaven is told that whatever he asks for, Hitler will get double. He asks that one of his testicles be removed." This kind of incontrovertible data strongly supports the idea that testicles and eyes are in some sense interchangeable. We can now better understand the modern Greek formula cited earlier, in which it is wished that the possessor of the evil eye suffer crushed genitals or burst breasts, in other words, that his or her vital fluids be wasted. (The wish for breasts to burst may also imply a wish for the death of a female evil eye caster's infant—an event which might tend to cause the mother's unused breasts to swell to the bursting point.)

One detail we have not yet explained is the singularity of the evil eye, and I mean singularity in the literal sense. Why the evil *eye* instead of evil eyes? In most languages the idiom for *evil eye* expresses the notion of a single eye. To my knowledge, none of the previous scholarship devoted to the evil eye has even raised this elementary but intriguing question. Any plausible theory of the evil eye should be able to account for it.

To better understand this facet of the evil eye belief complex, we may profitably examine ancient Egyptian beliefs. According to Moret (1902:40–47), all living things were created by eye and voice. Life was an emission of fecund light from the Master of rays. Above all, it was the sun Ra who was the primary creator, using his eye, the sun, "Eye of Horus." (For the sun as a heavenly eye generally, see Weinreich 1909.) The solar virtues of the gods were transmitted to the pharaoh through a magical fluid called *Sa*. That *Sa* which flowed in the veins of the pharaoh, son of Ra, was the "liquid of Ra," the gold of the sun's rays. *Sa* was emitted by a process termed *sotpou*, a verb used to describe the shooting forth of water, flames, and arrows and the ejaculation of semen (Moret 1902:47n.2; cf. Róheim 1972:162). Another source of life, incidentally, besides the liquid of Ra, was the milk of Isis (Moret 1902:48, n.1), which suggests that the symbolic equivalence of semen and milk is of considerable antiquity (cf. Jones 1951b:233; Legman 1975:139, 367).

The curious verb *sotpou* with all its nuances reminds us of the term *ejaculation* for the action of the evil eye. Francis Bacon in 1625 spoke of the act of envy producing an "ejaculation" of the eye; and many reports of the evil eye among Greeks and Greek-Americans use the term *ejaculate* in speaking of preventatives, e.g., ejaculating the phrase "garlic in your eyes" (Lawson 1910:14; Georges 1962:70). The eye shoots forth its rays just as the Egyptian sun, the eye of Horus, emitted its life-force liquid, *Sa*. The sun's rays, according to Ernest Jones (1951b:303), are often regarded as "a symbol of the phallus as well as of semen." The phallic interpretation of the sun with its rising perceived as a metaphorical form of erection was first suggested more than a hundred years ago (Schwartz 1874; cf. Jones 1951b:278, 285) and it certainly puts solar mythology in a new light! What is important in the present context is that the sun is both phallus and eye. Noteworthy also is that *jettatore*, the common term in southern Italy for the possessor of an evil eye, and *ejaculation* come from the same Latin root.

In 1910 Ernest Jones commented, in the course of discussing the power of the eye in hypnotism, on various beliefs in magical fluids including so-called magnetic fluid. (In this connection it is of interest that a report of the evil eye mechanism in Corsica [Rousseau 1976:6] suggests that the force involved may be a kind of fluid, a fluid that is released after an unguarded compliment or expression of admiration.) Jones noted (1910:239) that the magnetic fluid was principally emitted from the hypnotist's eye; and he suggested that such a belief in the influence of the human eye, for good or ill, had its origin in the notion that the eye and its glance were symbolically regarded as the expression of the male organ and its function. Freud too spoke of "the substitutive relation between the eye and the male member which is seen to exist in dreams and myths and phantasies" (1959:383–84). In the case of the phallus, one is tempted to observe, the glance might come from the glans. If one looks at the glans of a penis, it is not impossible to imagine it as an eye, the urinary meatus serving as a surrogate pupil.

What is startling about this notion is that iconographic representations of the phallus with an eye do occur. A number of scholars have noted the existence of the *phallus oculatus* (Seligmann 1910:2:28; Servadio 1936:405; Perdrizet 1922:31; Deonna 1965:70), but none have theorized about its significance. The idea of a phallus with an eye is no stranger than contemporary risqué puns on *cockeye* (Legman 1968:241). Even more germane is some striking evidence from Arabic folk speech. In the fifteenth-century Arabic classic *The Perfumed Garden* (Nefzawi 1963:166, 176), epithets for a man's sexual parts include *el aâouar*, "the one-eyed," and *abou aîne*, "he with one eye." The Arabic word for eye is similar to the Hebrew word *ayin*, which means both "eye" and "well" (Gifford 1958:81). One of the biblical verses used in phylacteries to ward off the evil eye was Genesis 49:22: "Joseph is a fruitful bough, even a fruitful bough by a well," because of the understood play on words. Joseph and his descendants were fruitful even though next to a well (= eye). The strength of the liquid metaphor even in the twentieth century is perhaps signalled by the fact that "*Maiyeh*, water, in colloquial Arabic is also used as the name of male semen, the life medium" (Canaan 1929:58).

The folk notion of the penis as the one-eyed also occurs in Walloon folklore. According to an anonymous report in *Kryptadia* (1902:24), a traditional epithet for the phallus is *li bwègne*, a dialect form of *le borgne*, which means "one-eyed." We are told that this remarkable appellation can be understood by the "ressemblance vague que la gland et ses lèvres présentent avec un oeil et ses paupières." However, the resemblance cannot be all that vague if we find the same one-eye idiom in other cultures! The tradition of the Walloon metaphor is confirmed by the reporting of an additional illustration: "sain-nî-s-bwégne," which is explicated as "saigner son borgne, c'est-à-dire pisser." If bleeding or, more figuratively, draining the one-eye refers to urination, then this would certainly support the idea that an eye containing liquid might represent a phallus!

We need not go so far afield as Arabic and Walloon folklore for the idea that a *third eye*, like a *third leg*, can be a circumlocution for the phallus. The fact that the phallus is the *third eye* or leg would be in accord with the phallicism of the number three in Indo-European tradition, with the phallus cum testiculis perceived as a triform cluster (Dundes 1968:420, n.1). The phallus as the one-eyed has been reported in American folklore. One of the "unprintable" folk beliefs from the Ozarks collected by Vance Randolph in 1946 has been published by G. Legman. It concerns the custom of the so-called dumb supper by means of which young women learn the identity of their future husbands. In most versions of the custom, the girls prepare a supper in total silence and then await the arrival of the first male visitor, who is supposedly a spouse-to-be. In Randolph's account of a prank played around the turn of the century, a "local ruffian" overhears the plans of two young girls near Green Forest, Arkansas. Here is part of the story: "Exactly at midnight the two girls sat down and bowed their heads. The door opened very slowly, and in came a big man walking backwards, clad only in a short undershirt. Approaching the table he bent forward, took his enormous tool in hand, and thrust it backwards between his legs, so that it stuck right out over the food on the table. One of the girls screamed and fled into the 'other house' crying 'Maw, maw, he's thar! He's come a long way, an' he's only got one eye!' " (Legman 1975:823). Whether or not the prank actually occurred is immaterial in the present context. What is important is that a narrative collected in 1946 refers to a phallus as a one-eyed man.

Even more striking is the widespread joke reported from both America and Europe in which fleas conceal themselves next day to compare notes. The flea who spent the night in the vagina reports that a bald-headed, and in some versions a one-eyed, man entered and spat on him (Legman 1968:585–586). This is not only another instance of the phallus described as one-eyed, it also exemplifies the equivalence of spitting and ejaculation.

If a healthy eye, that is, a phallus, can spit or ejaculate, then an unhealthy one cannot. Given this logic, it is not impossible to imagine that a larger, more powerful eye may rob a given eye of its ability to produce liquid, or of the precious liquid itself. The idea that an evil eye absorbs or sucks up liquid as opposed to a good eye, which emits liquid, is paralleled by an analogous folk belief attached to snakes and serpents. La Barre in his insightful discussion of the phallic symbolism of serpents observes that snakes are commonly endowed with such body image features as feathers or hair, despite the fact that "no snake in the world has either hair or feathers" (1962:61). Snakes are also believed to be able to suckle human breasts and to drink milk (La Barre 1962:94; cf. Aarne-Thompson tale type 285, The Child and the Snake, in which a snake drinks from the child's milk bottle). The point is that phalluses in the form of snakes or evil eyes are thought to have the power of stealing precious liquids.

If the phallus is the "one-eyed," then it is at least reasonable to speculate that one-eyed objects or persons in folklore might have phallic connotations. The tale of Polyphemus (cf. Aarne-Thompson tale type 1137, The Ogre Blinded) might be examined in these terms. Odysseus makes his escape by thrusting a burning mass into the giant's single eye. It may be of interest that one reported technique for removing the threat of an evil eye is to "blind the eye" (Westermarck 1926:1:434–35; Stillman 1970:90), while another entails a "symbolic burning of the eye" (Stillman 1970:85), which would be an extreme form of desiccating it. Analogous perhaps to the rationale of cremation discussed earlier, this technique would remove all liquid from the hostile eye.

With respect to Polyphemus, Comhaire (1958:26) remarks that while Homer consistently speaks of the one eye of the Cyclops, he does mention eyebrows in the plural. This suggests that the eye may be a nonliteral or symbolic one. As early as 1913, Reitler suggested that the eye of Polyphemus represented the father's phallus and that Odysseus's blinding of Cyclops represented a son's castration of his father (cf. Glenn 1978:151–52). Reitler's Freudian discussion began with a consideration of a curious Austrian folk toy. It is a little wooden man. When his head is pushed down, a potent phallus emerges from under his clothing. Not only does this toy equate the head with the phallus, but the head of the toy has three eyes. Besides the usual two, a third one appears above them right in the middle of the forehead. Reitler assumes the third eye represents the phallus (1913:161).

In folk tradition, the eye of the one-eyed giant is centered (cf. motif F531.1.1.1, Giant with one eye in middle of forehead). Onians presents much evidence to show that the head is the male genital organ displaced upward (1951:109–10, 234, n.6). If the head can represent the male genital organ, and if the phallus is perceived as a single eye, then it would be perfectly appropriate for the eye to be centrally located. One must remember, after all, that single eyes situated in the middle of foreheads do not occur in nature. We are dealing with fantasy. The importance of the middle of the forehead is also signalled by the idea in Lebanese-American custom that a counteractant blue bead (against the evil eye) "to be truly effective should suspend from the forehead to lie between the child's eyes" (Naff 1965:49). The location of the third eye in the middle of the forehead is also paralleled by the efficacy of the middle finger, the so-called digitus infamis or digitus impudicus (Seligmann 1910:2:183–84), in warding off or curing the ill effects of the evil eye. Typically, spittle is placed on the middle finger and applied to the infant's forehead (Napier 1879:35). The phallus is often considered to be a third leg placed obviously in the middle between the two regular legs.

The equivalence of eye and phallus may be suggested in ancient Egyptian mythology when Horus battles Set. Set tears out one of Horus's eyes and Horus counters by tearing off one of Set's testicles. In this connection, it is interesting that the Eye of Horus presented to the deceased in Egyptian funeral ritual is said to be the one devoured by Set, who later vomited it up (Budge 1909:134–135, 255); and even more significantly, the deceased is told, "The Eye of Horus has been presented unto thee and it shall not be cut off from him by thee" (Budge 1909:128, 245). In a variant text, "The Eye of Horus hath been presented unto thee, and it shall not be cut off from thee" (Budge 1909:184).

In Irish mythology, we find Balor, a famous robber, who had an eye in the middle of his forehead (Krappe 1927:1–43). Interestingly enough, Balor's was an evil eye and he used it to steal a wonder cow. The use of an evil eye to steal cattle is, of course, very much a part of the evil eye complex in the Celtic world and elsewhere. The evil Balor is eventually slain by his grandson Lug who, as prophesied, "thrust a red-hot bar into Balor's evil eye and through his skull so that it came out on the other side" (Krappe 1927:4). The antiquity of this notion of a male third eye is suggested by its possible occurrence in Sumer, where Enki (Ea) allegedly bore the epithet "Nun-igi-ku, the god with the gleaming eye." Reportedly this was described as "the god with the holy eye in his forehead" (Van Buren 1955:164, 169). In Indic mythology, Siva has a third eye. In light of the hypothetical phallic association of the eye in the forehead, it is of more than passing interest that Siva's cult consisted largely of the worship of his phallus (O'Flaherty 1975:137). The third eye of Siva has been interpreted in an erotic sense (O'Flaherty 1969).

I should like to suggest a logical, albeit magical, paradigm that also supports the idea that there is a phallic component of the evil eye. The paradigm is based upon the principle of homeopathic magic, in which a form of a dangerous object is itself used as a prophylactic counteragent. In Turkey and surrounding areas, for example, blue eyes are considered to be dangerous, perhaps evil eyes (Westermarck 1926:1:440). Lawson (1910:9), who had blue eyes, reported how difficult this made the conduct of fieldwork in Greece. He was often taken aback at having his ordinary salutation, "Health to you," answered only by the sign of the cross. Yet the color blue in the Near East is also regarded as protective against the evil eye (Westermarck 1926:1:440; Lawson 1910:12–13). The "like against like" principle also applies to eyes themselves. Eye amulets are commonly used (Westermarck 1926:1:459; Elworthy 1958:133). Bonner has noted that "the commonest of all amulets to ward off the evil eye consists of an apotropaic design which has been found on numerous monuments, and which, though subject to slight variations, remains the same through several centuries. It represents the eye, wide open, subjected to various injuries and assailed by a variety of animals, birds and reptiles" (Bonner 1950:97, cf. 211). The technical name of this design, Bonner discovers, is reported in a passage in the *Testament of Solomon*, an important source for the study of demonology dating perhaps from early in the third century (McCown 1922:108). In this passage, each of the thirty-six decans, or segments, of the zodiac is required to tell the king his name, his power, and the means of guarding against him. The thirty-fifth says, "My name is Rhyx

Phtheneoth. I cast the glance of evil at every man. My power is annulled by the graven image of the much suffering eye." Conybeare's translation of the relevant passage (1899:38) is "The thirty-fifth said: 'I am called Phthenoth. I cast the evil eye on every man. Therefore, the eye much-suffering, if it be drawn, frustrates me.' "

The paradigm then can be sketched as follows. The color blue causes the evil eye but the color blue is used on amulets to ward off the evil eye. An eye causes the evil eye but an image of an eye is used to ward off the evil eye. Now something, that is, something analogous to an algebraic unknown, causes the evil eye, but an amulet or gesture representing a phallus or vulva wards off the evil eye. If our paradigm is valid and our reasoning is correct, then one of the "causes" of the evil eye must be the phallus or vulva.

The horseshoe and crescent moon—charms of both shapes are used to ward off the evil eye—could represent the female genitals. The symbolic equation of eye and female genitals is substantiated by a well-known pretended obscene riddle. A version recounted by Bessie Jones of Georgia to enliven a discussion workshop at a folk festival in Berkeley, California, in 1963, is representative: "What's round and hair all around it and nothin' but water comes out?" The answer is "Your eye." (Cf. riddles 1425, 1426, and 1443–44, "Hair Above, Hair Below" in Taylor 1951.) The vulva as maleficent object would also explain Frachtenberg's observation that "the glance of the eye of a woman during her menstruation period was extemely dreaded by the Zoroastrians" (1918:421). Clearly, a woman who was losing blood, a life fluid, would represent a threat to the life fluids possessed by others (potential victims of the evil eye). According to a limited-good worldview, the loss of menstrual blood would require making up the liquid deficit—at someone else's expense.

The association between the eye and the genital areas may also explain the curious belief that too much coital activity (Meerloo 1971:54) or excessive masturbation will lead to blindness. Masturbatory ejaculation causes a loss of liquid and the eye would reflect this by dimming with each successive loss. Gifford (1958:166) reminds us of Francis Bacon's note that the ancient authorities believed "much use of Venus doth dim the sight." Bacon was puzzled that eunuchs were also dim-sighted but if their organs could not produce semen, then this lack of liquid life force might be responsible for poor vision—at least according to the folk theory. The logic is remarkably consistent. If the loss of liquid causes blindness, then the addition of liquid can cure blindness. Urine, for example (cf. the trade name of a solution to refresh eyes: *Murine*!), was commonly used to cure the effects of the evil eye as well as for eye diseases generally (Gifford 1958:66). Mother's milk is as effective a form of eye medicine as liquid from a male source. Numerous reports relate that "a few drops of mother's milk directly from the breast is also a favorite remedy for inflamed eyes" (Gordon 1937:313). "If a few drops of his mother's milk are poured into his eyes, the child will have good eyesight" reads a typical Hungarian superstition (Róheim 1952:353). Urine and mother's milk are evidently effective male and female curative fluids.

The phallus or the vulva as a liquid-seeking evil eye would explain why the evil eye is singular. But it may not be entirely clear why a phallus or a vulva should be perceived as liquid-seeking. To understand this, it is necessary to consider an important folk theory of sexuality, namely, that coitus is dangerous and debilitating insofar as it may result in a loss of liquid. Legman refers to the fantasy that "sexual intercourse is 'weakening' to the man, but not to the woman, because he 'loses' a fluid, the semen, which she receives" (1975:653). Legman relates this fantasy to the notion of the succubus. Earlier Ernest Jones (1951b:120) had suggested that "the simple idea of the vital fluid being withdrawn through an exhausting love embrace" was related to the vampire belief. Jones also (1951b:179) cited the fascinating folk belief that the devil has no semen and that "he can impregnate a woman only by having first obtained some semen by acting as a Succubus to a man." The crucial point with respect to the evil eye complex is that it is not farfetched to claim that the eye as phallus or vulva poses a threat to the victim's vital fluids. The widespread idea that hunters should refrain from sexual intercourse just before a hunt (or warriors before a battle or athletes before a game) is very likely related to the notion that a man has a finite amount of energy and this energy might be siphoned off or drained by the female genitals. The empirically observable fact that a man can manage only a limited or finite number of erections, hence sexual acts, within a given period of time while a woman, at least in theory (and fantasy—cf. Legman 1968:356–60 for the "unsatisfiable female"), can indulge in an infinite number of sexual acts might account for the idea that males have "limited good" with respect to semen.

In like manner, the Arab practice of *Imsȧk*, the special art of delaying the male orgasm (Nefzawi 1963:30), is probably selfishly intended to decrease the loss of precious semen rather than altruistically increasing the sexual pleasure of females. The idea that "women emit a special fluid at orgasm similar to the semen in men," which Legman calls a superstition "once almost universally believed at the folk level" (1968:403), would encourage such a practice. If the male succeeded in drawing fluid from the female genital while at the same time retaining his own fluid, he would presumably suffer no diminution in the finite amount of his life force. The fact that most males are unable to prevent ejaculation no doubt accounts for the widespread fear of female demons who threaten to suck a male victim dry in one way or another (cf. Legman 1975:134).

This battle of the sexes for precious liquid of life is quite explicit in Chinese sexual theory. In this theory, the Yang-Yin distinction includes a male-female component. According to one authority, the Chinese believed that "while man's semen is strictly limited in quantity, woman is an inexhaustible receptacle of Yin essence" (Weakland 1956:241). Men were supposed to retain their semen insofar as possible and to use the sexual act as a means of "absorbing the woman's Yin essence." According to the folk theory, "this art of sexual intercourse with a woman consists of restraining oneself so as not to ejaculate, thus making one's semen return and strengthen one's brain" (Weakland 1956:240). Since men wanted children (especially sons), they were "supposed to ejaculate only on those days when the woman was most likely to conceive . . . On all other days the man was to strive to let the woman reach orgasm without himself emitting semen. In this way the man would benefit by every coitus because the Yin essence of the woman, at its apex during the orgasm, strengthens his vital power . . ." The goal is absolutely clear. Man was to retain his vital essence while drawing the essence from his female sexual partner. In Chinese folklore, one finds dangerous, beautiful women who delight in draining their male sexual victims dry (Weakland 1956:241–42). While the evil eye was reported "to be no less common amongst the native population of northern China than it was and still is in Europe" (Dennys 1876:49), it seems to be largely absent from China (cf. Seligmann 1910:1:43). But even though the evil eye complex is not a major element in the Chinese folk belief system, the

Chinese perception of coitus in terms of gaining or losing sexual fluids seems to be paralleled by similar folk theories among Indo-European and Semitic peoples.

In Uttar Pradesh in northern India, it is believed (Minturn and Hitchcock 1966:74) that excessive sexual activity may cause minor illness and that "sexual intercourse is thought to make men in particular weak and susceptible to disease because the loss of one drop of semen is considered the equivalent of the loss of 40 drops of blood." Moreover, "the longevity of several men is attributed to complete abstinence in their later years." Clearly the loss of vital fluids through ejaculation is believed to diminish a finite supply of life energy. An Andalusian expression (collected in Andalusia by my colleague Stanley Brandes in 1976) confirms that the same reasoning is traditional in Spain: "Si quieres llegar a viejo, guarda la leche en el pellejo." "If you want to reach old age, keep your semen within your skin."

Essentially the same folk idea is described in Kinsey's *Sexual Behavior in the Human Male.*

> "For many centuries, men have wanted to know whether early involvement in sexual activity, or high frequency of early activity, would reduce one's capacities in later life. It has been suggested that the duration of one's sexual life is definitely limited, and that ultimate high capacity and long-lived performance depend upon the conservation of one's sexual powers in earlier years. The individual's ability to function sexually has been conceived as a finite quantity which is fairly limited and ultimately exhaustible. One can use up those capacities by frequent activity in his youth, or preserve his wealth for the fulfillment of the later obligations and privileges of marriage" (Kinsey, Pomeroy, and Martin 1948:297).

Kinsey goes on to remark that medical practitioners have sometimes claimed that infertility and erectal impotence were the results of the wastage of sperm through excessive sexual activity in youth and that Boy Scout manuals for decades informed countless youths "that in order 'to be prepared' one must conserve one's virility by avoiding any wastage of vital fluids in boyhood," which presumably was an attempt to appeal to self-interest to curb self-abuse, the common euphemism for masturbation. That a woman's genital area is perceived as a dangerous mouth posing a threat to the male genitals is confirmed not only by the vagina dentata motif (F547.1.1) but perhaps also by the use of the Latin *labia* for the outer and inner folds of skin and mucous membrane of the vulva. *Labia*, of course, means "lips" (cf. La Barre 1962:89n) and lips drink up liquid.

In the context of the evil eye belief complex, I suggest that showing the phallus or making the fica gesture (which symbolically shows a phallus in a vagina) affirms the prospective victim's ability to produce semen. The ability to produce a liquid is explicit in a curious detail in Lebanese-American custom. An exorcist who specialized in combatting the effects of the evil eye maintained that a child was not cured until he had urinated. She insisted that "no one should kiss a child while he is being read over and not until he has urinated after the eye has been expelled." Asked why this was necessary, she replied, "It's just natural. That's the way it is supposed to be" (Naff 1965:50). From the present perspective, the child's cure from the ill effects of the evil eye is demonstrated by his ability to make water, to produce liquid normally. (This would also be consonant with the fact that urine is sometimes reported to be an effective agent in curing the effects caused by the evil eye [cf. Pitrè 1889:245; Kirshenblatt-Gimblett and Lenowitz 1973:73].) It is, in sum, entirely consonant with the wet-dry hypothesis.

There is yet another way of blinding the evil eye and that is by defecating upon it. An unusual marble bas-relief reported by Millingen in his paper delivered in 1818 shows a man lifting his clothing to allow his bare buttocks to sit upon a large eye, which is also being attacked by a host of animals (cf. Elworthy 1958:138–41; Deonna 1955:93–94; 1965:180). This belongs to the same tradition as the painting unearthed at Pompeii next to a latrine, in which a man squats in a defecating position between two upright serpents next to a woman whose feet are pierced by a sword. Above the squatting man is inscribed *Cacator cave malum* (Magaldi 1931:97; cf. Deonna 1955:94). Seligmann (1910:1:302–3) notes that excrement is sometimes used to counteract the effects of the evil eye, e.g., in the case of a cow whose milk has gone dry, but he does not attempt to explain why excrement should be so used. Róheim (1955:28–31) suggests that "the magical value of excrement is based on the infantile anal birth theory" in which very young children equate the act of defecation with the act of giving birth. Thus, according to Róheim, "The defecating child is the mother; the excrement, the child." Róheim remarks that in Scotland, a calf can be protected against the evil eye if some of its mother's dung is put into its mouth (1955:25); and he interprets this as meaning the witch cannot "eat" the child with her evil eye because the child is eating the witch (bad mother, excrement). Says Róheim, "To possess the evil eye means to have oral aggression or a desire to eat the child" (1955:7). If the production of feces is equivalent to giving birth to a child, then defecation could be construed as an alternate means of proving one's fertility. But like spitting, the act of defecation can also have an insulting aspect. Defecating on the evil eye could also be a means of repudiating and defiling it. If the eye were that of an all-powerful and ever-watchful parent or all-seeing god, then a child (or an adult considering himself a child vis-à-vis his parents or a deity) might take pleasure in depositing feces in or on that eye (cf. Jones 1951b:176).

Deonna (1965:183) reminds us of a formula employed in Asia Minor by a mother attempting to keep the evil eye away from her child. The mother addresses the possible possessor of the evil eye as follows: "Que ton oeil soit derrière de mon enfant." Deonna wonders if wishing that the eye be positioned at the child's rear might be related to the curious custom of painting an eye at the bottom of chamber pots sold at fairs. Such chamber pots are reported in England, Scotland, and France, among other places, where they are commonly used in wedding customs (Monger 1975). In Stockport, Cheshire, a premarriage ceremony includes the groom's friends presenting him with a chamber pot. It is decorated with the names of the bride and groom and a large eye is painted on the bottom of it with the words "I can see you" (Monger 1975:52). Later the man and his friends take the pot to a tavern and everyone drinks from it. In Scotland, a chamber pot filled with salt was given as a wedding present to the groom. Miniature chamber pots were sold at the Aberdeen market in the mid 1930s "usually inscribed with the words 'For me and my girl' or with an eye at the bottom" (Monger 1975:56–57).

Van Gennep (1932:I:161–162) reported French versions of the custom, including one called *Saucée* (which one is tempted to translate as "soused" or "wet through"), from Revel-Tourdan in the Dauphiné district, in which melted chocolate was poured into a chamber pot with an eye design at the bottom in such a way as to leave the eye clear. After the chocolate hardened, other ingredients were added, such as white wine or champagne, grated chocolate, balls of chocolate, creams, etc. The concoction was taken later to the nuptial chamber after the bride and groom were considered to be asleep. The bride had to drink first, then the groom. Monger (1975:58) suggests a possible though admittedly highly speculative, connection to a supposed ancient eye-goddess cult in the Middle East (Crawford). However, it is more likely that it and the Scottish custom mentioned above are vestigial fertility rituals. Salt, as Ernest Jones convincingly demonstrated, is a symbolic substitute for semen (1951a:22–109), and thus a chamber pot filled with salt is a container full of semen given to the groom. Newlyweds are especially concerned with performing the sexual act satisfactorily. Tourney and Plazak observe that "the nuptial pair may fear impotence, frigidity and sterility" and that apotropaic charms are used to demonstrate that the threatened genitalia are safe (1954:491–92). If the eye at the bottom of the chamber pot represents the parental or peer group's attempt to observe the first connubial act of intercourse (cf. the words "I can see you") then the act of pouring in chocolate (a sweet, sublimated substitute for feces) might be analogous to defecating upon the evil eye.

If the evil eye represents the threat of impotence and/or the lack or loss of the necessary sexual fluids, then it would make sense to drink *from* an evil eye container. The chamber pot, an obvious receptacle for the passing of liquid, is converted through ritual reversal into a drinking goblet allowing for the incorporation of a potent liquid. (The ritual may also signal that a part of the body hitherto associated primarily with excretion will be employed in a new and different way.)

In the context of defecating upon the evil eye, it might be worth conjecturing that the common drinking toast "Here's mud in your eye" may stem from the same psychological source. The person who drinks is incorporating the liquid of life. The liquid is taken at someone else's expense. This other person, rather than taking in vital fluid, receives the end product of digestive incorporation in his eye. Certainly the above-mentioned wish "May your eye be at the posterior of my child" is not all that different from "Here's mud in your eye."

In terms of the possible symbolism of body parts, it is conceivable that the anus could constitute a metaphorical eye. This is suggested by a number of standard joke texts. One traced by Legman back to the late eighteenth century tells of a man who puts his artificial glass eye in a glass of water before retiring and swallows it by mistake. He visits a proctologist who after examining him exclaims, "I've been looking up these things for thirty years, but this is the first time anyone ever looked *back* at me!" (Legman 1975:515). Another involves a drunk who attempts to convince a bartender that he is sober: "Drunk? Hell, I'm not drunk. I can see. Look at that cat coming in the door there. It's got only one eye, hasn't it?" The bartender replies that the cat has two eyes, and besides, it is not coming in but going out (Legman 1975:822). In both Italian and Spanish, there are metaphorical references to the anus as an eye. From Liguria in Italy, we have the following example. A young girl refused to drink her coffee because she noticed coffee grounds in it. Her mother asked, "Ti ae puia che o te o l'euggio de cu?" which might be rendered "Are you afraid that it will stop up the eye of your ass?" i.e., cause constipation. Similarly, *ojo* means *culo* in Andalusia. In this connection one recalls Chaucer's reference at the end of his celebrated Miller's Tale to duped Absolon kissing Alison's "naked ers" with the words "And Absolon hath kissed hir nether ye." The nether eye was thus known in the fourteenth century.

To the extent that the evil eye has an anal cast, it would be perfectly reasonable to confront a threatening anus with anal power. In this light, an unusual Spanish ritual and charm against the evil eye might be cited (Diego Cuscoy 1969:502). According to this account, since individuals who give the evil eye are generally known as such, one turns a child's back or an animal's butt towards them when they are seen approaching. Then one thinks mentally or recites in a low voice the following text:

Tres garbanzitos
tiene en el culo:
quitale dos,
déjale uno.

Virate p'al monte
virate p'al mar,
virate el culo
y déjalo andar.

Three little chick peas
He has in the ass;
Away with two
Leave one.

Turn towards the mountain
Turn towards the sea
Turn your ass
And let it go.

This would seem to be consistent with the *Cacator cave malum* pattern noted earlier.

Most folklorists eschew symbolic analysis, and they may therefore be skeptical of the analysis of the evil eye proposed in this essay. But even leaving aside the symbolic considerations, one cannot avoid the obvious psychological aspects of the evil eye. Sometimes the possessor of an evil eye used the power for both psychological and mercenary advantage. In Scotland, fear of the evil eye led people to bribe or buy off the potential evil eye inflictor (Maclagan 1902:30–31, 47). One informant reported that Mrs. MacE. "was believed to have the Evil Eye very strongly, and people would do almost anything rather than offend her, so general was the impression that she could injure any person if she wished to do so" (Maclagan 1902:69). There are similar accounts from Italy. "I know also a most disagreeable woman whose daily task of running errands is made profitable by propitiatory tips, lest she blight her patrons, their children, or their cattle" (Mather 1910:42). In America (Gordon 1937:219), "one case in Philadelphia came up before a magistrate recently in which a dark-haired little old Italian woman was terrorizing the neighborhood. For many years she had extracted large sums of money from those who came under the influence of the evil eye. She also sold charms made out of bones of the dead, articles of ivory, stones, and herbs, wrapped in rag bags." These are surely examples of transforming what might be a liability into a kind of asset.

Occasionally, there have been attempts to put the power of the evil eye to good use. One of the most unusual of these attempts took place in Sassari in Sardinia near the end of the last century. According to the report (Edwardes 1889:326–27), the evil eye was enlisted to battle a plague of locusts: "Not long ago, Sassari elected a mayor who openly scoffed at the priests. This gentleman was not, however, a thorough type of the modern Sassarese. For though he condemned religion, he was sufficiently in the thrall of superstition to give his earnest sanction to the employment of a youth gifted with the evil eye. The country happened to be plagued with locusts. There was no remedy except the evil eye. And so the lad was perambulated about the district, and bidden to look his fiercest at the insufferable ravagers of vineyards, gardens, and the rich orchards of the north. Even when the locusts remained unmoved by this infliction, the mayor's faith in the remedy was unchanged. They had requisitioned an 'evil eye' of comparative impotency, that was all. It behooved them, therefore, to find a person better gifted than the lad they had used."

Evidently, humans are more likely to be intimidated by the evil eye than locusts are. In 1957, a committee of the U.S. Senate charged with investigating possible connections between organized crime and labor interviewed an Italian racketeer from New York City. The committee was told that the evil eye had been used to keep unhappy employees on the job. According to Gifford's account (1958:103), the racketeer was hired by one employer simply to come in once or twice every week or so to glare at the employees. The employer found that it was enough to have this individual come in and look at the workers to keep them at their work.

Most of the time, however, the possessor of the evil eye is shunned and ignored. In Morocco, "A person who is reputed to have an evil eye . . . is not allowed to take part in feasts or gatherings . . . he must not pitch his tent near the tents of others" (Westermarck 1926:426). Like accusations of witchcraft, accusations of possessing the evil eye give social sanction to ostracizing an individual, often transforming him into a pariah. Pitrè (1889:247) is one of the relatively few scholars to express sympathy for the poor soul who may be unfortunate enough to be victimized by an accusation of possessing the evil eye: "The *jettatore* has no name, no friends, nor the possibility of a social life . . ."

The evil eye, like so many forms of human custom and superstition, is condemned automatically by so-called educated members of Western elite societies. But it should be realized that the evil eye, like most customs, serves an invaluable projective function. When an infant becomes ill or dies, there is potentially a great deal of guilt and shame felt by parents. The evil eye belief complex provides a nearly foolproof mechanism that allows the anxious parents to shift the responsibility and blame for the misfortune upon someone else, perhaps even a total stranger whose eyes are a different color from the parents'. Similarly, if a cow's milk dries up or a favorite fruit tree withers, it is not the fault of the owner of the cow or the tree: the evil eye caused these calamities.

Even the diagnostic and protective techniques involved in the evil eye belief complex may provide important psychological supports. A small child who feels ill is assured of a great deal of parental attention. In Italian and Italian-American tradition, a bowl or shallow dish filled with water and a drop of olive oil may be placed on his head to determine whether or not his discomfort has been caused by the evil eye. Whether the child or parents believe in the efficacy of the procedure or not, most children surely enjoy being the cynosure of all eyes. Thus whatever evil results from the evil eye, there is also a beneficial aspect of the belief complex.

The concern in this essay has been not so much with the evil eye per se, but with the attempt to understand the folk ideas or worldview principles underlying it. The delineation of the wet-dry opposition and the idea of limited good is, however, not just an idle intellectual exercise. There are applications to be made that may lead to a better understanding of cultural differences. For example, in the United States, the idea of limited good is not as common as in the Old World. Instead, it has been argued that an idea of unlimited good prevails (Dundes 1971). In theory (as opposed to practice), there is enough "good" for everyone to have his fair share. One could also argue that the collective guilt felt by citizens of the United States for their relatively high standard of living accounts for their attempts to "tip" less fortunate countries by offering them substantial foreign aid. Just as many wealthy individuals turn to philanthropy as a means of salving their consciences (for enjoying the possession of more goods than they need for simple survival) so the have-nations feel impelled to help the have-nots by offering grain surpluses and other aid.

But there are some substantive differences. In American culture, praise is not only permitted but expected. One can praise the beauty of an infant or a friend's new house or dress without giving offense or causing anxiety. But Americans need to remember when they travel in other parts of the Indo-European and Semitic world that praise can be considered threatening. When a new acquaintance literally gives a visiting American the shirt off his back (which the American may have admired), it is not necessarily because of friendship so much as because of fear of the evil eye. By the same token, Americans, who from infancy are accustomed to hearing and receiving lavish praise for even the slightest deed, should not be offended when praise is not forthcoming from colleagues from cultures in which belief in the evil eye remains a vital force. One American woman married to an eastern European told me she had never understood why her in-laws so rarely praised her or her children. She took it personally, not realizing that their unwillingness to indulge in the public praising so common among Americans might have been due to the cultural imperatives demanded by the evil eye complex. To praise is to invite disaster in evil eye cultures.

The contrast between American conventions of socialization and those of evil eye cultures is quite pronounced. American children are typically asked to perform and show off in front of family and friends (and sometimes even strangers). Not so in evil eye cultures. The case of the Syrian and Lebanese Americans is instructive. "Experience taught that to show off a 'smart' child in front of people, especially strangers, is to invite the eye to strike him" (Naff 1965:49). The same is reported for northern India: "Because of the belief in the evil eye, a visitor who followed the American custom of admiring the baby, praising its unusual healthiness, good looks, or well-kept appearance would cause panic rather than pride, and a village mother would no more show off her baby to the admiration of a visitor than an American mother would deliberately expose an infant to a contagious disease" (Minturn and Hitchcock 1966:111–12).

For most of the Indo-European and Semitic world, the philosophy articulated by Herodotus and Horace prevails with respect to fame and fortune and the praise thereof. Herodotus in Book VII, chapter 10, of the *Persian Wars* speaks of lightning striking the tallest trees. "See how god with his lightning always smites the bigger animals, and will not suffer them to wax insolent, while those of a lesser bulk chafe him not. How likewise his bolts fall ever on the highest houses and the tallest trees. So plainly does he love to bring down everything that exalts itself." Horace says, "It is the mountaintop that the lightning strikes" (*Odes* 2.10). A low profile is essential to avoid the envy of one's peers or the gods. Certainly one element of the evil eye complex is the "fear of success" (Haimowitz and Haimowitz 1966). This is analogous to the underdog theme in American culture—politicians and athletic teams prefer to be the underdog because they ardently believe that front runners and the favored are likely to be overtaken and defeated. In the same ode Horace says, "Whoever cultivates the golden mean avoids both the poverty of a hovel and the envy of a palace." This is an ideal—to be neither envied nor envier.

One needs enough liquid to live but that means not too little and not too much. But eventually the finite amount is depleted. "For dust thou art, and unto dust shalt thou return." If drying is dying, then death is dust. The American slang idiom "to bite the dust" reflects not only the convulsive act of a dying man whose mouth may touch the earth, but also the same wet-dry continuum that I have suggested underlies the whole evil eye belief complex.

In the Judeo-Christian tradition, ideas of the after life include a solution to the problem of the imagined thirst of the dead. For heaven or paradise or the promised land is one which flows with milk and honey (Genesis 3:6, Exodus 33:3, Jeremiah 11:5, etc.). The phrase "and the hills shall flow with milk" (Joel 3:18) strongly suggests that there may be an infantile prototype for this metaphor, namely, the initial postnatal breast-feeding constellation. In the idealized afterlife, one is finally safe from the evil eye. Here there is plenty of milk and honey—enough for an eternity of replenishment. With unlimited liquid, one is free to enjoy life eternal. On the other hand, in hell, we have excessive heat—fire and water are presumably in opposition. And one thinks of the plight of the unfortunate Tantalus, perpetually consumed by thirst he is unable to slake because the waters cruelly recede whenever he bends down to drink.

In conclusion, it seems reasonable to argue that the wet-dry opposition is just as important as the hot-cold opposition, which has been frequently studied by anthropologists and students of the history of medicine. Perhaps it is even more important. Classical humoral pathology in fact included all four distinctions: heat, dryness, moistness, and cold (cf. Story 1860:697, Lloyd 1964). In this connection, it is noteworthy that a reported native classification of foods in northern India included hot, cold, dry, and wet (Minturn and Hitchcock 1966:73). If the wet-dry distinction does underlie the evil eye belief, then the distribution and age of the complex would tend to suggest that the wet-dry opposition is much older than its articulation among the ancient Greeks concerned with humoral pathology.

Rather, it would appear that the formulations of humoral pathology simply formalized a folk theory already in existence. One must keep in mind that all of the so-called humors were fluids, and for that matter, the term *humor* itself comes from the Latin *umor*, meaning "fluid" or "moisture." It is even possible that the idea of an exceptionally dry sense of humor might imply that the normal state of humor was wet!

Foster (1978) has assumed that the wet-dry distinction has disappeared in Latin America. He asks, "But why have the moist/dry qualities disappeared—apparently everywhere—in contemporary systems?" Foster answers his own question by suggesting that the moist-dry component so basic to classical humor pathology is less critical than the hot-cold distinction. "Heat and cold, and not moistness or dryness, are the primary causes of illness," argues Foster, who is, of course, speaking only of conscious articulation of theories of illness causation. If the wet-dry opposition is related to the evil eye belief complex (not to mention beliefs about the dead), one might take issue with the idea that the wet-dry distinction has disappeared and also with the idea that it is less critical than the hot-cold dichotomy with respect to folk theories of disease. On the contrary, I believe there is ample evidence to support the notion that the opposition between wet and dry is a fundamental folk idea, albeit an unconscious one, in Indo-European and Semitic worldview, a folk idea which is, metaphorically at any rate, a matter of life and death. With respect to the ideal of moderation, I can only hope in closing that my argument holds water but that my ideas are not all wet. God forbid that anyone who disagrees with me should give me a withering look, or tell me to go dry up and blow away.

REFERENCES

Abraham, Karl 1913. *Dreams and Myths: A Study in Race Psychology*. New York: Journal of Nervous and Mental Disease Publishing Company.

Andree, Richard 1878. *Ethnographische Parallelen and Vergleiche*. Stuttgart: Verlag von Julius Maier. [evil eye, pp. 35–45]

Anon. 1902. Chez les Wallons de Belgique. *Kryptadia* 8:1–148.

Anon. 1887. The Evil Eye. *The Celtic Magazine* 12:415–18.

Arditi, Michele 1825. *Il fascino, e l'amuleto contro del fascino presso gli antichi*. Naples.

Ball, R.A. 1967. The Evil eye in *Cristabel. Journal of the Ohio Folklore Society* 2:47–71.

Basil, Saint 1950. *Ascetical Works.* Translated by Sister M. Monica Wagner. New York: Fathers of the Church, Inc.

Bel, Alfred 1903. La Djâzya, Chanson Arabe. *Journal Asiatique*, Dixieme Série, 1:311–66. [evil eye, pp. 359–65]

Bellucci, Giuseppe 1909. Sul Bisogno di Dissetarsi Attribuito All'Anima dei Morti. *Archivio per l'Antopologia e le Etnologia* 39:211–29.

Bergen, Fanny D. 1890. Some Saliva Charms. *Journal of American Folklore* 3:51–59.

Berry, Veronica 1968. Neapolitan Charms Against the Evil Eye. *Folk-Lore* 79:250–56.

Bienkowski, P. 1893. Malocchio. In *Eranos Vindobonensis*, pp. 285–303. Vienna: Alfred Holder.

Blackman, Aylward M. 1912. The Significance of Incense and Libations in Funerary Temple Ritual. *Zeitschrift für Ägyptische Sprache und Altertumskunde* 50:69–75.

Blum, Richard, and Blum, Eva 1965. *Health and Healing in Rural Greece.* Stanford: Stanford University Press.

——— 1970 *The Dangerous Hour: The Lore of Crisis and Mystery in Rural Greece*. London: Chatto & Windus.

Bonner, Campbell 1950. *Studies in Magical Amulets Chiefly Graeco-Egyptian*. Ann Arbor: University of Michigan Press.

Borneman, Ernest 1971. *Sex in Volksmund.* Hamburg: Rowohlt.

Brav, Aaron 1908. The Evil Eye among the Hebrews. *Ophthalmology* 5:427–35.

Brown, H.R. 1909–1910. The Evil Eye. *Quarterly Journal of the Mythic Society* 1:57–77.

Browne, Peter 1716. *A Discourse of Drinking Healths*. London: Henry Clements.

Budge, E.A. Wallis 1909. *The Liturgy of Funerary Offerings.* London: Kegan Paul.

——— 1930. *Amulets and Superstitions*. London: Humphrey Milford. [evil eye, pp. 354–65]

Cadbury, Henry J. 1954. The Single Eye. *Harvard Theological Review* 47:69–74.

Cadoux, C.J. 1941–42. The Evil Eye. *The Expository Times* 53:354–55.

Callisen, S.A. 1937. The Evil Eye in Italian Art. *Art Bulletin* 19:450–62.

Camera Cascudo, Luis da 1949. Gorgoneion. In *Homenaje a Don Luis de Hoyos Sainz*, Vol. 1, pp. 67–77. Madrid: Gráficas Valera.

Campbell, Åke 1933. Det onda ögat och besläktade föreställningar i svensk folk-tradition. *Folkminnen ock folktankar* 20:121–46.

Canaan, T. 1914. *Aberglaube und Volksmedizin in Lande der Bibel.* Abhandlungen des Hamburgischen Kolonialinstituts, Band XX. Hamburg: L. Friederichsen. [evil eye, pp. 28–32]

——— 1929. Water and 'The Water of Life' in Palestinian Superstition. *Journal of the Palestinian Oriental Society* 9:57–69.

Caquot, André, and du Mesnil du Buisson, R. 1971. La seconde tablette ou 'Petite amulette' d'Arslan-Tash. *Syria* 48:391–406.

Casalis, Matthieu 1976. The Dry and the Wet: A Semiological Analysis of Creation and Flood Myths. *Semiotica* 17:35–67.

Charles, R. II. 1908. *The Testaments of the Twelve Patriarchs.* London: Adam and Charles Black.

Comhaire, Jean L. 1958. Oriental Versions of Polyphem's Myth. *Anthropological Quarterly* 31:21–28.

Conybeare, F.C. 1899. The Testament of Solomon. *The Jewish Quarterly Review* 11:1–45.

Coote-Lake, E.F. 1933. Some Notes on the Evil Eye Round the Mediterranean Basin. *Folklore* 44:93–98.

Corso, Rose 1959. The Evil Eye. *Polish Folklore* 4:6.

Coss, Richard 1974. Reflections on the Evil Eye. *Human Behavior* 3:16–22.

Crawford, O.G.S. 1957. *The Eye Goddess.* London: Phoenix House Ltd.

Crombie, J.E. 1892. The Saliva Superstition. In *The International Folk-Lore Congress 1891, Papers and Transactions*, edited by Joseph and Alfred Nutt, pp. 249–58. London: David Nutt.

Crooke, W. 1968. *The Popular Religion and Folklore of Northern India.* 2 vols. Delhi: Munshiram Manoharlal.

Cross, Frank Moore 1974. Leaves from an Epigraphist's Notebook. *Catholic Biblical Quarterly* 36:486–94.

Cutileiro, José 1971. *A Portuguese Rural Society.* Oxford: Clarendon. [evil eye, pp. 273–78]

Dawkins, R.M. 1937. Alexander and the Water of Life. *Medium Aevum* 7:173–92.

De Cunha, John 1886–89a. On the Evil Eye among the Bunnias. *Journal of the Anthropological Society of Bombay* 1:128–32.

——— 1886–89b. On the Belief in the Evil Eye among the Modern Persians. *Journal of the Anthropological Society of Bombay* 1:149–53.

Del Rio, Martinus Antonius 1599–1600. *Disquisitionum magicarum* libri sex. Lovanii.

Dennys, N.B. 1876. *The Folk-Lore of China.* London: Trübner.

Deonna, Waldemar 1939. Croyances Funéraires: La soif des morts; Le mort musicien. *Revue de l'Histoire des Religions* 119:53–81.

——— 1955. *De Télesphore au "moine bourre"; Dieux, génies et dëmons encapuchonnës.* Berchem-Bruxelles: Latomus.

——— 1965. *Le Symbolisme de l'Oeil.* Paris: Editions E. de Broccard.

Diego Cuscoy, Luis 1969. Mal de Ojo, Amuletos, Ensalmos y Santiguadores en la Isla de Teneriffe. In *Etologia y Tradiciones Populares*, pp. 499–520. Zaragoza: Institución "Fernando El Católico."

Dionisopoulos-Mass, Regina 1976. The Evil Eye and Bewitchment in a Peasant Village. In *The Evil Eye*, edited by Clarence Maloney, pp. 42–62. New York: Columbia University Press.

Djordjevíc, Tihomir R. 1934. Zle oĉi verovanju muslimana u Ohridu. *Glasnik Etnografski Muzej* 9:1–30.

——— 1938. Zle oĉi verovanju juẑnih Slovena. *Srpski etnografski zbornik* 53:1–347.

Dodwell, Edward 1819. *A Classical and Topographical Tour Through Greece, During the Years 1801, 1805, and 1806.* 2 vols. London: Rodwell and Martin.

Donaldson, Bess Allen 1938. *The Wild Rue: a Study of Muhammadan Magic and Folklore in Iran.* London: Luzac & Co. [evil eye, pp. 13–23]

Doutté, Edmond 1909. *Magie et Religion dans l'Afrique du Nord.* Alger: Typographie Adolfe Jourdan. [evil eye, pp. 317–27]

Dundes, Alan 1962. From Etic to Emic Units in the Structural Study of Folktales. *Journal of American Folklore* 75:95–105.

——— 1968. The Number Three in American Culture. In *Every Man His Way*, pp. 401–24. Englewood Cliffs, N.J.: Prentice-Hall.

——— 1971. Folk Ideas as Units of Worldview. *Journal of American Folklore* 84:93–103.

Ebeling, Erich 1949. Beschwörungen gegen den Fiend und den bösen Blick aus dem Zweistromlande. *Archiv Orientální* 17:172–211.

Edwardes, Charles 1889. *Sardinia and the Sardes.* London: Richard Bentley and Son.

Edwards, Dennis 1971. The 'Evil Eye' and Middle Eastern Culture. *Folklore Annual* (Austin, Texas) 3:33–40.

Eiszler, Lydia 1889. Das böse Auge. *Zeitschrift des Deutschen Palestina-Vereins* 12:200–222.

Eisen, M.J. 1927. Kuri silm. *Eesti Kirjandus* 21:34–43, 153–60.

Elworthy, Frederick Thomas 1958. *The Evil Eye: The Origins and Practices of Superstition.* 1895. Reprint. New York: Julian Press.

Erikson, Erik H. 1977. *Toys and Reasons: Stages in the Ritualization of Experience.* New York: Norton.

Evans, H.C. 1925. The Evil Eye. *Psyche* 6 (1):101–6.

Feilberg, H.F. 1901. Der böse Blick in nordischer überlieferung. *Zeitschrift für Volkskunde* 11:304–30, 420–30.

Ferenczi, Sandor 1956. On Eye Symbolism. In *Sex and Psycho-Analysis*, pp. 228–33. New York: Dover.

Fodor, Alexander 1971. The Evil Eye in Today's Egypt. *Folia Orientalia* 13:51–65.

Foster, George M. 1965. Peasant Society and the Image of Limited Good. *American Anthropologist* 67:293–315.

——— 1972. The Anatomy of Envy: a Study in Symbolic Behavior. *Current Anthropology* 13:165–202.

——— 1978. Hippocrates' Latin American Legacy: "Hot" and "Cold" in Contemporary Folk Medicine. In *Colloquio in Anthropology*, Vol. 2, edited by R.K. Wetherington, pp. 3–19. Dallas: Southern Methodist University, The Fort Burgwin Research Center.

Foulks, Edward; Freeman, Daniel M.A.; Kaslow, Florence; and Madow, Leo 1977. The Italian Evil Eye: Mal Occhio. *Journal of Operational Psychiatry* 8(2):28–34.

Frachtenberg, Leo J. 1918. Allusions to Witchcraft and Other Primitive Beliefs in the Zoroastrian Literature. In *The Dastur Hoshang Memorial Volume*, pp. 399–453. Bombay: Fort Printing Press. [evil eye, pp. 419–24]

Freud, Sigmund 1959. The 'Uncanny,' *Collected Papers*, Vol. 4, pp. 368–401. New York: Basic Books.

Frey, Dagobert 1953. *Dämonie de Blickes*. Akademie der Wissenschaften und der Literatur. Abhandlungen der Geistes- und Sozialwissenschaftlichen Klasse. Jahrgang 1953, no. 6. Mainz: Verlag der Akademie der Wissenschaften und der Literatur in Mainz.

Friedenwald, Harry 1939. The Evil Eye (Ayin Hara-ah). *Medical Leaves* 44–48.

Fries, Karl 1891. The Ethiopic Legend of Socinius and Ursula. *Actes de Huitième Congrès International des Orientalistes*, Vol. 2, Section Semitique, pp. 55–70. Leiden: E.J. Brill.

Frommann, Joannes Christianus 1675. *Tractatus de Fascinatione*. Norimbergae.

Gaidoz, Henri 1912. Jules Tuchmann. *Mélusine* 11:148–51.

Gallini, Clara 1973. *Dono e Malocchio*. Palermo: S.F. Flaccovio.

Gardiner, Alan H. 1916. A *Shawahti*-Figure with Interesting Names, The Evil Eye in Egypt. *Proceedings of the Society of Biblical Archaeology* 38:129–30.

Gaster, M. 1900. Two Thousand Years of a Charm Against the Child-Stealing Witch. *Folk-Lore* 11:129–62.

Gaster, Theodor H. 1973. A Hang-up for Hang-ups. The Second Amuletic Plaque from Arslan Tash. *Bulletin of the American Schools of Oriental Research* 209:18–26.

Gennep, Arnold van 1932. *Le Folklore du Dauphiné*. 2 vols. Paris: G.P. Maisonneuve.

——— 1967. *The Semi-Scholars*. London: Routledge & Kegan Paul.

Georges, Robert A. 1962. Matiasma: Living Folk Belief. *Midwest Folklore* 12:69–74.

Giancristofaro, Emiliano 1970. Viaggio nel Mondo Magico Abruzzese: II malocchio. *Rivista Abruzzese* 23:180–93.

Gifford, Edward S. 1957. The Evil Eye in Medical History. *American Journal of Ophthalmology* 44:237–43.

——— 1958. *The Evil Eye: Studies in the Folklore of Vision*. New York: Macmillan.

——— 1971. The Evil Eye in Philadelphia. *Pennsylvania Folklife* 20:58–59.

Glenn, Justin 1978. The Polyphemus Myth: Its Origin and Interpretation. *Greece & Rome* 25:141–55.

Gollancz, Hermann 1912. *The Book of Protection: Being a Collection of Charms*. London: Oxford University Press.

González Palencia, Angel 1932. La Doncella Que Se Sacó Los Ojos. *Revista de la Biblioteca, Archivo Y Museo* 9:180–200, 272–94.

Gordon, Benjamin I. 1937. Oculus fascinus (Fascination, Evil Eye). *Archives of Ophthalmology* 17:290–319.

Gouldner, Alvin W. 1965. *Enter Plato*. New York: Basic Books.

Grebe, Mariá Ester, Rajs, Dana, and Segura, José 1971. Enfermedades populares chilenas. Estudio antropológico de cuatro casos. *Cuadernos de la Realidad Nacional* 9:207–38. [evil eye, pp. 227–30]

Greenacre, Phyllis 1925–26. The Eye Motif in Delusion and Fantasy. *American Journal of Psychiatry* 82:553–79.

Gregory, Lady 1920. *Visions and Beliefs in the West of Ireland*, First Series, Vol. 1. New York: G.P. Putnam. [evil eye, pp. 127–52]

Grierson, George A. 1900. The Water of Life. *Folk-Lore* 11:433–34.

Grossi, Vincenzo 1886. *Il Fascino e La Jettatura nell' Antico Oriente*. Milano-Torino: Fratelli Dumolard Editori.

Grünbaum, M. 1877. Beiträge zur vergleichenden Mythologie aus der Hagada. *Zeitschrift der Morgenländischen Gesellschaft* 31:183–359. [evil eye, pp. 258–66]

Gubbins, J.K. 1946. Some Observations on the Evil Eye in Modern Greece. *Folk-Lore* 57:195–97.

Günther, R.T. 1905. The Cimaruta: Its Structure and Development. *Folk-Lore* 16:132–61.

Gutierrez, Joannes Lazarus 1653. *Opusculum de Fascino* . . . Lugduni.

Haimowitz, Morris L., and Haimowitz, Natalie Reader 1966. The Evil Eye: Fear of Success. In *Human Development; Selected Readings*, edited by

Morris L. Haimowitz and Natalie Reader Haimowitz, 2d ed., pp. 677–85. New York: Thomas Y. Crowell.

Hampden, Doreen 1955. The Evil Eye. *The Countryman* 51:272–74.

Hanauer, J.E. 1935. *Folk-Lore of the Holy Land*. London: The Sheldon Press.

Hand, Wayland D. 1976. The Evil Eye in its Folk Medical Aspects: A Survey of North America. *Actas del XLI Congreso Internacional de Americanistas*, Mexico, 2 al 7 de Septiembre de 1974. Vol. 3, pp. 183–89. Mexico City.

Hardie, Margaret M. [Mrs. F.W. Hasluck] 1923. The Evil Eye in Some Greek Villages of the Upper Haliakmon Valley in West Macedonia. *Journal of the Royal Anthropological Institute* 53:160–72.

Harfouche, Jamal Karam 1965. *Infant Health in Lebanon: Customs and Taboos*. Beirut: Khayats. [evil eye, pp. 81–106]

Hartman, Peter, and McIntosh, Karyl 1978. Evil Eye Beliefs Collected in Utica, New York. *New York Folklore* 4:60–69.

Hauschild, Thomas 1979 *Der Böse Blick: Ideengeschichtliche und Sozialpsychologische Untersuchungen*. Beiträge zur Ethnomedizin, Ethnobokanik und Ethnozoologie VII. Hamburg: Arbeitskreis Ethnomedizin.

Hazard, Willis Hatfield 1890–91. A Syriac Charm. *Journal of the American Oriental Society* 15:284–96.

Hemmer, Ragnar 1912 [1913]. Det onda ögat i skandinavisk folktro. *Brage Årsskrift* 7:52–75..

Henderson, George 1911. *Survivals in Belief Among the Celts*. Glasgow: James Maclehose and Sons.

Herber, J. 1927. La Main de Fathma. *Hespéris* 7:209–19.

H[ermann], A[ntal] 1888. Rumänische Besprechungsformel gegen den bösen Blick. *Ethnologische Mitteilungen aus Ungarn* 1:175–76.

Hildburgh, W.L. 1908. Notes on Some Contemporary Portuguese Amulets. *Folk-Lore* 19:213–24.

——— 1944. Indeterminability and Confusion as Apotropaic Elements in Italy and Spain. *Folk-Lore* 55:133–49.

——— 1946. Apotropaism in Greek Vase Paintings. *Folk-Lore* 57:154–78, 58:208–25.

——— 1951a. Psychology Underlying the Employment of Amulets in Europe. *Folk-Lore* 62:231–51.

——— 1951b. Some Spanish Amulets Connected with Lactation. *Folk-Lore* 62:430–48.

Hirsch, Emil G. 1892. The Evil Eye. *The Folk-Lorist* I:69–74.

Hocart, A.M. 1938. The Mechanism of the Evil Eye. *Folk-lore* 49:156–57.

Honea, Kenneth 1956. Buda in Ethiopia. *Wiener Völkerkundliche Mitteilungen* 4:20–24.

Hopkins, E. Washburn 1905. The Fountain of Youth. *Journal of the American Oriental Society* 26:1–67, 411–15.

Hornell, James 1923. Survivals of the Use of Oculi in Modern Boats. *Journal of the Royal Anthropological Institute* 53:289–321.

——— 1924. The Evil Eye and Related Beliefs in Trinidad. *Folk-Lore* 35:270–75.

——— 1938. Boat Oculi Survivals: Additional Records. *Journal of the Royal Anthropological Institute* 68:339–48.

Ibn Khaldûn 1967. *The Muqaddimah: An Introduction to History*. Vol. 3, 2nd ed. Translated by Franz Rosenthal. Princeton: Princeton University Press.

Jahn, Otto 1855. Über den Aberglauben des bösen Blicks bei den Alten. *Berichte über Verhandlungen der koniglich sächsischen Gesellschaft der Wissenschaften zu Leipzig*, Philologisch-Historische Classe 7:28–110.

Johnson, Clarence Richard 1924–25. The Evil Eye and Other Superstitions in Turkey. *Journal of Applied Sociology* 9:259–68.

Jones, Ernest 1910. The Action of Suggestion in Psychotherapy. *Journal of Abnormal Psychology* 5:217–54.

——— 1951a. *Essays in Applied Psycho-Analysis*. Vol. 2, Essays in Folklore, Anthropology and Religion. London: Hogarth Press.

——— 1951b. *On the Nightmare*. New York: Liveright Publishing Corporation.

Jones, Louis C. 1951. The Evil Eye among European-Americans. *Western Folklore* 10:11–25.

Jorio, Andrea de 1832. *La Mimica degli Antichi*. Naples: Dala stamperia e cartiera del Fibreno.

Joshi, Purushottam Balkrishma 1886–89. On the Evil Eye in the Konkan. *Journal of the Anthropological Society of Bombay* 1:120–28.

Kinsey, Alfred C., Pomeroy, Wardell B., and Martin, Clyde E. 1948. *Sexual Behavior in the Human Male*. Philadelphia: W.B. Sanders.

Kirshenblatt-Gimblett, Barbara, and Lenowitz, Harris 1973. The Evil Eye (The Good Eye) Einehore. *Alcheringa* 5:71–77.

Klein, Melanie 1957. *Envy and Gratitude: A Study of Unconscious Sources*. New York: Basic Books.

Knortz, Karl 1899. Der böse Blick. *Folkloristische Streifzüge*, pp. 280–291. Oppeln und Leipzig: Georg Maske.

Koenig, Otto 1975. *Urmotiv Auge*. Munich: R. Piper & Co.

Krappe, Alexander Hagerty 1927. *Balor with the Evil Eye*. New York: Columbia University Institut des Études Français.

Kuriks, O. 1930. Kuri silm ja tema pilgu maagiline moju. *Eesti Arst* 9:265–75.

La Barre, Weston 1962. *They Shall Take Up Serpents: Psychology of the Southern Snake-Handling Cult*. Minneapolis: University of Minnesota Press.

Landtman, Gunnar 1939. Tron pa det onda ögat i svenska Finland. *Bodkavlen* 18:34–42.

Lane, Edward William 1895. *An Account of the Manners and Customs of the Modern Egyptians*. London: Alexander Gardner.

Lawson, John Cuthbert 1910. *Modern Greek Folklore and Ancient Greek Religion*. Cambridge: Cambridge University Press. [evil eye, pp. 8–15]

Legman, G. 1968. *Rationale of the Dirty Joke: An Analysis of Sexual Humor*. New York: Grove Press.

——— 1975. *No Laughing Matter: Rationale of the Dirty Joke: 2nd Series*. New York: Breaking Point.

Leite de Vasconcellos, J. 1925. *A Figa: Estudio de Etnografia Comparativa*. Porto: Araujo & Sobrinho.

Lévi-Strauss, Claude 1969. *The Elementary Structures of Kinship*. Boston: Beacon Press.

Lilienthal, Regina 1924. Eyin ho-re. *Yidishe filologye* 1:245–71.

Lindquist, Edna W. 1936. Rue and the Evil Eye in Persia. *The Moslim World* 26:170–75.

Lloyd, G.E.R. 1964. The Hot and the Cold, the Dry and the Wet in Greek Philosophy. *Journal of Hellenic Studies* 84:92–106.

Lopasic, Alexander 1978. Animal Lore and the Evil-eye in Shepherd Sardinia. In *Animals in Folklore*, edited by J.R. Porter and W.M.S. Russell, pp. 59–69. Totowa, New Jersey: Rowman and Littlefield.

Löwinger, Adolf 1926. Der Böse Blick nach judischen Quellen. *Menorah* 4:551–69.

McCartney, Eugene S. 1943. Praise and Dispraise in Folklore. *Papers of the Michigan Academy of Science, Arts and Letters* 28:567–93.

McCown, Chester Charlton 1922. *The Testament of Solomon*. Leipzig: J.C. Hinrichssche Buchhandlung.

McDaniel, Walter Brooks 1918. The *Pupula Duplex* and Other Tokens of an "Evil Eye" in the Light of Ophthalmology. *Classical Philology* 13:335–46.

MacHovel, Frank J. 1976. The Evil Eye: Superstition or Hypnotic Phenomenon. *American Journal of Clinical Hypnosis* 19:74–79.

McKenzie, Dan 1927. *The Infancy of Medicine: An Enquiry into the Influence of Folk-Lore upon the Evolution of Scientific Medicine*. London: Macmillan. [evil eye, pp. 225–62]

Mackenzie, William 1895. *Gaelic Incantations, Charms and Blessings of the Hebrides*. Inverness: Northern Counties Newspaper and Printing and Publishing Company.

Maclagan, R.C. 1902. *Evil Eye in the Western Highlands*. London: David Nutt.

Magaldi, Emilio 1932. Di un particuloare ignorato e strano del culto della dea Fortuna. *Il Folklore Italiano* 7:97–110.

Maloney, Clarence, ed. 1976. *The Evil Eye*. New York: Columbia University Press.

Mallowan, M.E.L. 1947. Excavations at Brak and Chagar Bazar. *Iraq* 9:1–266.

Marugj, Giovanni Leonardo 1815. *Capricci sulla jettatura*. Naples: Dalla tipographia de L. Nobile.

Mather, Frank Jewett 1910. The Evil Eye. *Century Magazine* 80:42–47.

Meerloo, Joost A.M. 1971. *Intuition and the Evil Eye: The Natural History of a Superstition*. Wassenaar: Servire.

Meisen, Karl 1950. Der böse Blick und anderer Schadenzauber in Glaube and Brauch der alten Völker und in frühchristlicher Zeit. *Rheinisches Jahrbuch für Volkskunde* 1:144–77.

——— 1952. Der böse Blick, das böse Wort und der Schadenzauber durch Berührung im Mittelalter und in der neueren Zeit. *Rheinisches Jahrbuch für Volkskunde* 3:169–225.

Meltzl de Lomnitz, Hugo 1884. Le mauvais oeil chez les Arabes. *Archivio per lo Studio delle Tradizioni Popolari* 3:133–34.

Michaelis, A. 1885. Sarapis Standing on a Xanthian Marble in the British Museum. *Journal of Hellenic Studies* 6:287–318.

Millingen, James 1821. Some Observations on an Antique Bas-relief, on which the Evil Eye, or Fascinum, is represented. *Archaeologia* 19:70–74.

Minturn, Leigh, and Hitchcock, John T. 1966. *The Rajputs of Khalapur, India.* New York: John Wiley.

Modi, Jivanji Jamshedji 1924. A Few Notes From and On Recent Anthropological Literature. *Journal of the Anthropological Society of Bombay* 13:113–31. [evil eye, pp. 123–28]

Monger, G.P. 1975. Further Notes on Wedding Customs in Industry. *Folk-Lore* 86:50–61.

Montgomery, James A. 1910–11. Some Early Amulets from Palestine. *Journal of the American Oriental Society* 31:272–81.

——— 1913. *Aramaic Incantation Texts from Nippur*. University of Pennsylvania, The Museum, Publications of the Babylonian Section, Vol. 3. Philadelphia: University Museum.

Moret, Alexandre 1902. *De Charactère Religieux de la Royauté Pharaonique.* Annales de Musee Guimet 15. Paris: Ernest Leroux.

Moretti, Pietrina 1955. Contro il Malocchio del Bestiame in Sardegna. *La Lapa* 3:105.

Mundt, Theodor 1870. Der Blick ist der Mensch. *Europa* 10:298–306.

Murgoci, A. 1923. The Evil Eye in Roumania, and its Antidotes. *Folk-Lore* 34:357–62.

Naff, Alixa 1965. Belief in the Evil Eye among the Christian Syrian-Lebanese in America. *Journal of American Folklore* 78:46–51.

Napier, James 1879. *Folk-Lore or Superstitious Beliefs in the West of Scotland within this Century*. Paisley: Alex. Gardner.

Nefzawi, Shaykh 1963. *The Perfumed Garden of the Shaykh Nefzawi*. Translated by Richard F. Burton. Edited by Alan Hull Walton. London: Neville Spearman.

Nicholson, Frank W. 1897. The Saliva Superstition in Classical Literature. *Harvard Studies in Classical Philology* 8:23–40.

Odelstierna, Ingrid 1949. *Invidia, Invidiosus, and Invidiam facere: A Semantic Investigation*. Uppsala Universitets 1919:10. Uppsala: A.-B. Lundequistska.

O'Flaherty, Wendy Doniger 1969. The Symbolism of the Third Eye of Siva in the Purānas. *Purāna* 11:273–84.

——— 1975. *Hindu Myths*. Baltimore: Penguin.

O'Neil, Bernard 1908. The Evil Eye. *The Occult Review* 8:5–18.

Onians, Richard Broxton 1951. *The Origins of European Thought About the Body, the Mind, the Soul, the World, Time, and Fate*. Cambridge: Cambridge University Press.

Oyler, D.S. 1919. The Shilluk's Belief in the Evil Eye. *Sudan Notes and Records* 2:122–28.

Park, Roswell 1912. The Evil Eye. In *The Evil Eye, Thanatology and Other Essays*, pp. 9–31. Boston: Gorham Press.

Parry, Albert 1933. *Tattoo: Secrets of a Strange Art as Practised among the Natives of the United States.* New York: Simon and Schuster.

Percy, J. Duncan 1942–43. An Evil Eye. *The Expository Times* 54:26–27.

Perdrizet, Paul 1900. Mélanges Epigraphiques. *Bulletin de Correspondance Hellénique* 24:285–323. [evil eye, pp. 291–99]

——— 1922. *Negotium Perambulans in Tenebris:* Études de démonologie gréco-Orientale. Strasbourg: Librairie Istra.

Pitrè, Giuseppe 1889. La Jettatura ed il Malocchio. *Biblioteca delle Tradizioni Popolari Siciliane*, Vol. 17, pp. 235–49. Palermo: Libreria L. Pedone Lauriel.

——— 1913. Jettatura e. Malocchio. Scongiuri, Antidoti ed Amuleti. *Biblioteca delle Tradizioni Popolari Siciliane*, Vol. 25, pp. 193–211. Palermo: Libreria Internazional A. Reber.

Plutarch 1969. *Plutarch's Moralia*. Vol. 7. Translated by Paul A. Clement and Herbert B. Hoffliet. London: William Heinemann.

Potts, William John 1890. The Evil Eye. *Journal of American Folklore* 3:70.

Probst-Biraben, J.H. 1933. La Main de Fatma et Ses Antécédents Symboliques. *Revue Anthropologique* 43:370–75.

——— 1936. Les Talismans contre le Mauvais Oeil. *Revue Anthropologique* 46:171–80.

Quatremère, Étienne Marc 1838. Proverbes Arabes de Meidani. *Journal Asiatique*, III Série, 5:209–58. [evil eye, pp. 233–43]

R., E. 1879. The Evil Eye. *Cornhill Magazine* 39:184–98.

Reitler, Rudolf 1913. Zur Augensymbolic. *Internationale Zeitschrift für Ärztliche Psychoanalyse* 1:159–61.

Reminick, Ronald A. 1974. The Evil Eye Belief Among the Amhara of Ethiopia. *Ethnology* 13:279–91.

Riemschneider, Margarete 1953. *Augengott und heilige Hochzeit*. Leipzig: Koehler und Amelang.

Roback, A.A. 1938. *Psychological Aspects of Jewish Protective Phrases*. Bulletin of the Jewish Academy of Arts and Sciences, no. 4. New York: Jewish Academy of Arts and Sciences.

Roberts, John M. 1976. Belief in the Evil Eye in World Perspective. In *The Evil Eye*, edited by Clarence Maloney, pp. 223–78. New York: Columbia University Press.

Róheim, Géza 1952. The Evil Eye. *American Imago* 9:351–63.

——— 1955. *Magic and Schizophrenia*. New York: International Universities Press.

——— 1972. *The Panic of the Gods and Other Essays*. New York: Harper Torchbooks.

Rolfe, Eustace Neville, and Ingleby, Holcombe 1888. *Naples in 1888*. London: Trübner. [evil eye, pp. 106–26]

Rolleston, J.D. 1942. Ophthalmic Folk-Lore. *The British Journal of Ophthalmology* 26:481–502.

Rousseau, Pierrette Bertrand 1976. Contribution à l'étude de mauvais oeil en Corse. *Ethnopsychologie: revue de psychologie des peuples* 31:5–18.

Rypka, Jan 1965. Der böse Blick bei Nizmi. *Ural-Altaische Jahrbücher* 36:397–401.

Salillas, Raphael 1905. *La Fascinación en España*. Madrid: Eduardo Arias.

Salomone-Marino, Salvatore 1882. Rimedj e Formole contro le Jettatura. *Archivio per lo Studio delle Tradizioni Popolari* 1:132–34.

Sastriar, E.N. Mahadeva 1899. The Evil Eye and the Scaring of Ghosts. *Journal of the Asiatic Society of Bengal* 68(3):56–60.

Schmidt, Bernhard 1913. Der böse Blick und Ähnlicher Zauber im Neugriechischen Volksglauben. *Neue Jahrbücher für das Klassische Altertum Geschichte und Deutsche Literatur* 31:574–613.

Schnippel, Emil 1929. Dill als Mittel gegen den bösen Blick. *Zeitschrift für Volkskunde* 39:194–95.

Schoeck, Helmut 1955. The Evil Eye: Forms and Dynamics of a Universal

Superstition. *Emory University Quarterly* 11:153–61.

Schwartz, W. 1877. Der (rothe) Sonnenphallos der Urzeit. Eine mythologisch-antropologische Untersuchung. *Zeitschrift für Ethnologie* 6: 167–88, 409–10.

Seligmann, S. 1910. *Der Böse Blick und Verwandtes: Ein Beitrage zur Geschichte des Aberglaubens aller Zeiten und Völker.* 2 vols. Berlin: Hermann Barsdorf Verlag.

——— 1913. Antike Malocchio-Darstellungen. *Archiv für Geschichte der Medizin* 6:94–119.

——— 1922. *Die Zauberkraft des Auges and das Berufen: Ein Kapitel aus der Geschichte des Aberglaubens*. Hamburg: L. Friederichsen & Co.

Servadio, Emillio 1936. Die Angst vor dem bösen Blick. *Imago* 22:396–408.

Shrut, Samuel D. 1960. Coping with the 'Evil Eye' or Early Rabbinical Attempts at Psychotherapy. *American Imago* 17:201–13.

Simeon, George 1973. The Evil Eye in a Guatemalan Village. *Ethnomedizin* 2:437–41.

Simon, Maurice 1948. *Berakoth (The Babylonian Talmud).* London: Soncino Press.

Smith, C. Ryder 1941–42. An Evil Eye (Mark vii. 2). *The Expository Times* 53:181–82.

——— 1942–43. The Evil Eye. *The Expository Times* 54:26.

Smith, Kirby Flower 1902. Pupula Duplex. In *Studies in Honor of Basil L. Gildersleeve*, pp. 287–300. Baltimore: Johns Hopkins Press.

Spiegelberg, Wilhelm 1967. Der böse Blick in altägyptischen Glauben. *Zeitschrift für Ágyptische Sprache und Altertumskunde* 59:149–54.

Spooner, Brian 1976. Anthropology and the Evil Eye. In *The Evil Eye*, edited by Clarence Maloney, pp. 279–85. New York: Columbia University Press.

Stein, Howard F. 1974. Envy and the Evil Eye Among Slovak-Americans: An Essay in the Psychological Ontogeny of Belief and Ritual. *Ethos* 2(1):15–46.

Stillman, Yedida 1970. The Evil Eye in Morocco. In *Folklore Research Center Studies*, Vol. 1, edited by Dov Noy and Issachar Ben Ami, pp. 81–94. Jerusalem: Magnes Press.

Stocchetti, Sara 1941. Interpretazione Storico-critica di una Diffusa Superstitione Popolare. *Lares* 12:6–22.

Story, William W. 1860. Roba di Roma: The Evil Eye and Other Superstitions. *Atlantic Monthly* 5:694–704.

——— 1877. *Castle St. Angelo and the Evil Eye*. London: Chapman and Hall.

Sumner, Willian Graham 1960. *Folkways*. 1906. Reprint. New York: Mentor.

Taylor, Archer 1951. *English Riddles from Oral Tradition*. Berkeley and Los Angeles: University of California Press.

Thompson, Arthur 1907. The Secret of the Verge Watch: A Study in Symbolism and Design. In *Anthropological Essays Presented to Edward Burnett Taylor*, pp. 355–59. Oxford: Clarendon Press.

Thompson, R. Campbell 1904. *The Devils and Evil Spirits of Babylonia*. Vol. 2. London: Luzac and Co.

——— 1908. *Semitic Magic: Its Origins and Development*. London: Luzac & Co.

Thompson, Stith 1955–58. *Motif-Index of Folk Literature*. 6 vols. Bloomington: Indiana University Press.

Thurston, Edgar 1907. *Ethnographic Notes on Southern India*. Madras: Government Press. [evil eye, pp. 253–58]

——— 1912. *Omens and Superstitions of Southern India*. London: T. Fisher Unwin. [evil eye, pp. 109–20]

Tourney, Garfield, and Dean J. Plazak 1954. Evil Eye in Myth and Schizophrenia. *Psychiatric Quarterly* 28:478–95.

Tuchmann, Jules 1884–1901. La Fascination. *Mélusine* 2–10 passim.

Tylor, E.B. 1890. Notes on the Modern Survival of Ancient Amulets Against the Evil Eye. *Journal of the Royal Anthropological Institute* 19:54–56.

——— 1892. Exhibition of Charms and Amulets. In *Papers and Transactions of the International Folklore Congress 1891*, pp. 387–393. London: David Nutt.

Vairus, Leonardus 1589. *De Fascino Libre tres* . . . Venetiis.

Valla, Filippo 1894. La Jettatura (*Ocru malu*) in Sardegna (Barbagia). *Archivio per lo Studio delle Tradizioni Popolari* 13:419–32.

Valletta, Nicola 1787. *Cicalata sul Fascino Volgarmente detto Jettatura*. Naples.

Van Buren, E. Douglas 1955. New Evidence Concerning an Eye-Divinity. *Iraq* 17:164–75.

Vega, Juan José Hurtado 1968. 'El Ojo': Creencias y Prácticas Médicas Populares en Guatemala. *Tradiciones de Guatemala* 1:13–25.

Vereecken, J.L. Th. M. 1968. A Propos du mauvais oeil. *L'hygiène mentale* 57(1):25–38.

Vijaya-Tunga, J. 1935. The Evil Eye. *The Spectator* 154:1011–12.

Villena, Enrique de 1917. Tres Tratados. 1422. Reprint. *Revue Hispanique* 41:110–214.

Vuorela, Toivo 1967. *Der Böse Blick im Lichte der Finnischen Überlieferung*. Folklore Fellows Communication 201. Helsinki: Academia Scientiarum Fennica.

Wace, Alan J.B. 1903–1904. Grotesques and the Evil Eye. *The Annual of the British School at Athens*, no. 10. (Session 1903–1904), pp. 103–14.

Wagner, Max Leopaldo 1913. Il Malocchio e credenze affini in Sardegna. *Lares* 2:129–50.

Weakland, John H. 1956. Orality in Chinese Conceptions of Male Genital Sexuality. *Psychiatry* 19:237–47.

Weinreich, Otto 1909. Helios, Augen heiland. *Hessische Blätter für Volkskunde* 8:168–73.

West, John O. 1974. Mal Ojo. In *The Folklore of Texas Cultures*, Publications of the Texas Folklore Society 38, edited by Francis Edward Abernethy, pp. 82–84. Austin: The Encino Press.

Westermarck, Edward 1904. The Magic Origin of Moorish Designs. *Journal of the Royal Anthropological Institute* 34:211–22.

——— 1926. *Ritual and Belief in Morocco*. Vol. 1. London: Macmillan. [evil eye, pp. 414–78]

Weston, Stephen 1821. Further Observations on the Bas-relief, supposed to represent the Evil Eye. *Archaeologia* 19:99–101.

Williamson, Marjorie 1932. Les Yeux arrachés, *Philological Quarterly* 11:149–62.

Wolters, Paul 1909. Ein Apotropaion aus Baden im Aargau. *Bonner Jahrbücher* 118:257–74.

Woodburne, A. Stewart 1935. The Evil Eye in South Indian Folklore. *International Review of Missions* 24:237–47.

Zammit-Maempel, G. 1968. The evil eye and protective cattle horns in Malta. *Folk-Lore* 79:1–16.